ZAGAT®

America's Top Golf Courses

2007/08

GOLF EDITORS
Joseph Passov, Craig Better and Tom Mackin

STAFF EDITORS
Shelley Gallagher with Robert Seixas

Published and distributed by
Zagat Survey, LLC
4 Columbus Circle
New York, NY 10019
T: 212.977.6000
E: golf@zagat.com
www.zagat.com

ACKNOWLEDGMENTS

We thank Sara and Roxie Better, Nick Nicholas and Betsy Ryan Passov, as well as the following members of our staff: Emily Parsons (senior associate editor), Jessica Grose (editorial assistant), Sean Beachell, Maryanne Bertollo, Sandy Cheng, Reni Chin, Larry Cohn, Jeff Freier, Caroline Hatchett, Roy Jacob, Natalie Lebert, Mike Liao, Dave Makulec, Andre Pilette, Becky Ruthenberg, Thomas Sheehan, Kilolo Strobert, Yoji Yamaguchi, Sharon Yates and Kyle Zolner.

The reviews published in this guide are based on public opinion surveys, with numerical ratings reflecting the average scores given by all survey participants who voted on each establishment and text based on direct quotes from, or fair paraphrasings of, participants' comments. Phone numbers, addresses and other factual information were correct to the best of our knowledge when published in this guide; any subsequent changes may not be reflected.

Contents

Ratings & Symbols

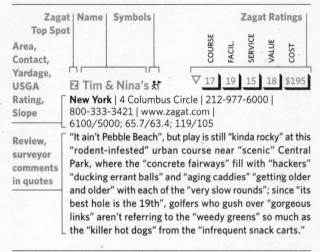

	Zagat Top Spot	Name	Symbols						Zagat Ratings

Area, Contact, Yardage, USGA Rating, Slope

	COURSE	FACIL.	SERVICE	VALUE	COST
	▽ 17	19	15	18	$195

Z Tim & Nina's 🏌

New York | 4 Columbus Circle | 212-977-6000 | 800-333-3421 | www.zagat.com | 6100/5000; 65.7/63.4; 119/105

Review, surveyor comments in quotes

"It ain't Pebble Beach", but play is still "kinda rocky" at this "rodent-infested" urban course near "scenic" Central Park, where the "concrete fairways" fill with "hackers" "ducking errant balls" and "aging caddies" "getting older and older" with each of the "very slow rounds"; since "its best hole is the 19th", golfers who gush over "gorgeous links" aren't referring to the "weedy greens" so much as the "killer hot dogs" from the "infrequent snack carts."

Ratings

Course, Facilities, Service and **Value** are rated on a scale of 0 to 30. Properties listed without ratings are **newcomers** or survey **write-ins.**

0 – 9	poor to fair
10 – 15	fair to good
16 – 19	good to very good
20 – 25	very good to excellent
26 – 30	extraordinary to perfection
▽	low response	less reliable

Cost is the price per non-member or non-guest to play 18 holes on a weekend in high season (excluding the extra cost of a cart), i.e. the highest possible price of play.

Symbols

Z	Zagat Top Spot (highest ratings, popularity and importance)
🏌	caddies/forecaddies
🛺	carts only
🔑	guests only
⏱	restricted tee times (call ahead for public hours)

Top Lists and Indexes

Properties throughout Tops Lists and Indexes are followed by nearest major city/area. The alphabetical index at the back of the book lists their page numbers.

About This Survey

Here are the results of our 2007/08 America's Top Golf Courses Survey, your guide to the best places to play near home or on the road from fellow roundsmen who've been there before.

 WHAT IT COVERS: 1,075 of the top courses in the U.S., including the Virgin Islands and Puerto Rico. Besides ratings and reviews of the best public, semi-private and resort layouts, it includes listings of urban driving ranges and 100 leading private courses in case you have friends who are members.

HELPFUL LISTS: Whether you're planning a luxurious golf vacation or looking for the best value, our lists can help you zero in on exactly the right choice. See Most Popular (page 9), Top Ratings (pages 10–18) and 45 handy indexes (pages 239–300).

WHO PARTICIPATED: Input from over 6,250 avid golfers forms the basis for the ratings and reviews in this guide (their comments are shown in quotation marks within the reviews). Of these surveyors, 80% are men, 20% women; the breakdown by age is 7% in their 20s; 23%, 30s; 24%, 40s; 28%, 50s; and 18%, 60s and above. Collectively they bring an impressive total of roughly 560,000 annual rounds worth of experience to this Survey. We sincerely thank each of these participants – this book is really "theirs."

OUR EDITORS: We're also grateful to our editors, Joseph Passov, author of *The Unofficial Guide to Golf Vacations in the Eastern U.S.*; Craig Better, managing editor of GolfVacationInsider.com and contributor to *Golf Odyssey: The Insider's Guide to Sophisticated Golf Travel*; and Tom Mackin, former associate editor at *Golf Magazine*.

ABOUT ZAGAT: This marks our 28th year reporting on the shared experiences of consumers like you. What started in 1979 as a hobby involving 200 people rating NYC restaurants has come a long way. Today we have over 250,000 surveyors and now cover dining, entertaining, golf, hotels, movies, music, nightlife, resorts, shopping, spas, theater and tourist attractions worldwide.

MAKE YOUR OPINION COUNT: We invite you to join any of our upcoming surveys – just register at **zagat.com,** where you can rate and review establishments year-round. Each participant will receive a free copy of the resulting guide when published.

AVAILABILITY: Zagat guides are available in all major bookstores, by subscription at **zagat.com,** and for use on BlackBerry, Palm, Windows Mobile devices and mobile phones.

FEEDBACK: There is always room for improvement, thus we invite your comments and suggestions about any aspect of our performance. Just contact us at golf@zagat.com.

New York, NY
March 28, 2007

Nina and Tim Zagat

What's New

Tiger Woods drew legions of fans to the sport of golf when he burst onto the pro scene a decade ago, and thanks in part to his appeal, the game remains a way of life for many Americans. In fact, this **2007/08 America's Top Golf Courses Survey** indicates that 72% of participants have played for 10 years or more. It's no wonder, then, that there are now so many new and improved courses.

PUTTIN' ON THE RITZ: One of the most respected names in the hospitality industry continues to bring its superior reputation to golf course management. Fast on the heels of the Ritz-Carlton Orlando comes the new Ritz-Carlton Members Club near Sarasota. With 49% of our respondents reporting that accommodations are a key factor (after course cost and quality) in choosing a golf vacation destination, look for other venues to replicate the Ritz's emphasis on luxury.

FIRST RESORT: Several of this year's new courses are offering a complete resort experience. The North layout at Connecticut's Lake of Isles is affiliated with Foxwoods Resort & Casino. Alabama's Ross Bridge is located at the luxe Renaissance Resort & Spa, while Idaho's Osprey Meadows track is tucked away at the Tamarack Resort, where there's hiking, fishing and rafting at the 19th hole.

BRING THE KIDS: Catering to family-minded golfers, courses like Florida's SouthWood, the layouts at North Carolina's Pinehurst Resort and the Robert Trent Jones track at South Carolina's Palmetto Dunes have established a separate set of kids' tees. The Baytowne option at Florida's Sandestin resort goes further, offering a children's yardage book.

ON THE MEND: After repairing Hurricane Katrina damage, the major Gulf Coast golf clubs are back in business. Following a 2006 renovation, TPC Louisiana will once again host a PGA Tour event. Carter Plantation near Baton Rouge is better than ever, while Tom Fazio's Fallen Oak course at Beau Rivage Resort in Mississippi finally made its debut.

ROTATING RATES: Taking a cue from the airline industry, some courses are adjusting fees to reflect the most in-demand times and seasons. All of New Jersey's Crystal Springs courses have prime, twilight and super-twilight rates, Arizona's Troon North changes its prices eight times per year and Minnesota's The Wilds runs an autumn special where the greens fee is equal to the outside temperature.

PRICE POINTS: At $19 per round, the Reynolds course at North Carolina's Tanglewood Park proves there's a layout for even the smallest budget. But with 64% of our respondents saying they'd travel specifically to play a top-ranked track, premium prices at courses like Nevada's Cascata ($500) and California's Pebble Beach ($475) aren't going out of style.

Phoenix, AZ   Joseph Passov
March 28, 2007

Golf Travel Tips

LEAVE YOUR STICKS AT HOME: For trips with  fewer than three rounds, consider using rental sets. Rental quality has improved markedly in recent years, and "borrowed-club syndrome" suggests you'll play better with someone else's clubs. Plus, you'll save yourself some heavy lifting. If you must bring your clubs, don't trust the airlines – instead, consider a club-shipping service.

GET THE BEST RATES: It's all about the discounts. Check into special rates via corporate affiliations, affinity groups, senior citizenship and frequent-flier clubs. Try calling resorts directly rather than a chain's toll-free number, and when a rate is quoted, always ask: "Is this the lowest price you have?"

RESEARCH ONLINE: The Internet can be your best friend when it comes to getting the lowdown on the links. Most courses have their own Web sites providing descriptions, photos and course maps, as well as online-only bargains. Throughout this guide, we've provided these Web site addresses for your use.

GO AGAINST THE SLOPE: Following the crowd can cost you. If you go to Palm Springs or Scottsdale on a winter weekend, you'll pay top dollar, wait to play or face other booking restrictions. On the other hand, you'll get better value and easier access during shoulder seasons and weekdays, especially if you try some of the less well-known destinations, which are listed herein. And anywhere you go, look for twilight and replay discounts.

DON'T COUNT ON A CAREER ROUND: You shouldn't expect to score well your first time on any course. GPS, yardage books and pin position sheets can only do so much. Consider planning two rounds at a track, or if you're with a group, try a scramble format or a betting game that keeps everyone interested. Remember, golf is supposed to be fun, especially when you're on vacation.

FLASH SOME GREEN: Sometimes, to be treated like a king you need to show the money. Golf isn't a high-paying industry unless your name is Tiger or Jack, so a few bucks' tip can often make a difference in how you're treated (TIP = To Improve Performance).

TAP-INS – A FEW FINAL THOUGHTS: Getting stuck on the back nine during a downpour without a jacket can ruin any round, so don't forget the rain gear and pack an extra pair of golf shoes if you're playing more than three rounds. A good travel planner can also make your life easier, as will calling the course a few days in advance to double-check your tee time, make sure the greens aren't being aerated that day and so on. Lastly, and we can't stress this enough – enjoy yourself no matter how you play. After all, it sure beats working!

Key Newcomers

With interesting arrivals spread coast to coast, golfers across the nation should have no problem finding new challenges. Here's our take on the past year's most notable newcomers. (For a full list of additions to this book, see page 258.)

Beau Rivage, Fallen Oak | *Gulfport, MS*

Broadmoor, Mountain | *Colorado Springs, CO*

Callippe Preserve | *San Francisco Bay Area, CA*

Classic Club | *Palm Springs, CA*

Erin Hills | *Milwaukee, WI*

Golf Resort at Indian Wells, Celebrity | *Palm Springs, CA*

Lake of Isles, North | *New London, CT*

Lakota Canyon Ranch | *Grand Junction, CO*

Marquette, Greywalls | *Upper Peninsula, MI*

Old Greenwood | *Lake Tahoe, CA*

Oxford Greens | *New Haven, CT*

Redstone, Tournament | *Houston, TX*

Reunion Resort, Independence | *Orlando, FL*

Ritz-Carlton Members Club | *Sarasota, FL*

Ross Bridge | *Birmingham, AL*

Shoals, Fighting Joe | *Huntsville, AL*

SilverRock, Arnold Palmer Classic | *Palm Springs, CA*

Soldier Hollow, Gold | *Salt Lake City, UT*

Sunday River | *Central ME*

Tamarack Resort, Osprey Meadows | *Boise, ID*

Trump Nat'l | *Los Angeles, CA*

We-Ko-Pa, Saguaro | *Scottsdale, AZ*

Wolfdancer | *Austin, TX*

The year to come shows plenty of potential with a number of high-profile projects in the works: Tom Fazio's **Butterfield Trail** will spruce up the sand dunes adjacent to El Paso International Airport in May 2007; Robert Trent Jones Jr.'s **Chambers Bay,** located just outside of Tacoma with panoramic vistas of the Puget Sound and Olympic Mountains, will open in June 2007; **Pound Ridge,** a design from father-and-son team Pete and Perry Dye for Ken Wang (brother of Vera Wang), will debut in rolling, rocky northern Westchester County; **The Crossings at Carlsbad** will arrive north of San Diego and feature ocean views from many of its holes; **Olivas Links** will skirt the banks of the Santa Clara River in Ventura north of LA; and central Pennsylvania's historic **Bedford Springs Resort,** with an architectural pedigree that includes A.W. Tillinghast and Donald Ross, will complete its much-anticipated restoration.

Most Popular

Each surveyor has been asked to name his or her five favorite courses.
This list reflects their choices.

1. Pebble Beach | *Monterey Peninsula, CA*
2. Bethpage, Black | *Long Island, NY*
3. Spyglass Hill | *Monterey Peninsula, CA*
4. Bandon Dunes, Pacific Dunes | *Coos Bay, OR*
5. Bandon Dunes, Bandon Dunes Course | *Coos Bay, OR*
6. Whistling Straits, Straits | *Kohler, WI*
7. Kiawah Island, Ocean | *Charleston, SC*
8. Spanish Bay | *Monterey Peninsula, CA*
9. Torrey Pines, South | *San Diego, CA*
10. Kapalua, Plantation | *Maui, HI*
11. Bethpage, Red | *Long Island, NY*
12. Poppy Hills | *Monterey Peninsula, CA*
13. TPC Sawgrass, Stadium | *Jacksonville, FL*
14. Montauk Downs | *Long Island, NY*
15. Pasatiempo | *Santa Cruz, CA**
16. Troon North, Monument | *Scottsdale, AZ*
17. Pinehurst, No. 2 | *Pinehurst, NC*
18. Aviara | *San Diego, CA*
19. Crystal Springs, Ballyowen | *NYC Metro, NJ*
20. We-Ko-Pa, Cholla | *Scottsdale, AZ*
21. Doral, Blue Monster | *Miami, FL*
22. Caledonia Golf & Fish | *Pawleys Island, SC*
23. Torrey Pines, North | *San Diego, CA**
24. Bulle Rock | *Baltimore, MD*
25. Golf Course at Glen Mills | *Philadelphia, PA*
26. Sea Pines, Harbour Town Golf Links | *Hilton Head, SC*
27. Harding Park | *San Francisco Bay Area, CA*
28. Blackwolf Run, River | *Kohler, WI*
29. Half Moon Bay, Ocean | *San Francisco Bay Area, CA**
30. Princeville, Prince | *Kauai, HI**
31. Pine Hill | *Camden, NJ*
32. Centennial | *NYC Metro, NY*
33. Bandon Dunes, Bandon Trails | *Coos Bay, OR*
34. Challenge at Manele | *Lanai, HI*
35. Harbor Links | *Long Island, NY*
36. Architects | *NYC Metro, NJ*
37. Whistling Straits, Irish | *Kohler, WI*
38. Twisted Dune | *Atlantic City, NJ*
39. Seaview Marriott, Pines | *Atlantic City, NJ*
40. PGA West, TPC Stadium | *Palm Springs, CA*

---

* Indicates a tie with course above

Top Ratings (Excluding courses with low voting)

TOP-RATED COURSES

30
Bandon Dunes, Pacific Dunes | *Coos Bay, OR*
Whistling Straits, Straits | *Kohler, WI*

29
Bandon Dunes, Bandon Dunes Course | *Coos Bay, OR*
Arcadia Bluffs | *Traverse City, MI*
Bethpage, Black | *Long Island, NY*
Cascata | *Las Vegas, NV**
Kiawah Island, Ocean | *Charleston, SC*
Pebble Beach | *Monterey Peninsula, CA*
Kapalua, Plantation | *Maui, HI*
Shadow Creek | *Las Vegas, NV*
Longaberger | *Columbus, OH*
Wolf Creek | *Las Vegas, NV*
Spyglass Hill | *Monterey Peninsula, CA*
Circling Raven | *Coeur d'Alene, ID*
Lake of Isles, North | *New London, CT*
Caledonia Golf & Fish | *Pawleys Island, SC*
Bulle Rock | *Baltimore, MD*
Old Kinderhook | *Lake of the Ozarks, MO*

28
Kiva Dunes | *Mobile, AL*
Challenge at Manele | *Lanai, HI*
TPC Sawgrass, Stadium | *Jacksonville, FL*
Paa-Ko Ridge | *Albuquerque, NM*
Homestead, Cascades | *Roanoke, VA*
Golden Horseshoe, Gold | *Williamsburg, VA*
Ocean Hammock | *Daytona Beach, FL*
Blackwolf Run, River | *Kohler, WI*
Red Sky, Fazio | *Vail, CO*
Taconic | *Berkshires, MA*
Troon North, Monument | *Scottsdale, AZ*
World Woods, Pine Barrens | *Tampa, FL*
Barton Creek, Fazio Canyons | *Austin, TX*
Eagle Ridge, The General | *Galena, IL*
Greenbrier, Greenbrier Course | *White Sulphur Springs, WV**
Cog Hill, No. 4 (Dubsdread) | *Chicago, IL*
Red Sky, Norman | *Vail, CO*
We-Ko-Pa, Cholla | *Scottsdale, AZ*
Reynolds, Great Waters | *Lake Oconee, GA*
Pinehurst, No. 2 | *Pinehurst, NC*
Sea Island, Seaside | *Lowcountry, GA*
Pasatiempo | *Santa Cruz, CA*
Belgrade Lakes | *Central ME*
Pumpkin Ridge, Ghost Creek | *Portland, OR*
Links at Lighthouse Sound | *Ocean City, MD*
Stonewall Orchard | *Chicago, IL**
Branson Creek | *Springfield, MO*
Madden's at Gull Lake, Classic | *Brainerd, MN*
Pinehurst, No. 8 | *Pinehurst, NC*
Shepherd's Hollow | *Detroit, MI*
Crumpin-Fox | *Berkshires, MA*
Gold Canyon, Dinosaur Mountain | *Phoenix, AZ**
Reynolds, Oconee | *Lake Oconee, GA**

ARIZONA

28 Troon North, Monument | *Scottsdale*
We-Ko-Pa, Cholla | *Scottsdale*
Gold Canyon, Dinosaur Mountain | *Phoenix*
27 Ventana Canyon, Mountain | *Tucson*
Troon North, Pinnacle | *Scottsdale*
26 Boulders, South | *Phoenix*
Grayhawk, Talon | *Scottsdale*
Vistoso | *Tucson*
Boulders, North | *Phoenix*
Eagle Mountain | *Scottsdale*

CALIFORNIA

29 Pebble Beach | *Monterey Peninsula*
Spyglass Hill | *Monterey Peninsula*
28 Pasatiempo | *Santa Cruz*
27 CordeValle | *San Francisco Bay Area*
Maderas | *San Diego*
Desert Willow, Firecliff | *Palm Springs*
Torrey Pines, South | *San Diego*
26 PGA West, TPC Stadium | *Palm Springs*
Lost Canyons, Sky | *Los Angeles*
Spanish Bay | *Monterey Peninsula*

FLORIDA

28 TPC Sawgrass, Stadium | *Jacksonville*
Ocean Hammock | *Daytona Beach*
World Woods, Pine Barrens | *Tampa*
27 Orange County Nat'l, Panther Lake | *Orlando*
Arnold Palmer's Bay Hill | *Orlando*
26 Westin Innisbrook, Copperhead | *Tampa*
World Woods, Rolling Oaks | *Tampa*
Tiburón, Black | *Naples*
Orange County Nat'l, Crooked Cat | *Orlando*
World Golf Village, King & Bear | *Jacksonville*

HAWAII

29 Kapalua, Plantation | *Maui*
28 Challenge at Manele | *Lanai*
27 Mauna Kea, Mauna Kea Course | *Big Island*
Kauai Lagoons, Kiele | *Kauai*
Experience at Koele | *Lanai*
Princeville, Prince | *Kauai*
26 Hualalai | *Big Island*
Mauna Lani, South | *Big Island*
Poipu Bay | *Kauai*
Turtle Bay, Arnold Palmer | *Oahu*

MID-ATLANTIC (DC, DE, MD, PA, VA, WV)

29 Bulle Rock | *Baltimore, MD*
28 Homestead, Cascades | *Roanoke, VA*
Golden Horseshoe, Gold | *Williamsburg, VA*
Greenbrier, Greenbrier Course | *White Sulphur Springs, WV*
Links at Lighthouse Sound | *Ocean City, MD*
27 Olde Stonewall | *Pittsburgh, PA*

Golf Course at Glen Mills | *Philadelphia, PA*
26 Greenbrier, Old White | *White Sulphur Springs, WV*
Nemacolin Woodlands, Mystic Rock | *Pittsburgh, PA*
Stonewall | *Leesburg, VA*

MIDWEST (IA, IL, IN, KS, MI, MN, MO, ND, NE, OH, OK, SD, WI)

30 Whistling Straits, Straits | *Kohler, WI*
29 Arcadia Bluffs | *Traverse City, MI*
Longaberger | *Columbus, OH*
Old Kinderhook | *Lake of the Ozarks, MO*
28 Blackwolf Run, River | *Kohler, WI*
Eagle Ridge, The General | *Galena, IL*
Cog Hill, No. 4 (Dubsdread) | *Chicago, IL*
Stonewall Orchard | *Chicago, IL*
Branson Creek | *Springfield, MO*
Madden's on Gull Lake, Classic | *Brainerd, MN*

NEW ENGLAND (MA, ME, NH, RI, VT)

28 Taconic | *Berkshires, MA*
Belgrade Lakes | *Central ME*
Crumpin-Fox | *Berkshires, MA*
27 Ranch | *Springfield, MA*
Pinehills, Nicklaus | *Boston, MA*
26 Sugarloaf | *Central ME*
Blackstone Nat'l | *Worcester, MA*
Farm Neck | *Martha's Vineyard, MA*
Red Tail | *Worcester, MA*
25 Pinehills, Jones | *Boston, MA*

NEW YORK & ENVIRONS (CT, NJ, NY)

29 Bethpage, Black | *Long Island, NY*
Lake of Isles, North | *New London, CT*
27 Pine Hill | *Camden, NJ*
Turning Stone, Shenendoah | *Finger Lakes, NY*
Conklin Players Club | *Finger Lakes, NY*
Crystal Springs, Ballyowen | *NYC Metro, NJ*
26 Bethpage, Red | *Long Island, NY*
Montauk Downs | *Long Island, NY*
Hominy Hill | *Freehold, NJ*
Richter Park | *Danbury, CT*

PACIFIC NORTHWEST (OR, WA)

30 Bandon Dunes, Pacific Dunes | *Coos Bay, OR*
29 Bandon Dunes, Bandon Dunes Course | *Coos Bay, OR*
28 Pumpkin Ridge, Ghost Creek | *Portland, OR*
27 Sunriver, Crosswater | *Bend, OR*
26 Gold Mountain, Olympic | *Bremerton, WA*
Bandon Dunes, Bandon Trails | *Coos Bay, OR*
25 McCormick Woods | *Bremerton, WA*
Trophy Lake | *Bremerton, WA*
Washington Nat'l | *Tacoma, WA*
24 Black Butte Ranch, Big Meadow | *Bend, OR*
Langdon Farms | *Portland, OR**

ROCKY MOUNTAINS (CO, ID, MT, NV, UT, WY)

29 Cascata | *Las Vegas, NV*
Shadow Creek | *Las Vegas, NV*

Wolf Creek | *Las Vegas, NV*
Circling Raven | *Coeur d'Alene, ID*
28 Red Sky, Fazio | *Vail, CO*
Red Sky, Norman | *Vail, CO*
27 Coeur d'Alene | *Coeur d'Alene, ID*
Broadmoor, East | *Colorado Springs, CO*
Falls at Lake Las Vegas | *Las Vegas, NV*
Rio Secco | *Las Vegas, NV*

SOUTHEAST (AL, AR, GA, KY, LA, MS, NC, SC, TN)

29 Kiawah Island, Ocean | *Charleston, SC*
Caledonia Golf & Fish | *Pawleys Island, SC*
28 Kiva Dunes | *Mobile, AL*
Reynolds, Great Waters | *Lake Oconee, GA*
Pinehurst, No. 2 | *Pinehurst, NC*
Sea Island, Seaside | *Lowcountry, GA*
Pinehurst, No. 8 | *Pinehurst, NC*
Reynolds, Oconee | *Lake Oconee, GA*
27 Cuscowilla | *Lake Oconee, GA*
Tidewater | *Myrtle Beach, SC*

SOUTHWEST (NM, TX)

28 Paa-Ko Ridge | *Albuquerque, NM*
Barton Creek, Fazio Canyons | *Austin, TX*
27 Barton Creek, Fazio Foothills | *Austin, TX*
La Cantera, Palmer | *San Antonio, TX*
26 Tribute | *Dallas, TX*
La Cantera, Resort | *San Antonio, TX*
Cowboys | *Dallas, TX*
25 Twin Warriors | *Albuquerque, NM*
Augusta Pines | *Houston, TX*
24 Texas Star | *Dallas, TX*

TOP COURSES BY SPECIAL FEATURE

In some categories, clubs with more than one course are listed once, with their highest Course rating.

BUDGET ($50 AND UNDER)

26 Willinger's | *Minneapolis, MN*
25 Eaglesticks | *Columbus, OH*
Cooks Creek | *Columbus, OH*
24 Tanglewood Park, Championship | *Winston-Salem, NC*
Oxmoor Valley, Valley | *Birmingham, AL*
Riverdale, Dunes | *Denver, CO*
23 Oxmoor Valley, Ridge | *Birmingham, AL*
Edinburgh USA | *Minneapolis, MN*

CONDITIONING

30 Bandon Dunes, Pacific Dunes | *Coos Bay, OR*
Whistling Straits, Straits | *Kohler, WI*
29 Bandon Dunes, Bandon Dunes Course | *Coos Bay, OR*
Bethpage, Black | *Long Island, NY*
Cascata | *Las Vegas, NV**
Kiawah Island, Ocean | *Charleston, SC*
Shadow Creek | *Las Vegas, NV*
Longaberger | *Columbus, OH*

ENVIRONMENTALLY FRIENDLY

29 Bethpage | *Long Island, NY*
    Kiawah Island | *Charleston, SC*
    Pebble Beach | *Monterey Peninsula, CA*
    Kapalua | *Maui, HI*
    Longaberger | *Columbus, OH*
    Spyglass Hill | *Monterey Peninsula, CA*
28 TPC Sawgrass | *Jacksonville, FL*
    Golden Horseshoe | *Williamsburg, VA*

EXPENSE ACCOUNT ($200 AND OVER)

30 Bandon Dunes, Pacific Dunes | *Coos Bay, OR*
    Whistling Straits, Straits | *Kohler, WI*
29 Bandon Dunes, Bandon Dunes Course | *Coos Bay, OR*
    Cascata | *Las Vegas, NV*
    Kiawah Island, Ocean | *Charleston, SC*
    Pebble Beach | *Monterey Peninsula, CA*
    Kapalua, Plantation | *Maui, HI*
    Shadow Creek | *Las Vegas, NV*

FINE FOOD TOO

30 Bandon Dunes | *Coos Bay, OR*
    Whistling Straits | *Kohler, WI*
29 Cascata | *Las Vegas, NV*
    Kiawah Island | *Charleston, SC*
    Caledonia Golf & Fish | *Pawleys Island, SC*
28 TPC Sawgrass | *Jacksonville, FL*
    Homestead | *Roanoke, VA*
    Blackwolf Run | *Kohler, WI*

INSTRUCTION

29 Kiawah Island | *Charleston, SC*
    Pebble Beach | *Monterey Peninsula, CA*
    Shadow Creek | *Las Vegas, NV*
    Spyglass Hill | *Monterey Peninsula, CA*
28 TPC Sawgrass | *Jacksonville, FL*
    Troon North | *Scottsdale, AZ*
    Reynolds | *Lake Oconee, GA*
27 Orange County Nat'l | *Orlando, FL*

NEWCOMERS/TOP RATED

29 Lake of Isles, North | *New London, CT*
26 Ross Bridge | *Birmingham, AL*
25 Old Greenwood | *Lake Tahoe, CA*
    Broadmoor, Mountain | *Colorado Springs, CO*
22 Oxford Greens | *New Haven, CT*
    SilverRock, Arnold Palmer Classic | *Palm Springs, CA*
    Trump Nat'l | *Los Angeles, CA*
    Callippe Preserve | *San Francisco Bay Area, CA*

19TH HOLES

29 Cascata | *Las Vegas, NV*
    Kiawah Island | *Charleston, SC*
    Pebble Beach | *Monterey Peninsula, CA*
28 TPC Sawgrass | *Jacksonville, FL*
    Homestead | *Roanoke, VA*
27 Desert Willow | *Palm Springs, CA*

26 Spanish Bay | *Monterey Peninsula, CA*
   Poppy Hills | *Monterey Peninsula, CA*

OUTSTANDING ACCOMMODATIONS

30 Whistling Straits | *Kohler, WI*
29 Kiawah Island | *Charleston, SC*
   Pebble Beach | *Monterey Peninsula, CA*
28 Challenge at Manele | *Lanai, HI*
   Golden Horseshoe | *Williamsburg, VA*
   Troon North | *Scottsdale, AZ*
27 Broadmoor | *Colorado Springs, CO*
26 Aviara | *San Diego, CA*

PRACTICE FACILITIES

29 Kiawah Island | *Charleston, SC*
   Longaberger | *Columbus, OH*
28 TPC Sawgrass | *Jacksonville, FL*
   World Woods | *Tampa, FL*
   Reynolds | *Lake Oconee, GA*
   Sea Island | *Lowcountry, GA*
27 Orange County Nat'l | *Orlando, FL*
26 Grayhawk | *Scottsdale, AZ*

PRO SHOPS

30 Bandon Dunes | *Coos Bay, OR*
   Whistling Straits | *Kohler, WI*
29 Kiawah Island | *Charleston, SC*
   Pebble Beach | *Monterey Peninsula, CA*
28 TPC Sawgrass | *Jacksonville, FL*
   Troon North | *Scottsdale, AZ*
   Pinehurst | *Pinehurst, NC*
27 Broadmoor | *Colorado Springs, CO*

SCENIC

30 Bandon Dunes, Pacific Dunes | *Coos Bay, OR*
   Whistling Straits, Straits | *Kohler, WI*
29 Bandon Dunes, Bandon Dunes Course | *Coos Bay, OR*
   Arcadia Bluffs | *Traverse City, MI*
   Cascata | *Las Vegas, NV*
   Kiawah Island, Ocean | *Charleston, SC*
   Pebble Beach | *Monterey Peninsula, CA*
   Kapalua, Plantation | *Maui, HI*

WOMEN-FRIENDLY

29 Pebble Beach | *Monterey Peninsula, CA*
   Longaberger | *Columbus, OH*
   Bulle Rock | *Baltimore, MD*
28 Challenge at Manele | *Lanai, HI*
   Ocean Hammock | *Daytona Beach, FL*
   Sea Island, Seaside | *Lowcountry, GA*
   Pumpkin Ridge, Ghost Creek | *Portland, OR*
   Reynolds, Oconee | *Lake Oconee, GA*

Facilities include clubhouses, pro shops, practice areas, restaurants and, at resorts, lodging and other amenities. Clubs with more than one course are listed once, with their highest Facilities rating.

29
- Greenbrier | *White Sulphur Springs, WV*
- Cascata | *Las Vegas, NV*
- Hualalai | *Big Island, HI*
- Pinehurst | *Pinehurst, NC*

28
- Golf Club at Newcastle | *Seattle, WA*
- Whistling Straits | *Kohler, WI*
- Blackwolf Run | *Kohler, WI*
- Ross Bridge | *Birmingham, AL*
- Reynolds | *Lake Oconee, GA*
- CordeValle | *San Francisco Bay Area, CA*
- Sea Island | *Lowcountry, GA*
- Coeur d'Alene | *Coeur d'Alene, ID*
- Shadow Creek | *Las Vegas, NV*

27
- Aviara | *San Diego, CA*
- Bandon Dunes | *Coos Bay, OR*
- Broadmoor | *Colorado Springs, CO*
- Pebble Beach | *Monterey Peninsula, CA*
- Tiburón | *Naples, FL*
- Four Seasons at Las Colinas | *Dallas, TX*
- Nemacolin Woodlands | *Pittsburgh, PA*
- La Cantera | *San Antonio, TX*
- Grand Nat'l | *Auburn, AL*
- Spanish Bay | *Monterey Peninsula, CA*
- Barton Creek | *Austin, TX*
- Longaberger | *Columbus, OH*
- Bay Harbor | *Petoskey, MI*
- Grayhawk | *Scottsdale, AZ*
- Kingsmill | *Williamsburg, VA*
- Kapalua | *Maui, HI*
- Boulders | *Phoenix, AZ*
- Arcadia Bluffs | *Traverse City, MI*

26
- Troon North | *Scottsdale, AZ*
- Bulle Rock | *Baltimore, MD*
- Capitol Hill | *Montgomery, AL*
- Challenge at Manele | *Lanai, HI*
- La Paloma | *Tucson, AZ*
- Red Sky | *Vail, CO*
- Grand Cypress | *Orlando, FL*
- World Golf Village | *Jacksonville, FL*
- Phoenician | *Scottsdale, AZ*
- Great River | *New Haven, CT*
- Ritz-Carlton Orlando | *Orlando, FL*
- Kiva Dunes | *Mobile, AL*
- Princeville | *Kauai, HI*
- TPC Sawgrass | *Jacksonville, FL*
- Turning Stone | *Finger Lakes, NY*
- Barefoot | *Myrtle Beach, SC*
- Pinehills | *Boston, MA*
- Experience at Koele | *Lanai, HI*
- Sunriver | *Bend, OR*

Clubs with more than one course are listed once, with their highest Service rating.

__29__ Greenbrier | *White Sulphur Springs, WV*
Cascata | *Las Vegas, NV*
Hualalai | *Big Island, HI*
Bandon Dunes | *Coos Bay, OR*
Sea Island | *Lowcountry, GA*

__28__ Whistling Straits | *Kohler, WI*
Coeur d'Alene | *Coeur d'Alene, ID*
Ritz-Carlton Members Club | *Sarasota, FL*
Shadow Creek | *Las Vegas, NV*

__27__ Pinehurst | *Pinehurst, NC*
Aviara | *San Diego, CA*
Reynolds | *Lake Oconee, GA*
CordeValle | *San Francisco Bay Area, CA*
Ritz-Carlton Orlando | *Orlando, FL*
Homestead | *Roanoke, VA*
Blackwolf Run | *Kohler, WI*
Spanish Bay | *Monterey Peninsula, CA*
Circling Raven | *Coeur d'Alene, ID*
Pebble Beach | *Monterey Peninsula, CA*
Experience at Koele | *Lanai, HI*
Challenge at Manele | *Lanai, HI*

__26__ Lake of Isles | *New London, CT*
Tiburón | *Naples, FL*
Boulders | *Phoenix, AZ*
Four Seasons at Las Colinas | *Dallas, TX**
Kiawah Island | *Charleston, SC*
Bulle Rock | *Baltimore, MD*
Bear's Best Atlanta | *Atlanta, GA*
Kingsmill | *Williamsburg, VA*
La Cantera | *San Antonio, TX*
Barton Creek | *Austin, TX*
Wynn Las Vegas | *Las Vegas, NV*
Grand Cypress | *Orlando, FL*
Troon North | *Scottsdale, AZ*
Grayhawk | *Scottsdale, AZ*
Broadmoor | *Colorado Springs, CO*
Golf Club at Newcastle | *Seattle, WA*
Caledonia Golf & Fish | *Pawleys Island, SC*
Ross Bridge | *Birmingham, AL*
Madden's on Gull Lake | *Brainerd, MN*
Longaberger | *Columbus, OH*
Cowboys | *Dallas, TX*

__25__ Grand Nat'l | *Auburn, AL*
Golden Horseshoe | *Williamsburg, VA*
Treetops | *Gaylord, MI*
Arcadia Bluffs | *Traverse City, MI*
Spyglass Hill | *Monterey Peninsula, CA*
World Golf Village | *Jacksonville, FL*
Princeville | *Kauai, HI*
Wailea | *Maui, HI*

29	Cambrian Ridge	*Montgomery, AL*
28	Bethpage, Red	*Long Island, NY*
	Gold Mountain, Olympic	*Bremerton, WA*
	Bethpage, Black	*Long Island, NY*
	Circling Raven	*Coeur d'Alene, ID*
	Riverdale, Dunes	*Denver, CO*
	Grand Nat'l, Links	*Auburn, AL*
	Pacific Grove	*Monterey Peninsula, CA*
27	Capitol Hill, Judge	*Montgomery, AL*
	Charleston Springs, South	*Freehold, NJ*
	Grand Nat'l, Lake	*Auburn, AL*
	Lawsonia, Links	*Madison, WI*
	Oxmoor Valley, Ridge	*Birmingham, AL*
	World Woods, Rolling Oaks	*Tampa, FL*
	Montauk Downs	*Long Island, NY*
	Capitol Hill, Senator	*Montgomery, AL*
	Univ. of NM Championship	*Albuquerque, NM*
	World Woods, Pine Barrens	*Tampa, FL*
	Bandon Dunes, Pacific Dunes	*Coos Bay, OR*
	Rustic Canyon	*Los Angeles, CA*
	Baker Nat'l	*Minneapolis, MN*
26	Oxmoor Valley, Valley	*Birmingham, AL*
	Conklin Players Club	*Finger Lakes, NY*
	Bethpage, Blue	*Long Island, NY*
	Capitol Hill, Legislator	*Montgomery, AL*
	Bandon Dunes, Bandon Dunes Course	*Coos Bay, OR*
	Bethpage, Green	*Long Island, NY*
	Paa-Ko Ridge	*Albuquerque, NM*
	Orange County Nat'l, Panther Lake	*Orlando, FL*
	Pilgrim's Oak	*Lancaster, PA*
25	Charleston Springs, North	*Freehold, NJ*
	Willinger's	*Minneapolis, MN*
	Shepherd's Crook	*Chicago, IL*
	Black Butte Ranch, Big Meadow	*Bend, OR*
	Bandon Dunes, Bandon Trails	*Coos Bay, OR*
	Mt. Woodson	*San Diego, CA*
	Chaska Town	*Minneapolis, MN*
	Elk Ridge	*Gaylord, MI*
	Neshanic Valley	*Bridgewater, NJ*
	PGA of So. Cal., Legends	*San Bernardino, CA**
	Vineyard	*Cincinnati, OH**
	Arroyo Trabuco	*Orange County, CA*
	Gateway Nat'l	*St. Louis Area, IL*
	Branson Creek	*Springfield, MO*
	Dancing Rabbit, Azaleas	*Jackson, MS**
	Univ. Ridge	*Madison, WI*
	Orchard Valley	*Chicago, IL*
	Orange County Nat'l, Crooked Cat	*Orlando, FL*
	Poquoy Brook	*Boston, MA**
	Eaglesticks	*Columbus, OH*
	Rancho Park Golf	*Los Angeles, CA**

ALPHABETICAL
DIRECTORY

Alabama

TOP COURSES IN STATE

_28_	Kiva Dunes	_Mobile_
_27_	Cambrian Ridge	_Montgomery_
	Capitol Hill, Judge	_Montgomery_
_26_	Grand Nat'l, Lake	_Auburn_
	Ross Bridge	_Birmingham_

Auburn

Grand National, Lake   26 | 26 | 25 | 27 | $62

Opelika | 3000 Sunbelt Pkwy. | 334-749-9042 | 800-949-4444 |
www.rtjgolf.com | 7149/4910; 74.9/68.7; 138/117

This is "golf the way God intended it to be" testify followers of this
"scenic, challenging beauty" just east of Auburn, a "top" layout on the
RTJ Trail "requiring management and shot-making" in order to tackle
"lots of water"; insiders insist you must "play late afternoon/early
evening to see the abundant wildlife" and also check out the "unbelievable" par-3 short course; overall, the consensus is "you'd normally
pay at least $150 per round for this kind of quality."

⚡ Grand National, Links   26 | 27 | 25 | 28 | $62

Opelika | 3000 Sunbelt Pkwy. | 334-749-9042 | 800-949-4444 |
www.rtjgolf.com | 7311/4843; 75.1/69.6; 135/113

"Unbelievable golf for those of us who don't drive a Lexus" lures linksters to "one of the best values in the game", a "tricky", "deceptively
undulating" layout that keeps players on their toes, especially as they
take on the "monster of a Jekyll-and-Hyde back nine"; if some puzzle
over the name and wonder why it's called "links-style when it's not",
most look the other way and decree "this is Robert Trent Jones Sr.
at his best."

Birmingham

Capstone Club of Alabama ⏱   - | - | - | - | $49

Brookwood | 16000 Capstone Blvd. | 205-462-0590 |
www.capstoneclub.com | 7100/5700; 75.2/70.7; 143/135

Bearing the design imprint of Gil Hanse, this track situated just east of
Tuscaloosa offers many challenges that include a 120-ft. drop to the
fifth green and a testing slope rating from the tips; meanwhile, penny-
watching types should note that prices are a bargain here (with twilight and super-twilight rates), while the clubhouse's Bear's Den restaurant is yet another reason to stop in for a round.

Limestone Springs   ▽ 29 | 25 | 23 | 27 | $89

Oneonta | 3000 Colonial Dr. | 205-274-4653 | www.limestonesprings.com |
6987/5042; 74.2/69.6; 139/128

"The best course in Alabama that no one knows about" is this "gem"
built from an old limestone quarry; yes, it's "in the middle of nowhere"
an hour north of Birmingham, but it's "worth the drive" for the "incredible views", "elevation changes", challenging conditions (i.e. "valleys,
ridges and water hazards") and "great practice facility"; perhaps best
of all, it feels just a little bit "like Augusta."

	COURSE	FACIL.	SERVICE	VALUE	COST

Oxmoor Valley, Ridge

| 23 | 22 | 22 | 27 | $43 |

Birmingham | 100 Sunbelt Pkwy. | 205-942-1177 | 800-949-4444 | www.rtjgolf.com | 7055/4974; 73.5/69.1; 140/122

With "undulating fairways" and "not a level lie" to be had, "you need to be a goat" to traverse this "long", "well-maintained" RTJ Trail track tucked into the "rolling hills" near Birmingham; while a few feel you should "play with someone who knows the course, because some of the shots are unexpected", satisfied swingers swoon over the "great clubhouse", "breathtaking views" and "excellent facilities", all of which adds up to "one of the best values in golf."

Oxmoor Valley, Valley

| 24 | 22 | 23 | 26 | $43 |

Birmingham | 100 Sunbelt Pkwy. | 205-942-1177 | 800-949-4444 | www.rtjgolf.com | 7292/4899; 74.6/69.4; 130/122

Contented club-wielders find this track "fun to play and easier to enjoy than its Ridge counterpart"; while detractors decry the "elevation changes" that "lead to plenty of blind shots and awkward lies", concluding that "it's not as good as" some other courses, even they are able to appreciate that it's "located in Birmingham, so it's easy to get to."

NEW Ross Bridge

| 26 | 28 | 26 | 22 | $125 |

Bessemer | 4000 Grand Ave. | 205-949-3085 | www.rtjgolf.com | 8200/5500; 78.5/70.2; 135/123

"Play this long, spectacular course one time and you will relive it for years to come" insist supporters of this Birmingham-area behemoth on the RTJ Trail that comes off as "golfer-friendly even though it's nearly 8,200 yards" thanks to "plenty of area for wayward shots"; the experience is enhanced by a "gorgeous setting" on the grounds of the Renaissance Resort & Spa, so while "it's not inexpensive", coming here is an "investment" that pays off in "long-term memories."

Silver Lakes

| ∇ 26 | 25 | 25 | 28 | $65 |

Glencoe | 1 Sunbelt Pkwy. | 256-892-3268 | www.rtjgolf.com
Backbreaker/Heartbreaker | 7674/4907; 77.7/68.8; 151/124
Heartbreaker/Mindbreaker | 7407/4865; 76.6/68.3; 148/122
Mindbreaker/Backbreaker | 7425/4686; 76.1/67.5; 155/118

"Get ready for a golf outing that will break your will" marvel masochists about this aptly named 27-hole RTJ Trail track situated 90 minutes northeast of Birmingham; it boasts a "helpful staff", an "excellent driving range" and "a variety of tee boxes that allows for a fair length for everybody", and though "some of the fairway bunkers have been filled in", these three nine-hole courses will still "test your skills."

Huntsville

Hampton Cove, Highlands

| ∇ 24 | 25 | 23 | 27 | $55 |

Owens Cross Roads | 450 Old Hwy. 431 | 256-551-1818 | 800-949-4444 | www.rtjgolf.com | 7262/4765; 75.7/68.3; 136/113

"All the RTJ Trail courses are very good and reasonably priced", but some require a fair amount of travel like this "out-of-the-way" track situated five miles from Huntsville in far northern Alabama; experts call the "interesting" layout "a battle for your golf soul" given its cavernous bunkers and "challenging, elevated greens" ("use the bunt swing" and "keep the ball on the course"), concluding this one is "not for the beginner."

Hampton Cove, River
_ _ _ _ $55

Owens Cross Roads | 450 Old Hwy. 431 | 256-551-1818 | 800-949-4444 | www.rtjgolf.com | 7667/5278; 77.8/70.4; 136/119

"Fantastically unique" declare delighted duffers looking for something different – and finding it – at this RTJ Trail "value" in northern Alabama that, as its name suggests, "plays along the river"; wise whackers warn "it looks easy, but it's hard to score well", and they caution it's "very difficult the first time" because "water is everywhere" (be sure to "bring lots of balls!").

NEW Shoals, Fighting Joe
_ _ _ _ $63

Muscle Shoals | 990 Sunbelt Pkwy. | 256-446-5111 | www.rtjgolf.com | 8092/4500; 78.7/49.7; 138/102

"Magnificent lakes and tall brush attract migratory birds", which "enhances the experience" at this links-style layout, perhaps the "most beautiful" track on the RTJ Trail; beware the "slippery areas around the greens that swallow balls in watery graves", but don't let that – or its remote location 90 minutes west of Huntsville – dissuade you from playing this "outstanding value."

Mobile

Craft Farms, Cotton Creek ⌂
▽ 21 19 18 21 $82

Gulf Shores | 3840 Cotton Creek Blvd. | 251-968-7500 | 800-327-2657 | www.craftfarms.com | 7028/5175; 73.3/70.9; 133/122

The King (as in Arnold Palmer) is the mind behind this "well-maintained" 18-hole course near the Gulf of Mexico; it features roomy, rippled fairways and contoured putting surfaces, along with a few other pluses for putters: a bird's-eye view of the newly built, nearby osprey platform and Southern cooking at the course's namesake restaurant.

☑ Kiva Dunes
28 26 25 24 $92

Gulf Shores | 815 Plantation Dr. | 251-540-7000 | 888-833-5482 | www.kivadunes.com | 7092/5006; 73.9/68.5; 132/115

Combine "a great routing over the natural dunes" with a "beautiful" and "demanding links-type course" and you have Alabama's top-rated Course, this "wonderful layout" near the Gulf of Mexico that's now "fully recovered from Hurricane Katrina"; aces advise "be careful" as there's "plenty of wind to complicate club selection", but all in all, it's a "fine" experience that's enhanced by "super" service, a "great pace of play" and "views of the gulf and bay."

Peninsula Golf & Racquet ⌂
21 22 22 20 $90

Gulf Shores | 20 Peninsula Blvd. | 251-968-8009 | www.peninsulagolfclub.com
Cypress/Lakes | 7055/4978; 72.4/69.6; 124/121
Lakes/Marsh | 7026/5072; 72.6/70.1; 125/120
Marsh/Cypress | 7179/5080; 73.2/68.7; 121/115

"This is a well-managed operation at a very reasonable price" say sensible swingers who tip their caps to this "challenging" 27-holer along Mobile Bay in Gulf Shores; if "nothing special" to some ("bypass it and go the extra miles to Kiva Dunes"), the "professional staff", "fun" ambiance and new clubhouse may give the track added appeal.

	COURSE	FACIL.	SERVICE	VALUE	COST

Rock Creek 🏌

▽ 24 | 22 | 23 | 25 | $69

Fairhope | 140 Clubhouse Dr. | 251-928-4223 | www.rockcreekgolf.com | 6920/5831; 72.2/67.3; 129/119

Thanks to "good conditions", "the best service you could hope for", "facilities like those of a private club" and "wonderful views" of the forested fringes of Mobile Bay, this Fairhope foray adds up to "one of the best in southern Alabama for the money"; in fact, enthusiasts go so far as to claim that even "the few houses on the course can't detract from the interesting play."

TimberCreek

▽ 20 | 21 | 21 | 21 | $59

Daphne | 9650 Timbercreek Blvd. | 251-621-9900 | 877-621-9900 | www.golftimbercreek.com
Dogwood/Magnolia | 7062/4885; 72.2/66.7; 130/106
Magnolia/Pines | 7090/4990; 72.2/67.8; 126/107
Pines/Dogwood | 6928/4911; 71.8/66.7; 122/105

Carved from rolling, forested terrain on Mobile Bay's eastern shore, this "wonderful" Daphne diversion offers the flexibility of three distinctive nines (with Dogwood/Magnolia the toughest combo), making it "a good course for 4-Ball charity tournaments"; while it's a "nice complex", the surrounding woods and water make it a wise idea to "bring bug spray."

Montgomery

☒ Cambrian Ridge

27 | 24 | 24 | 29 | $68

Greenville | 101 Sunbelt Pkwy. | 334-382-9787 | www.rtjgolf.com
Canyon/Sherling | 7427/4857; 75.4/68.1; 142/127
Loblolly/Canyon | 7297/4772; 74.6/67.8; 140/126
Sherling/Loblolly | 7232/4785; 73.9/67; 133/119

"From the 200-ft. elevated tee on the 1st, you're in for a treat" laud linksters who "thought [they] 'had game'" until they played this "tough" RTJ Trail course, whose "interesting terrain", "beautiful layout", "great elevation changes" and "well-run" clubhouse make it this Survey's Top Value and well worth the 40-mile drive south from Montgomery; P.S. some say Sherling, which "wraps around a lake", is "the best of the three nines."

Capitol Hill, Judge

27 | 25 | 22 | 27 | $74

Prattville | 2600 Constitution Ave. | 334-285-1114 | 800-949-4444 | www.rtjgolf.com | 7794/4955; 77.8/68.3; 144/121

With the jury ruling it "a superb course at a ridiculously affordable price", it's no wonder that this Montgomery-area mainstay is considered one of "the best on the RTJ Trail"; while weaker whackers warn it'll "wear you down" ("the traps will gobble you up", so "bring extra balls – lots of extra balls"), most legal eagles can't wait to bang their drivers all the way "from the 200-ft. cliff-drop tee shot on the 1st to the scenic elevated green on the 18th."

Capitol Hill, Legislator

24 | 25 | 23 | 26 | $62

Prattville | 2600 Constitution Ave. | 334-285-1114 | 800-949-4444 | www.rtjgolf.com | 7417/5488; 74.1/70; 126/121

"Another good course on the Robert Trent Jones Golf Trail", this "bargain" option provides "some nice holes"; while vets vote it "pedestrian", adding it's the "easiest of the three Capitol Hill layouts" (i.e. "Judge lite"), the majority maintains this "wonderful facility" is "worth it."

Capitol Hill, Senator | 26 | 26 | 22 | 27 | $62 |

Prattville | 2600 Constitution Ave. | 334-285-1114 | 800-949-4444 | www.rtjgolf.com | 7697/5122; 76.6/68.8; 131/112

You can practically hear the bagpipes playing at the "Scotland of the South", this "beautiful", "cleverly done", "open, links-style" layout that dishes out "lots of mounds, dunes and high grass"; "be prepared to lose a couple of balls" as it's "somewhat punitive" with its "thick and deep rough", but overall, it's "a good change of pace from the parkland style of the other Capitol Hill courses."

Alaska

Anchorage

Eagleglen ☉ | - | -- | - | - | $42 |

Anchorage | 4414 First St. | 907-552-3821 | www.elmendorfservices.com | 6689/5443; 71.6/70.9; 126/123

"If you can put up with the F-16s and bald eagles soaring overhead, you're golden" say surveyors who support this "old-style" "challenge" designed by Robert Trent Jones Jr.; if some sniff it's "not bad for Alaska but it wouldn't rank high in the [lower] 48", aces appreciate that there are "no crowds" at what they consider the "best course in the Anchorage area."

Arizona

TOP COURSES IN STATE

28	Troon North, Monument	*Scottsdale*
	We-Ko-Pa, Cholla	*Scottsdale*
	Gold Canyon, Dinosaur Mountain	*Phoenix*
27	Ventana Canyon, Mountain	*Tucson*
	Troon North, Pinnacle	*Scottsdale*
26	Boulders, South	*Phoenix*
	Grayhawk, Talon	*Scottsdale*
	Vistoso	*Tucson*
	Boulders, North	*Phoenix*
	Eagle Mountain	*Scottsdale*

Bullhead City

NEW Laughlin Ranch | - | - | - | - | $145 |

Bullhead City | 1360 William Hardy Dr. | 928-754-1243 | www.laughlinranch.com | 7155/4980; 73.4/68.1; 142/117

Although acolytes "can't believe" a course this memorable "is in this location" – draped across the hills overlooking the Colorado River and nearby casinos – this Bullhead City arrival has established itself as a "very dramatic" option featuring rugged desert terrain, elevation changes and undulating greens; some duffers dismiss it as "overpriced for the neighborhood", but this semi-private experience includes a luxe clubhouse with pool, day spa and gym facilities.

Phoenix

Arizona Biltmore, Adobe 🏨

| 18 | 21 | 21 | 16 | $175 |

Phoenix | 2400 E. Missouri Ave. | 602-955-9655 | www.arizonabiltmore.com | 6428/5417; 70.3/70.7; 123/120

Situated amid the "marvelous setting of the Arizona Biltmore in Phoenix, this "beautiful", "tourist-friendly" option is one of the oldest resort courses in the state, offering "wide, flat fairways" that make this "moderately difficult" experience just "easy" enough "for couples" to play; yes, traditionalists tend to say the layout's "just ok", but they also add that the "heavy-on-the-wallet" fees "keep the crowds down."

Arizona Biltmore, Links 🏨

| 20 | 22 | 23 | 16 | $175 |

Phoenix | 2400 E. Missouri Ave. | 602-955-9655 | www.arizonabiltmore.com | 6300/4747; 69.7/66.8; 126/110

Loyalists insist this "fairly short" Arizona Biltmore course is "better than the Adobe" (its older counterpart), with "rolling, up-and-down terrain" that can be "fun" to play; still, dissenters expect more "considering the quality of the hotel" and feel the track "needs to be updated."

ASU Karsten

| 19 | 20 | 21 | 24 | $105 |

Tempe | 1125 E. Rio Salado Pkwy. | 480-921-8070 | www.asukarsten.com | 7057/4765; 74.1/62.7; 132/103

"I wish I went to school here just for the cheap golf" exclaims one enthusiast enthralled with the "excellent value" to be had at ASU's "classic Pete Dye" layout loaded "with the familiar railroad ties, mounds and moguls"; while a few bristle at "too many power lines" along the track, others say it's a "good test" with a "final stretch that'll chew you up", concluding "no wonder the school sports a good team – this is where they practice."

Boulders, North

| 26 | 26 | 26 | 19 | $290 |

Carefree | 34831 N. Tom Darlington Dr. | 480-488-9028 | www.thebouldersclub.com | 6811/4900; 72.6/68.5; 137/115

The "postcard-worthy" "natural rock outcroppings" around this "terrific" Carefree resort resemble the "set for *The Flintstones* movie", but you'll find "everything here is real", particularly the "difficult target course" where it's "important to hit it straight or you'll be runnin' from the rattlers"; while you "may have to mortgage the house" to play here, the track is "one of the best manicured" around and the service is "unmatched", making this the place to go for a "day of pampered golf."

Boulders, South

| 26 | 27 | 26 | 19 | $290 |

Carefree | 34831 N. Tom Darlington Dr. | 480-488-9028 | www.thebouldersclub.com | 6726/4684; 71.9/68.7; 140/117

"Great facilities" and a "top-notch staff" that "makes you feel special" complement this "tight", "difficult" course "enveloped in natural desert"; though "no weekend hacker should even try" this track, those who do call it "desert golf at its best" and advise you "bring your camera", "climb the elevated tees" and take a few snapshots of the "rock and boulder features that give the resort its name."

	COURSE	FACIL.	SERVICE	VALUE	COST

Dove Valley Ranch
18 | 17 | 18 | 18 | $135

Cave Creek | 33750 N. Dove Lakes Dr. | 480-488-0009 |
www.dovevalleyranch.com | 7011/5337; 72.7/70.8; 131/120
A RTJ Jr. design just north of Phoenix, this Jekyll-and-Hyde layout features "two distinct nines": a flattish, "open" front and a "closed", rolling back hemmed in by desert; there are plenty of "nice views", and while some lament the "humble amenities" and "houses that are built a little too close" to the "tight fairways", those who prefer "no-frills" golf gush that it's "a great alternative to high-priced Scottsdale courses."

Estrella Mountain Ranch
25 | 20 | 21 | 22 | $139

Goodyear | 11800 S. Golf Club Dr. | 623-386-2600 |
www.estrellamountainranch.com | 7139/5124; 73.6/68.2; 136/116
Though "off the beaten track" in Goodyear, this Phoenix-area "favorite" is "worth the drive", for once you "wind your way through a seemingly endless real estate development", you'll find a Jack Nicklaus Jr. design with "beautiful views", "rebuilt greens" and solitude (it will feel like "your group is the only one on the course"); P.S. play it soon – "it'll be crowded" once "housing construction is complete."

☒ Gold Canyon, Dinosaur Mountain 🏨
28 | 20 | 22 | 21 | $185

Gold Canyon | 6100 S. Kings Ranch Rd. | 480-982-9449 | 800-827-5281 |
www.gcgr.com | 6653/4833; 71.3/67.4; 143/115
"Bring your camera" to "one of the most beautiful layouts in the area" say surveyors smitten with this "hidden treasure" in the "middle of nowhere" 40 minutes east of Phoenix; it's a "good, fair test" sporting "spectacular views and elevation changes", and though it's "not cheap" and the "pro shop needs updating", most agree "if you can endure the drive, it's a desert-mountain bundle of joy."

Gold Canyon, Sidewinder 🏨
▽ 23 | 23 | 25 | 24 | $105

Gold Canyon | 6100 S. Kings Ranch Rd. | 480-982-9449 | 800-827-5281 |
www.gcgr.com | 6509/4426; 71.6/66.1; 132/110
Unobstructed views of the Superstition Mountains make this serpentine track a "great second when playing its sister course", Dinosaur Mountain; cognoscenti caution you should "be careful of [tackling] this course when it's hot", as you're in a part of the desert where "there are no trees"; you'll discover, however, that there's plenty of wildlife to make it worth the "long drive from Phoenix."

Las Sendas 🏨
24 | 19 | 19 | 21 | $150

Mesa | 7555 E. Eagle Crest Dr. | 480-396-4000 | www.lassendas.com |
6914/5100; 72.5/69.9; 145/128
"Play from the tips at your own peril" and "make sure you have plenty of balls" at this RTJ Jr. design in Mesa that's "one of the toughest tracks in the desert", given that it pairs its "beautiful scenery" with "murderous greens" that can make for a "very long day"; although critics carp the clubhouse is "not much to look at" and "there's not enough staff", most agree it's still "worth the drive from Phoenix or Scottsdale."

Longbow
23 | 21 | 20 | 24 | $99

Mesa | 5601 E. Longbow Pkwy. | 480-807-5400 | www.longbowgolf.com |
7003/5202; 72.2/70.2; 129/124
This "shortish", "well-thought-out" Ken Kavanaugh design in Mesa is a "nice desert course with good mountain views", "no two holes

that are similar" and, though "very difficult from the back tees", a lay-out that's also "attractive to the higher handicap player"; meanwhile, the staff is both "friendly and helpful", and arms enthusiasts get a kick out of seeing "Apache Longbow helicopters lift off and hover" over the nearby Boeing plant.

Los Caballeros

COURSE	FACIL.	SERVICE	VALUE	COST
-	-	-	-	$135

Wickenburg | 1551 S. Vulture Mine Rd. | 928-684-2704 | www.loscaballerosgolf.com | 7015/5064; 73/70.6; 135/125
"If this course were 20 miles nearer to Phoenix, it would have hosted a big tournament" say geographically aware aces who appreciate this desert-mountain track nearly an hour northwest of the city; mature trees, a "great staff" and an on-site resort/dude ranch renowned for its horseback riding program leads cowboys to crow "it's off the beaten path, but it's a value."

Marriott's Wildfire, Faldo Championship

COURSE	FACIL.	SERVICE	VALUE	COST
23	24	23	19	$205

Phoenix | 5350 E. Marriott Dr. | 480-473-0205 | 888-705-7775 | www.wildfiregolf.com | 6846/5245; 71.6/69.6; 127/120
"Bring a pail, a bucket and SPF 30, because never before have I seen so many sand traps" brays one birdie-seeker of this "well-maintained", "wide-open" resort spread situated against the "beautiful backdrop of Desert Ridge" in Phoenix; yes, it may be "on the expensive side compared to some of Arizona's best", but most concur "Nick Faldo knows how to design a course that's fun without being a pushover."

Marriott's Wildfire, Palmer Signature

COURSE	FACIL.	SERVICE	VALUE	COST
25	25	24	20	$205

Phoenix | 5350 E. Marriott Dr. | 480-473-0205 | 888-705-7775 | www.wildfiregolf.com | 7170/5505; 73.3/70.1; 135/116
In the shadow of Arizona's largest hotel (the 900-plus room JW Marriott Desert Ridge Resort & Spa) sits this "flat", "fairly open" layout with "big greens" and fairways framed by desert flora; although "pricey", loyalists who have sampled this Arnold Palmer design call it "fun to play and yet a test" and praise the course's "excellent conditions" as well as its "first-class" facilities and service.

Ocotillo

COURSE	FACIL.	SERVICE	VALUE	COST
22	22	23	20	$165

Chandler | 3751 S. Clubhouse Dr. | 480-917-6660 | 888-624-8899 | www.ocotillogolf.com
Gold/Blue | 7016/5128; 72.2/69.6; 133/124
Gold/White | 6804/5124; 71.5/69.3; 128/118
White/Blue | 6782/5134; 71.3/70.2; 130/117
Go ahead and rub your eyes, for this 27-holer has fairways so "lush and green" you'll think you're "playing in Florida" as you take in the sight of this "oasis of water in the middle of the desert" near Chandler; as you might expect, you can "lose lots of balls in one of the 14 water holes", but this "nice surprise" "for golfers of all abilities" seems "designed to challenge and not to frustrate."

Papago Municipal

COURSE	FACIL.	SERVICE	VALUE	COST
▽ 18	7	8	24	$38

Phoenix | 5595 E. Moreland St. | 602-275-8428 | 7068/5937; 73.6/72.4; 132/119
"A great discovery in the land of high-priced golf", this "hidden oldie" "in the heart of Phoenix" sports "exceptional holes", many "with a

view of the red rocks of Papago [Butte]"; for some, this "overused" public course "needs money dumped into it" and requires "interminable waits", but those in-the-know praise a layout that's "unbelievable for a muni" – this "Valley of the Sun steal" is a "true bang for your buck."

Pointe at Lookout Mountain ▨ | 20 | 22 | 21 | 18 | $149

Phoenix | 11111 N. Seventh St. | 602-866-6356 | 800-947-9784 | www.pointehilton.com | 6535/4557; 70.1/66.3; 131/110

Look both ways before playing, as this "short but tricky" layout in Phoenix feels "like two different courses from the front to the back", with some holes that are flat with wall-to-wall grass and others that represent "target golf at its toughest, with a lot of grade change"; aces attest that the place has something up its sleeve, however – a "treat of a back nine."

Raven at South Mountain | 23 | 24 | 24 | 20 | $180

Phoenix | 3636 E. Baseline Rd. | 602-243-3636 | www.ravenatsouthmountain.com | 7078/5800; 73.9/72.9; 133/124

If you're "looking for South Carolina golf in Arizona, this is the place" say bi-coastal baggers who believe in this "really fun", "well-kept" course where "you'd never know you were in Phoenix" given that "it's lined with pine trees rather than palms"; although the flattish layout is considered "pleasant if uninspired", the club itself is an "exemplar of what service should be" – after all, it pioneered the use of "ice-cold, mango-scented towels."

Raven at Verrado | ▽ 24 | 25 | 25 | 25 | $179

Buckeye | 4242 N. Golf Dr. | 623-388-3000 | www.ravenatverrado.com | 7258/5402; 73.8/69.8; 132/118

"Winding through canyons" on the western edge of metro Phoenix, this "wonderful desert" design from Tom Lehman and John Fought offers up "beautiful views of the nearby mountains" to go with its many "challenging holes"; although critics chirp that it's "still young", the rest of the flock agrees that the venue's unique, "all-inclusive package that includes unlimited golf", use of the "nice" practice facilities and two full meals makes this an "excellent value."

Whirlwind, Cattail | ▽ 28 | 27 | 26 | 26 | $150

Chandler | 5692 W. North Loop Rd. | 480-940-1500 | www.whirlwindgolf.com | 7218/5383; 73.4/70.8; 132/123

You'll find "more trouble than anticipated" on this "good desert course" that's the younger of the two tracks at the Sheraton Wild Horse Pass hotel 30 minutes south of Phoenix; a "very nice" layout "for a resort", this overall "great play" and its risk/reward holes tested the Nationwide Tour pros until 2005; the clubhouse's Sivlik Grill, a soothing spa and a "nearby casino" offer further enticement.

Whirlwind, Devil's Claw | ▽ 26 | 24 | 26 | 25 | $150

Chandler | 5692 W. North Loop Rd. | 480-940-1500 | www.whirlwindgolf.com | 7029/5540; 72.6/71.4; 129/121

Perhaps it's the "great course conditions" (including "superb, fast greens") or the fact that this "beautiful" Gary Panks design offers panoramic vistas of the Estrella and Superstition Mountains, but whatever their reasoning, desert-dwellers have decided that this Sheraton Wild

	COURSE	FACIL.	SERVICE	VALUE	COST

Horse Pass resort track is a "decent" Phoenix-area option and "an excellent value for the price."

Wigwam, Gold

COURSE	FACIL.	SERVICE	VALUE	COST
19	21	20	18	$160

Litchfield Park | 451 N. Litchfield Rd. | 623-935-9414 | 800-909-4224 | www.wigwamresort.com | 7430/5885; 74.5/72.3; 135/125

"By far the best of Wigwam's three courses", this "long", flat, tree-lined "walk in the park" from Robert Trent Jones Sr. may "seem out of place in the land of desert/target golf", but players praise the west-of-Phoenix layout as a "tough track" with a "super-friendly staff"; complaints of "old everything", meanwhile, should be silenced by a recent, multimillion-dollar renovation that reshaped bunkers and expanded both the greens and practice facilities.

San Carlos

Apache Stronghold

COURSE	FACIL.	SERVICE	VALUE	COST
▽ 24	15	15	25	$55

San Carlos | Hwy. 70 (5 mi. east of Hwy. 77) | 928-475-7800 | 800-272-2438 | www.golfapache.com | 7519/5535; 74.5/70.9; 146/123

A "shining" example of a desert course, this Tom Doak design inspires roundsmen to make the drive "way out of Phoenix" (it's located two hours east of the city) for an "excellent" layout; it's a "good course for the money", but the consensus seems to be that the club needs to pache up the "dodgy conditions" and "turf problems."

Scottsdale

Camelback, Club

COURSE	FACIL.	SERVICE	VALUE	COST
20	22	23	19	$125

Scottsdale | 7847 N. Mockingbird Ln. | 480-596-7050 | www.camelbackinn.com | 7014/5808; 72.6/71.5; 122/118

"Wide fairways make it hard to lose a ball" on this "straightforward" 29-year-old course at the Marriott Camelback Inn in Scottsdale where pines, palms, greenside bunkers and mountain views greet golfers on every hole; although low-handicappers feel "it could use a little more shot selection", for others it's "nice to play [while] on holiday."

Camelback, Resort

COURSE	FACIL.	SERVICE	VALUE	COST
20	23	21	18	$169

Scottsdale | 7847 N. Mockingbird Ln. | 480-596-7050 | www.camelbackinn.com | 6903/5132; 72.8/68.6; 132/114

Like the eponymous mountain nearby, this "nice course with nicer personnel" is "gorgeous", offering "pristine tees, fairways and greens", mature trees and "spectacular sunsets"; though some scoffers sniff "it's more like camel breath compared to other courses in the area" (especially "for the price"), the resort and spa amenities are "magnificent" enticements.

Eagle Mountain

COURSE	FACIL.	SERVICE	VALUE	COST
26	24	24	22	$195

Fountain Hills | 14915 E. Eagle Mountain Pkwy. | 480-816-1234 | www.eaglemtn.com | 6802/5065; 71.7/68.2; 139/118

"Always in excellent condition", this Fountain Hills "jewel" is a "must-play for anyone visiting Phoenix" fawn fans who extol its "lofty tee boxes", "awesome hills and canyons" and "superb views"; the fairways are "very forgiving", while the "elevation changes will make your ears pop", and though some find the practice facilities merely "adequate", the service is "great from the bag drop to the rangers."

Gainey Ranch 🏨 ⛳

| | | | | $140 |

Scottsdale | 7600 E. Gainey Club Dr. | 480-951-0022 |
www.gaineyranchcc.com
Arroyo/Dunes | 6662/5515; 71.9/69.8; 128/123
Arroyo/Lakes | 6800/5312; 71.9/69.8; 129/123
Dunes/Lakes | 6614/4993; 71/68.1; 125/120

"Stay and play here if you can" advise road warriors who've sampled the "three distinct nines" (available only to guests of the Hyatt Regency Scottsdale) on this "flat but fun" course attached to a "beautiful clubhouse"; the discontented deem it "undemanding" and "short", but the majority maintain they'd "go back without question."

Grayhawk, Raptor

26 | 25 | 25 | 19 | $210

Scottsdale | 8620 E. Thompson Peak Pkwy. | 480-502-1800 | 800-472-9429 |
www.grayhawkgolf.com | 7135/5309; 74.1/71.3; 143/127

"Bring your expense account" for a "memory you will not forget" at this "top-notch" desert design in Scottsdale where "impeccable service", a "superb driving range", "upscale pro shop" and memorabilia-laden Phil's Grill (named for Phil Mickelson) make it "worth the splurge"; Tom Fazio's "strategic layout" is "not for the faint of heart" with its "many forced carries", but the "wide fairways and undulating greens" make it a local "must-play."

Grayhawk, Talon

26 | 27 | 26 | 21 | $210

Scottsdale | 8620 E. Thompson Peak Pkwy. | 480-502-1800 | 800-472-9429 |
www.grayhawkgolf.com | 6973/5143; 73.6/70; 143/121

In addition to an "awesome" "desert layout" with "beautiful views", this "phenomenal" Scottsdale destination boasts a "spectacular clubhouse" and service that "exceeds other courses"; though some duffers moan that "most driveways are wider than these fairways", others insist the course "has some room and is not too penal", making it "tough but fun"; it's "pricey", but "worth the outlay for the experience."

Kierland

23 | 24 | 23 | 20 | $199

Scottsdale | 15636 N. Clubgate Dr. | 480-922-9283 | www.kierlandgolf.com
Acacia/Ironwood | 6974/4985; 72.5/67.8; 128/118
Acacia/Mesquite | 6913/4898; 72.2/67.7; 131/116
Ironwood/Mesquite | 7017/5017; 73/68.1; 130/114

"Resort golf at its finest" can be found in "the middle of Scottsdale" at this 27-holer whose "three gorgeous nines" are "immaculately maintained" and "can be enjoyed by players at all levels" given fairways that allow you to "bomb your drive" since "every ball comes back to the center"; while "the pace may be a bit slow" at times, the "air-conditioned golf carts are a blessing in the summer" and the Segways are a "must-try" at any time of year.

Legend Trail

23 | 20 | 21 | 19 | $170

Scottsdale | 9462 Legendary Ln. | 480-488-7434 | www.legendtrailgc.com |
6845/5001; 73.2/68.2; 135/122

Wake up to this "real sleeper" designed by Rees Jones that features a "fantastic back nine" that "winds up a mountain", offering "great views of the surrounding valley"; although "you don't feel like you're in the middle of the desert" due to a "profusion of condos lining the fairways" (a "downside" for many), most prefer to focus instead on the "female-friendly" layout and "excellent teaching facility."

	COURSE	FACIL.	SERVICE	VALUE	COST

Phoenician, The 🏌

| 23 | 26 | 25 | 17 | $195 |

Scottsdale | 6000 E. Camelback Rd. | 480-423-2449 | 800-888-8234 |
www.thephoenician.com
Canyon/Desert | 6068/4777; 69.4/67.7; 131/117
Desert/Oasis | 6310/5024; 70.3/68.7; 130/117
Oasis/Canyon | 6258/4871; 70.1/68.4; 130/114

"Set beautifully" on the grounds of Scottsdale's "wonderful"
Phoenician hotel and spa, this "unique but short" "combination of
three nine-hole layouts" represents "resort golf at its finest"; although
"one nine is lined with a collection of cacti, waterfalls and ponds", all
of the holes offer "the ultimate in lush greens", "spectacular" mountain views and access to both the renowned Mary Elaine's restaurant
and the 19th Hole Grill, a "lovely place for a cocktail after a round."

Sanctuary at Westworld

| 22 | 18 | 19 | 23 | $119 |

Scottsdale | 10690 E. Sheena Dr. | 480-502-8200 | www.sanctuarygolf.com |
6624/4926; 71.2/67.8; 139/117

"You better hit them straight or you're in for a long day" at this hilly
"hidden treasure" in the Scottsdale desert that features protected
wetlands, "tight fairways, elevated tees and good risk/reward" opportunities, plus "a great finish" in the form of a "blind 18th"; while the
"overhead high-tension wires destroy the view" for one myopic
mashie-toter, there are enough unobstructed mountain vistas for
most to say they "could play this course every week."

SunRidge Canyon 🏌

| 26 | 23 | 22 | 21 | $195 |

Fountain Hills | 13100 N. Sunridge Dr. | 480-837-5100 | 800-562-5178 |
www.sunridgegolf.com | 6823/5193; 72.6/70.1; 142/128

"Be prepared to be challenged" by "difficult carries off the tee boxes",
"tight fairways" and some of "the toughest green complexes in the
area" at this "scenic" desert course offering "incredible views" as it
"winds through spectacular canyons"; though "challenging" and "not
for beginners", "it's interesting at all times" and well "worth the
money" and "the drive to Fountain Hills"; P.S. "after a long uphill grind
on the back nine, the great food is a fine reward!"

Talking Stick, North

| 23 | 22 | 23 | 21 | $170 |

Scottsdale | 9998 E. Indian Bend Rd. | 480-860-2221 |
www.talkingstickgolfclub.com | 7133/5532; 72.7/70.6; 123/117

This "low-slung desert" delight designed by Bill Coore and Ben
Crenshaw draws mixed reviews from Scottsdale swingers: while
some find the "links-style layout" to be a "tough, flat" and "beautiful"
"purist's course", others consider it "uninspiring" ("almost every hole
is straight") with views that are "not as spectacular as some"; nevertheless, golfers agree it maintains "impeccable standards, from
the clubhouse to the practice range" to grounds that are "thankfully
free of McMansions."

Talking Stick, South

| 22 | 24 | 24 | 21 | $170 |

Scottsdale | 9998 E. Indian Bend Rd. | 480-860-2221 |
www.talkingstickgolfclub.com | 6833/5428; 71.5/69; 125/120

"Somewhat unique for a desert course", this "classic" parkland-style
design from Bill Coore and Ben Crenshaw features "wide", tree-lined
fairways, "large, undulating greens" and just enough water; while one

discontented duffer dismisses the North's younger sibling as "flat" and "boring", most appreciate its "great course conditions", "gracious personnel" and "cool", "rustic" setting – it's "close to everything", yet has views of "wild horses nearby."

TPC Scottsdale, Stadium

| 25 | 25 | 24 | 17 | $238 |

Scottsdale | 17020 N. Hayden Rd. | 480-585-4334 | www.tpc.com | 7216/5567; 74.6/72.9; 138/130

You'll "feel like a tour pro" at this "home of the FBR Open", a "true desert-style layout" where the "generous fairways" and "fabulous greens" are kept in "pristine shape"; although a few find the prices "ridiculous" – "bring your PGA-sized checkbook with you" – most agree this Weiskopf/Morrish design is "worth it once" to indulge in "top-notch facilities" (including a "well-run pro shop") and a surplus of "great history, especially on the par-3 16th."

☑ Troon North, Monument ⏱

| 28 | 26 | 26 | 20 | $295 |

Scottsdale | 10320 E. Dynamite Blvd. | 480-585-5300 | www.troonnorthgolf.com | 7028/5050; 73.3/68.5; 147/117

"Be treated like a sun god" at this "always magnificent" desert design from Weiskopf and Morrish that's Arizona's top-rated Course; according to its loyal following, it's "first-class all the way", from the "perfectly manicured grounds" and "great pro shop" to the "wonderful service" and "starkly beautiful" setting, with "a quietude found only in the mountains" amid the "rattlers, coyotes" and saguaros; "brace yourself for ridiculously high fees", but rest assured it's "worth the splurge."

Troon North, Pinnacle ⏱

| 27 | 26 | 26 | 20 | $295 |

Scottsdale | 10320 E. Dynamite Blvd. | 480-585-5300 | www.troonnorthgolf.com | 7044/4980; 73.4/68.6; 147/120

"Fabulous like its sister course", Monument, this "visually arresting" Weiskopf/Morrish design plays over "spectacular", "varied terrain" that offers "great vistas" of the surrounding desert and mountains; the "incredibly difficult" track is "a true test of your game and wallet" "but worth it" for "amazing conditioning", "top-notch facilities" and "excellent service" that more than make up for the sight of "a few too many houses"; P.S. stay at the Four Seasons and "take the shuttle – what could be better?"

☑ We-Ko-Pa, Cholla

| 28 | 24 | 24 | 24 | $195 |

Fort McDowell | 18200 E. Toh Vee Circle | 480-836-9000 | www.wekopa.com | 7225/5337; 73/69.9; 136/126

They should "call it 'Wow-Ko-Pa'" aver acolytes of this "incredible, undulating, lush course" next to Fort McDowell Casino; it's clear that "slot-machine money has been lavished" on a "gorgeous layout" ("views for miles") that's "worth the extra drive" for its "demanding approaches", "carpetlike fairways", "wonderful practice facilities" and, "best of all, no houses"; just "be prepared to walk, as it's cart-path-only" and "mighty hilly."

NEW We-Ko-Pa, Saguaro

| – | – | – | – | $195 |

Fort McDowell | 18200 E. Toh Vee Circle | 480-836-9000 | www.wekopa.com | 6912/5061; 72.1/68.4; 137/112

Architects Bill Coore and Ben Crenshaw have carved out a modern (if slightly retro) design from the saguaro-studded Sonoran Desert with this rolling yet walkable layout – a rarity in these parts – where Scottish-style run-up shots are encouraged; what the course shares with its sibling, Cholla, are fairways bracketed by dense, thorny underbrush and backdropped by the Four Peaks Mountain and Wilderness Area, with nary a home or road in play.

Sedona

Sedona Golf Resort

| 23 | 20 | 20 | 22 | $95 |

Sedona | 35 Ridge Trail Dr. | 928-284-9355 | 877-733-9885 | www.sedonagolfresort.com | 6646/5059; 70.6/68.9; 128/126

Sporting "absolutely stunning" "vistas of the red rock formations", this "picturesque" Sedona spread is "so beautiful that it's hard to concentrate on your game"; distractions aside, this "hilly" "desert course nestled into an upscale resort home" development is "replete with water, sand and all the necessary challenges to make this an unforgettable playing experience"; plus, given "costs that keep the crowds away", you may just have the "friendly staff" and "immaculate grounds" all to yourself.

Tucson

Arizona National 🏌

| 25 | 22 | 22 | 21 | $165 |

Tucson | 9777 E. Sabino Greens Dr. | 520-749-3636 | www.arizonanationalgolfclub.com | 6785/4469; 72.4/66.3; 146/116

"Beautiful mountain" scenery, "variety in hole design" and "great elevation changes" spur swingers to visit this "well-kept" Robert Trent Jones Jr. layout that's one of "the best courses in the Tucson area"; while straight arrows advise you "stay out of the rough", crooked drivers suggest you "play the 18th from the tips" to take in views that reach clear to Mexico.

El Conquistador, Conquistador 🏌

| 19 | 18 | 19 | 19 | $125 |

Tucson | 10555 N. La Cañada Dr. | 520-544-5000 | www.hiltonelconquistador.com | 6781/4821; 72.7/69; 126/121

Just a "good course for a fun round", this desert layout located a few minutes from a Hilton-affiliated resort in Tucson sports "rolling hills, big greens and views"; although bored baggers bemoan the "uncreative" design and "uneventful holes", others find it a "challenge" and suggest playing "in summer" when "you can find some great deals."

La Paloma 🏌 ⛳

| 25 | 26 | 25 | 18 | $215 |

Tucson | 3660 E. Sunrise Dr. | 520-299-1500 | 800-222-1249 | www.lapalomacc.com
Canyon/Hill | 6997/5057; 73.1/70.6; 149/126
Hill/Ridge | 7017/4878; 72.3/68.5; 144/123
Ridge/Canyon | 7088/5075; 73.2/70.1; 154/123

Offering "incredible variations in altitude" and "target golf throughout", this "early Nicklaus design" in the desert near Tucson is "one of the best group of resort nines around", a facility where you "need to be a mountain climber" to negotiate some of the "deep grassy moguls surrounding the greens"; though the fees may "burn a hole in your pocket", an "excellent" staff that "provides cold towels drenched in ice" helps most keep their cool.

	COURSE	FACIL.	SERVICE	VALUE	COST

Omni Tucson National, Catalina ▽ 24 | 23 | 23 | 21 | $181

Tucson | 2727 W. Club Dr. | 520-297-2271 | www.tucsonnational.com |
7262/5414; 74.8/65.5; 138/125

Home to 40 years of events featuring champions like Arnold Palmer, Lee
Trevino and Johnny Miller, this "PGA Tournament–quality" resort layout
in Tucson offers "solid golf" before a multilayered mountain backdrop;
keep in mind, however, that watery finishes on each nine means "you
must be careful not to allow the 9th and 18th to destroy your score."

NEW Omni Tucson National, Sonoran ▽ 23 | 22 | 22 | 20 | $181

Tucson | 2727 W. Club Dr. | 520-297-2271 | www.tucsonnational.com |
6552/4579; 70/64; 127/109

"It may not have the history of the Catalina course", but the newer of
the two tracks at Omni Tucson National "provides what you came to
Arizona for: desert golf"; hilly with steep elevation changes and vistas
of the surrounding mountains, this 2006 Tom Lehman design (an expansion of an existing nine) is "friendly to all levels" and has swingers
swearing it "will really be something fun when it matures."

Starr Pass 🏌 23 | 21 | 21 | 18 | $190

Tucson | 3645 W. Starr Pass Blvd. | 520-670-0400 | 800-503-2898 |
www.starrpasstucson.com
Coyote/Rattler | 7002/5262; 73/70.8; 138/125
Coyote/Roadrunner | 6753/4963; 71.7/67.6; 143/120
Rattler/Roadrunner | 6731/5039; 71.7/68.2; 142/120

"The occasional quail or roadrunner" sighting is part of the "incredible
views" at this "fun desert course" tucked "in the Tucson foothills"; part
of "Marriott's new resort", the three "challenging" nines are "playable" but feature "ravines and barrancas" that may make it "tough for
the average golfer"; still, most warm to the "lush greens" and "first-
rate" clubhouse restaurant, where you can "eat dinner while watching
the sun come down over the mountains."

Ventana Canyon, Canyon 🏌 26 | 25 | 25 | 21 | $225

Tucson | 6200 N. Club House Ln. | 520-577-1400 |
www.thelodgeatventanacanyon.com | 6819/4939; 72.6/70.2; 140/119

Set in "one of the most magical locations in the world", this "incredible" Tom Fazio track is so "picturesque, it takes one's mind off balls
lost" in the North Tucson desert; "a pleasure to play" with its "beautiful conditioning" and "high shot value", it both "looks and feels like a
private club – which it is" ("members can play either course", but
guests of the two on-site hotels "are assigned to one per day");
N.B. expect new USGA ratings for the 2007 season.

Ventana Canyon, Mountain 🏌 27 | 24 | 24 | 21 | $225

Tucson | 6200 N. Club House Ln. | 520-577-1400 |
www.thelodgeatventanacanyon.com | 6907/4676; 73/68.3; 147/119

For "desert golf at its finest", head to this "scenic" Tom Fazio design
that's "as good as it gets in southern Arizona – or most places!" –
owing to its "spectacular vistas" and "memorable holes"; for some, it
seems to be "all about dodging boulders", but the vast majority consider it a "challenging course" that offers "excellent facilities", a "great
dining room" and luxe accommodations at the Lodge at Ventana
Canyon and Loews Ventana Canyon hotels.

	COURSE	FACIL.	SERVICE	VALUE	COST

Vistoso
26 | 21 | 22 | 23 | $175

Tucson | 955 W. Vistoso Highlands Dr. | 520-797-7900 | 877-548-1110 | www.vistosogolf.com | 6954/5095; 72.1/68.7; 147/120

Though "out of the way" in North Tucson, this "testy little" track is "worth the visit" insist swingers satisfied with the "target golf" – lots of bunkering, cacti and long carries – offered up by Tom Weiskopf's "beautiful, challenging" desert design; detractors dis the "cheesy housing" that's "starting to encroach" on the fairways, but more maintain they "would return", seeing as the "quality course" is kept in "consistently great shape" and "is just plain fun."

Arkansas

Fayetteville

Stonebridge Meadows
▽ 22 | 16 | 19 | 23 | $49

Fayetteville | 3495 E. Goff Farm Rd. | 479-571-3673 | 866-589-7753 | www.stonebridgemeadows.com | 7150/5215; 74.8/70.7; 138/128

"This place is the best in class" say swinging students of this Randy Heckenkemper course near the University of Arkansas, where the low-handicap Razorbacks golf team is tested by watery par 3s, densely wooded risk/reward par 5s and some of "the fastest greens" around; for those who "can easily get distracted by beauty", the architect built wide fairways, making this a "friendly family course."

California

TOP COURSES IN STATE

29 Pebble Beach | *Monterey Peninsula*
   Spyglass Hill | *Monterey Peninsula*
28 Pasatiempo | *Santa Cruz*
27 CordeValle | *San Francisco Bay Area*
   Maderas | *San Diego*
   Desert Willow, Firecliff | *Palm Springs*
   Torrey Pines, South | *San Diego*
26 PGA West, TPC Stadium | *Palm Springs*
   Lost Canyons, Sky | *Los Angeles*
   Spanish Bay | *Monterey Peninsula*

Lake Tahoe

Coyote Moon
26 | 19 | 21 | 18 | $150

Truckee | 10685 Northwoods Blvd. | 530-587-0886 | www.coyotemoongolf.com | 7177/5022; 74.1/68.4; 138/127

"Run, don't walk" to this "Tahoe-area jewel" that resembles "a walk in the park – Yosemite National Park" – with its "unbelievably beautiful mountain vistas, creeks and natural features"; some insist it was "a [better] value when it opened" in 2000, but it's "a must-play at least once" for its "many memorable holes" (like the "eye-opening par-3 13th with a 227-ft. drop") that feature "spacious fairways", "wonderful greens" and, best of all, "no houses!"

	COURSE	FACIL.	SERVICE	VALUE	COST

NEW Old Greenwood — `25` `23` `23` `18` `$170`

Truckee | 12915 Fairway Dr. | 530-550-7010 | 800-754-3070 |
www.oldgreenwood.com | 7518/5419; 75.8/69.8; 149/133

Situated "in a meadow at 6,000 feet with fairways that weave through
pines" and lakes, this "gorgeous" mountain "must-play" "just north of
Truckee" is "classic Nicklaus": "long", "tough" and "designed for low-
handicappers"; the "traditional" track is "so attractive that it (almost)
doesn't matter what you shoot" – "where else can you see a bald eagle
overhead?" – which has penny-pinchers admitting that it's "well
worth" its "pricey" fees.

Whitehawk Ranch — `25` `19` `21` `22` `$130`

Clio | 768 Whitehawk Dr. | 530-836-0394 | 800-332-4295 |
www.golfwhitehawk.com | 6927/4816; 72.6/65.4; 133/122

"One of the nicest mountain courses in the Sierras, period", this
"beautiful place to play" provides "visual delights" and a "great vibe"
on a track that "feels as if you're wandering through the woods of
Georgia"; although the course's facilities are decidedly "no-frills",
most find them "fittingly humble" – after all, this "great getaway location" "out of the way" in North Tahoe is "all about a comfortable, enjoyable round of golf."

Los Angeles

Angeles National 🔍 — `23` `12` `18` `17` `$110`

Sunland | 9401 Foothill Blvd. | 818-951-8771 | www.angelesnational.com |
7143/4899; 74.7/68.9; 143/116

"Seemingly above the LA smog", this "wonderful new" "Steve Nicklaus
design (not Jack)" just north of Burbank is a "long, tough" "layout for
thinking people" where "wayward shots are punished mercilessly" –
so "bring lots of balls"; the desert-style "escape" also includes "beautiful greens" and "great practice facilities" and has plans to build a
mission-style clubhouse that fans expect will "be world-class" – and it
may be, considering the temporary facility already hosts "many a
celeb nursing a cold one."

Industry Hills, Eisenhower — `-` `-` `-` `-` `$119`

City of Industry | 1 Industry Hills Pkwy. | 626-810-4653 | www.ihgolfclub.com

Industrious types will use every tool in their arsenal as they take on
this 1979 William F. Bell design that underwent a recent makeover, re-
opening in November 2006 with improved drainage, cleaned-out
rough and revamped bunkering; just 25 miles east of LA, this hilly layout remains a relentlessly rugged (if more player-friendly) test that rewards you at the finish with the luxe Pacific Palms Resort; N.B. the
course will receive new USGA ratings in late February 2007.

Lost Canyons, Shadow — `23` `24` `22` `20` `$125`

Simi Valley | 3301 Lost Canyon Dr. | 805-522-4653 | www.lostcanyons.com |
7005/4795; 75/69.1; 149/125

"Bring balls, lots of balls", to "one of the most enjoyable ways to get
beat up": this "starkly beautiful" Pete Dye design where "accuracy is
at a premium" given its "many blind shots" and landing areas that "are
surrounded by precipitous drops or heavy underbrush"; conveniently
located "close to LA in Simi Valley", this is one "tough course that of-

	COURSE	FACIL.	SERVICE	VALUE	COST

fers a lot for the money", including a "friendly" staff and "great facilities"; P.S. "watch out on windy days!"

Lost Canyons, Sky

| 26 | 23 | 22 | 20 | $125 |

Simi Valley | 3301 Lost Canyon Dr. | 805-522-4653 | www.lostcanyons.com |
7285/4885; 75.6/70; 147/120

Nicknamed "'Lost Balls Canyons'" by one witty whacker, this "incredibly difficult", "hilly" design from "evil genius Pete Dye" is loaded up
with "long carries" over "gulches and natural terrain", "narrow fairways" and "huge, undulating greens"; nevertheless, a prime Simi
Valley location "only 45 minutes from Downtown LA" plus "Monet-
type landscapes" and a "nice restaurant" have most touting it as "the
toughest course you'll ever love."

Los Verdes

| 20 | 13 | 12 | 25 | $28 |

Rancho Palos Verdes | 7000 W. Los Verdes Dr. | 310-377-7888 |
www.americangolf.com | 6617/5772; 71.7/67.7; 121/113

"The best bang for your buck near Los Angeles" is this "drop-dead
beautiful" muni in Rancho Palos Verdes that pairs its "serene and unobstructed vistas of the Pacific" and Catalina Island with "sidehill lies"
and "tricky greens that all slope toward the ocean"; unfortunately,
you'll also discover the meaning of "mandatory fivesomes" and "slow
play" – "but if you have six hours to spend on a round", just "be patient
and admire the views."

Moorpark 🏌

| 24 | 23 | 22 | 21 | $105 |

Moorpark | 11800 Championship Dr. | 805-532-2834 |
www.moorparkgolf.com
Canyon Crest/Creekside | 6939/4867; 73.8/69; 136/118
Canyon Crest/Ridgeline | 6902/4839; 73/68.6; 138/116
Creekside/Ridgeline | 6977/4722; 73.8/68.5; 142/118

"This is the Wild West!" gush gunslingers about this "pristine course"
that "feels like the countryside even though you're only 45 miles from
LA"; the 27-holer offers a "nice balance" on its three nines, but "the
Creekside gets your attention" with its "elevated tees with drops of
100-plus feet" and long carries over arroyos; meanwhile, the facility's
"beautiful views" of the "local hills" and orchards make it "a great
place to show visitors"; P.S. it can get "very windy."

Ojai Valley Inn & Spa

| 24 | 24 | 24 | 20 | $170 |

Ojai | 905 Country Club Rd. | 805-646-2420 | 800-422-6524 |
www.golfojai.com | 6292/5211; 71/70.7; 132/129

"Bring your best girl" to this "wonderful resort" "nestled in the Ojai
hills" because the "outstanding experience" includes a "good spa",
"great food and lodging" and a "classic" 1923 track that "winds its way
through the California oaks" – it's "quiet, serene and with the right
partner, romantic"; it can also be "pricey", but the "challenging" "old
gal keeps getting better": two 'lost holes' from the original design were
restored in 1999 and "are a revelation."

Palos Verdes Golf Club ◷

| 23 | 19 | 19 | 18 | $210 |

Palos Verdes Estates | 3301 Via Campesina | 310-375-2533 |
www.pvgc.com | 6219/4696; 70.5/63.6; 129/111

Given its rolling, eucalyptus-dotted terrain, "small greens" and "heavy
afternoon breezes", this "beautiful" 1920s-era layout located "on

| | COURSE | FACIL. | SERVICE | VALUE | COST |

cliffs overlooking the ocean" in Palos Verdes Estates is considered to be architect George C. Thomas' "baby Riviera" (after his famed private design); a few are put off by the course's "exclusive attitude" – it's open to the public only on weekdays – but most "consider it a privilege to play here."

Rancho Park
18 | 12 | 12 | 25 | $28

Los Angeles | 10460 W. Pico Blvd. | 310-839-9812 | www.rpgc.org | 6628/6300; 71.7/69; 126/120

"A great way to brush up on your game without leaving the city", "LA's most conveniently located municipal – which means it's also the hardest at which to land a tee time" – is a "classic layout" with a "country feel" that delivers "some history" and "lots of bang for your buck"; though a "great course if you can get on", the "short, tight" track is "famously busy" – so "be prepared for a five-hour round with five of your closest friends."

Robinson Ranch, Mountain
24 | 21 | 23 | 19 | $117

Santa Clarita | 27734 Sand Canyon Rd. | 661-252-7666 | www.robinsonranchgolf.com | 6508/5076; 72.3/69.5; 137/121

One half of "the best set of courses in Santa Clarita" is this "classic, old-school" layout that's "enjoyable" but also "very challenging" – "when the wind blows, it has all you can handle"; contrarians claim the "hilly" track is "too short and tight" (hitting "straight off the tee is a must"), but it's "always in great shape" with "some of the best-kept greens in SoCal" and "excellent service" to boot, making it worth the "long drive [north] from LA."

Robinson Ranch, Valley
24 | 23 | 23 | 20 | $117

Santa Clarita | 27734 Sand Canyon Rd. | 661-252-7666 | www.robinsonranchgolf.com | 6903/5408; 74.4/72.2; 149/126

"This is what high-end public access golf should be" declare duffers delighted by this "enjoyable course" designed by Ted Robinson Jr. and Sr.; offering "remarkable scenery" and "very pure greens" that are "fast and fair", the "solid" "test of golf skills" "mixes it up" with "interesting" "short and long holes" (some with "oaks in the middle of the fairway"), "lots of risk/reward" opportunities and "a tough closing stretch" aptly dubbed 'Death Row.'

Rustic Canyon
24 | 16 | 17 | 27 | $55

Moorpark | 15100 Happy Camp Canyon Rd. | 805-530-0221 | www.rusticcanyongolfcourse.com | 6988/5283; 73.3/69.4; 128/113

For a bit of "Scotland in the San Fernando Valley", venture to this "amazing" "canyon links" "with a rustic flair" and a layout "unlike any course" around: "generous fairways", "huge, undulating", "impossible greens" and "large run-off areas" that "make for interesting choices"; some would-be Scots scoff at the "nonexistent facilities", but most find the "test" "a welcome change of pace" with an "out-of-the-way location that translates to modest greens fees."

NEW Trump National Golf Club
22 | 24 | 23 | 11 | $300

Rancho Palos Verdes | 1 Ocean Trails Dr. | 310-265-5000 | www.trumpnational.com | 7300/4600; 75/68.6; 146/124

Truly a "special-occasion" course, this Trump design in Rancho Palos Verdes doles out "breathtaking" "views of the Pacific from every hole" plus an "amazing clubhouse" and "service that would satisfy 'The Donald'" himself; the "meticulously groomed" layout is "not for the faint of heart", with "tight fairways" flanked by "the most unforgiving rough this side of Ireland", and if some purists perceive it as "unremarkable" and "overpriced", others conclude that it's "ultimately worth the cost for a hassle-free, calm and unhurried round."

Monterey Peninsula

Bayonet Black Horse, Bayonet

| 25 | 15 | 18 | 24 | $102 |

Seaside | 1 McClure Way | 831-899-7271 | www.bayonetblackhorse.com | 7117/5763; 75.6/74.3; 136/129

For "a long march down narrow fairways", head to this "old-school" spread set on "a former army base near Monterey" that's "difficult but not punishing" with "lots of doglegs", "fast greens", "fog that rolls in" and "trees for hazards"; the front nine is currently closed for "major renovations" as part of a two-year property redo (to be completed in 2009) that will make over both courses and add a hotel and condos – so "wait until it's completed, then go!"

Bayonet Black Horse, Blackhorse

| 23 | 15 | 17 | 24 | $102 |

Seaside | 1 McClure Way | 831-899-7271 | www.bayonetblackhorse.com | 7009/5648; 74.9/73; 137/126

"Just one notch below" "the tougher Bayonet", this "classic course" may not provide the same "relentless pounding" but it does have "better Monterey Bay views" and offers "all the old-style features", including "tall trees lining" the long fairways and "smallish greens"; though its facilities lead some to say it "seems like it's still owned by the Army", it will be even more of "an overall great golfing experience" (and "bargain") after upcoming renovations.

Pacific Grove Municipal

| 21 | 13 | 15 | 28 | $40 |

Pacific Grove | 77 Asilomar Blvd. | 831-648-5777 | www.ci.pg.ca.us | 5727/5305; 67.5/70.2; 118/116

"Your wallet will thank you" as you play this "treasure of a muni" that "deserves its moniker as the 'poor man's Pebble Beach'"; the "best value on the Monterey coast", this "delightful course" pairs its "standard" inland front with a "wonderful back" boasting "spectacular" oceanside holes complete with "rolling dunes" and "million-dollar views" of "waves crashing on the rocks"; the "high volume of play" leads to "so-so conditioning", but a "new clubhouse and restaurant add much" to the experience.

⊠ Pebble Beach ⚬⏱

| 29 | 27 | 27 | 16 | $475 |

Pebble Beach | 1700 17-Mile Dr. | 831-624-3811 | 800-654-9300 | www.pebblebeach.com | 6737/5198; 73.8/71.8; 142/129

"The crème de la crème of American golf" is "all it's cracked up to be", so "do whatever you need to do" to play this "legendary" "slice of heaven" – California's top-rated Course and the Most Popular in this Survey – where "the hype, the history and the drama" "ooze out of every inch of turf"; given the "unbelievable coastal views" and "unending memories", you'll want to "walk so you can savor every footstep" of a "luxurious experience" that is sure to "change your life . . . and your credit card statement."

	COURSE	FACIL.	SERVICE	VALUE	COST

☑ Poppy Hills 🏌

	26	23	22	24	$195

Pebble Beach | 3200 Lopez Rd. | 831-625-1513 | www.poppyhillsgolf.com | 6833/5403; 74.2/71.6; 144/131

Perhaps "the best value on 17-Mile Drive" is this "very picturesque" "Robert Trent Jones Jr. gem" that's nestled "among Pebble's pines rather than on the Pacific"; it dishes out "morning mist", "big", "hilly greens" and "lots of doglegs", making it "brutal if you're wild off the tee" or "when the wind blows"; still, though there are "no views of the ocean", "watch out for the deer" as "they own the fairways" (i.e. the same ones "the pros walk in the AT&T National Pro-Am").

Quail Lodge 🔑⏱

	21	23	23	18	$200

Carmel | 8000 Valley Greens Dr. | 831-620-8808 | 888-828-8787 | www.quaillodge.com | 6449/5488; 71.4/72; 128/127

"The unspoiled and untouristy Carmel Valley" "is the perfect setting for golf and relaxation and Quail Lodge provides both in grand manner" aver acolytes of this "great little" riverside track that's "very playable with some interesting water holes" and "easy greens [that] equal better scores"; all in all, it's a "well-maintained" and "fun course along the mountains" that most say they'd definitely "play again"; P.S. they offer some "nice" package deals.

San Juan Oaks

	22	21	19	20	$80

Hollister | 3825 Union Rd. | 831-636-6118 | 800-453-8337 | www.sanjuanoaks.com | 7133/4770; 75.6/64.5; 145/115

"What a gem!" exclaim enthusiasts of this "challenging" "coastal hills course in the middle of nowhere" – actually, "halfway between Monterey and San Jose" – that parcels out "a great variety" of "hard and more forgiving holes" on a "flat front and a very hilly back"; "just remote enough to keep the crowds away", this "beautiful" layout is "usually easy to get on", although it's also easy "to be blown off" by "strong afternoon winds."

☑ Spanish Bay 🏌

	26	27	27	18	$240

Pebble Beach | 2700 17-Mile Dr. | 831-647-7500 | 800-654-9300 | www.pebblebeach.com | 6821/5332; 74.1/72.1; 146/129

"It's links, it's ocean, it's hard . . . but you've gotta play" RTJ Jr.'s "Monterey Coast masterpiece" as it will "challenge your mind" with its "seaside routing through dunes and forest" and "enlighten your senses" with its "serene beauty"; "a treat" for low-handicappers, shotmakers and short-gamers, this "windy", misty "taste of Scottish golf with California style" – "at sunset, the bagpiper will bring a tear to your eye" – is best "followed with cocktails by the fire pit at the Inn at Spanish Bay."

☑ Spyglass Hill 🏌

	29	23	25	20	$300

Pebble Beach | Spyglass Hill Rd. | 831-625-8563 | 800-654-9300 | www.pebblebeach.com | 6938/5379; 75.5/72.9; 147/133

"Wowza!" – this "ridiculously beautiful" "thinking-man's track" designed by Robert Trent Jones Sr. starts off with five "ruggedly spectacular" holes that "hug the ocean", then "effortlessly segues" into a virtual "nature preserve" that's "routed through tall pines" ("à la the Carolinas") "requiring precise driving"; in short, this Pebble Beach layout "is damn hard" – for "serious golfers only!" – and "staggeringly expensive", although swingers insist "you'll not find a better test of golf on the planet" or possibly "in the universe."

Orange County

Arroyo Trabuco
23 | 22 | 22 | 25 | $94

Mission Viejo | 26772 Avery Pkwy. | 949-305-5100 |
www.arroyotrabuco.com | 7011/5045; 73.7/59.8; 134/121

"Orange County's best deal" may be this "beautiful if tough" track that "winds through canyons" – with "no houses" and "great nature views" – and features "huge, rolling greens", "carries over barrancas" and "great service from top to bottom"; while some argue that it's too "crowded" and "not fully mature", those hungry for more can "follow the yummy scent of BBQ" to the "cool clubhouse" for some "outstanding food from O'Neill's."

Black Gold
20 | 20 | 20 | 18 | $104

Yorba Linda | 17681 Lakeview Ave. | 714-961-0060 |
www.blackgoldgolf.com | 6756/4937; 73.1/69.3; 133/124

Situated on an old oil field, this "surprisingly" "great course" "in a less-than-glamorous area" "above Yorba Linda" is a "decent" Arthur Hills design featuring "steep hills" "and more hills", along with "lovely views over Orange County" and of "oil wells and golfers both pumping away"; some describe the layout as "quirky" with its "many blind shots" and "OB on both sides" of the fairways, but most gold-diggers declare it "a wonderful experience."

Monarch Beach
22 | 23 | 23 | 15 | $210

Dana Point | 50 Monarch Beach Resort N. | 949-240-8247 |
www.monarchbeachgolf.com | 6601/5050; 72.8/70.4; 138/125

"Part of the top-notch" St. Regis resort in Dana Point, this "short but fun layout" designed by Robert Trent Jones Jr. has a "great location" with "wonderful views" "of the [sea] from several holes"; although some say it's "too expensive for what it is" – it charges "ocean prices for an inland course" with "no driving range" – the majority maintains the "well-kept" tourist "favorite" is "as good as it looks" . . . and "this baby is gorgeous!"

Oak Creek
22 | 23 | 22 | 18 | $145

Irvine | 1 Golf Club Dr. | 949-653-7300 | www.oakcreekgolfclub.com |
6850/4989; 72.7/69; 132/120

"No longer an Orange County secret", this "nice Tom Fazio course" "has really matured" into an "enjoyable" option thanks to its "nicely varying terrain (amazing, in pancake-flat Irvine)", "wide fairways and accessible greens" as well as its "great service" and "outstanding practice facility"; while "you may have a brush with nature" if you go out of bounds, keep your ears open for another hazard: "trains that pass by as you address your ball" – "toot toot!"

Strawberry Farms
20 | 20 | 20 | 17 | $150

Irvine | 11 Strawberry Farms Rd. | 949-551-1811 |
www.strawberryfarmsgolf.com | 6700/4832; 72.7/68.7; 136/114

Owner and former baseball great "Doug DeCinces did a great job with this course" insist swingers sweet on this "Orange County sleeper" that's "built on the site of an old strawberry farm" and offers "two totally different nines": a "narrow" front that "runs up and down a creek" and "a back that opens up spectacularly" as it encircles a 35-acre reservoir; a "good pace" of play and "nice touches" like the "complimentary bowl of fruit" make it ripe for a return visit.

Talega 🏌

| 22 | 19 | 21 | 19 | $125 |

San Clemente | 990 Avenida Talega | 949-369-6226 | www.talegagolfclub.com | 6951/5245; 73.6/71.1; 137/121
There's "something for everyone" on this "tough" but "fun" "test" offering "many interesting shots" and "elevation changes" as it tumbles over and through San Clemente's hills, canyons and marshes with its "well-trapped" "front nine that's all about precision and a back that's all about driving the ball long and straight off the tee"; given the "friendly, down-to-earth" staff and a new double-ended driving range, supporters are certain "you'll enjoy this course."

Tijeras Creek

| 20 | 18 | 18 | 18 | $95 |

Rancho Santa Margarita | 29082 Tijeras Creek | 949-589-9793 | www.tijerascreek.com | 6918/5130; 73.4/70.9; 136/130
"You'll look forward to returning" to this "interesting, challenging" Rancho Santa Margarita mainstay that's "very well-maintained" "for the amount of play" it receives; "an enjoyable course for everyone", it offers "two completely different nines": a "fairly open", "straightforward front" that's routed "amongst housing" and "pretty lakes" and a "gem" of a back that's "true target golf" as it races "through tree-filled canyons."

Palm Springs

NEW Classic Club 🏌

| - | - | - | - | $195 |

Palm Desert | 75-200 Northstar Resort Pkwy. | 760-601-3600 | www.classicclubgolf.com | 7305/5421; 75.3/73.2; 142/132
Only 10 weeks after opening in October 2005, this Palm Desert addition acted as host for the PGA Tour's Bob Hope Chrysler Classic – and it did so admirably, thanks to a challenging Arnold Palmer design that unfolds over the desert floor amid pine, olive and pepperwood trees and also through transition areas sprinkled with shrubs; given the plethora of lakes and sprawling bunkers, you'd think you were in Florida . . . if not for the mountain vistas.

Desert Dunes 🏌

| 21 | 19 | 17 | 20 | $100 |

Desert Hot Springs | 19300 Palm Dr. | 760-251-5367 | 6876/5359; 73.8/70.7; 142/122
"Put lead in your golf shoes" before stepping onto this "fun desert course" just north of Palm Springs, because "when the wind is blowing, it can literally knock you over"; nine of its holes "remind you of links golf" while the others "are more parklike", but this "wonderful track" designed by Robert Trent Jones Jr. features "nice large greens" and strategic bunkering throughout; plus, it "offers a reasonable value" "among the pricey courses in this area."

Desert Falls 🏌

| 21 | 21 | 20 | 20 | $165 |

Palm Desert | 1111 Desert Falls Pkwy. | 760-340-4653 | www.desert-falls.com | 7084/5273; 74/72.1; 133/125
There's "something about the air there – the ball just flies high and far" – insist stratosphere-seeking swingers of this "beautiful links-

style course in a desert setting" southeast of Palm Springs; with "water to clear" and "killer greens", there are "plenty of chances to score (or implode)", and though cynics say "you could skip this one and not miss anything", most consider it "a fun, interesting" layout that can be a "value in the summer off-months."

Desert Willow, Firecliff 🖶

27	25	23	22	$175

Palm Desert | 38995 Desert Willow Dr. | 760-346-7060 | 800-320-3323 | www.desertwillow.com | 7056/5079; 73.6/69; 138/117

"It's hard to believe this is actually a muni" marvel fans of this desert course, "the ultimate Coachella Valley golf experience" given its "fantastic conditions", "excellent clubhouse", "terrific pro shop" and "lush" "Southwestern landscaping"; the Hurdzan/Fry design is "a challenge, with many sand traps" that will "bring you to your knees if you don't bring your A-game", but you can recover at "the 19th hole, a great place for drinks, food and views."

Desert Willow, Mountain View 🖶

25	24	23	21	$175

Palm Desert | 38995 Desert Willow Dr. | 760-346-7060 | 800-320-3323 | www.desertwillow.com | 6913/5040; 73.4/68.9; 130/116

So striking you may "feel like [you're] in a painted desert diorama at Disneyland", this "scenic" Palm Desert "beauty" offers "terrific" golf thanks to a "playable" Hurdzan/Fry design featuring "wide-open fairways" and many "well-placed bunkers"; P.S. don't worry if you arrive without clubs because "you can get a really good rental set."

🆕 Escena

21	9	19	19	$115

Palm Springs | 1000 N. Gene Autry Trail | 760-778-2737 | 866-557-8870 | www.escenagolf.com | 7173/5541; 74.2/72.1; 130/127

Although "not as challenging as others in the Coachella Valley", this "benevolent" design from the Nicklaus team nevertheless draws "grip-it-and-rip-it" types who come here to "fire away at the open fairways" on a layout that's "in good shape for a brand-new course"; just remember to "bring your wind game", however, to conquer "the home par 5, a beauty with a creek running down the left side"; N.B. the clubhouse is slated for completion in spring 2007.

🆕 Golf Resort at Indian Wells, Celebrity 🖶

-	-	-	-	$170

Indian Wells | 44-500 Indian Wells Ln. | 760- 346-4653 | www.golfresortatindianwells.com | 7088/5316; 74.2; 138

Whether you're a celebrity or not, you're liable to appreciate this entirely new layout from architect Clive Clark that's built on the site of the resort's former West course; as with its predecessor, this Indian Wells track winds around hotels and offers majestic views of the surrounding mountains, but the current version – scheduled to host the LG Skins Game in November 2007 – has a bit more elbow room and is drenched in floral displays and rock-lined lakes; N.B. it does not yet have USGA ratings for the forward tees.

La Quinta, Dunes 🖶 ⏱

21	24	24	17	$145

La Quinta | 50-200 Avenida Vista Bonita | 760-564-7610 | www.laquintaresort.com | 6682/4930; 72.4/69.3; 136/124

An "interesting layout with spectacular views" of the Santa Rosas, this "nice example of a Pete Dye design" may "play second fiddle to the

Mountain" course, but it's nevertheless "fun to play", especially on the watery par-4 "No. 17, still one of the great holes in golf"; less-kind linksters say the "classic" La Quinta layout "needs a face-lift", but even they admit it's still "enjoyable" as part of a package that includes a "fantastic room" at the "excellent hotel."

La Quinta, Mountain 🏳️⏱️ | 26 | 24 | 23 | 19 | $199

La Quinta | 50-200 Avenida Vista Bonita | 760-564-7610 | www.laquintaresort.com | 6756/4894; 72.6/68.9; 135/120

"One of Pete Dye's best" is this "memorable" La Quinta layout featuring a "unique", "breathtaking back nine" "that winds up and down the mountains" with "several remote holes" and "gorgeous" views; though there are "too many expensive homes" near the course, its "well-manicured greens" and "impeccable service" help to make it "a must-play"; P.S. winter fees "will burn the numbers right off your credit card", but it's relatively "cheap" in summer.

Marriott Desert Springs, Palm 🏳️ | 21 | 23 | 22 | 17 | $155

Palm Desert | 74855 Country Club Dr. | 760-341-2211 | 800-331-3112 | www.desertspringsresort.com | 6761/5492; 72.1/71.9; 130/125

As the name suggests, there's "plenty of agua" and palm trees on this "beautiful desert resort course" that "wraps around a hotel" in Palm Desert with "spectacular views" of the Santa Rosa Mountains; the "well-maintained" layout is "challenging enough for low-handicappers but not too daunting" overall (think "wide", "forgiving" fairways), and it's part of a complex that boasts "excellent service, facilities" and other amenities; in short, "everything is great but the price."

Marriott Desert Springs, Valley 🏳️ | 20 | 23 | 23 | 18 | $155

Palm Desert | 74855 Country Club Dr. | 760-341-2211 | 800-331-3112 | www.desertspringsresort.com | 6627/5262; 71.5/70.2; 127/118

Although players "can't get used to seeing so much water in the desert", they find this lagoon-laced resort course "a great way to start a Palm Desert vacation"; "interesting but forgiving", this "beautifully landscaped" layout offers "awesome views" of the surrounding mountains as well as "terrific service (e.g. the restaurant and pro shop)"; the catch: "it's pricey to play – except in the hot summer off-months."

Marriott Shadow Ridge 🏳️ | 25 | 25 | 24 | 20 | $165

Palm Desert | 9002 Shadow Ridge Rd. | 760-674-2700 | www.golfshadowridge.com | 7006/5158; 73.9/68.7; 134/118

"This Nick Faldo design is a jewel" insist swingers who've taken a shine to this "enjoyable" layout "in a Marriott time-share development" in Palm Desert; it has "one of the best practice facilities in the Coachella Valley" (including a "great golf school"), but don't overlook the course's other facets: a "wonderful variety of holes", dramatic bunkering and "surprising elevation changes" – be sure to "bring your best putting game"; P.S. "it can get windy here."

PGA West, Jack Nicklaus Tournament 🏳️ | 24 | 24 | 22 | 18 | $235

La Quinta | 56-150 PGA Blvd. | 760-564-7170 | 800-742-9378 | www.pgawest.com | 7204/5023; 75.3/69.4; 143/124

"A real bear in the desert", this "exciting" La Quinta course represents "Jack at his best", offering the "right mix of challenges and design" courtesy of "elevated greens", "deep pot bunkers" and "sand on either side of the fairways" – "it can really beat you up", so "you must hit the ball well to score"; it's "expensive", but the "beautiful" layout comes with "mountain backdrops", a "great practice range" and "comfortable facilities."

☒ PGA West, TPC Stadium ⛳

| 26 | 25 | 23 | 19 | $235 |

La Quinta | 56-150 PGA Blvd. | 760-564-7170 | 800-742-9378 |
www.pgawest.com | 7300/5092; 75.9/70; 150/124

"When you feel like being humbled, play this" "iconic" La Quinta "collector's item" "from Pete Dye's 'unplayable' period" that is "all the course anyone could want (even from the middle tees)" given its "many moguls, railroad ties" and "bunkers you've never seen before" plus a "tough island-green 17th"; foozlers feel that "no course should be this hard" – "too many forced carries" – but the majority maintains that "while it may not be fair, it's certainly fun."

NEW SilverRock Resort, Arnold Palmer Classic

| 22 | 18 | 20 | 19 | $160 |

La Quinta | 79-179 Ahmanson Ln. | 760-777-8884 | www.silverrock.org |
7578/4884; 76.3/68.4; 139/118

"Arnie's army has another fine recruit" with this "spectacular" new Arnold Palmer design in La Quinta featuring "generous landing areas but well-guarded greens" – "the bunkers and wandering water make this course tough"; although it's "in the process of expanding its amenities" (they'll be adding a "permanent clubhouse"), it already boasts "beautiful desert and mountain views" and seems "destined to be a fun, challenging" choice.

Trilogy at La Quinta ⛳

| 21 | 21 | 20 | 19 | $155 |

La Quinta | 60-151 Trilogy Pkwy. | 760-771-0707 | www.trilogygolfclub.com |
7174/4998; 74.3/68.5; 130/116

"Test your game from the tees" used during the PGA Tour's 2006 LG Skins Game at this "beautiful" La Quinta course that's "fun" but "doesn't beat you up" as it winds through the desert landscape; although a few find it "bland" with too many "cookie-cutter homes lining the fairways", those with "no complaints" laud its "friendly, accommodating staff" and "nice clubhouse and range", saying the "relatively new course" "will improve with age."

Westin Mission Hills, Gary Player

| 22 | 22 | 23 | 20 | $165 |

Rancho Mirage | 70705 Ramon Rd. | 760-770-9496 |
www.westinmissionhillsgolf.com | 7062/4907; 73.4/68; 131/118

"Fun and playable", this "solid Westin course" in Rancho Mirage offers "resort golf at its best" courtesy of a "long, wide-open" desert design from Gary Player that proves "good for women" and "friendly to both the duffer and the experienced golfer"; sure, it's a short "drive from the Mission Hills property" and "surrounded by $$$ homes", but the "absolutely lovely" staff, "great facilities", mountain views and package "deals aplenty" make it "a must."

Westin Mission Hills, Pete Dye

| 22 | 24 | 22 | 19 | $165 |

Rancho Mirage | 71501 Dinah Shore Dr. | 760-328-3198 |
www.westinmissionhillsgolf.com | 6706/4841; 72.2/67.6; 131/117

A "Coachella Valley favorite", this "dye-abolical" design "requires good course management" to deal with its "many traps" and "signature Pete Dye features" – so be sure to "pick the proper tee"; some say this "wonderful", "walkable" course "looks more like Florida than the desert", but as it's "well-maintained" with a "helpful, professional staff", it's considered by most to be a "great venue"; P.S. unlike its sibling, it's located "at the same site as the hotel."

Sacramento

DarkHorse

| | | 24 | 12 | 16 | 20 | $79 |

Auburn | 13450 Combie Rd. | 530-269-7900 | www.darkhorsegolf.com | 7218/5058; 75/68.3; 140/122

"A marvelous, undulating design among the oaks" and pines northeast of Sacramento, this "fairly priced" Keith Foster course is a long, "beautiful, challenging" mountain layout where "creativity is demanded" and "excellent shot values" prevail; lagging amenities lead a few to fuss that it's a bit "overrated", but most "hope [the facility] can make it work" and are eagerly "waiting for the new clubhouse" to open in 2007.

Diablo Grande, Legends West ⊙

| | | 26 | 20 | 20 | 22 | $125 |

Patterson | 9521 Morton Davis Dr. | 209-892-4653 | www.diablogrande.com | 7112/4905; 74.4/69.3; 147/123

This "outstanding" Jack Nicklaus/Gene Sarazen design "far removed from civilization" delivers a "challenge" and "captivates the mind and body with twists, turns and target golf", all in a "beautiful setting" 90 miles south of Sacramento; even though this legend is "miles away from any metro area", city slickers say it's "worth the effort", while loyalists advise "this is a hidden gem – stay away and it'll stay that way!"; N.B. closed to the public on weekends.

Diablo Grande, Ranch

| | ∇ | 24 | 17 | 20 | 23 | $100 |

Patterson | 9521 Morton Davis Dr. | 209-892-4653 | www.diablogrande.com | 7246/5112; 75.8/70; 144/124

Located "in the middle of nowhere" near Patterson, this "superb" "diamond in the dry valley rough" proves itself to be well "worth the drive" if only for the "gem" of a layout and views of 400-year-old oaks and grapevines; while anti-progressives argue that "new housing construction interferes with the golf", others conclude that it's "still a great value" even if "you have to travel two hours from the Bay Area" just to get there.

San Bernardino

Oak Quarry 🏌

| | | 26 | 18 | 20 | 23 | $95 |

Riverside | 7151 Sierra Ave. | 951-685-1440 | www.oakquarry.com | 7002/5408; 73.9/71.9; 137/121

"What a great find" fawn fans of this "gorgeous" "must-play" that offers "dramatic", "vivid and exciting golf" in the form of a "unique" layout that is laced with "many elevation" changes, "tricky greens" (be sure to "listen to the locals' tips") and "spectacular quarry views"; all in all, it's a "decent value" featuring "breathtaking holes" that include an all-carry 14th – "one of the country's great par 3s"; the "only drawback": its Riverside location "is far from anywhere that's anywhere."

	COURSE	FACIL.	SERVICE	VALUE	COST

Oak Valley ♠

	23	17	17	24	$85

Beaumont | 1888 Golf Club Dr. | 951-769-7200 | www.oakvalleygolf.com | 7003/5349; 73.8/71.9; 140/128

This course "would be $250 a round" "if it were in Palm Springs", but since this under-the-radar Schmidt-Curley "classic" is just south of San Bernardino, it's actually "a great value for the money", offering a "wonderful course" with "excellent shot-making opportunities" and "great conditions" at "very reasonable rates"; the unconvinced counter it's "understaffed" and too "far away", but as it's "not crowded during the week, it's well worth the drive."

PGA of Southern California, Champions

	25	23	21	23	$85

Beaumont | 36211 Champions Dr. | 951-845-0014 | 877-742-2500 | www.scpgagolf.com | 7377/5274; 76.1/72.4; 139/128

"If only I had a helicopter" sighs one swinger set on reducing the commute to this "PGA winner" "stuck out in the middle of nowhere" in Beaumont; considered by some to be "the best value between LA and Palm Springs", this "amazing", "tough, windswept course" offers up "some beautiful holes" laced with plenty of bunkers and "a few forced carries"; "scenic" views of the surrounding oak groves and mountains make it even more of a "pleasure to play."

PGA of Southern California, Legends

	25	24	23	25	$75

Beaumont | 36211 Champions Dr. | 951-845-0014 | 877-742-2500 | www.scpgagolf.com | 7442/5169; 75.9/70.9; 141/130

Although the nearby mountains, oak-studded woodlands and coursing streams have golfers gushing about "the astonishing acreage surrounding many of its holes", this "true test" of skill provides plenty of on-course attractions as well, including formidable bunkers, "changing elevations" and "rolling greens" – "a nightmare for putting"; although affordable at all times, this "nice" layout is "an amazing deal in the off-season"; P.S. "watch out when the winds blow!"

San Diego

☑ Aviara ♠

	26	27	27	19	$215

Carlsbad | 7447 Batiquitos Dr. | 760-603-6900 | www.fourseasons.com | 7007/5007; 75/69.3; 144/127

Whether it's the "Augusta of the West" or "golf in the Garden of Eden", aesthetes agree that "no course has prettier flowers and waterfalls" than this "relaxing", "must-play Palmer" paradise at the Four Seasons resort north of San Diego; although the "memorable" experience comes with "out-of-sight greens fees", the layout's "fabulous facilities" and "flawless service" - along with the chance to "get an amazing spa treatment after playing 18" - will "make you feel good about what you paid."

Barona Creek

	23	22	22	22	$120

Lakeside | 1932 Wildcat Canyon Rd. | 619-387-7018 | 888-722-7662 | www.barona.com | 7088/5296; 74.5/70.6; 140/126

"I went for the gambling [but] I'd return for the golf" insists one born-again bettor about this "fine desert layout" that's "part of a resort complex in a beautiful" "Wild West–looking" setting northeast of San Diego; although the fairways can get "a little dried out in summer", the "open, rolling" track is generally "well-manicured" and features "women-friendly tee boxes" and "firm", "super-fast greens"; N.B. it is set to host the Nationwide Tour Championship in 2007.

CrossCreek

| 24 | 20 | 22 | 24 | $105 |

Temecula | 43860 Glenn Meadows Rd. | 951-506-3402 | www.crosscreekgolfclub.com | 6833/4606; 73.1/67.4; 140/118

This Arthur Hills "gem" is "not easy to find", but it's "well worth the drive" west of Temecula for "a beautiful course" where "the solitude" is so complete, "you'd never know you were near civilization"; "cut through canyons", this "unique", "nicely laid out" track makes "great use of the hills, creeks" and mature oak trees, offering "challenging holes to test your nerves" amid "perfect surroundings: no homes"; P.S. there are "great hash browns in the clubhouse!"

La Costa, North 🎎

| 22 | 24 | 24 | 17 | $200 |

Carlsbad | 2100 Costa Del Mar Rd. | 760-438-9111 | 800-854-5000 | www.lacosta.com | 7094/5939; 74.9/76.3; 141/137

Combine this "lovely", "straightforward" layout with the amenities of a "beautiful resort" north of San Diego (including a "world-class spa") and "it's paradise without getting on an airplane"; the "solid course" features "lush" grounds, "incredible facilities", "history and challenge" – it's the former host of the PGA Tour's Accenture Match Play Championship – and though a few find it "pricey" and a bit "tired", they're outvoted: "you pay to play, but what a place to stay."

La Costa, South 🎎

| 22 | 24 | 23 | 16 | $200 |

Carlsbad | 2100 Costa Del Mar Rd. | 760-438-9111 | 800-854-5000 | www.lacosta.com | 7077/5612; 74.8/74.2; 140/134

"Great golf, great hotel, great spa, great location" neatly sums up the appeal of this recently "remodeled resort" where the PGA Tour touched down from 1968–2006 to take on a boldly bunkered layout composed of holes from both the North and South; though a few duffers are "disappointed" by "deteriorating course conditions", supporters cite a "hospitable staff" and a "beautiful setting" north of San Diego as proof that this "costly experience" is "worth it."

Maderas 🏌

| 27 | 23 | 25 | 21 | $195 |

Poway | 17750 Old Coach Rd. | 858-451-8100 | www.maderasgolf.com | 7115/4967; 75.6/69.8; 145/127

"The Angelina Jolie of courses", this "premier" layout in the mountains north of San Diego is "beautiful, tough" and "extremely well-maintained"; it's also "not for the faint of handicap", featuring "more twists and turns than a pretzel", dramatic "elevation changes" and "fast", "challenging greens"; sure, it's "expensive", but it's also a "favorite" for its "canyon views", "excellent staff" and "great" facilities; P.S. there are "six sets of tees for every level of golfer."

Mt. Woodson 🏌

| 24 | 16 | 19 | 25 | $85 |

Ramona | 16422 N. Woodson Dr. | 760-788-3555 | www.mtwoodson.com | 6004/4842; 69.1/68.1; 134/122

"Bring your smile" to this "little secret" northeast of San Diego, as the "smart and twisty" "target course" is "a really fun place to play"; there are "lots of options off the tee" at this "shot-makers' delight" that's "short yet challenging" and nestled in a "unique" setting that's "part-mountain, part-desert" and includes a 450-ft.-long "trellis bridge" through the treetops; many "wish it had a driving range" and club-house, but it's still "one of the best values" around.

Pala Mesa 🏌

20	17	19	20	$79

Fallbrook | 2001 Old Hwy. 395 | 760-728-5881 | 800-722-4700 | www.palamesa.com | 6502/5096; 71.9/64.3; 128/108

You'll need to be able "to move the ball both ways to manage the many doglegs on this old-fashioned, tree-lined layout", but even less-sophisticated shot-makers can appreciate this "gem" of a resort course, a "tight, fun track" just north of San Diego that features "lots of hills", "fast greens" and "beautiful gardens"; although "freeway noise spoils the tranquility" for a few, "nice stay, play and eat pack-ages" can make for "a most enjoyable visit."

Rancho Bernardo Inn

19	22	23	19	$115

San Diego | 17550 Bernardo Oaks Dr. | 858-487-1611 | www.jcgolf.com | 6631/4949; 72.3/68.5; 133/119

"Enjoyable but not too challenging", this "course is nevertheless worth visiting" due to its "surrounding ambiance": a resort where "every-thing is first-class", from the "excellent service" to the "very comfort-able facilities" to a "wonderful restaurant noted for its fine wine cellar"; detractors dub it "unremarkable", but the San Diego spread proves "user-friendly", "walkable" and "sooo beautiful" – after all, you simply "can't beat the location and weather."

Redhawk 🏌

22	18	19	20	$85

Temecula | 45100 Redhawk Pkwy. | 951-302-3850 | 800-451-4295 | www.redhawkgolfcourse.com | 7095/5515; 75.1/72.1; 145/125

A "cool putting green" framed by fountains and flowers sets the tone for this "super layout" in Temecula "where you'll use every club" as you tackle 18 "challenging but fair" holes featuring "incredible greens" that are "big, with undulations and levels"; while dissenters declare there are "too many houses" dotting the design, the mountain views and "value" pricing leads others to say they "would enjoy playing it more often."

SCGA Golf Course

22	18	19	24	$80

Murrieta | 39500 Robert Trent Jones Pkwy. | 951-677-7446 | 800-752-9724 | www.scgagolfcourse.com | 7036/5355; 74.6/71.7; 137/128

"Put your thinking cap on when you play" this RTJ Sr. design, as the long, "traditional layout" located between LA and San Diego doles out "great variety" via "elevation, wind, water and well-placed bunkers" that "makes for a fun" day; weather-watchers warn those days can get "very hot in summer", so it's nice that the "fabulous conditions" and "friendly staff" make it "an incredible value at any time."

Steele Canyon 🏌

22	18	19	21	$124

Jamul | 3199 Stonefield Dr. | 619-441-6900 | www.steelecanyon.com
Canyon/Meadow | 6479/4577; 72/67.1; 130/116
Meadow/Ranch | 6834/4790; 73.4/67.9; 141/124
Ranch/Canyon | 6767/4655; 73.1/66.8; 139/118

"A hidden gem in the canyons" "just [east] of San Diego", this "sce-nic", "semi-private" "bad boy" designed by Gary Player "is worth a visit" (and proves a "good alternative" "when June gloom hangs over the coast"); the three "interesting" nines feature a "variety of elevation changes, lateral hazards and excellent greens", so "bring your A-game", because as much as the "killer course" "rewards strong play", it also "punishes you if you stray" or "get sloppy."

Temecula Creek Inn — 20 | 20 | 20 | 21 | $85

Temecula | 44501 Rainbow Canyon Rd. | 951-694-1000 | 877-517-1823 | www.temeculacreekinn.com
Creek/Oaks | 6784/5712; 72.3/72.8; 127/118
Stonehouse/Creek | 6605/5686; 71.6/72.8; 130/120
Stonehouse/Oaks | 6693/5658; 72.2/73.1; 129/123

For "27 fun holes" that are "great in any combination", head to this Temecula track that's "not tough" but is "nice for a round of golf and a meal" of "wonderful food and wine" served by the "great inn staff"; some say "the Stonehouse nine is the best of the three" ("it will make you think"), but others find it delivers too "many blind shots and tricked-up holes", saying they "prefer the more traditional", "older-style" Oaks and Creek layouts.

☒ Torrey Pines, North — 26 | 19 | 19 | 23 | $100

La Jolla | 11480 N. Torrey Pines Rd. | 858-452-3226 | 800-985-4653 | www.torreypinesgolfcourse.com | 6874/6122; 72.1/75.4; 129/134

"Beautiful in its simplicity", this "traditional" "cliffside" course in La Jolla comes with "some amazing oceanside holes" that stun swingers with "million-dollar views" "at muni prices" ("the value depends on whether you're a city resident or not"); "more user-friendly than the longer South, but still very challenging", this "incredible" co-host of the PGA Tour's Buick Invitational "must be played at least once" – which may be all you can handle, as "getting a tee time is like trying to meet the Pope."

☒ Torrey Pines, South — 27 | 18 | 18 | 22 | $163

La Jolla | 11480 N. Torrey Pines Rd. | 858-452-3226 | 800-985-4653 | www.torreypinesgolfcourse.com | 7227/5542; 76.1/73.5; 139/128

"Elevating golf-related suffering to a category all its own", this "fierce" La Jolla "gem" "perched on the cliffs above the Pacific" "will beat you up" with its "length and gnarly rough" – although "you'll love every minute of it"; it's a "slice of heaven" with "spectacular views" and "a masterpiece" of a lodge, but "don't expect resort treatment" as the course "gets heavy play" and "the rest is municipal all the way"; nit-picking aside, however, "there's a reason why the 2008 U.S. Open is going to be held here."

San Francisco Bay Area

Bridges, The — 21 | 21 | 20 | 16 | $85

San Ramon | 9000 S. Gale Ridge Rd. | 925-735-4253 | www.thebridgesgolf.com | 6915/5229; 75/71.4; 148/123

With "narrow fairways bordered by canyons" and "wicked rough", this San Ramon "shot-makers'" spread from the "truly diabolical mind" of designer Johnny Miller is "target golf at its best", a "sadistic" layout that's "not for the novice"; still, most masochists who "hate this course" nevertheless "want to play it again", as the "humbling experience" may be "unfair" at times but is "nice when you know where to aim"; P.S. "make sure to bring enough balls."

NEW Callippe Preserve

| | 22 | 20 | 19 | 22 | $60 |

Pleasanton | 8500 Clubhouse Dr. | 925-426-6666 | www.playcallippe.com | 6748/4788; 73.4/68.4; 139/114

"Set in the hills east of San Francisco", this "beautiful new" muni is "already a favorite" – tee times are as endangered as the butterfly it's named after – thanks to a "fun", "eco-friendly" design that offers "character on almost every hole"; the "immaculate course" starts out "flat and modestly challenging", but the rolling back nine "will keep you humble" with its "narrow fairways" and "difficult greens"; already a "bang for the buck", "it will only improve with time."

Cinnabar Hills

| | 24 | 23 | 22 | 21 | $100 |

San Jose | 23600 McKean Rd. | 408-323-5200 | www.cinnabarhills.com
Canyon/Mountain | 6641/4859; 72.5/68.1; 137/118
Lake/Canyon | 6688/4959; 72.9/68.4; 138/121
Mountain/Lake | 6853/5010; 73.6/68.1; 142/120

"Leave the Silicon Valley behind and escape" to this "beautiful" "haven" "nestled in the hills south of San Jose"; the "three challenging nines" are "always in fine shape" ("lush fairways", "ultra-fast greens" "like undulating pool tables") and offer "lots of variety" as they tumble over "interesting terrain" that requires "an oxygen mask to counter all the elevation changes"; "amazing" "countryside views" and "nice" facilities also help to make this a "fantastic value."

CordeValle 🏌 ⚬⟍

| | 27 | 28 | 27 | 18 | $225 |

San Martin | 1 CordeValle Dr. | 408-695-4590 | 877-255-2626 | www.cordevalle.com | 7169/5385; 75.1/71; 138/120

"Golf as it was meant to be" includes "caddies, views and a challenging" RTJ Jr. creation that "was designed as a private club – and still feels that way" with its "strategic, well-trapped holes" kept "in outstanding shape" plus a "fabulous clubhouse" and "excellent service"; it's "expensive" and open only to members and guests who stay in the "fantastic" cottages and villas, but the "beautiful" San Martin resort has swingers saying "get me a loan so I can return."

☑ Half Moon Bay, Ocean

| | 25 | 23 | 24 | 18 | $180 |

Half Moon Bay | 2 Miramontes Point Rd. | 650-726-4438 | www.halfmoonbaygolf.com | 6649/4872; 72.5/69; 128/119

You'll be "transported to Scotland" on this "wonderful seaside links course" that's "near authentic" with its "chilly weather", "wicked winds" and "unpredictable fog" that can sometimes spoil the "dramatic ocean vistas" "from every hole"; the Arthur Hills design is "very expensive" and the "lack of a driving range is a drawback", but most maintain the "views alone are worth the cost"; P.S. complete your "great golf weekend" with "superb" accommodations at the nearby (but unaffiliated) Ritz-Carlton Half Moon Bay.

Half Moon Bay, Old Course 🏞

| | 24 | 22 | 24 | 18 | $180 |

Half Moon Bay | 2 Miramontes Point Rd. | 650-726-4438 | www.halfmoonbaygolf.com | 7003/5279; 75.3/72.1; 135/120

With "a much different layout than its sister", this "traditional course" tumbles over lakes and through pines, providing a "challenging" but "playable" experience with a "reward at the end": the "most breathtaking finishing hole outside of Pebble Beach", a 418-yard par 4 that hugs the coastal cliffs; it may have "too many houses" and "lack a driving range", but swingers insist "if you like mist and fog" and "can't afford Scotland, come here"; N.B. it's no longer affiliated with the nearby Ritz-Carlton.

☑ Harding Park

| 25 | 17 | 16 | 22 | $155 |

San Francisco | 99 Harding Rd. | 415-661-1865 | www.harding-park.com | 6845/5375; 72.8/70.4; 126/116

"Since the remodel" for the PGA Tour's 2005 World Golf Championship, this "muni on steroids" is "a rejuvenated jewel" and "a blessing for the San Francisco everyman" owing to "gorgeous views of Lake Merced", a "nice new clubhouse" and a "beautiful layout" lined with "majestic" "100-year-old cypress trees"; while critics rip the "poor service" and "continual" noise from the "next-door skeet shooting range", most find it an "outstanding value" – "but only if you're a card-carrying resident."

Poppy Ridge

| 23 | 21 | 20 | 24 | $87 |

Livermore | 4280 Greenville Rd. | 925-447-6779 | www.poppyridgegolf.com
Chardonnay/Merlot | 7106/5212; 74.8/70.2; 141/120
Merlot/Zinfandel | 7128/5265; 74.8/70.2; 141/120
Zinfandel/Chardonnay | 7048/5267; 74.8/70.2; 141/120

"Way out of town" in the rugged foothills east of San Francisco, Rees Jones' "great 27-hole layout" offers "nothing to disturb you" but the course's combination of "undulations, bikini-waxed greens" and "afternoon wind that brings you to your knees"; though a few find it "solid if unspectacular", most "want to come back" as it's a "great value" ("particularly for NCGA members") that offers "lovely vistas" of the surrounding wineries; P.S. "it's nearly treeless", so "bring sunscreen!"

Presidio

| 19 | 16 | 17 | 19 | $90 |

San Francisco | 300 Finley Rd. | 415-561-4670 | www.presidiogolf.com | 6424/5705; 72.3/69.6; 136/128

"Skyscrapers surround you" on this "charming" "urban oasis" that "flows through the redwoods and oaks of the Presidio" "in the heart of San Francisco"; though "a must if you like tough old courses" "with lots of history", the former "military gem" is "cold and foggy much of the time", "six-hour rounds are not uncommon" and the grounds can be a "mud bath"; nevertheless, given its "breathtaking city views, how can you not have an enjoyable day?"

Roddy Ranch

| 21 | 9 | 16 | 20 | $75 |

Antioch | 1 Tour Way | 925-978-4653 | www.roddyranch.com | 7024/5390; 74.5/71.7; 136/120

"Pool tables for greens is all you need to know" about this "challenging course" where club-goers cue up on "hard", "wicked-fast" putting surfaces that "roll true"; tucked into a "gorgeous" cattle-ranch setting "in the working part of the Bay Area", this "enjoyable" "test" is "wide-open" and "well-maintained" with "great bunkering" and "murderous rough" – literally, so "watch out for rattlesnakes"; sure, it's "without a clubhouse, but the golf is a great value."

Sonoma Golf Club ⚬⃥

| 22 | 22 | 21 | 16 | $160 |

Sonoma | 17700 Arnold Dr. | 707-996-0300 | www.sonomagolfclub.com | 7103/5555; 75.2/71.9; 137/125

"A wine country delight", this "classic" "walking course" doles out "fabulous views of the vineyards and surrounding mountains" and is the host to the PGA Champions Tour's season-ending Charles Schwab Cup; considering the "favorite" features "true greens" that are "like putting on glass" plus "new clubhouse facilities that are top-of-the-line", surveyors say it's "too bad" this "long" parklander is "very pricey" and "you can't play unless you stay" a night at the affiliated Fairmont Sonoma Mission Inn.

StoneTree

| 20 | 19 | 21 | 17 | $115 |

Novato | 9 Stone Tree Ln. | 415-209-6090 | www.stonetreegolf.com | 6810/5232; 73.3/66.4; 143/127

"Winding through canyons and across fields" "just north of San Francisco", this "fantastic" "ass-kicker" is "really two courses in one": while the front is "flat" and "boring", the layout will "eat you up by" the time you reach the "narrow" back with its "trees, outcroppings", "elevation changes" and "trouble everywhere"; it "needs a driving range", but "superior drainage and maintenance" keep the spread "in country-club condition"; P.S. "go now before more homes" "blight the hillsides."

Wente Vineyards

| 24 | 23 | 23 | 20 | $105 |

Livermore | 5050 Arroyo Rd. | 925-456-2478 | 800-999-2885 | www.wentegolf.com | 7181/5637; 75.8/68.7; 145/124

A "beautiful Greg Norman layout that weaves through the vineyards and the hills" east of San Francisco is just the beginning at this "upscale" experience where "golf in the afternoon" accompanied by "panoramic views" and followed by "some wine tasting afterwards" and a "spectacular dinner at the restaurant" "makes for a perfect day"; as for the Shark's "excellent design", swingers say it's "harder than it looks", with "steep", "narrow fairways", "wicked rough" and "lots of elevation changes."

San Luis Obispo

Hunter Ranch

| 24 | 19 | 19 | 23 | $78 |

Paso Robles | 4041 E. Hwy. 46 | 805-237-7444 | www.hunterranchgolf.com | 6741/5639; 72.6/72; 136/128

"Providing a rewarding golf experience at an affordable price", this "pleasant, hilly", oak-lined layout "in the sleepy community of Paso Robles" is "not for beginners" with its "wicked doglegs", "multilevel greens" and "killer afternoon wind"; given that the "nicely kept" track boasts "a beautiful location" "in the middle of wine country", oenophiles also find it to be a convenient and "worthwhile stop when [traveling] on the central coast."

NEW Monarch Dunes

▽ | 24 | 20 | 22 | 22 | $68 |

Nipomo | 1606 Trilogy Pkwy. | 805-343-9459 | www.monarchdunes.com | 6810/4702; 73/69.2; 137/132

"Anything but monotonous", this "wonderful", "fun new course" 30 minutes south of San Luis Obispo offers Pacific vistas, coastal dunes and eucalyptus forests on a "challenging" layout chock-full of "interesting holes" and "wickedly subtle", "lightning-fast greens" – "you better practice putting beforehand"; despite "some blind shots", players have "come to appreciate" this "links-ish design" that's already "in great shape" and "will only get better."

	COURSE	FACIL.	SERVICE	VALUE	COST

Santa Barbara

Glen Annie

	19	18	19	20	$85

Santa Barbara | 405 Glen Annie Rd. | 805-968-6400 |
www.glenanniegolf.com | 6420/5036; 71.2/69.4; 130/123

You'll "pray for level lies" at this "beauty of a course in the hills above Santa Barbara" that combines "towering shots from elevated tee boxes" and "challenging", "rolling fairways" with "stunning views" "overlooking the Pacific Ocean" and the Channel Islands; although some consider it "perfectly average", most maintain it's "truly a central coast hidden gem" and "a great value when compared to neighboring courses."

La Purisima

	25	16	18	24	$78

Lompoc | 3455 E. State Hwy. 246 | 805-735-8395 | www.lapurisimagolf.com |
7105/5763; 75.6/75.6; 143/135

"Be prepared for a humbling round" at the "best challenge" and "best-kept secret" in the area, this "magnificent" layout that's "long, winding and treacherous with fast greens" and "afternoon winds that wreak havoc on your game"; though the layout is "not for high-handicappers", it is a "fantastic course for the money" with a "serene" setting – "no houses" and "lush fairways that contrast with the arid hills" – that makes it "worth the drive" north of Santa Barbara.

Rancho San Marcos

	24	17	20	20	$85

Santa Barbara | 4600 Hwy. 154 | 805-683-6334 | 877-766-1804 |
www.rsm1804.com | 6817/5004; 73.2/69.8; 136/119

A "great escape from wine-tasting when in the Santa Ynez Valley", this "typical Trent Jones Jr. layout with beautiful mountain views and no homes" features "a flat front and a rolling back" that are "fun" but "a real challenge from the tips"; still, some feel this track "needs a little TLC" (with the exception of its "unbelievable practice range"), and "perhaps new owner Ty 'Beanie Baby' Warner can re-create the magic" once course renovations begin in March 2007.

River Course at Alisal

	19	16	18	19	$75

Solvang | 150 Alisal Rd. | 805-688-6042 | 6830/5710; 73.1/73.8; 129/128

With "the wineries really, really close by", this "wide-open", "ego-pumping" course is "very convenient for the weekend winos" and "*Sideways* followers" who flock to "the hills oustide Solvang"; though "too windy" and perhaps "too rustic for the serious golfer (with holes adjacent to a dude ranch)", most find it "a pleasant four hours in the sun" and "marvel at the architect's ability to design" a "fun, lovely lay-out" on such "a narrow strip of land."

Sandpiper

	24	17	18	19	$155

Goleta | 7925 Hollister Ave. | 805-968-1541 | www.sandpipergolf.com |
7068/5701; 74.7/68.4; 136/121

Considering its "priceless ocean vistas", this links-style "grande dame" "just north of Santa Barbara" is "a joy to play" as you "skirt the bluffs" and hit "tee shots toward the beach"; "now that they've raised their fees", the "poor man's Pebble Beach" "moniker no longer fits", but it's still "worth the drive" for a "memorable round" that can be "difficult when windy"; it may be "in need of a face-lift", but swingers say you play here "for the scenery – the golf is incidental."

	COURSE	FACIL.	SERVICE	VALUE	COST

Santa Cruz

⊠ Pasatiempo 🎏 ⏱

| 28 | 19 | 21 | 21 | $175 |

Santa Cruz | 18 Clubhouse Rd. | 831-459-9155 | www.pasatiempo.com |
6432/5680; 71.9/73.7; 138/133

"It's all about the golf" at this "phenomenal Alister MacKenzie design"
"in the hills above Santa Cruz" where "you can see the ocean from the
first tee" on an "absolute must-play" layout featuring "narrow fairways, lots of trees, no rough" and "lightning-quick greens" – "you
won't leave without a three-putt"; some say the "facilities hold it
back", but most find it "a pleasure" "from bag drop to finishing hole."

Santa Rosa

Links at Bodega Harbour

| 22 | 15 | 18 | 18 | $75 |

Bodega Bay | 21301 Heron Dr. | 707-875-3538 |
www.bodegaharbourgolf.com | 6275/4801; 71.4/70.5; 127/121

"Spectacular views across Bodega Harbour" are a highlight of this
"tough, tight treat" where architect RTJ Jr. "went all out" on an "undulating layout" featuring "lots of elevation", "fast, true greens" and a
"fantastic finish along the ocean"; though it's "covered with houses"
and has "no driving range", most consider it a "no-frills gem" on which
it's "easy" to get a tee time; P.S. "when the wind blows, look out."

Stockton

Saddle Creek

| 26 | 23 | 22 | 21 | $135 |

Copperopolis | 1001 Saddle Creek Dr. | 209-785-3700 | 888-852-5787 |
www.saddlecreekgolf.com | 6826/4486; 72.9/66.7; 136/117

Architect Carter Morrish's multilobed bunkers are a highlight of this
"interesting" course "in the Sierra foothills" that offers an "excellent
layout" with "no two holes alike" and a multitude of "tee box options"; a
two-hour drive east from the Bay Area, this "serene" resort has views
of the surrounding mountains and what players opine are a "friendly
staff" and "Downtown amenities away from it all."

Stevinson Ranch

| 23 | 16 | 19 | 22 | $85 |

Stevinson | 2700 N. Van Clief Rd. | 209-668-8200 | 877-752-9276 |
www.stevinsonranch.com | 7206/5461; 74.7/71.9; 138/124

A "surprisingly nice course" "in the middle of nowhere" south of
Stockton, this "wonderful track winds itself around marshes and
streams" on a linksy layout that "makes the words 'risk or reward' come
alive from the tips"; "killer greens", native "grass rough" and "lots of
wind" make it "challenging", but the toughest task on this environmentally friendly design may be trying to "putt while swatting mosquitos."

Colorado

TOP COURSES IN STATE

28	Red Sky, Fazio	*Vail*
	Red Sky, Norman	*Vail*
27	Broadmoor, East	*Colorado Springs*
	Raven at Three Peaks	*Vail*
26	Ridge at Castle Pines N.	*Denver*

| | COURSE | FACIL. | SERVICE | VALUE | COST |

Boulder

Indian Peaks
▽ 22 | 17 | 18 | 21 | $44

Lafayette | 2300 Indian Peaks Trail | 303-666-4706 |
www.indianpeaksgolf.com | 7083/5420; 73.9/70.8; 134/122

Three-time U.S. Open champion Hale Irwin designed this "challenging
layout" in Lafayette that boasts a half-dozen lakes, "wide-open fairways, well-kept greens" and "great views of the Rocky Mountains"; although a few skeptics knock it for being "set in a housing development",
acolytes agree it's "well-managed and -staffed" and insist that "playing 18 at sunset is a religious experience."

Mariana Butte
▽ 22 | 15 | 18 | 24 | $36

Loveland | 701 Clubhouse Dr. | 970-667-8308 | www.golfloveland.com |
6604/5067; 70.8/68.4; 130/117

Sitting "more than a mile high", this "well-maintained" layout has "lots
of ups and downs" and "a number of interesting holes, especially
along the river", and while you "don't go there for the service or facilities", for many it's still "worth the drive" 45 minutes north of Boulder;
it's "short from the regular men's tees", but "don't be afraid" "to un-
leash your cannon on the wide fairways", and "don't worry about the
rattlesnakes" because the "bull snakes eat them."

Colorado Springs

Broadmoor, East 🏌 ⌐
27 | 27 | 26 | 21 | $180

Colorado Springs | 1 Lake Ave. | 719-577-5790 | www.broadmoor.com |
7310/5738; 74/72.8; 135/148

This "timeless", "truly great" "Donald Ross/Robert Trent Jones Sr.
combo" and affiliated resort "deserve the acclaim" for the "breathtaking views" and "immaculate" conditions that are part of this "classic"
Colorado Springs design that also boasts some of the "most difficult
greens on the planet"; though the prices are "outrageous", "if you're
staying at the Broadmoor anyway, why not?"; N.B. it's scheduled to
host the 2008 U.S. Senior Open.

NEW Broadmoor, Mountain 🏌
25 | 25 | 25 | 21 | $180

Colorado Springs | 1 Lake Ave. | 719-577-5790 | www.broadmoor.com |
7637/4928; 75.7/67.7; 149/124

A "stunning beauty in the Rockies" with "magnificent views" to admire
"while you search for your ball", this recently redesigned resort course
is situated "away from the main lodge" amid a natural setting that
might make you "forget about golf"; it's "difficult" and "long" with
large greens (you'll "need a cart" and a caddie), but most agree it's
"worth playing" – especially since "the ball goes further" when you
"hit atop a mountain."

Broadmoor, West 🏌 ⌐
25 | 26 | 26 | 22 | $180

Colorado Springs | 1 Lake Ave. | 719-577-5790 | www.broadmoor.com |
7016/5162; 70.8/68.6; 130/120

In a "setting that can't be beat", this "fabulously maintained" and
"very difficult" Broadmoor sibling designed by Donald Ross and Robert
Trent Jones Sr. is a "true mountain experience" that "will get your attention", as it's "quite a challenge from the tips" and the "lightning-

fast greens make it a bear"; fortunately, there are also views so "beautiful", you may be tempted to "ignore the marshal's pleas to pick up the pace."

Walking Stick

▽ 22 | 15 | 18 | 25 | $30

Pueblo | 4301 Walking Stick Blvd. | 719-584-3400 | www.golfinpueblo.com | 7147/5181; 73.5/68.5; 131/121

Host to the 2006 U.S. Women's Amateur Public Links Championship, this Arthur Hills/Keith Foster collaboration is a "windy", "challenging and enjoyable" course set on gently rolling, mostly treeless desert terrain just a short drive south of Colorado Springs; it's "good for spring and fall golf", and the "staff really makes you feel at home", but cognoscenti caution: "just don't try to find your wayward ball in the arroyo."

Denver

Arrowhead 🖾

23 | 19 | 19 | 16 | $135

Littleton | 10850 W. Sundown Trail | 303-973-9614 | www.arrowheadcolorado.com | 6682/5465; 70.9/71.1; 134/127

A federation of fans feel like they're "playing in a *Star Trek* episode" at this Robert Trent Jones Jr.–designed "beauty" south of Denver where the hilly terrain has "slabs of rock [that] shoot right out of the ground" and necessitate "shots through boulders"; "slow play" and "poor" conditions are exacerbated by "rising greens fees", but most are content to "pay for scenery" that's "stunning" enough to "take your mind off a bad round."

Buffalo Run

▽ 21 | 19 | 18 | 22 | $40

Commerce City | 15700 E. 112th Ave. | 303-289-1500 | www.golfexperience.com/buffalorun | 7411/5227; 74.5/68.8; 129/117

Situated on the "high plains" with "water and sand traps" but "not a tree anywhere", this "unique, links-style" muni designed by Keith Foster is "challenging" enough to "play every day and have fun"; regulars report it's "better conditioned" than in the past but still "rough" in some spots, and notwithstanding the sight of "too many houses that distract from its pleasant setting", many feel the Commerce City spread is a "good value near the airport."

Fossil Trace

23 | 20 | 20 | 21 | $56

Golden | 3050 Illinois St. | 303-277-8750 | www.fossiltrace.com | 6831/4681; 72.5/66.5; 139/121

"Dinosaur tracks", "coyotes running around the fairways" and the "smell of Coors Light being brewed" nearby are just some of the things that give this "funky" and "beautiful" Jim Engh design in Golden "lots of character"; though it can be "expensive for non-residents" and "sometimes difficult to get weekend tee times", the "unique", "challenging" course, "helpful" service and "nice facilities" make it one of the "best muni values in the state."

Fox Hollow at Lakewood

22 | 17 | 18 | 23 | $52

Lakewood | 13410 Morrison Rd. | 303-986-7888 | www.lakewoodgolf.org
Canyon/Meadow | 6808/4473; 71.7/64.4; 133/112
Links/Canyon | 7030/4802; 72.9/66.7; 132/118
Meadow/Links | 6888/4835; 72/66.5; 131/116

"A cut above most" munis, this "great up-and-down course" in Lakewood has "a lot of variety in its three different nines", though most deem the "Canyon/Meadow combo the best", as "you are rewarded for solid play but severely punished for wayward shots"; despite being "heavily trafficked" and especially "crowded on weekends", it's nevertheless a "well-maintained", "dependable" option that offers "something for everyone."

Green Valley Ranch
| 22 | 22 | 20 | 24 | $55 |

Denver | 4900 Himalaya Rd. | 303-371-3131 | www.gvrgolf.com | 7144/5670; 72.7/66.4; 131/107

"Bring your A-game" to the "home of the Colorado Open", this "tough", "surprisingly good" Perry Dye design that stretches out over a prairie landscape near Denver's airport; despite "some real snoozer holes" nested "in the middle of a housing development", this public course is a "great place to learn" thanks to Mike McGetrick's "great teaching facility", while other amenities such as the "fabulous brunches" also make it a "very good value."

Legacy Ridge
| 20 | 17 | 18 | 20 | $45 |

Westminster | 10801 Legacy Ridge Pkwy. | 303-438-8997 | www.golfwestminster.com | 7157/5315; 73.4/71.5; 144/127

This "interesting" layout built near a wildlife sanctuary in Westminster represents "Arthur Hills at his best": "very open but tricky" with a "killer" back nine, plenty of water and sand and "variety at every turn" to make it a "solid test of golf from the tips"; critics complain it's "getting crowded out by the development" and "conditions can be somewhat sporadic", but no one objects to the "great rates."

Murphy Creek
∇ | 21 | 19 | 19 | 23 | $40 |

Aurora | 1700 S. Old Tom Morris Rd. | 303-361-7300 | www.golfaurora.com | 7456/5335; 74.6/69.8; 131/127

A "very tough course with interesting contours", this "flat and treeless" links design from Ken Kavanaugh is "maturing nicely" in the eastern suburb of Aurora; sprawling, jagged bunkers and rusted farm equipment dot the high-prairie landscape, and while "the greens took a beating last winter, most have come back" just in time for the layout to host the 2008 U.S. Amateur Public Links Championship.

Pole Creek
∇ | 24 | 18 | 20 | 24 | $85 |

Winter Park | 5827 County Rd. 51 | 970-887-9195 | 800-511-5076 | www.polecreekgolf.com
Meadow/Ranch | 7106/5008; 73.7/69; 145/130
Ranch/Ridge | 7212/5058; 73.8/69.2; 139/128
Ridge/Meadow | 7100/5002; 73/69; 136/128

Set against the "spectacularly beautiful" backdrop of the Winter Park ski area, with "trees framing the mountain views", these "three great nines" offer a "wonderful variety of holes" – "especially the Ridge" course, which some find "more interesting and scenic" than its siblings; despite the "distraction [of] the houses", this 27-holer is an "enjoyable experience" with "friendly" service and a layout that's kept in "terrific shape."

Red Hawk Ridge
| 23 | 17 | 21 | 22 | $64 |

Castle Rock | 2156 Red Hawk Ridge Dr. | 303-663-7150 | www.redhawkridge.com | 6942/4636; 71.8/67; 130/107

"You'll score well" on this "well-maintained", "short but interesting" Jim Engh design that's less than an hour's drive south of Denver with "beautiful views", "good greens" and "nice elevation changes"; while a few hawkish hackers harrumph about "sketchy" greens, most "really enjoy" winging it on the watery closer and the other "great holes with topographical challenges."

Ridge at Castle Pines North

| 26 | 24 | 23 | 19 | $125 |

Castle Rock | 1414 Castle Pines Pkwy. | 303-688-0100 | www.theridgecpn.com | 7013/5011; 73/67.6; 140/123

"Hitting from mountaintop to mountaintop" and over "huge ravines" is a "real challenge" at this "solid" Tom Weiskopf design in Castle Rock where the "distinctly different nines" (the "front is rolling hills", while the back is "in the woods") are both "fun, interesting and tough"; it's "expensive" and "too hilly to walk", but "top-notch service and conditions" and "great views" of Pike's Peak and Devil's Head make it "worth the day in gold."

⚡ Riverdale, Dunes

| 24 | 20 | 17 | 28 | $41 |

Brighton | 13300 Riverdale Rd. | 303-659-6700 | www.riverdalegolf.com | 7067/4884; 73.3/67.6; 134/123

"Pete Dye is sinister" and you've "got to love him" (and his son, Perry) "to love this" "22-year-old gem" in Denver's northern suburbs; a "solid muni" and a "great deal", this "challenging links" is like the "British Open in Colorado" with its "fast, true greens" and "traditional Scottish feel", and while some find the course a "bit on the short side", it's "always in top-notch shape."

Saddle Rock

| ▽ 23 | 19 | 19 | 24 | $42 |

Aurora | 21705 E. Arapahoe Rd. | 303-699-3939 | www.auroragov.org | 7351/5407; 74.7/71.9; 140/126

While a few fanatics tout this 1997 Dick Phelps design as one of "the best courses" around, more reserved sorts say this former host of the Colorado Open is simply "nice for a muni"; it's situated in a "seemingly desolate location" in Aurora and has many elevation changes and environmental areas that can make it "very tough to score."

Grand Junction

NEW Lakota Canyon Ranch

| ▽ 25 | 10 | 19 | 20 | $85 |

New Castle | 1000 Club House Dr. | 970-984-9700 | www.lakotacanyonranch.com | 7111/4744; 72.2/68.5; 137/123

"One of the best new courses in the state", this "great risk/reward layout" by Jim Engh ("the master of difficult sites") offers "dramatic vistas and breathtaking elevation changes"; while critics warn the "front nine is for mountain goats", fans insist "you can't go wrong" with holes that are "so well laid out, you won't even know I-70 is below you"; plus, the "very friendly staff" makes it "worth a long drive" to New Castle in "the western slope."

Redlands Mesa

| ▽ 29 | 24 | 22 | 25 | $76 |

Grand Junction | 2325 W. Ridges Blvd. | 970-263-9270 | www.redlandsmesa.com | 7007/4916; 71.7/69; 135/115

This "picturesque" Jim Engh–designed course "close to the Colorado National Monument" is a "blast to play", even if it's "hard to concentrate with such beauty all around" courtesy of "spectacular views" that make "you feel like you're playing in the middle of the Grand

	COURSE	FACIL.	SERVICE	VALUE	COST

Canyon"; despite recent housing development that "detracts greatly" from the "absolutely stunning setting", most find the "excellent" lay-out a "great value for the money."

Vail

Beaver Creek 🏕 ⏲

| 22 | 21 | 21 | 16 | $165 |

Beaver Creek | 103 Offerson Rd. | 970-845-5775 | www.beavercreek.com | 6784/5088; 71/69.3; 140/131

It's "almost like playing golf in heaven" at this "majestic", "high-altitude" course in Colorado's Vail Valley, but "bring lots of golf balls" and "beware of the elevation changes" on the "smart" RTJ Jr. design where the "forested" "first three holes are killers" and the "hilly terrain and streams" require "careful ball placement"; while many feel it's "not as difficult as some of the non-municipal tracks" in the area, the "incredibly scenic" surroundings make it "memorable."

Breckenridge

| 24 | 21 | 20 | 22 | $99 |

Breckenridge | 200 Clubhouse Dr. | 970-453-9104 |
www.breckenridgegolfclub.com
Bear/Beaver | 7276/5063; 73.9/69.2; 147/124
Beaver/Elk | 7145/4908; 73.5/67.4; 151/129
Elk/Bear | 7257/5045; 74/67.8; 145/130

Fans find it "amazing" that this "well-managed", "extraordinary Nicklaus course" in Breckenridge is "actually a municipal", for it's "one of the best in the mountains", offering "great golfing" amid "beautiful scenery"; the "tight fairways" on these "tough" 27 holes "require a variety of shots", and while the rarefied air at 9,324 feet might "make you hit the same as Tiger", "you'll shoot a high score" and "need lots of balls."

Cordillera, Mountain 🏌 🏕 ⏲

| 22 | 24 | 22 | 18 | $235 |

Edwards | 650 Club House Dr. | 970-926-5100 | www.cordillera-vail.com | 7457/5200; 75.6/68.9; 147/130

A "challenging course" in "superb condition" and a "breathtaking environment" with "to-die-for views" make up a "winning combination" at this Cordillera sibling crafted by Hale Irwin; some find this Edwards layout "tricked-up", but putters praise the "incredible greens" and suggest you may just "need all the clubs in your bag" for this "excellent" if "pricey" "test of golf."

Cordillera, Summit 🏌 🏕 ⏲

| 24 | 24 | 23 | 19 | $237 |

Edwards | 190 Gore Trail | 970-926-5300 | www.cordillera-vail.com | 7530/5239; 74.4/69.4; 137/129

"Watch your ball sail into the wild blue yonder" at this "magnificent" Jack Nicklaus design, where the views are "fantastic" at "9,200 feet" and it "feels like playing on the moon"; while some critics complain the "snobbish" "staff doesn't care" and "you would expect more for all that money", most find it "spectacular", but warn that "the Golden Bear might have broken par when he first played it – but I doubt you will!"

Cordillera, Valley 🏌 ⛳

| – | – | – | – | $215 |

Edwards | 0101 Legends Dr. | 970-926-5950 | www.cordillera-vail.com | 7091/5017; 73.2/67.2; 138/123

Christened by Phil Mickelson and Colin Montgomerie in a 1998 exhibition match, this part-links, part-mountain Tom Fazio design unfolds

	COURSE	FACIL.	SERVICE	VALUE	COST

along 400 acres of desert terrain on the Vail Valley floor; a nearby highway can occasionally distract from the layout's aesthetic appeal – arroyos, streams and native grasses predominate – but at least its 7,150-ft. elevation (which is lower than that of its resort siblings) ensures a long playing season.

Eagle Vail ♿

| 19 | 16 | 18 | 21 | $94 |

Avon | 431 Eagle Dr. | 970-949-5267 | 800-341-8051 | www.eaglevailgolfclub.com | 6819/4856; 71.3/67.4; 131/123

"A great place to take your family", this "older", "pretty" layout "spread out along the Vail Valley floor" is a "pleasant change from the overpriced mountain courses"; though "lined with houses" and "cramped" (the "narrow fairways" "require a sniper's accuracy"), most find the Avon alternative "rugged, fun" and, most importantly, "a value."

Keystone Ranch, Ranch

| 23 | 22 | 21 | 20 | $130 |

Keystone | 1239 Keystone Ranch Rd. | 970-496-4250 | www.keystonegolf.com | 7090/5582; 72.5/69.9; 137/128

Fans flying high on this "fairly flat" Keystone course describe it as "fun at 9,300 feet", a Robert Trent Jones Jr. layout offering "true links" golf on the front nine and "beautiful views all around" on an experience that's "not easy from the back tees" given "lodgepole pine–lined holes" that "make it tough if you miss the fairway"; though a couple of connoisseurs complain about "typical resort slow play", most agree the conditions are "excellent."

Keystone Ranch, River

| 24 | 20 | 20 | 20 | $145 |

Keystone | 155 River Course Rd. | 970-496-4250 | www.keystonegolf.com | 6886/4762; 70.8/65.1; 132/123

"The elevated first tee makes your blood rush and the elevated 18th makes you wish the end wasn't so near" gush fans of this "family-friendly" Keystone resort course that's highlighted by "dramatic elevation changes" and "huge drops" – which will "include your jaw", as you take in the "spectacular" "views of snow-capped peaks from just about every hole"; the only thing "ordinary" here is the "self-serve" food operations.

Raven at Three Peaks ☺

| 27 | 24 | 23 | 21 | $139 |

Silverthorne | 2929 N. Golden Eagle Rd. | 970-262-3636 | www.ravenatthreepeaks.com | 7413/5235; 73.4/69.9; 142/129

Aspen groves, distinctive bunkers, "creeks, lakes" and "many ups and downs" (all at some 9,000 feet above sea level) are all part of this "challenging" "mountain course" in Silverthorne that was designed by Hurdzan and Fry in consultation with Tom Lehman; a "great clubhouse and service" contribute to what many consider "the best all-around golf experience in Colorado", a "gorgeous" adventure that may just "distract you enough to relax and shoot one of your best scores."

☑ Red Sky, Fazio ♿ ⚬

| 28 | 26 | 24 | 22 | $225 |

Wolcott | 376 Red Sky Rd. | 970-477-8425 | 866-873-3759 | www.redskygolfclub.com | 7113/5265; 72/68.2; 135/125

It "feels like you died and went to golf heaven" at this "intriguing" Tom Fazio layout – the top-rated Course in Colorado – where "perfectly manicured" sagebrush- and aspen-framed fairways offer glimpses of Vail's back bowls; aficionados advise it may take "awhile to get used to putting into the mountainside or valley" and "you need to control your distance to score well", but with "great views and wildlife" and a "fantastic guest clubhouse", this "country-club experience" in Wolcott comes "highly recommended."

⛳ Red Sky, Norman 🏌 ⛳

28	26	25	23	$225

Wolcott | 376 Red Sky Rd. | 970-477-8400 | 866-873-3759 | www.redskygolfclub.com | 7580/5269; 74.2/68.5; 144/124

For "world-class golfing in the Rockies", fans tout this "thrilling" Greg Norman design set amid alpine backdrops and wildflower-filled meadows, a "truly unique experience" offering "fantastic views" and "awesome", "tough-to-read greens" kept in "immaculate condition"; factor in an "incredibly warm, caring staff" and some of the "best facilities" around, and it's easy to see why this Wolcott resort "favorite" is so "difficult to get on."

Sonnenalp ⏱

24	21	21	21	$175

Edwards | 1265 Berry Creek Rd. | 970-477-5370 | www.sonnenalp.com | 7059/5293; 72.3/70; 138/115

"Well maintained" and "never crowded", this "tough", "traditional links layout" from Jay Morrish and Bob Cupp is "reasonably priced" and "may be the best all-around value in the Vail Valley" according to its fans; located at the Sonnenalp resort in the midst of mountains, meadows and streams that overshadow the "upscale houses on the holes", it's a "great course at 9,000 feet" – as long as you "make sure there's a drink holder on your oxygen tank."

Connecticut

Danbury

Richter Park

26	15	16	23	$68

Danbury | 100 Aunt Hack Rd. | 203-792-2552 | www.richterpark.com | 6744/5114; 73.3/69.8; 134/126

"Set on a reservoir" with "serene views" of the surrounding park, this "pristine" "beauty of a muni" offers "challenging, memorable" holes with "plenty of blind shots, water and elevation changes"; while some "can't think of anything bad to say about" this woodsy Danbury "value", others aren't sure whether the "pedestrian facilities" ("no driving range") and "unfriendly staff" are worth "the pain and suffering of procuring a [non-resident] tee time."

East Haddam

Fox Hopyard

25	25	22	21	$118

East Haddam | 1 Hopyard Rd. | 860-434-6644 | 800-943-1903 | www.golfthefox.com | 6912/5111; 74.1/70.7; 136/123

"Absolutely beautiful", "especially during the fall foliage", this "foxy lady" lures visitors "off the beaten track" to East Haddam with her "country club-like setting" and "traditional, tree-lined" layout on which "familiarity breeds content" as you tackle "lots of elevation changes" and "forced carries over wetlands" (it "gets better each time you play"); with a "top-notch pro shop" and "courteous staff", it "feels almost like a resort" – with "pricey greens fees" to match.

Hartford

Gillette Ridge

| 21 | 19 | 20 | 20 | $80 |

Bloomfield | 1360 Hall Blvd./Rte. 218 | 860-726-1430 |
www.gilletteridgegolf.com | 7191/5582; 74.8/67.2; 135/117
"A beauty to behold" just 15 minutes north of Hartford, this "fairly
new" Arnold Palmer layout is a "thoughtful" but "extremely challenging" design that delivers "excellent risk/reward options" and "variety"
but can prove "difficult for the average weekend golfer" with its "bizarre routing" and "impossibly hard forced carries"; though "poor conditions have plagued it" ("a little love would go a long way"), most
agree this "course is finally coming into its own."

Lyman Orchards, Gary Player 🏌

| 21 | 19 | 19 | 21 | $63 |

Middlefield | 1 Lyman Rd. | 888-995-9626 | www.lymangolf.com |
6725/4900; 72.7/68.3; 133/118
"Bring a bag in the fall and grab some apples from the orchards"
through which this "unique, beautiful" Gary Player design makes its
"bizarre routing"; the "challenging" "target golf heaven" just 30 minutes south of Hartford may disconcert with its "forced carries" and
"tough blind shots", but the "family-run" facility will make you feel entirely "at home" with its "very personal" service and "great practice"
area; P.S. be on the lookout for their "can't-beat" specials.

Lyman Orchards, Robert Trent Jones

| 22 | 19 | 20 | 22 | $49 |

Middlefield | 1 Lyman Rd. | 888-995-9626 | www.lymangolf.com |
7011/5812; 73.2/72; 129/124
"You'll be struck by the beauty" of this "mature", "traditional", "typical
Trent Jones Sr." affair featuring "wide fairways and gnarly greens"
to make it a "challenge"; "the back nine can be a bog in wet weather",
but a "nice" staff, "great facilities" and plenty of orchard-related
activities lead swingers to say it's "an excellent value" overall; in short:
"if you live in Connecticut, you should be playing here – and getting
your cider here."

Wintonbury Hills

| 24 | 19 | 20 | 24 | $75 |

Bloomfield | 206 Terry Plains Rd. | 860-242-1401 |
www.wintonburyhillsgolf.com | 6709/5005; 72.8/68.2; 130/112
Considered "a wonderful addition to the state's golf scene", this "beautiful" Pete Dye design just north of Hartford "is truly a find" – "his work
belies the $1 compensation he received" – that pairs "generous", tree-
lined fairways with "fast, sloped", "tough-to-read greens"; though the
muni draws duffers' ire for its "spare clubhouse" and "mess" of a driving range (getting to it may "require a taxi ride"), it's nevertheless "a
lot of fun" and "a great value for your $$$."

New Haven

Great River

| 25 | 26 | 23 | 17 | $125 |

Milford | 130 Coram Ln. | 203-876-8051 | 877-478-7470 |
www.greatrivergolfclub.com | 7191/5170; 75.2/68; 150/118
"The best thing to happen to Connecticut in years, golfwise", this "fan-
tastic Tommy Fazio course" in a "picturesque" Milford "setting along
the Housatonic River" "will challenge the best and kill the rest" thanks

to holes like the "mischievous and deceptive 12th" "with a big approach over water"; a "super clubhouse", "unbelievable practice facilities" and "outstanding dining" add up to a "country-club experience for the public player" at prices that are "worth every penny."

NEW Oxford Greens 🏴 | 22 | 20 | 20 | 20 | $89 |

Oxford | 99 Country Club Dr. | 203-888-1600 | www.oxfordgreens.com | 7186/5188; 74.9/69.9; 134/122

"This will be a great course in a few years" predict players who "love the layout" of this "beautiful addition" northwest of New Haven, a "still maturing" track that traverses varied terrain with its "rolling fairways and challenging, undulating greens"; though "not completely grown in yet", "conditions are improving", which leads some to suspect that "others [may] soon find out about" this "hidden" "value"; P.S. a "new driving range has improved the experience."

New London

Z NEW Lake of Isles, North 🏴 | 29 | 25 | 26 | 21 | $195 |

North Stonington | 1 Clubhouse Dr. | 888-475-3746 | www.lakeofisles.com | 7250/4937; 75.8/69; 143/127

"Such a challenge that grown golfers weep openly", Connecticut's top-rated Course is "one of the hardest layouts" in the state, with a "beautiful but difficult target" design from Rees Jones that involves "long forced carries" and "deep sand everywhere"; though the "amazing" experience "lives up to the hype" via "immaculate conditions", "impeccable service" and a location "right across from Foxwoods Resort & Casino", "pricey" fees make it "too expensive to play often"; N.B. it has a private South sibling.

Shennecossett | 21 | 13 | 15 | 23 | $42 |

Groton | 93 Plant St. | 860-445-0262 | www.shennygolf.com | 6562/5571; 71.5/72.4; 122/122

"Old, old, old tradition" sets the distinguished tone for this "wonderful links" that was originally built in 1898 and redesigned by Donald Ross in 1916; winding "along the Connecticut coast" near Groton, this "pleasant muni" is "packed with players" who appreciate "lots of bunkers", "rough that will drive you crazy" and "lovely views of the Long Island Sound" from the "great back nine"; while some note it "could upgrade its clubhouse" and "limited services", most find it "a real value."

Stamford

Sterling Farms | 19 | 17 | 16 | 21 | $50 |

Stamford | 1349 Newfield Ave. | 203-329-7888 | www.sterlingfarmsgc.com | 6327/5495; 71.4/72.8; 126/125

"The best reason to be a resident of Stamford" is this "short but plenty challenging layout" that offers "some hills, some water" and greens that "are consistently the best of any muni" around; it's "not easy to get a tee time" on this "really crowded" "value" ("expect five-hour rounds"), but it's kept "in great shape for the amount of play it gets" and boasts a "pleasant restaurant" and a "very nice driving range" replete with heated hitting stations.

	COURSE	FACIL.	SERVICE	VALUE	COST

Delaware

Rehoboth Beach

NEW Bayside 🏕

∇ 24 | 19 | 21 | 17 | $160

Selbyville | 31806 Lakeview Dr. | 302-436-3400 | 877-436-9998 | www.livebayside.com | 7545/5165; 76.5/64.9; 139/112

Situated just west of Fenwick Island with views of Assawoman Bay from several of its holes, this "great Golden Bear" design starts with a bang courtesy of a tree-lined opener that curves around a lake and is peppered with 11 bunkers; the rest of the course meanders through woodlands, meadows and marshland with fescue and bluegrass rough, and though a few critics complain of "some goofiness", most bear no grudge against the semi-private spread.

Baywood Greens

26 | 26 | 23 | 22 | $95

Long Neck | 32267 Clubhouse Way | 302-947-9800 | 888-844-2254 | www.baywoodgreens.com | 6983/5136; 73.2/70.9; 129/124

"You'll think you're at Augusta" as you tee it up at what fanatics feel is "the best-manicured, -landscaped and -valued course" on the Delaware shore; pleasing to the eye with its "simply awesome" flowers ("especially those lining the bridge"), this "open" layout also "challenges every type of game" with a woodsy front half and a back that's "awash in water" – so "be sure to bring your waders"; "it's a little pricey, but worth it to treat yourself!"

Bear Trap Dunes

22 | 22 | 21 | 20 | $120

Ocean View | Central Ave. | 302-537-5600 | 877-232-7872 | www.beartrapdunes.com
Black Bear/Kodiak | 6853/5074; 72.4/69.1; 130/118
Grizzly/Black Bear | 6901/5094; 72.7/69.4; 130/121
Grizzly/Kodiak | 6834/5208; 72.1/69.8; 126/120

A "great experience at the beach", this "links-style" layout offers three nines, each of which "has individual character" as it "meanders over relatively flat ground" near Bethany Beach, and all of which are "open and affected by the ocean breezes" with "very large traps and water that need to be carried"; if perhaps "prices are on the high end" and "new construction" is "taking away some of the tranquility", it's otherwise a "wonderful facility" with "good twilight" deals.

Florida

TOP COURSES IN STATE

28 | TPC Sawgrass, Stadium | *Jacksonville*
Ocean Hammock | *Daytona Beach*
World Woods, Pine Barrens | *Tampa*
27 | Orange County Nat'l, Panther Lake | *Orlando*
Arnold Palmer's Bay Hill | *Orlando*
26 | Westin Innisbrook, Copperhead | *Tampa*
World Woods, Rolling Oaks | *Tampa*
Tiburón, Black | *Naples*
Orange County Nat'l, Crooked Cat | *Orlando*
World Golf Village, King & Bear | *Jacksonville*

Daytona Beach

LPGA International, Champions 🔊   22 | 21 | 22 | 19 | $100

Daytona Beach | 1000 Champions Dr. | 386-274-5742 |
www.lpgainternational.com | 7088/5131; 74.6/70.2; 137/125

This "fairly easy", "straightforward" links design from Rees Jones is a
"very good", "very playable" option with few trees, "mounds in the
middle of nowhere" and undulating greens; though it "rewards strong
play if the wind isn't up", this "inland" Daytona Beach layout nevertheless "suffers by comparison to [sibling] Legends" (there's "not one
place where you say, 'man, nice hole!'"), although it profits from its
connection to the LPGA's "great" national headquarters.

LPGA International, Legends 🔊   25 | 25 | 25 | 21 | $100

Daytona Beach | 1000 Champions Dr. | 386-274-5742 |
www.lpgainternational.com | 6984/5155; 74.1/70.2; 142/123

Although it's part of the LPGA's headquarters, this "tough but fun"
Arthur Hills design is "not only for the females": men and women alike
praise the tight, tree-lined track as being "harder than the Champions
course" with "lots of carries" – "brush up on your iron play" – and an
emphasis "on ball placement"; all in all, it's "one of the great courses
and facilities" around, but if you plan to take advantage of the twilight
specials, "bring bug spray!"

☑ Ocean Hammock   28 | 24 | 24 | 19 | $265

Palm Coast | 105 16th Rd. | 386-447-4611 | 888-515-4579 |
www.oceanhammock.com | 7201/5115; 77/71.5; 147/131

"Wow!" – it's "worth a detour" 45 minutes north of Daytona Beach
to tackle this "relatively unknown masterpiece" that's "one of the
more picturesque courses in Florida" with its six "magnificent oceanside holes"; the "tremendous" resort design is "Nicklaus at his friendliest" but is nevertheless quite "challenging" as it plays around
wetlands, lakes and coquina-sand bunkers; it's "pricey", but its "first-
rate facilities" are just one reason swingers insist "if you can get on,
then play it."

Victoria Hills   ▽ 25 | 20 | 19 | 25 | $110

Deland | 300 Spalding Way | 386-738-6000 | 866-295-4385 |
www.stjoegolf.com | 6989/4852; 73.5/67.2; 142/124

"You'll forget you're in Florida" exclaim escapists about this "absolutely beautiful" Ron Garl design 20 miles southwest of Daytona Beach
that "feels like Pinehurst" thanks to its undulating fairways, slope-
filled green surrounds and tall pines; although "it's a long way from
Orlando", many "love this course" and "would come back again."

Ft. Lauderdale

Club at Emerald Hills 🔊   25 | 19 | 20 | 21 | $175

Hollywood | 4100 N. Hills Dr. | 954-961-4000 |
www.theclubatemeraldhills.com | 7280/5012; 76.3/70.1; 146/116

The "best-kept secret in South Florida" is this "interesting" spread just
south of Ft. Lauderdale that strikes some as "all the course a vacationing golfer would want"; kept in "excellent condition", the "challenging,
older" layout (built in 1969 and reconstructed 30 years later) offers

	COURSE	FACIL.	SERVICE	VALUE	COST

rolling fairways, lots of water and "nice", "fast greens"; a few foozlers feel the facilities "need more love", but overall it's a "very nice" track and a "sensible value."

TPC Heron Bay ⚑

| 19 | 23 | 22 | 16 | $141 |

Coral Springs | 11801 Heron Bay Blvd. | 954-796-2000 | 800-511-6616 | www.tpcheronbay.com | 7268/4961; 74.9/68.7; 127/113

"You can always get on" this "pleasant" Mark McCumber layout in the "cow country west of Ft. Lauderdale"; it's a "deal in the summer", but critics advise "bringing your camel and suntan lotion", as only "Lawrence of Arabia would like all the sun and wind" and "Sahara's worth of bunkers" on this "flat", "rather uninspiring" course with "no trees or water."

Jacksonville

Amelia Island Plantation, Long Point ⚑ ⚯

| 25 | 23 | 22 | 20 | $160 |

Amelia Island | 6800 First Coast Hwy. | 904-277-5908 | 888-261-6161 | www.aipfl.com | 6775/4927; 73/70.2; 135/123

A "beautiful Tom Fazio" design, "the most difficult of the Amelia Island courses" offers "a perfect combination of ocean, marsh and woodsy holes" (the seaside section is "particularly dramatic") with large, undulating greens and "lush", "well-manicured" fairways that are "like hitting onto soft shag carpeting"; a "first-rate clubhouse" and "professional atmosphere" are two more reasons why this "fun and interesting" choice is some resort guests' "favorite."

Amelia Island Plantation, Oak Marsh ⚑ ⚯

| 23 | 23 | 24 | 20 | $140 |

Amelia Island | 6800 First Coast Hwy. | 904-277-5907 | 888-261-6161 | www.aipfl.com | 6580/4983; 72.3/69.7; 136/122

With "lots of overhanging oaks and Spanish moss", this "playable" but "very tight" Pete Dye design is "so beautiful, golfers just laugh when they lose balls" on one of the "relatively isolated holes"; while there's "no ocean" to be had on this "average length" spread, over half of the resort course has water in play, providing "spectacular views across the marsh" "at or near sunset"; factor in "good conditions and service", and this is "a great place to go" for a round.

Amelia Island Plantation, Ocean Links ⚑ ⚯

| 24 | 23 | 23 | 20 | $140 |

Amelia Island | 6800 First Coast Hwy. | 904-277-5907 | 888-261-6161 | www.aipfl.com | 6108/4341; 69.3/66.4; 128/118

"Probably the most scenic" of the three Amelia Island courses with "stunning views" from "five beautiful holes along the ocean", this "terrific" Pete Dye/Bobby Weed collaboration is "fun and interesting" "but not too hard" – that is, until you encounter the "really challenging on-shore breezes"; although a few feel the tree-laden track "could have been in better shape", most maintain they "had a ball!"

◪ TPC Sawgrass, Stadium ⛳ ⚯

| 28 | 26 | 25 | 20 | $371 |

Ponte Vedra Beach | 110 TPC Blvd. | 904-273-3230 | www.tpcsawgrass.com | 6954/5000; 75/65.3; 149/125

"Ok, I'm not Vijay" reveal fans who nonetheless "shoot 100 and love it" "on this "beautiful but difficult-to-master diva" "where the big boys play"; Florida's top-rated Course is "Pete Dye at his diabolical best", a Ponte Vedra Beach brute boasting "18 terrific holes" that are a "dream come true" and "worth it even in the rain" (the island-green "17th alone is worth it"); still, you'd best "bring your corporate credit card"; N.B. a 2006 renovation rebuilt the greens and enhanced drainage.

TPC Sawgrass, Valley 🏌 ⚙ ⊙ | 24 | 25 | 24 | 21 | $182

Ponte Vedra Beach | 110 TPC Blvd. | 904-273-3230 | www.tpcsawgrass.com | 6864/5126; 72.8/65; 130/115

"A great course in its own right", this "impressive" Pete Dye/Bobby Weed layout is "more forgiving" and "not as well known as big brother Stadium", but "with similar features", it's "just as fun and challenging" - so "keep it in the fairway or take your medicine"; even with "facilities that should be better after renovations are completed", many conclude "it's a step down from the Stadium, but a step up from most."

World Golf Village, King & Bear 🏌 ⊙ | 26 | 25 | 25 | 21 | $175

St. Augustine | 1 King Bear Dr. | 904-940-6200 | www.wgv.com | 7279/5119; 75.2/70.1; 141/123

There's "a good reason to take the trip to North Florida", and that's to tackle this "golf-lover's must", a "Jack and Arnie" co-design where it's sport to "guess which legend designed which hole"; boasting "the best of both" architects, this St. Augustine resort course is in "perfect shape" and has rapt roundsmen raving about both its "great customer service" and its luxe spa, where you can take a "tranquil break from golf."

World Golf Village, Slammer & Squire 🏌 ⊙ | 24 | 26 | 25 | 21 | $150

St. Augustine | 2 World Golf Pl. | 904-940-6100 | www.wgv.com | 6939/4996; 73.8/69.1; 135/116

Although "playing in the footsteps of the game's greatest players" may be the ultimate enticement to visit this World Golf Village venue, don't underestimate Bobby Weed's "beautiful" woods-and-wetlands design; some say the Jacksonville-area layout is "in better shape than Augusta", and all agree that it offers "great facilities" and "unbelievable service" from "the nicest" staff.

Miami

Biltmore | 19 | 20 | 19 | 19 | $54

Coral Gables | 1210 Anastasia Ave. | 305-460-5364 | www.biltmorehotel.com | 6701/6301; 72/70; 126/123

"If you like traditional courses with history, this is the place for you" aver acolytes of this 1924 Donald Ross design that "takes you back in time" with a "unique layout that circles" the "antique Biltmore Hotel" "in the middle of Coral Gables"; though "you'll want to slow [down] to take in the million-dollar homes", a few feel the city-owned spread needs to be "kept in better condition" - they've "updated, but Babe Ruth would still recognize some of the holes."

Crandon 🏌 | 24 | 16 | 16 | 21 | $148

Key Biscayne | 6700 Crandon Blvd. | 305-361-9120 | www.miamidade.gov/parks/golf.asp | 7301/5423; 76.2/71.8; 145/130

"A true island paradise" that's "routed around the mangroves" on "exotic Key Biscayne", this "picturesque and challenging" park-owned

	COURSE	FACIL.	SERVICE	VALUE	COST

property is considered by some to be "one of the best bangs for the buck in South Florida", offering "views of the Bay from many holes" plus "lots of wildlife" like "iguanas running across the fairways"; some two-legged types tut "it's too crowded" with "spotty conditions", but even they admit the "new pro shop and guest center" was "a major upgrade."

☑ Doral, Blue Monster 斗 | 25 | 24 | 21 | 15 | $295 |

Miami | 4400 NW 87th Ave. | 305-592-2030 | 800-713-6725 | www.doralresort.com | 7288/5392; 74.5/73; 130/124

"Restored to its former glory" "in summer 2006", "da Monster" is back with "sharper teeth" due to a "complete greens" and bunker renovation and fresh landscaping; now "everybody wants to play" this "killer course" in Miami that's hosted the PGA Tour since 1962 and "will be home to the WGC-CA Championship in 2007"; of course, you'll "have your hands full" with "water everywhere", "deep rough" and "sand, sand, sand", but it's a "must-play once in a lifetime" – which may be plenty, as it "also costs a pretty penny."

Doral, Gold 斗 | 22 | 24 | 23 | 17 | $250 |

Miami | 4400 NW 87th Ave. | 305-592-2030 | 800-713-6725 | www.doralresort.com | 6602/5179; 73.3/71.4; 129/123

It "packs none of the bite" of big brother Blue, yet "you won't regret" playing this "solid" gold sister that's "a little easier", "much more fun" and comes at "a better price"; highlighted by the "great island-green 18th", this "lovely" "typical resort course" draws "families and groups" and, fortunately, "handles a lot of people well"; although "not the Monster" and located in the flight "path for MIA", this "wonderful facility" will leave you "with a smile."

Doral, Great White 斗 | 22 | 24 | 21 | 15 | $275 |

Miami | 4400 NW 87th Ave. | 305-592-2030 | 800-713-6725 | www.doralresort.com | 7171/5026; 74.5/67.8; 134/117

"A desert course in a tropical climate", this "unique" Greg Norman design "in the heart of Miami" is "fun" and "playable for the average Joe and Jane"; nevertheless, swingers suggest you "hit it straight" or "bring a shovel with your sand wedge", as the "rough is ground coquina shells" and there's "more [of it] than water"; a few grouse about the "premium prices", but the resort experience includes "an awesome clubhouse, friendly staff and well-stocked pro shop."

Naples

Lely, Flamingo Island | 21 | 21 | 20 | 19 | $164 |

Naples | 8004 Lely Resort Blvd. | 239-793-2600 | 800-388-4653 | www.lely-resort.com | 7171/5377; 75/71.4; 136/123

"Try it, you'll like it" entreat admirers of this Robert Trent Jones Sr. semi-private spread sporting "long holes" with "strategically placed bunkers" and "considerable water" – as well as "alligators [that] voraciously eat golf balls"; the "challenging" layout is nevertheless "fair" and "women-friendly", and while it's "expensive in winter", more reasonable "summer prices" ensure it's a "great Naples-area value"; in fact, "the only thing warmer than the course is the weather and the nice people who work there."

	COURSE	FACIL.	SERVICE	VALUE	COST

Lely, Mustang 🛺

| 22 | 20 | 20 | 18 | $164 |

Naples | 8004 Lely Resort Blvd. | 239-793-2600 | 800-388-4653 |
www.lely-resort.com | 7217/5197; 75.2/70.5; 141/120

Located in a residential community halfway "between Naples and
Marco Island", this "tough", "well-groomed" Lee Trevino design is
routed through natural wetlands and rolling hills; "some blind tee
shots" and 12 lakes "make for a challenge" and ensure that "a large
number of balls can disappear from your bag" – so "brush up on the
'alligator sunning near ball' rule" before you go; a "good driving range
and practice area" and "excellent food" add to the appeal.

Tiburón, Black 🛺 ⏱

| 26 | 27 | 26 | 20 | $265 |

Naples | 2620 Tiburon Dr. | 239-594-2040 | www.wcigolf.com |
7005/4909; 74.2/69.7; 147/119

"Greg Norman does it right" with this "unreal" yet "unpretentious"
course "carved out" of some "expensive real estate" in Naples, creat-
ing "gorgeous" holes with "lots of natural beauty", "no rough",
"mounded greens" and "tight fairways" that give "an advantage to the
straight hitter"; as "part of the Ritz-Carlton", it's a "first-class facility"
with "unparalleled service" ("families are welcome"), but you might
have to "bring the trust fund" if you want to play in season.

Tiburón, Gold 🛺 ⏱

| 26 | 27 | 25 | 20 | $265 |

Naples | 2620 Tiburon Dr. | 239-594-2040 | www.wcigolf.com |
7288/5148; 74.7/69.2; 137/113

Peripatetic players insist "it's worth a 1,400-mile drive to play" this
"outstanding", "well-designed" Greg Norman layout that some call
"the best in the Naples area"; because it's "all fairway", it's "player-
friendly", and because "it's Tiburón", you "just cannot beat" the "phenomenal service and facilities" – it's part of the "upscale" Ritz-Carlton
resort – that make it "almost worth the price in the high season" and a
"real steal" "in the summer heat."

Ocala

El Diablo

| 21 | 11 | 15 | 22 | $55 |

Citrus Springs | 10405 N. Sherman Dr. | 352-465-0986 | 888-886-1309 |
www.eldiablogolf.com | 7045/5144; 75.3/69.8; 147/117

It's "definitely worth the drive" to this "unknown gem" "in the middle
of nowhere" – actually, just southwest of Ocala – as this "great Jim
Fazio layout" offers a "challenging" "test of golf"; the devil is in the details, however, as what was "once a very nice course" is "no longer
properly maintained" and the clubhouse facilities feel "makeshift",
making this add up to "all you want in a golf course" "with little else."

Orlando

Arnold Palmer's Bay Hill 🏌 🔑

| 27 | 25 | 25 | 22 | $214 |

Orlando | 9000 Bay Hill Blvd. | 407-876-2429 | www.bayhill.com |
7267/5235; 75.3/70.8; 140/128

"The King's finest" is "simply the best in Orlando", a "traditional"
"PGA Tour-tough" track where "you might even see" "Mr. Palmer at
work" or "on an adjacent fairway"; "you must stay to play", but the
"fantastic lodge" provides "a resort experience" and the "accommo-

dating" staff "treats guests like royalty"; besides, "if you can get a tee time", "nothing beats" "sharing a locker with Tiger, Phil or any of the pros" who come here for the annual Arnold Palmer Invitational.

Baytree National 🏌

▽ 25 | 22 | 21 | 25 | $69

Melbourne | 8207 National Dr. | 321-259-9060 | www.baytreenational.com | 7043/4803; 74/68.4; 135/121

Blast off at this "nice" Gary Player design situated in the heart of Florida's Space Coast about 45 minutes southeast of Orlando; playing "through a semi-private neighborhood" "next to I-95", the layout has mounds framing its fairways, over 80 bunkers, distinctive red shale waste areas and large, flat greens; the course has had a recent "change in ownership", but the rugged lake- and wetlands-skirting par-4 18th remains the same.

Black Bear 🏌

▽ 24 | 20 | 20 | 23 | $55

Eustis | 24505 Calusa Blvd. | 352-357-4732 | 800-423-2718 | www.orlando-golf.com | 7002/5044; 73.8/69.3; 131/122

Located "in the middle of nowhere" 40 miles northwest of Orlando, this "wide-open" "links course" "doesn't feel like Florida golf (besides the humidity)" thanks to a "fun" P.B. Dye design with "some serious elevations to it"; the "well-kept" layout is set on "rolling terrain" "without trees" or water but with "over 100 bunkers, undulating greens" and wind that's "usually in play", making it a "very challenging" but "excellent course for the money."

Celebration Golf Club

23 | 22 | 23 | 21 | $139

Celebration | 701 Golfpark Dr. | 407-566-4653 | www.celebrationgolf.com | 6772/4949; 73/68.5; 135/121

A "picturesque" layout "designed by the Jones boys" (Robert Trent Jones Sr. and Jr.), this "perfectly manicured course" plays through "beautiful homes" "in the center of 'Pleasantville'" – aka the "planned community" of Celebration southwest of Orlando; while a few "expected more" from what they call a "not overly challenging" experience, most find it "a fair test" featuring "huge, sloped greens" and "fairways lined with ball-eating grass"; even better, it has "an exceptionally nice staff" providing "typical Disney service."

ChampionsGate, International 🏌

24 | 25 | 23 | 19 | $170

Champions Gate | 1400 Masters Blvd. | 407-787-4653 | 888-558-9301 | www.championsgategolf.com | 7363/5618; 76.8/71.6; 143/118

"Greg Norman brought a taste of seaside links golf to central Florida" say swingers smitten with this "awesome" Omni Resort layout "about 20 minutes from Downtown Disney"; "precision is paramount" thanks to "sloping fairways" with "narrow landing areas", "water that threatens imperfect approaches" and wind and "pot bunkers that add to the misery" – it's "much more challenging than its sister course"; though a few cynics sneer "it's about as international as an IHOP", most find it "worth every nickel."

ChampionsGate, National 🏌

23 | 25 | 24 | 18 | $160

Champions Gate | 1400 Masters Blvd. | 407-787-4653 | 888-558-9301 | www.championsgategolf.com | 7128/5150; 75.2/69.4; 138/115

"Like its sister, it's an amazing" layout laud admirers of this "traditional" "Florida course" (read: "flat with sand and water") situated south of Disney; "much simpler than the International", this "enjoyable" Greg Norman design is also "more forgiving and less challenging" – "what you see is what you get"; factor in "great practice facilities" that include David Leadbetter's teaching headquarters and you have a truly "top-notch" resort destination.

DeBary ♠

| | | | | $69 |

DeBary | 300 Plantation Club Dr. | 386-668-1705 | www.debarycc.com | 6776/5060; 72.6/69.4; 140/118

Not many have ventured out to this "great course" that's "not too far off I-4" about 20 minutes north of Orlando, but those who have made the trip to this "underrated" destination tell a tale of undulating terrain, pine-framed fairways, "slick but fair greens" and a mere two holes with water: the 9th and the 18th; the "fun-to-play" semi-private even sports a "helpful staff" that contributes much to the "wonderful experience."

Diamondback ♠

24 | 17 | 19 | 22 | $69

Haines City | 6501 State Rd. 544 E. | 863-421-0437 | 800-222-5629 | www.diamondbackgolfclub.net | 6893/4872; 73.1/69.9; 131/119

This "wonderful out-of-the-way place" is "worth the drive" 45 minutes south of Orlando for a "course that never eases up" as it plays through "fabulous flora and fauna"; "bring a lot of golf balls", as this "challenging" layout is "tight" with tree-lined fairways and a "welcoming atmosphere", provided you're not herpetologically challenged – "if you're afraid of snakes, I wouldn't suggest playing here."

Falcon's Fire ♠

23 | 20 | 21 | 20 | $139

Kissimmee | 3200 Seralago Blvd. | 407-239-5445 | 877-878-3473 | www.falconsfire.com | 6901/5417; 73.8/71.6; 138/126

"A joy to play", this Rees Jones design delivers a "variety of holes" that are "just challenging enough to test" both the "average and experienced golfer" but also "playable enough to score on"; a "long" layout with "interesting" terrain and "a staff that treats you like a member", this Kissimmee course is "a great place to practice" and "an excellent way to get away from Disney but stay close enough to rejoin your family."

Grand Cypress ♣ ⏰

25 | 26 | 25 | 19 | $250

Orlando | 1 N. Jacaranda St. | 407-239-4700 | 800-835-7377 | www.grandcypress.com

East/North | 6955/5056; 74.2/69.4; 135/117
North/South | 6993/5328; 74.4/71.2; 136/120
South/East | 6906/5126; 73.8/69.8; 135/117

"If you can't make it to the other side of the pond", head to this "top-notch" Orlando facility with an "amazing" 27 holes – think "lots of water" and "six-ft.-tall pot bunkers" on the North/South nines and woodlands on the East; the "terrific" resort experience comes with an "excellent school" and "impeccable service and maintenance", making it a "good place to hide while the family's at Disney!"; P.S. "book a package in-season" or expect "very high fees."

Grand Cypress, New ♣ ⏰

25 | 26 | 26 | 18 | $250

Orlando | 1 N. Jacaranda St. | 407-239-4700 | 800-835-7377 | www.grandcypress.com | 6773/5314; 71.5/69.7; 122/113

"Jack does St. Andrews in Orlando" – "without the airfare", "rain or snow" – on this "awesome", "wide-open" "homage to the Old Course" where there's "a thrill a hole" as you "grip it and rip it" on "huge fairways" featuring "pot bunkers everywhere except the greens and tee boxes"; some purists pout that "like Disney, it's a theme park" where the "biggest problem is the number at the bottom of the receipt", but loyal linksters insist this "treasure" is "worth every penny."

Marriott Grande Pines

| | 22 | 21 | 21 | 20 | $130 |

Orlando | 6351 International Golf Club Rd. | 407-239-6108 | www.grandepines.com | 7012/5418; 74.3/71.6; 140/126

It's not easy to "avoid the sand" at this "challenging" Joe Lee design that Steve Smyers reworked a few years ago, adding lakes, pines and plenty of bunkers; though one holdout "liked it better before the redo", most agree it's "solid" with "great facilities" that include the Faldo Golf Institute; plus, it's "convenient to the hotels on International Drive South", making it "worth a round if you're in the Orlando area."

Mission Inn, El Campeón 🔒

| | 25 | 22 | 23 | 24 | $150 |

Howey-in-the-Hills | 10400 County Rd. 48 | 352-324-3101 | 800-874-9053 | www.missioninnresort.com | 7003/4811; 74.2/68.5; 136/123

"Wow . . . who knew" that just 40 minutes northwest of Orlando there was this "totally unique Florida golf course with real hills" that provide an "amazing" and "unusual" "50-plus feet of elevation change"; part of a "great resort", the "magnificent", "old-fashioned" layout is routed "over rolling terrain" with a "beautiful" woodland setting, "lots of water" and "some memorable holes" to make swingers say they "would go out of the way to play it again."

Mission Inn, Las Colinas 🔒

| | 21 | 20 | 22 | 21 | $125 |

Howey-in-the-Hills | 10400 County Rd. 48 | 352-324-3101 | 800-874-9053 | www.missioninnresort.com | 6876/4696; 73.3/66.8; 130/106

"A great second mate" and "nice complement to the El Campeón course", this "mature", tree-lined "test of golf" is less hilly than its sibling but nevertheless offers some "elevation changes" on its "scenic", gently rolling layout; while a few feel "there are better choices for the money", the track's "great pace of play and views", "friendly staff" and Spanish-style clubhouse have most insisting "you'll like it."

Orange County National, Crooked Cat 🔒

| | 26 | 24 | 24 | 25 | $140 |

Winter Garden | 16301 Phil Ritson Way | 407-656-2626 | 888-727-3672 | www.ocngolf.com | 7277/5236; 75.4/70.3; 140/120

"All about the golf", this "real player's paradise" was "used for the PGA Tour's Qualifying School" thanks to its "fun", "immaculately kept" layout with "tough" links-style holes (read: "elevation changes", "fast greens" and "windy conditions") as well as its "huge practice area" and "excellent pro shop"; still, it's located "out in the boonies" in Winter Garden with only "spartan accommodations", so some suggest you should "stay in Orlando, but play here."

Orange County National, Panther Lake 🔒

| | 27 | 24 | 24 | 26 | $150 |

Winter Garden | 16301 Phil Ritson Way | 407-656-2626 | 888-727-3672 | www.ocngolf.com | 7370/5359; 75.7/71.5; 137/125

"Don't tell anyone" plead players who propose this "superb" "test" is just about "the best deal anywhere" for a day of "golf for golf's sake", including "some risk/reward choices for long hitters"; though located "not far from Disney", you'll find "no mouse-shaped bunkers" and "no condos to spoil the view", making this "a nice alternative" that also boasts "an unbelievable range" and "great service"; in short, it's a "truly great course" you "could play every day."

Orange Lake, Legends 🏌

21	20	21	23	$105

Kissimmee | 8505 W. Irlo Bronson Memorial Hwy. | 407-239-1050 | 800-887-6522 | www.orangelake.com | 7072/5188; 74.3/69.6; 132/120

Designed by Arnold Palmer, this appropriately named resort layout features "several long, scenic drives between the holes" on its open, linksy front and a smaller but tighter back that's routed through oaks and pines; although some say it "was better before all of the condos" appeared, others still consider it an "excellent experience" and note that its Kissimmee location is so "close to Disney, you can sneak out and play instead of visiting Mickey."

Remington 🏌

▽ 21	18	21	25	$75

Kissimmee | 2995 Remington Blvd. | 407-344-4004 | www.remington-gc.com | 7111/5178; 73.9/69.8; 134/118

Ten minutes after touching down at Orlando International Airport, you can let 'er rip at this traditional Florida find where the "unique 'all you can play, eat and practice' special" makes it "a great value during the winter season"; flat and "playable" for all levels, the Kissimmee course comes with a few distinctive touches like its aqua driving range, although most say they return because the course is a "well-maintained" value.

NEW Reunion Resort, Independence ⌐

▽ 26	27	28	24	$155

Orlando | 7599 Gathering Dr. | 407-396-3195 | www.reunionresort.com | 7154/5395; 74.7/70.6; 140/119

A "fantastic design from Tom Watson", this links-style "Florida anomaly" in Orlando may have "no water" but "there must be 300 traps" plus "vast waste areas" where "you can still find your ball (and maybe have a shot to the green)"; between the mounded fairways and undulating dance floors, hackers harrumph that this "impeccably maintained" resort course (an "LPGA Tour stop") is "almost too tough", but they have no problems with the "great clubhouse and fantastic staff."

NEW Reunion Resort, Legacy 🏌⌐

▽ 26	24	26	21	$155

Orlando | 7599 Gathering Dr. | 407-396-3195 | www.reunionresort.com | 6916/4802; 73.4/67; 137/113

Co-host for the LPGA Tour's Ginn Open, "this challenging Arnie classic is a beauty" and "unusual for this part of Florida" – "you would think it's Augusta National with all of the pretty flowers" and "elevation changes"; though ongoing work at the resort community can make it seem like "a massive construction site", the layout's "wide, forgiving fairways", "beautiful landscaping" and "five-star treatment" means that, though not quite "Disney World, it sure seems like it."

Ritz-Carlton Orlando, Grande Lakes 🏌

23	26	27	19	$215

Orlando | 4048 Central Florida Pkwy. | 407-393-4900 | www.grandelakes.com | 7122/5223; 73.9/69.8; 139/115

"It's like being on a nature preserve" at this "beautiful Greg Norman course" "that even Tiger liked" – you can "see his letter in the

	COURSE	FACIL.	SERVICE	VALUE	COST

clubhouse" – for its "fantastic fairways and greens" that are routed through ponds, wetlands and oak trees; just as the "mandatory fore-caddies are a real treat", providing "a great perspective" and "a very pleasurable day", the Ritz-Carlton's "top-notch service and amenities" ensure "you get what you pay for – and you pay a lot."

Southern Dunes 🏌

| | 23 | 17 | 18 | 24 | $115 |

Haines City | 2888 Southern Dunes Blvd. | 863-421-4653 | 800-632-6400 | www.southerndunes.com | 7227/4987; 75.7/68.5; 138/118

As the name suggests, "sand is the name of the game" ("bring a sand wedge or two" or "a shovel and pail") on this "jewel" of a design that's also known for its "huge greens, wide fairways" and abundant bunkers; though it has so "many houses" they feel like they're "on top of you", this layout is "worth the drive" 45 minutes south from Orlando to play a course that "won't empty your wallet."

Walt Disney World, Eagle Pines 🏌

| | 24 | 24 | 25 | 21 | $149 |

Lake Buena Vista | 3451 Golf View Dr. | 407-939-4653 | www.disneyworldgolf.com | 6772/4838; 72.5/68; 135/111

"Walt would be proud" of this Pete Dye design in Lake Buena Vista that's "tougher than it looks", dishing out a "challenge" with its "pretty thick rough" and "prevalent sand and water"; yes, it's part of Disney (there are "Mickey Mouse golf carts, complete with red shorts and ears"), but the "phenomenal scenery" and a "considerate" staff that "couldn't be better" – "friendly, chatty, fun, helpful" – make this a "great vacation getaway."

Walt Disney World, Lake Buena Vista 🏌

| | 22 | 24 | 25 | 20 | $119 |

Lake Buena Vista | 2200 Club Lake Dr. | 407-939-4653 | www.disneyworldgolf.com | 6749/5194; 73/69.9; 133/122

"While the kids are in the parks", get "away from the crowds" and play this "great escape" in Lake Buena Vista, a "beautifully maintained" track that's "challenging" but perhaps "better for the casual golfer" (i.e. it's "fun to play" and "easy on the nerves"); a "good practice area" and the "extremely helpful", "renowned Disney service" factor in to the consensus: there's "never a bad round" here.

Walt Disney World, Magnolia 🏌

| | 23 | 23 | 23 | 19 | $155 |

Lake Buena Vista | 1950 Magnolia Palm Dr. | 407-939-4653 | www.disneyworldgolf.com | 7516/5232; 76.4/70.5; 140/123

"Disney did a nice job" with this "older" yet "beautiful" option that's "set up for all types of golfers" even though it has "lots of length", "water and sand"; a "longtime venue on the PGA Tour", it offers a "well-maintained" layout and "first-rate" staff and facilities, and while the experience is "a little pricey", the "Mickey Mouse–shaped bunker" at the par-3 6th may alone be worth the cost of admission.

Walt Disney World, Osprey Ridge 🏌

| | 26 | 24 | 24 | 20 | $165 |

Lake Buena Vista | 3451 Golf View Dr. | 407-939-4653 | www.disneyworldgolf.com | 7101/5402; 74.4/71.3; 131/127

"Tom Fazio presents myriad challenges" on what many consider "the Mouse's best", a "fantastic" layout that "requires precise shots" given its "raised, sloping greens, elevated tees, rolling fairways" and "rough

	COURSE	FACIL.	SERVICE	VALUE	COST

[that's] full of pine needles"; kids at heart claim "Disney's Imagineers earned their pay", especially when you take into account all of the "unbelievable scenery" and "excellent" service; P.S. "bring a full wallet."

Walt Disney World, Palm 🏌️

| | 22 | 24 | 24 | 19 | $139 |

Lake Buena Vista | 1950 Magnolia Palm Dr. | 407-939-4653 | www.disneyworldgolf.com | 6957/5311; 73.9/70.4; 138/124

"Mickey Mouse–shaped tee markers" are the tip-offs to the "fun" in store at Joe Lee's "long and narrow" PGA Tour course (where Tiger Woods, Jack Nicklaus and Vijay Singh have all walked and won); kept "in good shape" with "interesting, pretty holes on the back nine", this "challenging" choice comes with "typical Disney service" and somewhat "expensive" fees.

Palm Beach

Boca Raton Resort, Resort Course 🏌️ ⛳

| | 21 | 25 | 24 | 17 | $182 |

Boca Raton | 501 E. Camino Real | 561-447-3000 | 800-327-0101 | www.bocaresort.com | 6253/4577; 69.3/65.5; 128/112

"What a pleasant way to spend four hours" fawn fans of this "fancy", "well-groomed Eden" "in the heart" of Boca Raton's "mink-and-manicure district"; originally opened in 1926 and redesigned by Gene Bates in 1997, this "world-class retirement course" is "quite tight" and "a little short" – "leave your woods at home" – but can be "challenging from the back tees"; "for the $$$", however, this stay-to-play option "doesn't measure up to everything else" at the "wonderfully snobby" resort.

Breakers, The, Ocean 🏌️ ⛳

| | 19 | 23 | 24 | 17 | $195 |

Palm Beach | 2 S. County Rd. | 561-659-8407 | www.thebreakers.com | 6167/5254; 68.1/69; 127/123

"Wedged into a few of the world's most expensive acres", this "short", "tight", "old-school" course offers "holes next to the Atlantic Ocean" plus "lots of history": it's purportedly the oldest 18-holer in Florida, although it was redesigned by Brian Silva in 2000; "excellent for the casual golfer", this "beautifully manicured" Palm Beach layout is "not too difficult" – "you feel good playing here" – and "there's never a wait" once "they shuttle you" from the "great hotel."

Breakers, The, Rees Jones ⛳

| | 24 | 25 | 24 | 20 | $175 |

Palm Beach | 1550 Flagler Pkwy. | 561-653-6320 | www.thebreakers.com | 7104/5164; 74.9/70.7; 140/125

"One of the best tracks in Palm Beach County", this "challenging but fair" Rees Jones layout is "much more difficult than the Ocean course" with "lots of water", sprawling bunkers and "amazing greens and tee boxes"; as it plays through a residential community 10 miles west of The Breakers, some snipe there are "more houses near the fairways than trees", but most feel it constitutes "lovely", "manicured golf" with "excellent facilities and service."

Links at Madison Green, The 🏌️

| | 19 | 16 | 17 | 21 | $75 |

Royal Palm Beach | 2001 Crestwood Blvd. | 561-784-5225 | www.madisongreengolf.com | 7002/4800; 73.6/67.6; 144/114

Pack your atlas to find this "fun" track "hidden" 20 minutes west of Palm Beach, as "it's a demanding shot-maker's course" with small, "icy-fast greens", a variety of pot, beach and waste bunkers, tight fair-

	COURSE	FACIL.	SERVICE	VALUE	COST

ways and "lots of water to get in the way"; while one swinger scoffs that it's "still a bit young", the remainder rally behind the "imaginative layout" and its "nice staff", saying that overall it's a "wonderful value."

NEW North Palm Beach Country Club, Jack Nicklaus Signature

| – | – | – | – | $108 |

North Palm Beach | 951 US Hwy. 1 S. | 561-691-3420 | www.village-npb.org | 7071/5203; 74.8/70.7; 140/128

Longtime local resident Jack Nicklaus has taken this 1920s-era public layout and transformed it into a modern masterpiece – all for the fee of just one dollar, the Golden Bear's way of giving back to his adopted hometown; reopened in November 2006, the North Palm Beach muni features two holes along the Intracoastal Waterway, an additional 800 yards in length and an expanded practice and teaching facility, making it one of Florida's value experiences.

PGA National, Champion

| 25 | 24 | 21 | 18 | $318 |

West Palm Beach | 1000 Ave. of the Champions | 561-627-1800 | 800-633-9150 | www.pga-resorts.com | 7048/5145; 75.3/72.3; 147/136

Set to host the PGA Tour's 2007 Honda Classic, this "dynamite" Jack Nicklaus redesign is the "best of the bunch" at the "wonderful" home of the PGA of America, a "great" West Palm Beach resort that's "like camp for adults"; the "tough track" offers a "true test" with "water, water everywhere", especially on the "nightmare Bear Trap" (holes 15–17), so "take lots of balls" – and "lots of cash", as it will also "test the limits of your credit card."

PGA National, General

| 21 | 23 | 21 | 20 | $200 |

West Palm Beach | 1000 Ave. of the Champions | 561-627-1800 | 800-633-9150 | www.pga-resorts.com | 6768/5327; 73.1/71.3; 134/123

It's "terrific golfing all the way around" on this "challenging but fair" (and "fun") Arnold Palmer design that can be "hard for beginners with water on almost every" one of its links-style holes – so be sure to "look out for gators" as you play; kept in "great shape" and accompanied by "comfortable facilities" and resort accommodations, this "tough track" has "all of the pluses of the Champion course but with a slightly lower price tag."

PGA National, Haig

| 21 | 22 | 22 | 19 | $200 |

West Palm Beach | 1000 Ave. of the Champions | 561-627-1800 | 800-633-9150 | www.pga-resorts.com | 6806/5645; 73.5/73.1; 139/129

"The best choice at PGA National for the average player", this "fun" Tom Fazio design – a tribute to the legendary Walter Hagen – features plenty of bunkers, "lots of challenge" and perhaps "too much water" throughout; though "no big deal" to some and "not as nice as the Champion" to others, it's nevertheless an "ok" choice "for a warm-up or change of scenery" – and is "a better value" to boot.

PGA National, Squire

| 20 | 23 | 22 | 19 | $200 |

West Palm Beach | 1000 Ave. of the Champions | 561-627-1800 | 800-633-9150 | www.pga-resorts.com | 6465/4975; 72.5/70.2; 139/131

"Another wonderful PGA course", this "pretty" Tom Fazio design is "user-friendly but not easy", a "short, tight" track made "challenging" by "lots of water" and "houses too close to the fairways" – "you don't have to be a hacker to hit roofs"; laid out in homage to Hall-of-Famer Gene Sarazen, the "fun course" comes with "PGA National's first-rate facilities", making this "a great place to take a vacation."

Polo Trace 🚶⏲

| 23 | 19 | 19 | 16 | $159 |

Delray Beach | 13479 Polo Trace Dr. | 561-495-5300 | 866-465-3765 | www.polotracegolf.com | 7035/5099; 74.8/71.6; 139/125

"Worth the drive" 25 minutes south from Palm Beach, this "marvelous" Delray Beach design allows "daily players to enjoy the private-club sensation" while being a links-style "paradise for long drivers" with its many carries over water; while critics claim it's "pricey" and "too impressed with itself", the majority point to the "well-manicured" conditions, "fine practice facilities" and "very nice clubhouse" as reasons this is "a course you could enjoy playing every day."

Panhandle

Camp Creek 🔑

| – | – | – | – | $175 |

Panama City Beach | 684 Fazio Dr. | 850-231-7600 | www.campcreekflorida.com | 7159/5150; 75.1/70.4; 145/121

You can hardly call it roughing it at this Panama City Beach camp, where designer Tom Fazio has crafted a back-to-nature layout amid a pristine (and virtually treeless) landscape of lakes, wetlands, dunes and vast sandy waste areas dotted with stubby palmettos and native grasses; to experience this little slice of serenity, however, you'll need to be either a member or a guest of the nearby WaterColor Inn.

Kelly Plantation 🚶

| 23 | 21 | 20 | 18 | $123 |

Destin | 307 Kelly Plantation Dr. | 850-650-7600 | 800-811-6757 | www.kellyplantation.com | 7099/5170; 74.2/70.9; 144/114

"Everything you would want from a Freddie Couples course", this "elegant" layout is a "very fair test of golf" that's nevertheless "not a place to play if your game is sick", as it features bold bunkering and encroaching woods and wetlands; although the "nice" track touts a prime setting on the Choctawhatchee Bay in Destin, a couple of swingers conclude the "beautiful" option is "too expensive for the area."

Moors, The

| ▽ 24 | 22 | 21 | 23 | $49 |

Milton | 3220 Avalon Blvd. | 850-995-4653 | www.moors.com | 6830/5259; 73/70.2; 130/122

"If you like Scottish layouts, you may like this" links-style design from John B. LaFoy that serves up mounds, pot bunkers and native grasses plus a clubhouse and holes that pay homage to golf's ancient tracks; situated in a convenient location just 30 minutes north of Pensacola, the resort course also boasts British Open-themed lodge accommodations; N.B. Lee Trevino, Raymond Floyd and Gil Morgan all won Senior tournaments here.

Regatta Bay 🚶

| 23 | 23 | 21 | 19 | $124 |

Destin | 465 Regatta Bay Blvd. | 850-337-8080 | 800-648-0123 | www.regattabay.com | 6864/5092; 73.8/70.6; 149/118

It's "a pleasure to play" this "beautifully maintained" wild ride that's awash with forced carries over wetlands and water as well as plenty of free-form bunkers – especially at the option-laden par-5 18th; critics complain that's there's "a lot of repetition throughout the course", but at least it boasts a handsome location near Lake Regatta and three of the Panhandle's state parks (with "no extra charge for gnats"); in short: it's a "fun" experience at a "good value."

Sandestin, Baytowne

▽ 21 | 21 | 23 | 18 | $119

Destin | 9300 Emerald Coast Pkwy. W. | 850-267-8155 | www.sandestin.com | 6950/4770; 73.2/67.7; 138/120

Remodeled by original architect Tom Jackson in the summer of 2005, this mature resort course nestled near Choctawhatchee Bay in Destin "has more character than ever before"; there's still lots of water – though little of it is in play – and "surprising elevation changes for northwest Florida" (most memorably on the downhill par-3 14th), plus now it offers a fifth set of tees for kids, who also get their own yardage book to study as they negotiate the 3,002 yards.

Sandestin, Burnt Pine ⚬⊶ ⊙

23 | 21 | 21 | 18 | $145

Destin | 9300 Emerald Coast Pkwy. W. | 850-267-6500 | www.sandestin.com | 7001/5153; 74.7/71.2; 144/122

Sibling rivalry runs rampant on the Emerald Coast as those who have played this "great test of golf" designed by Rees Jones say it's "a lot of course" and "more challenging than its sister, Raven" (created by Rees' brother Robert Trent Jones Jr.), thanks in part to its "huge greens" and copious amounts of sand; while "the three holes on the bay" can be "brutal in the wind", at least the trio is "beautifully maintained" and provides "awesome views."

Sandestin, Raven

25 | 19 | 19 | 20 | $145

Destin | 9300 Emerald Coast Pkwy. W. | 850-267-8155 | www.sandestin.com | 6931/5106; 73.8/70.6; 137/126

"Poe would be proud" of "Sandestin's best", this "phenomenal resort course" that's "the host of a PGA Champions Tour event" (the Boeing Championship); "a nice layout" designed by Robert Trent Jones Jr., it features large, undulating greens, a smattering of lakes and wetlands and an assortment of bunker shapes, and while some turn up their beaks at "average maintenance", most sing a sweet song about this layout's "value for the money."

SouthWood 🏌

– | – | – | – | $70

Tallahassee | 3750 Grove Park Dr. | 850-942-4653 | www.southwoodflorida.com | 7172/4521; 74.3/66.2; 135/103

At Florida State University's home facility, co-designer "Fred Couples provides fairly large fairways and greens", but this Tallahassee track also features "lots of elevation changes [that force] some challenging shots"; the moss-drenched oaks and hardwoods are reminiscent of a Georgia layout, and though the "nice" course can be a test from the tips, children will find it a friendly option from the 2,968-yard Wee tees.

NEW Windswept Dunes 🏌

– | – | – | – | $65

Freeport | 11 Club House Dr. | 850-835-1847 | www.windsweptdunes.com | 7600/5199; 76.8/64.8; 143/105

"Play from the tips if you feel manly", as this somewhat under-the-radar site (it's just 12 miles from the Gulf of Mexico) is the longest track in Florida, with sprawling white sand dunes and waste bunkers that "will make you hit punishing second shots all day long" if you succumb to "waywardness"; still, there are "lots of tees to choose from" on this

FLORIDA

COURSE
FACIL.
SERVICE
VALUE
COST

"fair" and "well-designed" layout, and the staff's "Southern hospitality" easily soothes the occasional bruised ego.

Port St. Lucie

PGA Golf Club, Dye
25 | 23 | 23 | 24 | $99

Port St. Lucie | 1916 Perfect Dr. | 772-467-1300 | 800-800-4653 | www.pgavillage.com | 7150/5015; 74.7/68.4; 139/117

"Not for the faint of heart", this "brutally challenging" but "simply awesome" Pete Dye layout is loaded with a range of the architect's "classic" and "subtle strategies"; the tricky track will "test your mettle" on "undulating greens" that are surrounded by unique "coquina-shell areas", so "don't expect to have an easy time" at this "golf heaven" that's part of a "great PGA center" and resort complex in Port St. Lucie, but do anticipate that you will "love the course, the staff and the facilities"; N.B. play it now, as it's scheduled to undergo renovations in summer 2007.

PGA Golf Club, Ryder
23 | 23 | 23 | 24 | $99

Port St. Lucie | 1916 Perfect Dr. | 772-467-1300 | 800-800-4653 | www.pgavillage.com | 7026/4993; 74/68.8; 132/114

Formerly called the North course, this "very good" Tom Fazio design may be "even better" now that it's reopened after extensive landscaping and renovations to its greens and bunkers; routed over rolling, "variable terrain" with "wide", pine tree–lined fairways and "plenty of challenge", this "solid value" also features "friendly service" and "wonderful facilities" that have "both amateurs and professionals" wondering "what more could you ask for?"; N.B. they plan to expand the clubhouse in summer 2007.

PGA Golf Club, Wanamaker
25 | 23 | 24 | 24 | $99

Port St. Lucie | 1916 Perfect Dr. | 772-467-1300 | 800-800-4653 | www.pgavillage.com | 7076/4933; 74.7/69.4; 140/122

Renamed after "recent renovations, which involved replacing all of the greens" and reconstructing a number of the bunkers, this Tom Fazio design (formerly called the South course) remains a "solid" and "challenging" "gem" that's laced with palms, palmettos, wetlands and enormous traps that are sure to "kick your ass if you're not careful"; boasting all of the amenities of the "great PGA Village facility", including a 35-acre Learning Center, the layout proves "a wonderful value considering the quality."

Sarasota

Legacy at Lakewood Ranch ♠
22 | 21 | 22 | 19 | $119

Bradenton | 8255 Legacy Blvd. | 941-907-7920 | www.legacygolfclub.com | 7067/4886; 73.8/68.8; 140/115

"The first hole sets the tone for the rest of the course", so be forewarned that the rugged 454-yard par 4 is just one of many "hard but fun" holes that "will grind you down" on this Arnold Palmer design situated amid pines, oaks and grasslands 20 minutes north of Sarasota; the "well-maintained" layout features "lots of water" and just as much sand, so be sure to "take extra golf balls" – and extra money, as the course can be "pricey" in season.

	COURSE	FACIL.	SERVICE	VALUE	COST

NEW Ritz-Carlton Members Club 🎗 ⛳ 🕐

| 24 | 23 | 28 | 18 | $235 |

Bradenton | 7295 Lorraine Rd. | 941-309-2000 | www.ritzcarlton.com | 7414/5175; 75.6/68.3; 133/108

"True to style at a Ritz-Carlton", "everything is tops" at this "classy facility" that offers a "straightforward" Tom Fazio design that's kept in "country-club condition" and is "a pleasure to walk" given that there are "excellent caddies" "to carry the bag"; "only resort guests and members have the privilege of playing" and you'll do a "double-take" at the fees, so "add this to your once-in-a-lifetime list" and book a room, as the experience comes complete with "fantastic" service.

Riverwood 🏌

| - | - | - | - | $100 |

Port Charlotte | 4100 Riverwood Dr. | 941-764-6661 | www.riverwoodgc.com | 7004/4695; 74.8/68; 144/114

"Depending on the wind, it can bite you hard or serve up some birdies" vouch veterans who have played this "beautiful" and "beautifully maintained" Port Charlotte course that rambles through pines on the front and twists through lakes and marshes on the back; best of all, budget-conscious types say it's got "bang for the buck."

University Park Golf Course 🏌 ⛳ 🕐

| 25 | 21 | 20 | 24 | $125 |

University Park | 7671 The Park Blvd. | 941-359-9999 | 800-394-6325 | www.universitypark-fl.com
Course 10/Course 19 | 7247/4960; 74.8/68.3; 135/116
Course 19/Course 1 | 7152/4850; 74.8/67.5; 130/113
Course 1/Course 10 | 7001/4800; 74/68.4; 133/114

Just north of Sarasota there are "eagles flying, cranes squawking and gators snorting" at this "phenomenal" course where "golfers of all levels and handicaps" will find three "very nice nines"; fans fete the "beautiful design", especially the par-3 5th ("one of the most picturesque holes in golf"), and though some grumble about the "course ranger who's a poster child for micro-management", most consider it a "tremendous value in the off season."

Venetian Golf & River Club

| ▽ 21 | 16 | 21 | 21 | $90 |

North Venice | 103 Pesaro Dr. | 941-483-4811 | www.wcigolf.com | 6931/5038; 72.9/69.1; 127/115

On this Chip Powell design situated in a "nicely developing subdivision" in North Venice, you can expect "lots of traps" in the style of old masters Alister MacKenzie and A.W. Tillinghast, as well as "very challenging greens" that pay homage to Donald Ross and C.B. MacDonald; while some grumble that the "facilities are lacking" because the clubhouse "has yet to be completed", most tout it as a "fun course for all levels" that's "always in great shape."

Tampa

Bloomingdale 🏌

| ▽ 21 | 16 | 16 | 23 | $79 |

Valrico | 4113 Great Golfers Pl. | 813-685-4105 | www.bloomingdalegolf.com | 7100/5397; 74.4/72.1; 131/132

Situated "close to Tampa", this "good layout" "tests all aspects of your game" with a plethora of doglegs, difficult par 5s, moss-draped oaks and 14 lakes; set amid wooded marshland, the design accommodates the natural habitat (half of its 200-plus acres are a wildlife preserve), so expect the occasional four-footed spectator; shoppers say "the course is not always in the best of shape" but they remain sold on what they call a bit of "local fun."

Saddlebrook, Saddlebrook Course 🏨 | 20 | 22 | 22 | 19 | $145 |

Wesley Chapel | 5700 Saddlebrook Way | 813-907-4566 | 800-729-8383 | www.saddlebrookresort.com | 6564/4941; 72/70.6; 127/126

Ideal for those who bring "accuracy" to their game, this tree-lined Arnold Palmer design in a "magnificent resort" setting just 30 minutes north of Tampa is "a class act from start to finish"; although a few foozlers feel "there are better in the area" ("I wouldn't rush back to play it"), most appreciate the layout's "awesome" facilities and a "family" setup where there are "lots of activities for everyone."

TPC Tampa Bay | 24 | 22 | 23 | 21 | $159 |

Lutz | 5300 W. Lutz Lake Fern Rd. | 813-949-0090 | 866-752-9872 | www.tpc.com | 6898/4990; 73.6/69.7; 135/119

"A monster from even the whites", this "not-well-publicized" but "surprisingly wonderful" home of the Champions Tour's Outback Steakhouse Pro-Am is "worthy of the TPC name" and a "must-play" if "you have the means"; while it's in "excellent condition", a "ridiculous" amount of sand will "challenge your game" and crowds can lead to "six-hour rounds"; nevertheless, "the best draft beer in town" softens the sting of what some call the "toughest in the Tampa area."

Westin Innisbrook, Copperhead 🏨 ⛳ | 26 | 24 | 24 | 20 | $240 |

Palm Harbor | 36750 US Hwy. 19 N. | 727-942-2000 | 800-456-2000 | 7340/5605; 75.6/71.8; 134/130

"Not for the short hitter", this "superb" Palm Harbor host of the PGA Tour's PODS Championship will "test your shot-making" thanks to "thick rough", unusually hilly conditions and "water, water and more water"; in short, stay focused – the "beautiful" resort setting features lots of "wildlife that competes for your attention" – and "bring your A-game or get bitten"; given its "helpful staff", the only drawback here seems to be that the "on-course lodgings are outdated."

Westin Innisbrook, Island 🏨 | 23 | 24 | 24 | 21 | $210 |

Palm Harbor | 36750 US Hwy. 19 N. | 727-942-2000 | 800-456-2000 | 7063/5578; 74.1/73; 132/129

"Accuracy is at a premium" on this "underrated" second layout that some consider to be "almost as good" as its Westin Innisbrook partner (and others, "more challenging"); the Palm Harbor venue has "great terrain" with "lots of water", "gators and birds", so although one cynic says you should "spend the extra and play Copperhead", others call it a "very enjoyable course"; N.B. Phil Mickelson won the 1990 NCAA Championship here.

Z World Woods, Pine Barrens | 28 | 21 | 22 | 27 | $130 |

Brooksville | 17590 Ponce de Leon Blvd. | 352-796-5500 | www.worldwoods.com | 6902/5301; 73.7/70.9; 136/124

The "Tom Fazio genius" is readily apparent at this "hidden masterpiece", a "magnificent" "must-play" that's perfect for "purists" who like their course with "more sand than the Kalahari" and don't mind "the hike north" to the "middle of nowhere" near Brooksville; the re-

	COURSE	FACIL.	SERVICE	VALUE	COST

sort course makes up for its "disappointing clubhouse" with "phenomenal practice facilities" that have fans concluding this may be one of "the best for the money" around.

World Woods, Rolling Oaks

| 26 | 21 | 22 | 27 | $120 |

Brooksville | 17590 Ponce de Leon Blvd. | 352-796-5500 | www.worldwoods.com | 6985/5245; 73.9/70.1; 133/123

"You won't be disappointed" declare those golfers who agree that "dollar for dollar, this is the best overall course in Florida", an "invigorating" Tom Fazio design that's made for those who have appetites for "hills and valleys"; though hungry hackers hint "it needs a good hotel and restaurant", most maintain it's a "great" alternative to its "more glamorous" sister; P.S. "play this and Pine Barrens on the same day – what a deal!"

Georgia

TOP COURSES IN STATE

28	Reynolds, Great Waters	*Lake Oconee*
	Sea Island, Seaside	*Lowcountry*
	Reynolds, Oconee	*Lake Oconee*
27	Cuscowilla	*Lake Oconee*
	Reynolds, National	*Lake Oconee*

Atlanta

Barnsley Gardens, General

| 25 | 24 | 24 | 19 | $115 |

Adairsville | 597 Barnsley Gardens Rd. | 770-773-7480 | 877-773-2447 | www.barnsleyresort.com | 7180/5450; 74.5/71.7; 141/127

"Come for the golf and stay for the ambiance" – complete with "stunning views of the Georgia mountains" – at this "rural" "treat" situated on the grounds of an 1800s estate an hour north of Atlanta; designer Jim Fazio's "challenging", "well-maintained" layout "starts easy and gets progressively harder", and though fees are a "little high", the resort's cottages, beer garden and "friendly staff" make a trip here "worth it."

Bear's Best Atlanta 🏌 🏑

| 25 | 24 | 26 | 19 | $105 |

Suwanee | 5342 Aldeburgh Dr. | 678-714-2582 | 866-511-2378 | www.bearsbest.com | 7037/5076; 72.5/70; 140/127

Golden Bear–hunters head to this "interesting" collection of 18 replica holes that offers the best of "Jack's great designs all in one place"; while some say it's a "worthwhile experience" that's enhanced by a "friendly staff" and a "fantastic forecaddie system" (required until 1 PM), purists maintain it's "hard to get any rhythm since each hole is unique"; N.B. Nicklaus nuts will appreciate the photo- and memorabilia-filled clubhouse grill.

Brasstown Valley 🏑

| ▽ 23 | 19 | 21 | 24 | $90 |

Young Harris | 6321 US Hwy. 76 | 706-379-4613 | www.brasstownvalley.com | 6957/5028; 73.2/69.2; 139/116

A new management team is shining up this "gem in the Georgia mountains" that's set on 500 rolling resort acres near Young Harris and is a "great value"; though whackers warn of "traps galore" and "difficult, undulating fairways" that "force you to learn about uphill and downhill lies", high-scorers can always seek solace in the "scenic" Blue Ridge vistas or by the warmth of the lodge's 72-ft.-high stone fireplace.

Château Élan, Château

| | 22 | 23 | 21 | 20 | $80 |

Braselton | 6060 Golf Club Dr. | 678-425-0900 | 800-233-9463 | www.chateauelan.com | 7030/5092; 73.5/70.8; 136/124

Set on a 3,500-acre inn and winery about 50 miles north of Atlanta, this creek- and lake-dotted layout is labeled "a little less challenging than its sister course, Woodlands"; a few fret it's "not up to par", but most maintain it's "a nice course to play" considering its "excellent conditions", "great greens" and "lots of unusual and fun holes"; and given the resort's eight on-site restaurants and spa, it's also easy to see why clubbers dub it a "great facility."

Château Élan, Woodlands

| | 23 | 20 | 21 | 20 | $80 |

Braselton | 6060 Golf Club Dr. | 678-425-0900 | 800-233-9463 | www.chateauelan.com | 6735/4850; 72.5/68.4; 131/121

This "excellent tree-lined" Denis Griffiths design is a "well-maintained" "shot-makers' course" boasting "difficult elevation changes" that may make it "more challenging" than its older sibling, Château; one wood-chucker warns it's "losing its appeal" with "the encroachment of houses", but given the resort has a "friendly staff" and "lots of activities for the whole family", most still consider it part of a "great get-away close to Atlanta."

Cherokee Run

| | 23 | 20 | 19 | 24 | $53 |

Conyers | 1595 Centennial Olympic Pkwy. NE | 770-785-7904 | www.cherokeerun.com | 7016/4948; 75.1/70.6; 143/124

"Bring your A-game" to this "hidden gem" that putters point to as one of the "best bangs for the buck near Atlanta" and well worth the 30-minute "schlep of a drive"; set on a rolling "scenic" site thick with Georgia pines and granite outcroppings, the "fun" but "demanding" Arnold Palmer Signature features a "dramatic design" – the "unusual zoysia fairways really keep the ball up" – sure to "test any ability."

Cobblestone

| | 22 | 15 | 17 | 19 | $69 |

Acworth | 4200 Nance Rd. NW | 770-917-5151 | www.cobblestonegolf.com | 6759/5400; 73.5/71.5; 139/129

"Don't tell anyone about this sleeper" gush golfers who insist this "challenging woodland" muni is "one of the better values in metro Atlanta"; a Ken Dye design, it offers "a few scenic water" features and "elevation changes" that include a "daunting downhill finishing hole"; but whereas the staff is "friendly and helpful", the course conditions are not as polished: "they need to improve the greens and fairways."

Crooked Creek ◷

| | 21 | 19 | 18 | 18 | $93 |

Alpharetta | 3430 Hwy. 9 N. | 770-475-2300 | www.crookedcreekgolf.com | 6929/4987; 73.4/70; 141/120

Open to the public on weekdays only (and with plans to turn fully private by mid-2007), this "fine" Mike Riley design is "worth the drive" north of Atlanta; sure, a round here is "a little pricey", but suburban swingers can expect "polite service" and a "very pretty", "well-maintained" layout that boasts newly installed bunkers and "linoleum"-fast greens; despite the hazards, the four "short par 3s may earn golfers a few birdies."

	COURSE	FACIL.	SERVICE	VALUE	COST

Frog at The Georgian ⚑

	24	22	21	23	$79

Villa Rica | 1900 Georgian Pkwy. | 770-459-4400 | www.golfthefrog.com | 7018/5814; 73.7/70.5; 140/127

"Gorgeous and impeccably kept", this "consistent, quality" Tom Fazio design is "definitely worth the drive west of Atlanta" for "a great experience" "no matter what your level" (especially given the "nice, true greens"); "the lack of houses" on the tree-lined layout is a plus, as are a "helpful, friendly" staff and "value" prices; P.S. be forewarned: "frogs aren't the only critters in the swampy areas."

Nicklaus at Birch River ⚑

	23	23	22	23	$85

Dahlonega | 639 Birch River Dr. | 706-867-7900 | www.nicklausgolfbirchriver.com | 6964/4999; 73.5/68.8; 140/124

An "A+" is the grade some putting professors give to this Jack Nicklaus design that's considered "worth the drive" to "the low mountains" an hour northeast of Atlanta; the Chestatee River is in play on 16 of the "well-kept" holes and "the par 5s on the back nine can get mean", making this "fantastic course" as "challenging" as it is "scenic"; nevertheless, it's "playable" and "a good value for a Nicklaus course."

St. Marlo

	18	18	16	15	$89

Duluth | 7755 St. Marlo Country Club Pkwy. | 770-495-7725 | www.stmarlo.com | 6823/4969; 73.7/70.2; 140/121

Nestled inside a gated community, this "nice track on the north side" of Atlanta "plays through very hilly", "scenic" terrain featuring stone walls, hardwoods and a decorative waterfall; nevertheless, it's dubbed an "average course" by serious swingers, who say it has "too much traffic on the fairways" and "too small a plot" for its size; as for "the rest of the package", it offers "ok facilities" and service that's "spotty but congenial."

Columbus

Callaway Gardens, Lake View ⚑

	22	23	21	23	$85

Pine Mountain | US Hwy. 27 S. | 706-663-2281 | 800-225-5292 | www.callawaygardens.com | 6031/5285; 68.6/71.1; 123/121

"A good experience for the mid- and high-handicapper", this short 1952 layout is a horticultural delight given its "beautiful" landscape abloom with azaleas, dogwoods and seasonal flowers; set on a 13,000-acre resort, garden and nature preserve near the Appalachian foothills, it's a "fun course" with nine water holes to potentially soak your score and kids' tees to keep your family's spirits undampened.

Callaway Gardens, Mountain View ⚑

	23	22	22	21	$100

Pine Mountain | US Hwy. 27 S. | 706-663-2281 | 800-225-5292 | www.callawaygardens.com | 7057/4883; 73.7/69.4; 139/120

"Definitely not for the older folk", this former host of the PGA Tour's Buick Challenge features a "difficult" design by Dick Wilson and Joe Lee that prompts mountaineers to moan about "the most fairway bunkers ever seen"; while reactions aren't unanimous ("great course" vs. "left me flat"), most find the tree-lined track with its water-guarded par-5 15th to be a "true test" of skills; N.B. the resort recently added a new lodge and will open a spa facility in March 2007.

Lake Oconee

Cuscowilla 🏌🏤🕐

COURSE	FACIL.	SERVICE	VALUE	COST
27	22	22	20	$150

Eatonton | 354 Cuscowilla Dr. | 706-484-0050 | 800-458-5351 |
www.cuscowilla.com | 6847/5348; 72.3/69.6; 130/123

Sure, this decade-old Eatonton course "caters to the serious golfer" –
the "greens are like waxed turtle shells" and swingers should "stay out
of the native grass" – but this "awesome Coore/Crenshaw design" is
"a blast to play" and "worth the $150"; plus, those who consider it
"one of the best in the country" for its "great risk/reward options" also
find it "easy on the eyes" ("love those red sand traps"); the only com-
plaint: "it's hidden inside a real estate development."

Harbor Club

COURSE	FACIL.	SERVICE	VALUE	COST
▽ 21	20	19	21	$105

Greensboro | 1 Club Dr. | 706-453-4414 | 800-505-4653 |
www.harborclub.com | 7048/5169; 73.7/70; 139/120

"One of the best courses on Lake Oconee" is now even better thanks to
recent renovations that enlarged the greens on the tree- and water-
lined layout; host of the 1996 PGA Tour Qualifying School, this
Weiskopf/Morrish design is "tough but fair", with holes that include a
par-3 tee shot over the lake and an 18th that's cut in half by a creek.

Reynolds Landing

COURSE	FACIL.	SERVICE	VALUE	COST
-	-	-	-	$125

Greensboro | 1071 Plantation Ln. | 706-453-4564 | 866-405-7400 |
www.reynoldslanding.com | 7051/5235; 75.1/72.6; 142/133

The first course on Lake Oconee, this 1985 Bob Cupp classic was ac-
quired by Reynolds in 2005; it's routed through woodlands with three
holes along the shoreline, and those who have "enjoyed the course" in
the past will appreciate attempts to bring the destination up to "the
rest of Reynolds' facilities": new grasses were installed and a new
clubhouse will open in June 2007.

☑ Reynolds Plantation, Great Waters 🏌🍸

COURSE	FACIL.	SERVICE	VALUE	COST
28	27	26	22	$210

Greensboro | 100 Linger Longer Rd. | 706-467-1135 | 800-800-5250 |
www.reynoldsplantation.com | 7048/5082; 73.8/69.2; 135/114

"You will love" this "magnificent" Nicklaus layout that's "one of the
most beautiful courses" swingers "have ever seen" given its "immaculate conditions" and "great views of Lake Oconee"; considered "the
best of the four" at Reynolds Plantation – and voted Georgia's top-
rated Course – this "tough" track (the "back nine holes are all with water") is "expensive but worth it" and "playable for all skill levels";
N.B. a members-only Jim Engh spread is expected to debut in 2007.

Reynolds Plantation, National 🏌🍸

COURSE	FACIL.	SERVICE	VALUE	COST
27	23	26	22	$165

Greensboro | 100 Linger Longer Rd. | 706-467-1142 | 800-800-5250 |
www.reynoldsplantation.com
Bluff/Cove | 7034/5296; 73.8/71.5; 137/127
Ridge/Bluff | 6955/5318; 73.4/71.4; 137/124
Ridge/Cove | 7025/5386; 73.6/71.6; 136/126

"Marshals with cold, almond-scented towels are an awesome" touch
as you "walk the contours of this hilly" Tom Fazio design which has
only two of its nines open at a time; this "well-kept" track has "fast,
true greens" and "will test your shot-making skills" with holes that "offer a variety of challenges and terrific scenery" in the form of lake

views, pines and dogwoods; it's affiliated with the nearby Ritz-Carlton Lodge, "so prices aren't low", but it nevertheless remains a "favorite."

Reynolds Plantation, Oconee 彳 ⌒ | 28 | 28 | 27 | 22 | $260

Greensboro | 100 Linger Longer Rd. | 706-467-1135 | 800-800-5250 | www.reynoldsplantation.com | 7393/5198; 75.5/70; 143/126

Even "prettier than in the pictures", this "impeccably maintained" Rees Jones design is a "long" "Southern classic" that "showcases Georgia pines" and will do the same for the PGA Cup in 2007; "challenging" but "manageable", it's "perfect for experts or resort golfers" ("have the Ritz's valet whisk you over") who call it a "must-play"; and with "nice facilities" and a "fantastic restaurant on-site", "everything about it is great – except for the prices."

Reynolds Plantation, Plantation 彳 ⌒ | 24 | 26. | 26 | 21 | $165

Greensboro | 100 Linger Longer Rd. | 706-467-1135 | 800-800-5250 | www.reynoldsplantation.com | 6698/5121; 71.7/68.9; 128/115

The "easiest of the Reynolds" layouts, this "hidden gem" "actually plays extremely well", especially after a greens redo left the "newly designed back nine better than the front"; the "beautifully maintained" track is "a great experience" that "will test you with tight fairways and well-guarded greens", although more selective sorts say "don't waste your time when you have so many [other] great courses to play" here.

Lowcountry

Hampton Club ⌂ | ▽ 21. | 20 | 20 | 21 | $90

St. Simons Island | 100 Tabbystone | 912-634-0255 | 800-342-0212 | www.hamptonclub.com | 6465/5233; 71.7/71.3; 137/121

"Does it get any prettier?" than at this "well-done design" whose "scenery alone is worth" "driving to the north end of St. Simons" Island – as is the chance "to avoid Sea Island's absurd prices"; set on an 18th-century plantation, it "makes you remember you're in the South" as you traverse tidal creeks, lakes and lagoons or marsh island-hop during a four-hole signature spread (Nos. 12–15); just be fore-warned: the "horse flies can be the size of, well, horses."

Sea Island, Plantation 彳 ⌒ | 25. | 28 | 29 | 22 | $200

St. Simons Island | 100 Retreat Ave. | 912-638-5118 | 800-732-4752 | www.seaisland.com | 7058/5048; 73.9/70.4; 135/122

"Southern charm is alive and well" at this "great course for the have-it-alls and a special treat for the rest of us" on St. Simons Island; "a golfer's dream experience", the 1998 Rees Jones redesign (incorporating the original 1927 Plantation nine) offers "peaceful, undulating" terrain, a "stunning lodge" and an "amazing driving range", although some vets vent it may be "more history than challenge"; meanwhile, "awesome service" helps to justify the "expensive" fees.

Sea Island, Retreat 彳 ⌒ | 23 | 27 | 27 | 22 | $200

St. Simons Island | 100 Retreat Ave. | 912-638-5118 | 800-732-4752 | www.seaisland.com | .7000/5100; 73.9/70; 135/119

"Is that Davis Love III on the course?" – it probably is, as the designer of this "perfectly acceptable" spread "lives and practices" on St. Simons Island; though "overshadowed" by its sisters, the "spartan" layout is "in good condition", offering "challenging greens" that are "elevated and

	COURSE	FACIL.	SERVICE	VALUE	COST

hard to hold" as well as a "great practice area" and "excellent service" – "a ranger found me on the back nine and offered me an iced tea."

☒ Sea Island, Seaside 🎏 ⚬⌐   28 | 28 | 27 | 22 | $250

St. Simons Island | 100 Retreat Ave. | 912-638-5118 | 800-732-4752 | www.seaisland.com | 7005/5048; 72.3/68.8; 137/120

"Maybe the best daily fee in Georgia", this linksy layout is "more British" than its sisters, a "top-notch" track that was "made even better" by Tom Fazio's 1999 redesign; the "beautiful" course "can be punishing when the wind blows", but the oceanside spread is otherwise "perfect" ("not a misplaced blade of grass"); and given its "great clubhouse", "amazing facilities" and "superb service", the "pricey" play is "worth it"; P.S. "for the full experience, stay at the Lodge."

Savannah

Club at Savannah Harbor   25 | 24 | 24 | 22 | $145

Savannah | 2 Resort Dr. | 912-201-2007 | www.theclubatsavannahharbor.net | 7288/5261; 75.1/70.8; 137/124

"Watch for gators in the canals" as you play this Champions Tour host, a "beautiful" marsh-dotted track tucked between the Savannah and Back rivers; the Bob Cupp/Sam Snead design is "narrow", but it's a "top course" where "you'll feel like a pro", especially if you indulge in one of the "GPS- and a/c-outfitted carts on a hot day"; P.S. try relaxing with "a sauna and shower afterwards" at the layout's luxe Greenbrier Spa.

Valdosta

NEW Kinderlou Forest   - | - | - | - | $75

Valdosta | 4005 Bear Lake Rd. | 229-219-2300 | www.kinderlouforest.com | 7781/5364; 76.6/71.8; 144/134

"Don't miss this course" proclaim those who've tried out this relatively new design from Davis Love III; located on a historic south Georgia farm near the Florida border, this "great challenge" plays a whopping 7,781 yards from the tips and offers dramatic elevation changes, a wide-open front nine and a pine forest on the back; N.B. look for it to host the Nationwide Tour's South Georgia Classic in 2007.

Hawaii

TOP COURSES IN STATE

- <u>29</u> Kapalua, Plantation | *Maui*
- <u>28</u> Challenge at Manele | *Lanai*
- <u>27</u> Mauna Kea, Mauna Kea Course | *Big Island*
  Kauai Lagoons, Kiele | *Kauai*
  Experience at Koele | *Lanai*

Big Island

☒ Hualalai ⚬⌐   26 | 29 | 29 | 20 | $195

Kaupulehu-Kona | 100 Kaupulehu Dr. | 808-325-8480 | www.hualalairesort.com | 7117/5374; 73.7/65.8; 139/119

"Beautiful ocean views", "perfect weather" and what some call the "best-manicured course in all the Hawaiian islands" – "can it get any

	COURSE	FACIL.	SERVICE	VALUE	COST

better?" wonder fans of this "exquisite" track on the Big Island that boasts "one of the most picturesque holes in the world", the signature 17th; "sneaky, tough" winds and "tricky lava hazards" help make it "tons of fun", and while it's "pricey", you "can't beat the service" or "great lessons", and the "limited access" ("you have to stay at the hotel or know someone") means "it's almost never crowded."

Kona Country Club, Mountain 🏌

		-	-	-	-	$145

Kailua-Kona | 78-7000 Alii Dr. | 808-322-2595 | www.konagolf.com | 6634/5038; 72.9/65; 135/119

Situated on ground that was once a destination for Hawaiian royalty, the Ocean's shorter and younger sibling is a feast for the eyes thanks to a mountain setting that features black lava rock, three lakes and dramatic elevation changes, especially on the par-3 14th offering panoramic views of the Kona coastline; the Big Island resort's Vista Restaurant, meanwhile, sports sunset sightlines of Keauhou Bay, the birthplace of King Kamehameha III.

Kona Country Club, Ocean 🏌

	21	16	18	20	$160

Kailua-Kona | 78-7000 Alii Dr. | 808-322-2595 | www.konagolf.com | 6748/5436; 72.8/67.2; 129/118

For those who claim the "only way to play golf is in Hawaii", this "beautiful" Big Island spread may just fit the bill with its "terrific" mountain views and "no-frills" oceanside layout; but "bring your best game", because this course has plenty of sand bunkers and lava-rock formations plus a signature 13th complicated by a geyserlike blow hole; P.S. "get discounts through the concierge or else you'll pay too much!"

Mauna Kea, Hapuna 🏌

	24	22	24	19	$145

Kamuela | 62-100 Kauna'oa Dr. | 808-880-3000 | www.maunakearesort.com | 6875/6029; 73.3/64.3; 136/114

"Watch out for the lava-strewn rough" on this "hilly" Arnold Palmer/Ed Seay design that's "not your typical island course" given a layout that winds inland to 700 feet above sea level ("fantastic" ocean views); it's "less pleasant [now] due to adjacent housing construction", but it remains "a great round of golf" made "interesting" with "billy-goat lies, challenging greens" and "wind blowing down the mountain"; P.S. you get the "best value when staying at the hotel."

Mauna Kea, Mauna Kea Course 🏌

	27	22	23	20	$210

Kamuela | 62-100 Mauna Kea Beach Dr. | 808-882-5400 | www.maunakearesort.com | 7124/6365; 75.3/66.5; 142/118

A "must-play on the Big Island", this "dramatic" RTJ Sr. design is an "oldie but goodie" that proves "challenging, though not frustratingly so"; in fact, its setting – amid lava beds, "vegetation and sweeping views" – is so "beautiful", "you don't even mind losing a golf ball in the ocean" on the "picture-perfect 3rd" featuring a shot over surging inlet waters; a few moan that the "facilities are not up to par with the course", but most simply "savor the experience."

Mauna Lani, North

	25	25	25	20	$205

Kohala | 68-1310 Mauna Lani Dr. | 808-885-6655 | www.maunalani.com | 6913/5383; 74/70.6; 135/120

Though the lava rough at this "beautiful" Big Island "must-play" "is unique", it certainly "is not your friend", so "bring plenty" of "pre-

HAWAII

COURSE
FACIL.
SERVICE
VALUE
COST

scuffed balls" to this rolling track "carved out of" dormant volcano fields; though "a shade harder" than its South sibling, this still "playable" and "beautiful resort course" offers "varied hole designs", "panoramic views" and "excellent facilities", all of which more than compensate for the "condos lining the fairways."

Mauna Lani, South   26 | 24 | 25 | 19 | $205

Kohala | 68-1310 Mauna Lani Dr. | 808-885-6655 | www.maunalani.com | 6938/5128; 72.8/69.6; 133/117

"Beautiful ribbons of green on stark black lava" plus "breathtaking ocean holes" and "Mauna Kea views" make this Big Island resort track "a gem"; though "challenging" (especially "when the wind blows"), the course remains "satisfying" for all players, offering "unique hazards" – the "famous" par-3 15th features a carry over crashing surf – and an "attentive staff"; sure, it's "expensive", but hotel guests can take advantage of "special value packages."

Waikoloa Beach Resort, Beach   23 | 21 | 22 | 19 | $195

Waikoloa | 1020 Keana Pl. | 808-886-6060 | www.waikoloabeachresort.com | 6566/5094; 71.6/64.8; 134/115

"Hitting a golf ball down a bright-green fairway to a lava-rock coast just can't be beat", so "don't pass up" the chance to play this "beautiful" Big Island track; the RTJ Jr. effort is a "typical resort" layout that's "easy to play" and offers "a few great holes" – including a shoreline par-5 12th – but some feel it's "misleading to call this the Beach course" since "one hole leads you to the ocean and the next leads you away."

Waikoloa Beach Resort, Kings'   23 | 21 | 22 | 20 | $195

Waikoloa | 1020 Keana Pl. | 808-886-6060 | 877-924-5656 | www.waikoloabeachresort.com | 7074/5459; 73.4/66.3; 135/116

Offering "spectacular views of the mountains and ocean", this well-"manicured" Weiskopf/Morrish links-style layout is "the picture-perfect Hawaiian golf course"; although a few feel it's "nothing special", others counter it's a "challenging" track with blustery winds to "keep you on your toes" and ancient lava-rock rough to keep you "on the lookout"; all in all, it's deemed "a nice course if you're close" to the Kohala coast.

Kauai

Kauai Lagoons, Kiele   27 | 23 | 23 | 20 | $195

Lihue | 3351 Hoolaulea Way | 808-241-6000 | 800-634-6400 | www.kauailagoonsgolf.com | 7070/5417; 75.2/67.7; 140/121

"It's so beautiful, it's hard to focus on the golf" at this "perfect resort course" on Kauai, where the Golden Bear "did a great job taking advantage of" the "priceless" seaside scenery; "Nicklaus' sadistic treasure" is "brutal when the wind's up" – think "tee shots into the trades" – and a tad "expensive", but it's definitely "something to experience" and "worth playing more than once"; N.B. in 2007, the designer will oversee the relocation of holes 10, 14 and 15.

Kauai Lagoons, Mokihana   21 | 23 | 22 | 21 | $120

Lihue | 3351 Hoolaulea Way | 808-241-6000 | 800-634-6400 | www.kauailagoonsgolf.com | 6960/5607; 73.1/71.8; 127/116

"Not as challenging as its sister, Kiele", this "underrated" Jack Nicklaus design is nevertheless "a good course in its own right" for a "relaxing round" in a "beautiful setting"; although it has "no ocean views", you'll appreciate the links-style layout's combination of "mostly flat", "wide-open fairways" and undulating, heavily fortified greens, and if you find the track to be "less well-maintained" than its "braddah", you'll also discover that it's "less expensive" too.

Poipu Bay 🏌
26 | 25 | 25 | 19 | $185

Koloa | 2250 Ainako St. | 808-742-8711 | 800-858-6300 | www.poipubaygolf.com | 7123/5372; 73.9/70.4; 134/122

"First-class is written all over" this former host of the PGA Grand Slam of Golf that "lives up to its reputation", offering a "beautiful" RTJ Jr. design that's a "brutal test when the wind's up"; plus, the Kauai course's "last few holes are spectacular" – "bring your camera for the 15th and 16th" "along the water" – and the "excellent service" and facilities will "make your day a delight"; granted, it's "expensive", but "the major winners play here – shouldn't you?"

Princeville, Makai
24 | 22 | 23 | 22 | $175

Princeville | 5520 Ka Haku Rd. | 808-826-9644 | 800-826-4400 | www.princeville.com
Ocean/Lakes | 6953/5516; 73.2/69.9; 132/120
Ocean/Woods | 6942/5631; 72.9/67; 131/119
Woods/Lakes | 6901/5543; 72.5/66.3; 129/117

Though "clearly second banana" to its "spectacular" sibling, this "lovely" trio of "interesting nines" from RTJ Jr. is "better matched to the average golfer" than the Prince and proves itself particularly "good for beginners"; in fact, given the "wonderful service" and "great practice facilities", the only "problem is the scenery" – the resort's "paradise location" on Kauai's North Shore is so "amazing", "you'll forget to play golf."

🔢 Princeville, Prince 🏌
27 | 26 | 25 | 20 | $175

Princeville | 5520 Ka Haku Rd. | 808-826-9644 | 800-826-4400 | www.princeville.com | 7309/5346; 75.7/71.4; 140/124

"When God thought of golf, this is what was running through his head" fawn fans of this "memorable" RTJ Jr. creation on Kauai; but you'd better "bring aspirin", "a lot of golf balls" and "your sense of humor" to this "awesome" course, as it's a "treacherous test" that "wanders through the jungle" and features "long carries", wind and "frequent rain"; it's "pricey", but it comes with a "nice driving range" and "free spa pass."

Puakea 🏌
▽ 25 | 16 | 20 | 26 | $125

Lihue | 4150 Nuhou St. | 808-245-8756 | 866-773-5554 | www.puakeagolf.com | 6954/5225; 73.5/69.3; 135/113

With "a little bit of everything – ocean, valleys, mountains" – this "breathtaking" Kauai course offers "surprises on each hole" courtesy of its dramatic routing around jungle, ravines and streams; although considered "a must-play", "most people don't know" about this "hidden gem" from architect Robin Nelson, so "ask a local"; N.B. take advantage of the three-tiered pricing system and save $70 after 2 PM.

Wailua
- | - | - | - | $44

Kapaa | 3-5350 Kuhio Hwy. | 808-241-6666 | www.kauai.gov/golf | 6991/5974; 73.3/73.4; 129/119

"Locals are there at the crack of dawn" to play this "long" layout considered "the best value on Kauai" and the "the best muni" some swingers "have ever played"; running "parallel to the ocean" over rolling terrain, the tree-lined spread offers scenic vistas but few facilities, which may be why one tourist type concludes it's best to "bypass this and continue on to Princeville."

Lanai

⚡ Challenge at Manele ⛳ | 28 | 26 | 27 | 20 | $225 |

Lanai City | 1 Challenge Dr. | 808-565-2222 | www.lanai-resorts.com | 7039/5024; 73.7/68.8; 135/119

"Bring your camera and a lot of balls" to this Lanai "dreamland" (impressive enough to have been "Bill Gates' choice for a wedding" site), a "beautiful", "challenging" Nicklaus layout with "only two types of holes, ocean view or on the ocean", where the "whales and dolphins playing off shore" can be "distracting"; it's "high-priced" and the sight of nearby "housing construction" mars an otherwise "perfect setting", but for most surveyors, it's "worth it"; N.B. Four Seasons took over the hotel in 2006 and completed a $50-million-plus property renovation.

Experience at Koele ⛳ | 27 | 26 | 27 | 22 | $225 |

Lanai City | 1 Keamoku Dr. | 808-565-4653 | www.lanai-resorts.com | 7014/5425; 75.3/72.6; 143/130

"One of the most beautiful parkland courses you'll ever see" is this Greg Norman–designed "Shangri-la" in "upcountry" Lanai where the 17th, with a 250-ft. drop from tee to fairway, is so "spectacular" some "would like to be buried" there; while you may see "wild turkeys, chickens and deer", usually "no one else is there", making it "a joy to play"; P.S. at 2,000 feet above sea level, it's "typically cool", so "bring a jacket" or "pay a small fortune in the clubhouse."

Maui

Dunes at Maui Lani ⛳ | 21 | 19 | 20 | 22 | $120 |

Kahului | 1333 Maui Lani Pkwy. | 808-873-7911 | www.dunesatmauilani.com | 6841/4768; 73.5/67.9; 136/114

A "great alternative to the fancy resort courses", this "hidden treasure on Maui" is one of the "best values" on the island, offering "links golf with swaying palm trees" right "near the airport"; "trade winds play havoc on the ball most of the day", "a couple of holes are tricked-up with blind shots" and "18 is a killer", but all in all it's "real fun"; green golfers gripe about the "gasoline-powered carts", however.

Kapalua, Bay ⛳⛳ | 25 | 23 | 24 | 19 | $210 |

Kapalua | 300 Kapalua Dr. | 808-669-8044 | 877-527-2582 | www.kapaluamaui.com | 6600/5124; 72.1/69.6; 136/121

"Could it be more stunning?" ask aficionados of this "beautiful, rolling" Maui course whose "magnificent" ocean "views alone are worth" the "expensive" greens fees; it "can get ultrawindy" at Kapalua's original layout (blustery enough to "challenge just about anyone"), but it's also "fun" and "memorable" with "well-kept" greens; in fact, "when your ego is beaten up after playing Plantation", this "much more playable cousin can lift your spirits"; P.S. there are "good deals on twilight play."

HAWAII

	COURSE	FACIL.	SERVICE	VALUE	COST

☑ Kapalua, Plantation 🏌🏾⛳
29 | 27 | 25 | 19 | $295

Kapalua | 2000 Plantation Club Dr. | 808-669-8044 | 877-527-2582 | www.kapaluamaui.com | 7263/5627; 74.9/73.2; 138/129

For "serious golf with serious greens", head to Hawaii's top-rated Course, a "grueling" Coore/Crenshaw layout where you'll need the "generous fairways" given "constant" "merciless winds" and "hilly" terrain; "if the course doesn't kill you, you'll love" this "home of the Mercedes-Benz Championship" for its "amazing 17th and 18th holes", Golf Academy and "breathtaking" Maui setting; sure, it's "way too expensive", but "what can be better than walking in Tiger's footsteps" amid "gorgeous views of the Pacific?"

Makena, North ⛳
24 | 19 | 22 | 21 | $170

Makena | 5415 Makena Alanui | 808-879-3344 | 800-321-6284 | www.makenagolf.com | 6914/5303; 73.6/70.5; 138/120

"You always know you're on Maui" as you traverse this "exciting" RTJ Jr. resort design that winds "up and down Mt. Haleakala", "taking your breath away" with its "ocean views" and "lava everywhere"; natural gullies and kiawe trees help to make each hole "interesting", but some say the "fun-to-play" course could nevertheless "be in better shape"; P.S. "prepare for Hawaiian sticker shock", but remember: "teeing off [here] at sunrise is priceless."

Makena, South
24 | 19 | 22 | 20 | $170

Makena | 5415 Makena Alanui | 808-879-3344 | 800-321-6284 | www.makenagolf.com | 7014/5489; 73.8/71.7; 137/125

Players offer up "a *mahalo* for this lava-ly" oceanside spread that's "just a chip shot from spectacular"; "not as crowded as the neighboring Wailea courses", this "highly recommended" layout "is what life is all about", especially "at sunset" when playing the "beautiful par-3 15th" featuring a "green that's backed by the world's largest water hazard – the Pacific"; though the facilities seem "spartan", the "great staff" makes up for it with considerable "aloha spirit."

Wailea, Blue ⛳
22 | 20 | 23 | 19 | $160

Wailea | 100 Wailea Golf Club Dr. | 808-875-7450 | 888-328-6284 | www.waileagolf.com | 6765/5208; 72.2/69.3; 129/117

"The *menehune* magic is alive" at this "most forgiving of the Wailea courses" where Hawaii's mythical 'little people' have imbued the "fun" Maui layout – there are few hazards besides the "stunning views" of the ocean and Mt. Haleakala – with "feel-good" spirit; some say the oldest of the three resort tracks is "a bit tired", but the club's brand-new David Leadbetter Golf Academy is just one more reason for swingers to ask "how can I can get back here and how soon?"

Wailea, Emerald ⛳
26 | 24 | 24 | 21 | $190

Wailea | 100 Wailea Golf Club Dr. | 808-875-7450 | 888-328-6284 | www.waileagolf.com | 6825/5256; 71.7/69.5; 130/114

"A true gem" is the appraisal acolytes give to this "gorgeous" Wailea spread that "meanders through low foothills" and features tropical foliage and "lava everywhere"; a "perfect resort course", the RTJ Jr. layout is "challenging" but "fun" and "friendly to women" and the "occasional golfer"; it's "a bit pricey" but "worth every penny", especially given the "great driving range", pro shop and other facilities.

	COURSE	FACIL.	SERVICE	VALUE	COST

Wailea, Gold ⌘

	26	25	25	21	$190

Wailea | 100 Wailea Golf Club Dr. | 808-875-7450 | 888-328-6284 |
www.waileagolf.com | 7078/5317; 73.4/70.1; 137/119

The "hardest of the Wailea courses", this "exciting" layout is "good
enough to host the pros – which it has" as the former "home of the
Champions Skins Game"; "bring your camera" to this RTJ Jr. design,
because the "killer views" of "heavenly Maui" and the Pacific are
nearly as hazardous as the "many bunkers", the "break towards the
ocean" and the "sharp lava-rock rough"; it's "crowded" and "expensive", but expect "well-maintained" conditions and "amazing service."

Oahu

Kapolei ⌘

	22	21	20	21	$140

Kapolei | 91-701 Farrington Hwy. | 808-674-2227 |
7001/5490; 74.3/71.8; 135/124

This "nice, tight" "typical Ted Robinson design" on Oahu is a "great
course for women", which may explain why it's been a frequent host
of LPGA events; fans find it's usually in "perfect condition" (just
"watch out for the homes that line some of the fairways"), and a "helpful golf pro" and "great pro shop" complement the "wonderful" driving
range and "reasonable restaurant" serving Japanese and American
fare; most agree it's "expensive, but worth it."

Ko'olau ⌘

	26	20	21	23	$135

Kaneohe | 45-550 Kionaole Rd. | 808-247-7088 | www.koolaugolfclub.com |
7310/5102; 76.4/72.9; 152/134

"Not called the toughest course in the U.S. for nothing", this "breathtaking" Oahu "must-play" offers "target golf in a *Jurassic Park* environment" ("if you can't carry 150 yards over a ravine, play elsewhere");
"nothing can replace" the "jungle" setting and "views of the Ko'olau
mountains", however, so "bring your A-game" and "all your balls – golf
balls too" – because you're guaranteed a "memorable day"; P.S. "new
management" is planning course and practice facility improvements.

Ko Olina

	24	23	22	19	$170

Kapolei | 92-1220 Aliinui Dr. | 808-676-5309 | www.koolinagolf.com |
6867/5361; 72.3/71.8; 135/126

"A gem away from the city" of Honolulu, this "beautifully maintained"
Ted Robinson design was "sculpted from a sugar field" to include
"challenging" water hazards and multi-tiered greens; while a few
claim there's just "nothing spectacular or unusual" about the "expensive" "resort layout", most maintain it's "an all-around enjoyable experience", especially given its "friendly" staff.

Luana Hills ⌘

	26	16	18	20	$125

Kailua | 770 Auloa Rd. | 808-262-2139 | www.luanahills.com |
6595/4654; 73/64.1; 135/123

"In the jungle, the mighty jungle" of "lush" Maunawili Valley lies this
"tough" Pete Dye design featuring carries over water and ravines; the
"secluded, quiet course" is "a ball-eater" with a hilly "front nine that lulls
you into complacency and a back that takes it all away" as "it "snakes
through a rainforest" – "you have to think your way around"; all in all,
however, it's "a must-play" that's "worth the drive" from Waikiki.

	COURSE	FACIL.	SERVICE	VALUE	COST

Makaha ⚑
▽ 21 | 17 | 21 | 23 | $160

Waianae | 84-626 Makaha Valley Rd. | 808-695-9544 |
www.makaharesort.net | 7077/5856; 74.3/73.9; 137/129

Located "an hour from Waikiki" in west Oahu's "hidden" Makaha
Valley, this "tough, challenging" William F. Bell design is "worth the
drive" and "well worth playing" for its variety of holes and "beautiful"
mountain and ocean vistas; so snag an "early morning tee time" because this "great" resort track proves "less crowded than some of the
other courses on the island."

Pearl Country Club ⚑
19 | 15 | 16 | 20 | $75

Aiea | 98-535 Kaonohi St. | 808-487-3802 | www.pearlcc.com |
6787/5536; 72.7/67.1; 136/120

It may "not have the aura that surrounds other Hawaiian" layouts,
but for "a conventional round in an incredible setting", this course
situated at the base of the Ko'olau mountains certainly fits the bill;
"home to many local qualifiers" as well as the annual Pearl Open,
the "challenging" track forces players "to stretch their game" as
they traverse "hills, hills and more hills"; P.S. "the view of Pearl Harbor
is quite impressive."

Royal Kunia ⚑
▽ 24 | 11 | 18 | 22 | $120

Waipahu | 94-1509 Anonui St. | 808-688-9222 | www.royalkuniacc.com |
7007/4945; 73.8/68.1; 135/110

For "a new experience on an [already] mature course", head to this
Oahu layout that "took a long time to be released" – it was built in
1993 but didn't open until 2003; "every hole is different" on the Robin
Nelson design and it offers "great views" of Honolulu and Pearl
Harbor, but some fret over the "archaic" temporary facilities, saying it
will be "a whole lot better" once they move forward with plans to build
their new clubhouse.

Turtle Bay, Arnold Palmer
26 | 23 | 23 | 20 | $175

Kahuku | 57-049 Kuilima Dr. | 808-293-8574 | www.turtlebayresort.com |
7218/4851; 74.4/64.3; 143/121

This "pot of golf gold at the end of an hour's drive" to the North Shore
is "just breathtaking" given its "picturesque setting" surrounding a
wetlands bird sanctuary; although some wish the "challenging",
dogleg-heavy Arnold Palmer design was "routed closer to the ocean",
most find it "a wonderful escape from hotel- and condo-lined" layouts;
plus, it's especially "exciting to play a course" that's host to annual
LPGA and PGA Champions Tour events.

Turtle Bay, George Fazio
22 | 24 | 23 | 19 | $155

Kahuku | 57-049 Kuilima Dr. | 808-293-8574 | www.turtlebayresort.com |
6535/5355; 71.2/70.2; 131/116

"Almost as good as the Arnold Palmer course but not quite", this
1971 George Fazio–designed "little brother" is "fun to play" and well
"worth a 36-hole day if you're driving up" to the North Shore of
Oahu; although a few frustrated foozlers "expected more" of the
site of the very first Senior Skins Game, most agree this option makes
for a "fine" golfing experience that includes "more views" than its sibling (there are three oceanside holes); N.B. the twilight rates will
save you big bucks.

	COURSE	FACIL.	SERVICE	VALUE	COST

Idaho

Boise

NEW Tamarack Resort, Osprey Meadows ⛳

| - | - | - | - | $119 |

Donnelly | 2099 W. Mountain Rd. | 208-325-1030 | 877-826-7376 | www.tamarackidaho.com | 7319/5003; 81.5/63.6; 155/111

Framed by Idaho's Payette River Mountains with Lake Cascade nearby, this 7,319-yard Robert Trent Jones Jr. design traverses varied terrain that includes woodlands, marshes and meadows; it offsets its 100-plus bunkers and numerous water hazards with large, contoured greens and also boasts an elevated practice area where your drives will seemingly fly forever; if golf is not enough, the resort also offers hiking, whitewater rafting and trout fishing.

Coeur d'Alene

Z Circling Raven ⛳

| 29 | 26 | 27 | 28 | $85 |

Worley | US Hwy. 95 | 800-523-2464 | www.cdacasino.com | 7189/4708; 74.8/67.2; 140/126

"I'm told paradise is lost – I think I found it" asserts one admirer of this "outstanding" spread set in the "beautifully remote" "hills of a Native American reservation" "without any houses or buildings" in sight; a "work of art that moves effortlessly from rolling fields to forests", it's a "definite must-play" with four tricky par 3s to make it "engaging"; even better, it has a "fantastic staff" and is adjacent to a lavish casino resort, although "with a course like this, why gamble?"

Z Coeur d'Alene Resort 🏌

| 27 | 28 | 28 | 20 | $250 |

Coeur d'Alene | 900 Floating Green Dr. | 208-667-4653 | 800-688-5253 | www.cdaresort.com | 6735/4448; 71.1/64.4; 119/105

With a "spectacular lakeside setting" in the foothills of the Rocky Mountains and "pristine conditions", it's easy to understand this layout's "reputation for being the best-cared-for course in America"; although "superlatives abound, the track is not as difficult as one would expect" – "nonexistent rough makes for a happy vacation" – but its "interesting holes" include a par-3 14th with a floating, moveable green; the only problem: "mandatory forecaddies", which can make it "very expensive."

Sun Valley

Sun Valley Resort ⛳

| ▽ 23 | 20 | 21 | 17 | $145 |

Sun Valley | 1 Sun Valley Rd. | 208-622-2251 | 800-786-8259 | www.sunvalley.com | 6938/5408; 72.5/70.7; 141/127

"Your ball sure does carry at this elevation", but the thin Bald Mountain air at this Robert Trent Jones Jr. redesign of a 1936 original "is a good thing", not only for the "fantastic views" it provides, but also because "some of the holes [here] are nearly 600 yards long"; even more daunting, though, is the course's rugged Sun Valley terrain: it crosses Trail Creek a full 11 times and features a 244-yard 15th with a shot over the water from every tee.

Illinois

TOP COURSES IN STATE

Chicago

Big Run   23 | 12 | 17 | 22 | $68

Lockport | 17211 W. 135th St. | 815-838-1057 | www.bigrungolf.com |
7050/6200; 74.6/70.8; 142/132

"Bring your big stick" because this "beautiful old course" (built in 1930)
"is a big run indeed": the "challenging" "beast" measures over 7,000
yards; located north of Joliet "on rolling landscape with lots of mature
trees", this "local favorite" features "long par 5s" and "huge elevation
changes" ("even on the greens"); still, some lament that "they have no
driving range" and "no marshals" – "what a course this could be!"

Cantigny 🏌   26 | 24 | 25 | 21 | $85

Wheaton | 27 W. 270 Mack Rd. | 630-668-3323 | www.cantignygolf.com
Hillside/Lakeside | 6831/5183; 72.6/70.1; 131/119
Lakeside/Woodside | 7004/5425; 73.9/71.9; 138/127
Woodside/Hillside | 6961/5236; 73.5/70.3; 132/120

For "country-club atmosphere without the dues", head to "one of the
most scenic courses in Illinois", this "old-fashioned" 27-holer located
on the Wheaton-area estate of former *Chicago Tribune* honcho Robert
McCormick; fans "can't say enough" about the "pristine conditions",
"helpful staff" and caddie program, with the highest marks going to
the "superb Lakeside/Woodside combo" and signature "Dick Tracy
hole" (look for the uniquely shaped bunker).

Chalet Hills   22 | 19 | 19 | 20 | $84

Cary | 943 Rawson Bridge Rd. | 847-639-0666 | www.chaletgolf.com |
6877/4934; 73.6/69.1; 137/121

You may "want to take the cart" given the "great ups and downs" at
this "very scenic" spread set on rolling terrain in the far northern suburbs; featuring "tight" fairways lined with mature oak trees and water
on 13 holes, this "tough course" makes locals "proud to bring out-of-
town guests to play", especially when tackling what they call "two of
the best finishing holes in the Chicagoland area" (the 9th and 18th);
all in all, it's considered "a good value."

Cog Hill, No. 2 (Ravines) 🏌   24 | 22 | 20 | 24 | $53

Lemont | 12294 Archer Ave. | 630-257-5872 | www.coghillgolf.com |
6576/5639; 71.4/71.5; 124/117

Cog Hill's "second best" "lives under the shadow" of sister course
Dubsdread, but the "excellent" 1929 design situated southwest of
Chicago is "challenging enough" "if you want to practice your game";
what makes it a real "value", though, is its "woodsy, hilly", ravine-laced
setting ("unusual" for the area and "a nice change of pace") and its "excellent service" – "it's been there a long time, so it understands golfers."

	COURSE	FACIL.	SERVICE	VALUE	COST

☒ Cog Hill, No. 4 (Dubsdread) 🎒 | 28 | 21 | 21 | 22 | $135 |

Lemont | 12294 Archer Ave. | 630-257-5872 | www.coghillgolf.com |
6940/5590; 75.4/70.6; 142/133

"It's tough, it's long" and it "has enough sand to build a desert", but
somehow this "well-maintained" Cog Hill course "still manages to be
fun" and "fair"; "one of the very best in the Midwest", the regular PGA
Tour stop offers a "classic" design that will make you "feel like a pro"
as you test your shot-making skills; duffers dub the facilities "mar-
ginal", but upcoming renovations (to be overseen by Rees Jones) are
intended to "make it worthy of a major."

Glen Club 🎒 | 25 | 24 | 23 | 15 | $165 |

Glenview | 2901 W. Lake Ave. | 847-724-7272 | www.theglenclub.com |
7149/5324; 72.2/71.5; 132/127

Designer Tom Fazio "moved tons of earth" to turn "a flat Naval air-
strip" into this "challenging" "championship course" "not far from
Downtown" Chicago; site of the Nationwide Tour's LaSalle Bank Open,
the "fantastic" rolling layout offers "a refreshing mix" of holes that are
kept in "top-rate condition", plus a "lovely clubhouse" and "excellent
service"; nevertheless, its equally "premium prices" have some wary
types wondering why you'd "play this when you can play Cog Hill's
No. 4 for less?"

Harborside International, Port | 26 | 24 | 22 | 20 | $92 |

Chicago | 11001 S. Doty Ave. | 312-782-7837 |
www.harborsideinternational.com | 7164/5164; 75.1/70.8; 132/122

As "windy as the city's nickname", this "true links design" is a "fun"
but "challenging" layout that offers treeless expanses, tufted mounding and "deep, deep rough" – "don't bother looking" for errant balls; although situated atop a former landfill "in the heart of the industrial
district", the Scottish-style muni is "well worth playing" for its "great
views" of Chicagoland and its "friendly, attentive" staff; P.S. "nothing
beats the value at twilight."

Harborside International, Starboard | 24 | 23 | 22 | 20 | $92 |

Chicago | 11001 S. Doty Ave. | 312-782-7837 |
www.harborsideinternational.com | 7166/5110; 75/66.4; 132/116

"Like its sister course", this "phenomenal" links layout is a "fun, scenic, relatively affordable" "favorite" that's "convenient to Downtown
Chicago"; located "atop an old landfill", the "challenging" muni can be
"tough when the wind's blowing" with "very penal rough" ("stay out of
the fescue"), but given its "surreal" and "beautiful" environs, "views of
the city skyline" and "excellent facilities", one swinger swears it's the
"best dump I've ever played."

Heritage Bluffs | ▽ 26 | 14 | 17 | 28 | $46 |

Channahon | 24355 W. Bluff Rd. | 815-467-7888 | www.heritagebluffs.com |
7106/4967; 73.9/68.6; 138/114

"Run like an old-time public", this "local favorite" spread over rolling,
wooded terrain may "dollar for doller" be "the best value in the
Chicago area"; it's "a long ride" 50 miles southwest of the city, but the
"classic Dick Nugent design" is a "well-maintained" "must-play" offering a "challenging" "variety of holes" (including "some great ones on
the bluffs") that are laced with lakes, wetlands and elevation changes.

ILLINOIS

	COURSE	FACIL.	SERVICE	VALUE	COST

Oak Brook
	19	17	17	20	$51

Oak Brook | 2606 York Rd. | 630-368-6400 | www.oak-brook.org |
6541/5341; 71.1/70.7; 126/120

Though "a little short" at just over 6,500 yards, this "fun" track 25
miles west of Chicago is nonetheless difficult due to "great greens"
featuring "tough placements"; despite its generally "good upkeep",
the "abnormally slow play" and "typical muni" routing may "make you
wish you were playing at Butler National next door."

Orchard Valley
	26	21	22	25	$59

Aurora | 2411 W. Illinois Ave. | 630-907-0500 | www.orchardvalleygolf.com |
6745/5162; 72.8/70.9; 134/128

"As Midwest munis go, you won't get any better than this" "upscale
course" an hour west of Chicago that's considered "one of the most
challenging and best-run" public layouts in the state; "plenty of sand
traps" and "water, water everywhere" helps to keep the "fabulous" design "challenging" (especially on the "super back nine"), while "very
good conditioning" adds to its "excellent value."

Pine Meadow
	25	18	18	21	$79

Mundelein | 1 Pine Meadow Ln. | 847-566-4653 | www.pinemeadowgc.com |
7141/5203; 74.6/70.1; 138/126

If you're "tired of courses that are laid out around houses", head to this
"magnificent track" owned by Cog Hill's Jemsek family and located on
the "beautiful", tree-filled grounds of a seminary north of Chicago; although it "could use a new clubhouse", this "old-style" "gem" ("nothing
is tricked-up" here) is "truly a golfer's golf course" that's "worth playing";
"well-maintained" conditions and a "great practice area" are pluses.

Plum Tree National
	22	17	18	23	$65

Harvard | 19511 Lembcke Rd. | 815-943-7474 | www.plumtreegolf.com |
6648/5760; 71.8/74.9; 132/126

"A diamond in the rough, pun intended", this "enjoyable" "Joe Lee classic" situated in "rural" McHenry County on the Wisconsin border is "out
of the way" "but worth the ride"; although "a little run-down" at times,
the "old-style" parklander is "well-maintained" "with mature trees", hills
and lakes dotting its dogleg-filled layout; but though it's a "value", "the
money you save [on greens fees] may be spent on the gas to get here."

Prairie Landing
	24	25	22	20	$84

West Chicago | 2325 Longest Dr. | 630-208-7600 | www.prairielanding.com |
6950/4859; 73.2/68.3; 136/116

The "three-hole warm-up course eliminates excuses" at this "difficult"
Robert Trent Jones Jr. design where it's "not gossip but the steady flow
of corporate jets" at nearby DuPage Airport that gives it its "buzz"; "be
ready to carry rough, trees and water" – the "excellent finishing hole"
has a 235-yard shot over a lake – on this linksy layout that's "expensive
for a muni" but offers "a country-club experience" that includes "GPS
to assess distances" and "beautiful" facilities.

Ruffled Feathers
	24	23	22	17	$99

Lemont | 1 Pete Dye Dr. | 630-257-1000 | www.ruffledfeathersgc.com |
6898/5273; 74.1/71.7; 140/129

With a "course name [that] tells it like it is", this "difficult", waterlogged
layout from Pete and P.B. Dye – their "only facility in the Chicago

area" – "tests the skills" of swingers with "brutal par 3s" and "lots of challenges", but tests their patience with "target golf on a few holes"; located southwest of the city in Lemont ("an alternative to Cog Hill"), the "top-notch" track is "kept impeccably clean and beautiful", which may explain why it's also "a little pricey."

Schaumburg
▽ 21 | 21 | 20 | 24 | $50

Schaumburg | 401 N. Roselle Rd. | 847-885-9000 | www.parkfun.com
Baer/Players | 6525/4871; 70.4/67.4; 118/113
Players/Tournament | 6412/4892; 69.8/67.4; 119/112
Tournament/Baer | 6559/4900; 70.5/67.2; 121/114

This park district 27-holer situated "in a residential area" 30 miles northwest of Chicago is "a real pleasure" to play given its wide fairways, numerous water hazards and strategic bunkering; the "great muni" "really does go above and beyond here", offering a "country club–like" experience – "well-maintained" course conditions, a "friendly" staff and "great food" – without the attendant "snobbish air" or high prices.

Seven Bridges 🏌
22 | 21 | 21 | 18 | $99

Woodridge | 1 Mulligan Dr. | 630-964-7777 | www.sevenbridges.com | 7103/5262; 74.6/65.6; 135/114

"Golf is a water sport" on this "classic Jekyll and Hyde layout" where "one of the nines is a fair yet challenging track" set amid rolling, wooded terrain "and the other is target golf at its worst" courtesy of holes lined with water on either (or both) sides; located 30 miles southwest of Chicago, this "upscale public" also offers a "very good restaurant" and staff, but considering its "somewhat pricey" fees, a few question "how a high-end course can not have a driving range."

Shepherd's Crook
22 | 15 | 16 | 25 | $42

Zion | 351 Greenbay Rd. | 847-872-2080 | www.shepherdscrook.org | 6769/4901; 71.9/67.9; 125/116

"Another non-private must-play", this "all-around good deal" owned by the Zion Park District is located an hour north of Chicago; "links-like in some parts and woodsy in others", the "short" Keith Foster design is "fair but tough" with "many interesting holes" featuring "wide fairways" and "elephants buried under the greens"; but the lack of a driving range and the malodorous "ambiance from a [nearby] dump" can "detract from an otherwise" "nice course."

Steeple Chase
22 | 18 | 16 | 21 | $57

Mundelein | 200 N. La Vista Dr. | 847-949-8900 | www.mundeleinparks.org | 6827/4831; 73.1/68.2; 136/118

"A place you could feel good about playing on a regular basis", this "beautiful" "treat" set amid lakes, wetlands and woods an hour north of Chicago is a "decent" muni that will "challenge your game" with its "difficult greens" and "elevation changes"; "there aren't over-the-top amenities" here – there's no driving range, although they've recently added GPS to their carts – "but the prices aren't out of control either."

☑ Stonewall Orchard
28 | 23 | 22 | 22 | $74

Grayslake | 25675 W. Hwy. 60 | 847-740-4890 | www.stonewallorchard.com | 7074/5375; 74.1/71.2; 140/126

"Far from the world" "with few houses", this 1999 Arthur Hills design "has matured" into one of the "best public courses in Chicagoland"; located an hour north of the city in a setting that "combines beautiful wetlands, trees and more elevation" than you normally find in Illinois, this "awesome course" proves "special yet challenging" courtesy of elevated tees, rolling greens, forced carries over water and "deep rough" that all but "eats golf balls."

ThunderHawk

27	22	20	22	$98

Beach Park | 39700 N. Lewis Ave. | 847-872-4295 | www.lcfpd.org | 7031/5046; 73.8/69.2; 136/122

"Wow, what a course" coo club-wielders about this "masterpiece" "designed by RTJ Jr. for the Lake County Forest Preserve" and nestled "just far enough from Chicago to make it a secret" (about an hour north); "surrounded by flora and fauna", the "beautiful", "well-maintained" layout is "long and challenging" with "wide fairways", "excellent" serpentine bunkering and fast, marsh-guarded greens; all in all, it proves "a top value" – "especially for county residents."

Water's Edge

▽ 18	16	17	21	$65

Worth | 7205 W. 115th St. | 708-671-1032 | www.watersedgegolf.com | 6904/5332; 72.9/70.4; 131/122

"An asset for the southwest side of Chicago", this "fun" Rick Robbins/Gary Koch collaboration provides a "good test for amateur golfers"; located "along an old ship canal" with the Saganashkee Slough to its south, the "great" layout is routed through wetlands and forests with marshes, trees and water to guard its greens; a recently renovated clubhouse and lighted practice area round out the experience.

Galena

Eagle Ridge, North

24	22	22	19	$140

Galena | 444 Eagle Ridge Dr. | 815-777-2444 | www.eagleridge.com | 6875/5578; 73.2/72.1; 132/125

"Golf away your vacation" at this "nice" resort track situated in the far northwest corner of the state amid "rolling hills that don't look like Illinois"; given its undulating fairways and greens, you may not want to walk this "scenic course" – that is, "unless you have a pack mule" – although swingers love to "let loose" from the elevated tees, especially on the "gorgeous downhill par-3 8th with a view of" (and forced carry over) Lake Galena.

Eagle Ridge, South

▽ 21	22	21	19	$140

Galena | 444 Eagle Ridge Dr. | 815-777-2444 | www.eagleridge.com | 6762/5609; 72.7/72.3; 134/129

Shorter and tighter than its North sibling, Eagle Ridge's "solid" middle child is a "splendid way to spend your" day given its picturesque routing through a wooded, stream-laced valley; although lofters love the "downhill shot to the 11th green" ("birdie time") and the "drive over the creek from the 18th tee", the distribution of practice facilities among the resort's courses has ball whackers asking "where's the [driving] range?"

☑ Eagle Ridge, The General

28	24	24	20	$170

Galena | 444 Eagle Ridge Dr. | 815-777-2444 | www.eagleridge.com | 6820/5337; 73.7/71.8; 141/128

With "breathtaking changes in elevation", this "amazing" Eagle Ridge layout is an "unforgiving" (but "fun") track featuring "tight fairways", "fast, true greens" and several high-altitude tees that "make for some exciting shots as well as panoramic views of three states"; Illinois' top-rated Course also has "wildlife all over", lots of "solitude" and an "excellent staff", but a few say the experience can be "spoiled by a cart-path-only policy" that leads to "slow play."

Moline

TPC Deere Run

| 26 | 25 | 25 | 24 | $70 |

Silvis | 3100 Heather Knoll | 309-796-6000 | 877-872-3677 | www.tpcatdeererun.com | 7138/5179; 75.1/70.1; 134/119

Boasting "beautiful vistas as you play along the Rock River", this lay-out located just east of Moline is a "wonderful" golfing destination – and the "PGA agrees", having held its John Deere Classic here since 2000; designed by Illinois native D.A. Weibring, the "hilly" track trav-els over varied terrain and includes elevation changes, blind shots and bunkering that makes "straight shooting a must"; given its "top-notch facilities" and "know-how" staff, it's seen by many as "a steal."

Peoria

WeaverRidge

| 27 | 23 | 21 | 21 | $73 |

Peoria | 5100 Weaverridge Blvd. | 309-691-3344 | www.weaverridge.com | 7030/5046; 73.1/68.9; 136/115

Despite the "long drive from Chicago" to Peoria, this "great" Hurdzan/Fry design is definitely "worth doing once"; snaking over rolling hills and forested lowlands, the scenic layout offers "nice eleva-tion changes" and risk/reward shots courtesy of deep bunkers, ponds and the meandering Big Hollow Creek; despite its status as a local fa-vorite, a few still find it "overpriced for golf in central Illinois."

Rockford

Aldeen

| ▽ 23 | 19 | 19 | 28 | $45 |

Rockford | 1900 Reid Farm Rd. | 815-282-4653 | 888-425-3336 | www.aldeengolfclub.com | 7131/5075; 74.2/69.1; 134/117

Thank local philanthropists Norris and Margaret Aldeen for this "beautiful" and "challenging" 1991 park-district track that may be "out of the way" northwest of the Windy City but is considered "a bar-gain"; the upscale amenities include a 26-acre lighted practice facility, a 14,000-sq.-ft. putting green and handheld laser devices for measur-ing yardage on the "fun", walkable course.

Springfield

Piper Glen

| - | - | - | - | $33 |

Springfield | 7112 Piper Glen Dr. | 217-483-6537 | 877-635-7326 | www.piperglen.com | 6985/5138; 73.6/70.3; 132/123

Situated 90 minutes north of St. Louis, this host of the 2003 Illinois State Amateur Championship is considered "one of the most affordable courses" in the state; set on rolling, wooded countryside dotted with nat-ural ponds and crisscrossed by Polecat Creek, the Sangamon County course features water on 12 of its holes; also providing a challenge are its undulating greens, hidden bunkers and signature double doglegs.

St. Louis Area

Annbriar
27 | 21 | 23 | 24 | $69

Waterloo | 1524 Birdie Ln. | 618-939-4653 | 888-939-5191 |
www.annbriar.com | 6863/4792; 72.8/66.4; 136/110

Perhaps "the best public course in the St. Louis area", this "test of
golf" "rivals the local country clubs" and is "worth the drive" 30 minutes south of the city; you'll "feel like you're all by yourself" as you
traverse an "unspoiled" spread that's made up of "two distinct nines":
an easier "links-style front" and a "wooded back" that's "a true monster" with its "steep elevation changes"; a "personable" staff rounds
out the "enjoyable" experience.

Gateway National
24 | 20 | 20 | 25 | $69

Madison | 18 Golf Dr. | 314-421-4653 | www.gatewaynational.com |
7092/5187; 74.6/64.5; 138/109

"If you like NASCAR and golf, you can have a great time indulging both
passions" at Keith Foster's "tough" links-style layout located "imme-
diately behind the Gateway International Raceway"; also "very convenient to Downtown St. Louis" (read: "it gets a lot of play"), this "good
value" offers "something interesting on every hole" – from lakes and
"high rough" to deep bunkers and mounding – plus "views of the
Gateway Arch that can't be beat."

Spencer T. Olin 🏌
▽ 23 | 14 | 17 | 23 | $55

Alton | 4701 College Ave. | 618-465-3111 | www.spencertolingolf.com |
6941/5049; 73.5/65.6; 135/110

"As good as everybody has told you", this Arnold Palmer design – host
to the 1999 U.S. Amateur Public Links Championship – was named after a lifelong friend who paired with him in a 1955 pro-am; located 40
minutes north of St. Louis, the "well-maintained" community park
course features zoysia fairways, sloped greens and lots of wind, water
and fescue; it also offers "constant specials", which make it both "a
great value" and a bit "too crowded."

Stonewolf 🏌
▽ 21 | 20 | 18 | 19 | $65

Fairview Heights | 1195 Stonewolf Trail | 618-624-4653 | 877-721-4653 |
www.stonewolfgolf.com | 6943/4849; 73.4/68.2; 136/114

Set amid rolling hills 20 minutes east of St. Louis, this "very interesting" Jack Nicklaus design is "worth the drive" given its scenic routing
through a forest of mature oak trees; "a challenge" for all skill levels, it
features severe elevation changes, zoysia fairways fitted out with 69
bunkers and water on eight of its holes; although a few sections seem
"a little tricked-up", overall the spread is a "well-maintained" "value."

Indiana

Cincinnati Area

Belterra
– | – | – | – | $100

Florence | 777 Belterra Dr. | 812-417-7777 | 888-235-8377 |
www.belterracasino.com | 6925/5102; 73.3/69.2; 136/117

"Visually appealing" with views of the Ohio River and Log Lick Creek,
this "fun" Tom Fazio design winds through lakes and trees an hour

southwest of Cincinnati; the picturesque parklander sits adjacent to the Belterra casino and resort, which makes it "great for gambling and golf outings", so "look for specials" that include an overnight stay and breakfast and be sure to try your luck at the many slot machines and gaming tables.

French Lick

French Lick, Donald Ross
▽ 23 | 17 | 17 | 19 | $110

French Lick | 8670 W. State Rd. 56 | 800-457-4042 | 800-457-4042 | www.frenchlick.com | 6500/5400

"The most enjoyable aspect" of this "classic old" Donald Ross design "is walking the same hills Walter Hagen did when he won the 1924 PGA Championship", but a recent multimillion-dollar renovation is providing even more incentive to play this 1917 layout in French Lick; part of an overall resort expansion, the redo returned 35 of its original bunkers, reshaped and enlarged the greens and added championship tees (new USGA ratings will be available in summer 2007); N.B. a Pete Dye course is expected to open in 2008.

Indianapolis

Brickyard Crossing
26 | 21 | 23 | 22 | $90

Indianapolis | 4400 W. 16th St. | 317-484-6572 | www.brickyardcrossing.com | 6994/5038; 74.5/68.3; 137/116

A "must-play when you're in Indy", this "A+" "surprise" from designer Pete Dye is parked next to the Indianapolis Motor Speedway, with four of its holes right "in the middle of the 500 track" ("bring your earplugs"); the "setting is spectacular", but so is the "challenging course", offering plenty of water via Little Eagle Creek but remaining "playable for the average golfer"; it's "slightly overpriced", but their affordable "stay-and-play deals" take the checkered flag.

Fort, The
▽ 26 | 21 | 23 | 23 | $58

Indianapolis | 6002 N. Post Rd. | 317-543-9592 | www.thefortgolfcourse.com | 7148/5045; 74.5/69.8; 139/127

"One of the prettiest Pete Dye designs you'll find", this "awesome" and "well-maintained" course just minutes from Downtown Indianapolis in Fort Harrison State Park is "very scenic" with "lush trees lining every hole"; nonetheless, the public facility is also "one tough course", so "unless you're really good, bring plenty of balls" to this "hilly and narrow" track; factor in quaint lodgings at the seven-room Harrison House and it adds up to "a very good experience."

Heartland Crossing
- | - | - | - | $51

Camby | 6701 S. Heartland Blvd. | 317-630-1785 | www.heartlandcrossinggolf.com | 7267/5536; 75.4/69; 134/121

Although it's routed over rolling terrain just southwest of Indianapolis, "you'd think you were playing in Saudi Arabia" as you cross your heart and take on this "links-style" layout that garners mixed reviews for its liberal use of white-sand bunkers ("well-placed" vs. "too many"); they've recently removed 20 of the traps, however, so even whiny wedgers can agree that this fescue-, bluegrass- and wildflower-strewn spread is an "excellent value" "for the recreational golfer."

	COURSE	FACIL.	SERVICE	VALUE	COST

Otter Creek
▽ 25 | 18 | 19 | 20 | $75

Columbus | 11522 E. 50 N. | 812-579-5227 | www.ottercreekgolf.com
East/North | 7224/5581; 75.6/73; 137/125
North/West | 7258/5690; 75.6/73.5; 138/128
West/East | 7126/5403; 75/71.9; 137/123

"What great courses used to be like" gush golfers about this "awesome" "traditional" course that uses "lots of trees" and the namesake creek to create a "serene environment" south of Indianapolis; while some consider RTJ Sr.'s "original 18" to be "better than the newer East nine" designed by his son Rees Jones in 1995, all three offer a range of challenges and are kept in "good" if sometimes "scruffy" condition; N.B. play all day for $100.

Prairie View
▽ 25 | 18 | 26 | 21 | $90

Carmel | 7000 Longest Dr. | 317-816-3100 | www.prairieviewgc.com | 7073/5203; 74.5/65.8; 138/114

"Carmel residents are fortunate to have" this "great public course" "at their doorstep", but out-of-towners can also enjoy this RTJ Jr. design set on the banks of the White River in Hamilton County; the bunker-strewn woodlander features five lakes, wetlands and a meandering stream, but its "looks are deceiving" as the "open layout" proves "not overly difficult"; all in all, it's "fun" to play, especially given its "friendly staff" and "family atmosphere."

Purgatory
▽ 23 | 17 | 21 | 21 | $65

Noblesville | 12160 E. 216th St. | 317-776-4653 | www.purgatorygolf.com | 7754/4562; 78.1/66.9; 142/115

In between heaven and hell (and north of Indianapolis) is the longest course in Indiana, this "tough" 18-holer that measures 7,754 yards from the back tees; despite "lots of bunkers" – over 125 of them make for "way too much sand" – the parklander proves "challenging yet playable" by all levels thanks to "six sets of tees"; "very well-maintained" course conditions and a relatively new clubhouse also help to make it a "favorite."

Rock Hollow
- | - | - | - | $49

Peru | County Rd. 250 W. | 765-473-6100 | www.rockhollowgolf.com | 6944/4967; 74/69.1; 136/118

Owned by the father of PGA Tour player Chris Smith (who holds the course record of 63), this "Hoosier gem" is "worth the drive" 90 minutes north of Indianapolis; uniquely routed through a mined-out rock quarry, this design from Pete Dye protégé Tim Liddy is "a must for any golfer in the Midwest", especially those who appreciate a value-priced layout that's laced with lots of water, wetlands and, of course, rocks.

Trophy Club
▽ 25 | 17 | 21 | 23 | $60

Lebanon | 3887 N. US Hwy. 52 | 765-482-7272 | www.thetrophyclubgolf.com | 7280/5050; 75.3/69.3; 138/118

Admirers "travel 45 minutes from Indy to play" this "uncrowded links-style" layout whose "outstanding design" from Tim Liddy forces you to "work the ball both ways" before reaching its "tricky", "large and undulating greens"; with lakes, a creek and "a constant wind blowing" over the fescue- and bluegrass-framed fairways, it's a "challenging" track that's considered both a "favorite" and a "great value."

Iowa

Cedar Rapids

Amana Colonies 🏨

| | - | - | - | - | $52 |

Amana | 451 27th Ave. | 319-622-6222 | 800-383-3636 | www.amanagolfcourse.com | 6824/5228; 73.3/70; 136/119

Situated southwest of Cedar Rapids, this "great course" is nestled amid the landmarked villages of a local religious community; the "excellent grounds" offer "beautiful scenery" in the form of dense forests and undulating hills, while ponds, streams and strategic bunkering help to make it a "challenge"; N.B. they've recently added on-site condo lodging.

Des Moines

Harvester, The

| ▽ 29 | 24 | 24 | 24 | $79 |

Rhodes | 1102 330th St. | 641-227-4653 | www.harvestergolf.com | 7300/4950; 75.6/68.9; 137/120

"Every hole is challenging and fun" at this "Keith Foster gem" set on former farmland northeast of Des Moines; a "Midwest favorite", the "well-groomed course" offers plenty of risk/reward shots on an expansive, hilly layout that features bluegrass rough, a 60-acre lake and large, "very fast greens"; sure, it's "scary", but "in a good way."

Kansas

Garden City

Buffalo Dunes

| - | - | - | - | $25 |

Garden City | 5685 S. Hwy. 83 | 620-276-1210 | www.garden-city.org | 6774/5150; 72.1/69.5; 127/118

Some swingers are "surprised to find this jewel of a course in southwest Kansas", but at least one club-wielder is convinced this three-decade-old muni is "worth a drive to the in-laws" if only to "escape to play this course"; with undulating, "carpetlike fairways" twisting toward "excellent" rolling greens, this challenging layout is "great for the money"; N.B. they added new back tees in 2006.

Kansas City

Alvamar Public

| ▽ 24 | 18 | 18 | 27 | $39 |

Lawrence | 1800 Crossgate Dr. | 785-842-1907 | www.alvamar.com | 7092/4892; 74.5/68.1; 130/112

Home to the U. of Kansas golf team, this "hidden gem" in Lawrence is a "fair" foray that's in its "best shape in years" (with new turf on its "large greens"); the long parklander is "demanding from the black tees", but no matter where you play from, you'll find the same "zoysia fairways" plus "two great finishers"; P.S. "get an invite to the adjoining private course."

Deer Creek

| ▽ 21 | 21 | 23 | 19 | $69 |

Overland Park | 7000 W. 133rd St. | 913-681-3100 | www.deercreekgc.com | 6811/5126; 74.5/68.5; 137/113

"Neatly packed into a suburban neighborhood" just south of Kansas City, this "challenging" RTJ Jr. design can seem "very tight" given that its zoysia fairways are lined with "a lot of trees and sand" and crisscrossed by a meandering stream; a few find it "a bit pricey" for a club with "no driving range", but most consider it to be an overall "nice course."

Falcon Ridge

▽ 24 | 21 | 22 | 19 | $75

Lenexa | 20200 Prairie Star Pkwy. | 913-393-4653 | www.falconridgegolf.com | 6820/5160; 72.8/69.6; 130/119

Enjoy the views of Downtown Kansas City from the 4th tee at this "long, interesting" Lenexa layout that offers "elevation changes" on its hilly holes; although it's "very busy most of the time", the "fairways and greens are generally in good shape" and "GPS in the carts helps the pacing"; sure, it's "one of the higher-priced courses in the area", but it remains "a fun place to play if money isn't a consideration."

Prairie Highlands

▽ 24 | 18 | 19 | 22 | $50

Olathe | 14695 S. Inverness Dr. | 913-856-7235 | www.prairiehighlands.com | 7066/5122; 74.5/69.6; 129/114

There's "lots of trouble" to be had on this "great" linksy layout from designer/co-owner Craig Schreiner: the 7,066-yard effort features 60 bunkers, "blind shots", deep rough and windy conditions on its variety of holes; despite its routing over rolling hills on the west side of Olathe, this 2006 U.S. Senior Open qualifying site was constructed to "actually be walkable" and is considered well "worth the fees."

Sycamore Ridge

▽ 26 | 19 | 21 | 23 | $59

Spring Hill | 21731 Clubhouse Dr. | 913-592-5292 | www.sycamoreridgegolf.com | 7081/4877; 76.2/65.4; 150/118

One of the "best publics in Kansas City" is actually 40 minutes south of the metropolis, but once you make your way there, you'll find this "fun" muni "favorite" offers "two completely different nines"; just "don't get too overconfident" on the "links-style front" as the "awesome back" that's "threaded through the woods" and loaded "with doglegs, narrow fairways" and creek carries might just "kick your butt."

Topeka

Colbert Hills ⌂

▽ 29 | 20 | 25 | 25 | $79

Manhattan | 5200 Colbert Hills Dr. | 785-776-6475 | www.colberthills.com | 7525/4947; 77.5/65.1; 152/119

"Anyone who enjoys a challenge" along with "breathtaking scenery" should appreciate this "links-style course" in Manhattan that's home to the Kansas State Wildcats; with seven sets of tees ("beware the psychopath ones at 7,525 yards"), this "demanding test of golf" is "as difficult as you want it to be" with "forced carries", "well-trapped greens" and "prairie wind" to create "high risk/reward decisions"; N.B. alumni, students and staff all receive discounted greens fees.

Wichita

NEW Sand Creek Station

- | - | - | - | $49

Newton | 920 Meadowbrook Dr. | 316-284-6161 | www.sandcreekgolfclub.com | 7400/5500; 76.3/71.9; 136/124

Re-created holes from famed St. Andrews and North Berwick mix with modern designs on this Jeff Brauer effort just north of Wichita; strong breezes can wreak havoc on scores at this 2006 links that plays 7,400 yards from the tips with four holes that border the namesake creek and others that pay homage to the town's railroad history (a working train runs through the course); N.B. it's city-owned, so expect even weekend non-resident rates to be under $50.

Kentucky

Lexington

Marriott's Griffin Gate ⚐

	COURSE	FACIL.	SERVICE	VALUE	COST
▽	19	19	22	19	$69

Lexington | 1720 Newtown Pike | 859-288-6193 | www.marriott.com | 6784/5053; 72.2/68.6; 133/122

A "nice facility in Lexington" just four miles from Downtown Lexington, this "classic Rees Jones design" may be "high on the snob factor" – it is located in horse country, after all – but the layout is nonetheless a "decent" choice for a "fun" round; sure, the "short course" can feel "cramped" (unlike the "long weekend rounds"), but you can always melt away the aggravation over a relaxing meal at the luxe JW Steakhouse.

Old Silo

	COURSE	FACIL.	SERVICE	VALUE	COST
▽	23	21	23	23	$49

Mount Sterling | 350 Silver Lake Dr. | 859-498-4697 | www.oldsilo.com | 6977/5509; 74.5/67.8; 139/125

"Bring your best sand game or stay home" warn those who've tackled this "challenging" design from Champions Tour player Graham Marsh that features "hilly" terrain strewn with bunkers and a meandering creek; offering "nice views" of the horse country east of Lexington, this future site of the 2007 U.S. Open Qualifier is a "scenic", "affordable" course; N.B. stop by historic Mount Sterling before or after your round.

Louisiana

Baton Rouge

Bluffs, The

COURSE	FACIL.	SERVICE	VALUE	COST
25	20	19	20	$115

Saint Francisville | Hwy. 965 at Freeland Rd. | 225-634-5222 | www.thebluffs.com | 7184/4781; 75.3/68.6; 150/117

"Be patient, you will find it" reassure fans of this "remote" Arnold Palmer design that's "hard to get to" but "worth the drive" 40 miles northeast of Baton Rouge; you'll "feel like you're playing in the woods" as you walk this "beautiful, well-maintained course" that's routed over diverse, "rolling terrain" not typical of these parts; four sets of tees make it "user-friendly" for all levels, and it now boasts an "impressive new clubhouse" to go with its B&B-style lodgings.

Carter Plantation

COURSE	FACIL.	SERVICE	VALUE	COST
24	25	23	23	$95

Springfield | 23475 Carter Trace | 225-294-7555 | www.carterplantation.com | 7049/5057; 74.4/69.8; 140/122

This "interesting" destination may be "hard to find" 45 minutes east of Baton Rouge ("get explicit instructions"), but "once you're out on the course, you'll know it's worth it"; the spread provides "quality golf" on a layout that's routed over woods and wetlands "with some reachable par 5s" and water on 11 holes; a "great clubhouse" and "wonderful" villa accommodations also help to make it a "favorite."

	COURSE	FACIL.	SERVICE	VALUE	COST

Copper Mill

| | – | – | – | – | $55 |

Zachary | 2100 Copper Mill Blvd. | 225-658-0656 | www.coppermillgolf.com | 6902/4693; 73.7/67.6; 133/111

Featuring wide fairways that traverse grasslands, lakes and the Cypress Bayou, this newcomer 25 miles north of Baton Rouge is "very flat but nevertheless" quite "memorable" thanks to its inclusion of "three holes each of par 3s, 4s and 5s" "on each nine"; "not every hole" on this "open, linksy" spread "is great, but most are", leading at least one clubber to conclude the "creative layout" will only "get better as it matures."

Lake Charles

Gray Plantation

| | ▽ 25 | 22 | 24 | 25 | $41 |

Lake Charles | 6150 Graywood Pkwy. | 337-562-1663 | www.graywoodllc.com | 7233/5392; 75/71.9; 138/128

One of the "best courses in southwestern Louisiana", this spread near Lake Charles serves up "old-fashioned Southern hospitality" with just a tinge of "country-club" attitude; "always in great shape", the "beautiful" layout features tree-lined fairways, well-bunkered greens and water on 12 holes (the "mosquitos are as big as birds"); all in all, it's a "very nice course for the money", especially given a recent clubhouse expansion.

New Orleans

NEW Atchafalaya at Idlewild

| | – | – | – | – | $65 |

Patterson | 400 Cotten Rd. | 985-395-4653 | www.atchafalayagolf.com | 7533/5263; 77.6/71.8; 144/127

Stretching 7,533 yards, this Robert von Hagge behemoth 90 miles west of New Orleans tops off its longer front with a massive 50-yard-long green that's shared by the 9th and 18th holes; the 2005 Cajun country creation offers spectacular elevation changes on a layout that features no residential development and is part of Louisiana's environmentally friendly Audubon Golf Trail; N.B. a clubhouse is slated to open in 2007.

TPC Louisiana

| | 24 | 24 | 24 | 19 | $125 |

Avondale | 11001 Lapalco Blvd. | 504-436-8721 | 866-665-2872 | www.tpc.com | 7520/5121; 76.6/69.7; 138/119

Recently reopened after renovations to repair Katrina damage, this "tough" Pete Dye design in Avondale is "coming back well": landscaping has restored the "great scenery", the clubhouse has been redone and the look of four holes has been enhanced; its "hospitable" pre-hurricane staff has also made a return, as will the PGA Tour in April 2007; N.B. the course has yet to receive updated ratings from the USGA.

Maine

Central Maine

Z Belgrade Lakes 朩

| | 28 | 17 | 24 | 20 | $110 |

Belgrade Lakes | West Rd. at Clubhouse Dr. | 207-495-4653 | www.belgradelakesgolf.com | 6723/5168; 72.2/64.1; 135/126

This "don't-miss experience" north of Augusta is "one of the most spectacular courses you'll find", a "beautiful" layout where you "can't help but notice the lake views"; kept "in incredible condition", the "unique" spread is strewn with stones and boulders that golfers "love" even as the rocks "rocket the ball into the next county"; it has a "friendly staff" but "limited facilities" (there's "no driving range"), which can make it seem a tad "pricey" to some.

Kebo Valley

▽ 24 | 17 | 19 | 21 | $76

Bar Harbor | Eagle Lake Rd. | 207-288-3000 | www.kebovalleyclub.com | 6131/5473; 69.5/72.6; 124/128

Exemplifying "New England quirkiness at its finest", "the eighth oldest course in the country" "maintains its charm and allure" as it rolls "over beautiful terrain" "at the base of Cadillac Mountain"; "old-fashioned" but "challenging", this "prestigious" 1888 course features "a beast of a par-4 8th" along with "a mammoth sand trap" on the 17th; though it can "feel like you're paying a lot for its cachet", "new construction" – including a practice area – "promises even more fun."

Sugarloaf

26 | 22 | 23 | 20 | $115

Carrabassett Valley | 5092 Access Rd. | 207-237-2000 | 800-843-5623 | www.sugarloaf.com | 6910/5289; 74.4/72.5; 151/131

Nestled in a valley in northwestern Maine, this "remote" Robert Trent Jones Jr. design is a "very tight, unforgiving" course that's so "wild", you're advised to "bring extra balls"; a "great spot for fall golf", the "spectacular" resort course has a six-hole stretch along the Carrabassett River and "incredible views" of the surrounding mountains; although a few say "conditions need to improve", most feel it's a "hidden gem"; P.S. there's "a very good chance" you'll spy a moose.

NEW Sunday River

▽ 28 | 24 | 19 | 22 | $95

Newry | 18 Championship Dr. | 207-824-4653 | www.sundayriver.com | 7130/5006; 75.2/60.2; 146/118

Even though they "wish it weren't so far" away in western Maine, those who've played this "excellent new course" from RTJ Jr. just "can't wait to go back"; they advise first-timers to bring their "long shots to find the greens", as this "awesome" layout is packed with undulating fairways, severe sloping and forced carries over ravines; it also boasts "superior views" of the mountains and "good resort facilities."

Southern Maine

Dunegrass

25 | 20 | 20 | 23 | $79

Old Orchard Beach | 200 Wild Dunes Way | 207-934-4513 | 800-521-1029 | www.dunegrass.com | 6684/4818; 72.1/68; 137/113

For "a taste of Carolina in Maine" – think rolling terrain and pine trees – head to this "beautiful" layout that's "one of the better courses" in the state's southern reaches; "you almost never see another hole from the one you're on" as you traverse this "woody" wonder featuring "fast greens" and "tight fairways" laced with waste bunkers and ravines; P.S. the coastal setting can be "very wet", so expect "lots of mosquitos."

Ledges, The

25 | 20 | 21 | 21 | $65

York | 1 Ledges Dr. | 207-351-3000 | www.ledgesgolf.com | 6981/4997; 74/70.9; 138/126

Set on the rugged hillsides of southeastern Maine, this "cunning course" is carved from rock to have "lots of elevation change" and panoramic views of the surrounding area; with a tree-filled front and an open, windy back, the seasonal spread features "tough", "lightning-fast greens" that are as much of "a real challenge" as the "618-yard finishing hole"; ledge-sitters insist there's "not a lot of ambiance", but overall it's a "great" option.

Samoset

24	21	21	20	$130

Rockport | 220 Warrenton St. | 207-594-2511 | 800-341-1650 | www.samoset.com | 6548/5083; 70.8/70.2; 133/120

"No wonder they call this the Pebble Beach of the East" – you'll "play along the Atlantic on this spectacular" southeast Maine layout that provides "postcard views" of Penobscot Bay from 14 of its holes; the linksy spread is a bit "short" and gets "crowded in season, but it's worth it" to visit a "beautiful course" that also boasts "very good practice facilities" and a resort "stay-and-play package that includes dinner" at the upscale, on-site Marcel's.

Maryland

TOP COURSES IN STATE

29 Bulle Rock | *Baltimore*
28 Links at Lighthouse Sound | *Ocean City*
26 Beechtree | *Baltimore*
  Atlantic Golf at Queenstown, River | *Easton*
25 Rum Pointe | *Ocean City*

Baltimore

Beechtree

26	23	22	22	$95

Aberdeen | 811 S. Stepney Rd. | 410-297-9700 | 877-233-2487 | www.beechtreegolf.com | 7023/5363; 75.1/71.1; 142/126

This "great Tom Doak layout" is "well worth" the trip north of Baltimore for its "two very different nines": an "open but challenging" links-style front and a parkland back that plays through stately hardwoods; this "purist's delight" features "firm, fast greens" and "plenty of challenging holes" that are kept "in immaculate condition"; although it's "pricey", swingers say it's "almost as good as [nearby] Bulle Rock for half the price" – so "do yourself a favor and play this course twice."

⛳ Bulle Rock 🏌

29	26	26	20	$145

Havre de Grace | 320 Blenheim Ln. | 410-939-8887 | 888-285-5375 | www.bullerock.com | 7375/5426; 76.4/72; 147/126

"Everything you ever imagined and more", this "spectacular Pete Dye design" "can bully the best of players" with its "killer inclines" and "rough so dense you'll wish for a machete"; host of the LPGA Championship, the layout is ranked "best in the state" in this year's Survey courtesy of its "immaculate" course conditions, "first-class facilities" and service that's "off the charts"; sure, it's "expensive" and situated "in the middle of nowhere" northeast of Baltimore, but surveyors say it's "a must-play for serious golfers" in search of the "ultimate experience."

	COURSE	FACIL.	SERVICE	VALUE	COST

Greystone
`24` `23` `20` `24` `$74`

White Hall | 2115 White Hall Rd. | 410-887-1945 |
www.baltimoregolfing.com | 6925/4800; 73.5/67.5; 139/112

Situated "a long way from anywhere" in the "beautiful" horse country north of Baltimore, this "tough track" from designer Joe Lee is the "best value in the state"; "difficult" "but not overdone", the "fun" lay-out is laced with 80-plus bunkers and "thick rough" plus a number of "challenging par 3s"; a "courteous and helpful staff" works to keep it in "fine condition", which may be why some say it "feels more like a private club" than a county-owned course.

Timbers at Troy
`20` `17` `18` `21` `$45`

Elkridge | 6100 Marshalee Dr. | 410-313-4653 | www.timbersgolf.com |
6652/4865; 73.5/68.8; 138/114

"Leave the driver in the bag on the tree-lined fairways" of this "solid" countryside course southwest of Baltimore that has "good stuff for a muni", including just "enough challenge" as well as bentgrass turf from tee to green; although golfers agree it's "not one of the greatest" – the grounds can get "torn apart by heavy play" and there are just "too many houses and more all the time" – it remains an "interesting" option at a reasonable price.

Waverly Woods
`23` `18` `19` `20` `$79`

Marriottsville | 2100 Warwick Way | 410-313-9182 |
www.waverlywoods.com | 7024/4808; 73.1/67.8; 132/115

"A real hidden charm near Charm City", this "nice Arthur Hills design" in Marriottsville is a "challenging", "upscale daily fee" that rolls over the countryside, "requiring your best effort" as you tackle its "long, narrow fairways", "blind approaches" and "very fast greens"; still, although some "haven't found a flaw yet", a minority points to "pricey" fees, facilities that "need improvement" and "too many townhouses that ruin the views."

Cumberland

Rocky Gap Lodge ⌂
`24` `18` `17` `21` `$80`

Flintstone | 16701 Lakeview Rd. NE | 301-784-8500 | 800-724-8208 |
www.rockygapresort.com | 7002/5198; 74.2/70; 142/129

"The only Jack Nicklaus–designed course in the state", this "pleasant surprise" is "worth the trip" to "out-of-the-way" western Maryland's Rocky Gap State Park; a "drop-dead gorgeous" resort destination for "fun mountain golf", this "challenging" "range of holes" offers "dramatic elevation" changes on its wooded front, "hilly fairways" on the back and views of Evitt's Mountain and Lake Habeeb throughout.

DC Metro Area

Atlantic Golf at South River
`23` `20` `21` `17` `$91`

Edgewater | 3451 Solomons Island Rd. | 410-798-5865 | 800-767-4837 |
www.mdgolf.com | 6723/4935; 72.3/70.5; 138/123

It's "pretty far from the DC metro area, but once you arrive" at this "enjoyable" if "pricey" Edgewater layout, you'll find "a tremendous amount of nature" – mature trees, water, wildflowers – that belies its routing "through a neighborhood"; while the back nine of this "envi-

| | COURSE | FACIL. | SERVICE | VALUE | COST |

ronmentally friendly" layout has wetlands on seven of its holes (which can be "a little maddening" for those who dub it "target golf"), a "friendly" staff is available to soothe frayed nerves.

Swan Point   ▽ 22 | 20 | 21 | 20 | $80

Issue | 11550 Swan Point Blvd. | 301-259-0047 | www.swanpointgolf.com | 6859/4992; 73.1/69.3; 130/116

"As close to the Carolinas as you'll get this far north", this "hidden gem" on the shores of the southern Potomac River near Issue has a distinctly Lowcountry look with "lots of marsh and water" on its "wide fairways"; although veterans vent it's "like night and day compared to last year's staff and course" ("especially the normally beautiful" putting surfaces), you'll nevertheless appreciate a unique Bob Cupp design that includes a par-3 11th with a wraparound bunker that surrounds the green.

University of Maryland Golf Course   18 | 15 | 17 | 21 | $57

College Park | University of Maryland | 301-314-4653 | www.golf.umd.edu | 6759/5525; 71.6/71.7; 125/120

"Go Terps!" cheer alums who say "it's great to go back and play" this 1958 design that's a "solid" choice "for an inexpensive and challenging outing" 30 minutes northeast of DC; mature trees line the "rolling fairways" on a "variety of holes", but swingers say the "enjoyable but not exceptional" layout "can have drainage issues" and is "showing its age", despite the recent addition of a short-game practice area.

Easton

Atlantic Golf at Queenstown Harbor, Lakes   23 | 20 | 22 | 20 | $84

Queenstown | 310 Links Ln. | 410-827-6611 | 800-827-5257 | www.mdgolf.com | 6569/4606; 71/66.8; 126/108

"Almost the equal of the River course", this "challenging Eastern Shore" layout is located just across the bridge from Annapolis; the "lush" woodlander is "enjoyable for all levels of play" and features water on 15 of its "well-maintained" holes; a few find the facilities "so-so", but it's considered "well worth" the greens fee given a "friendly, helpful staff" and "magnificent Chesapeake Bay views."

Atlantic Golf at Queenstown Harbor, River   26 | 20 | 21 | 19 | $109

Queenstown | 310 Links Ln. | 410-827-6611 | 800-827-5257 | www.mdgolf.com | 7110/5026; 74.2/69.4; 137/123

"Francis Scott Key watched the bombs bursting in air" at nearby Ft. McHenry, but you can "launch your own bombs" on this "picturesque" "test" an hour north of Easton; "beautiful Chesapeake Bay vistas" and "perfect conditions" abound at this "enjoyable experience" that offers "challenging approach shots" as it "winds around" the Chester River; though it's "crowded" and "a little pricey", "the fee is small in relation to the quality of the golf."

Hog Neck   21 | 17 | 18 | 23 | $70

Easton | 10142 Old Cordova Rd. | 410-822-6079 | 800-280-1790 | www.hogneck.com | 7049/5435; 73.7/71.3; 131/125

For a "fun time with few crowds", take a detour to this "unexpectedly interesting" Eastern Shore muni that's "an excellent value for what it

	COURSE	FACIL.	SERVICE	VALUE	COST

is", which happens to be "two completely different nines": the front is "out in the open" with water views, while the back is "in the trees"; though one nitpicker notes that the "service is not up to its usual good standards", you'll nonetheless "enjoy the stroll" on this "older", "woman-friendly" course.

River Marsh ♨

	24	25	23	19	$140

Cambridge | 100 Heron Blvd. | 410-901-6397 | www.chesapeakebay.hyatt.com | 6801/4780; 72.5/67.8; 127/111

"Convenient to DC and Baltimore but miles away from city attitude", this "tough but doable" Keith Foster design is part of a "wonderful", "family-friendly resort" on the Eastern Shore; the experience "will cost you", but it's "worth it" for a "beautiful", "well-maintained course" whose wide fairways skirt the Choptank River; still, at least one swinger finds it "too modern, especially the 17th" (with a long carry over Shoal Creek) – "one Sawgrass 17th is enough."

Frederick

Maryland National ♨

	25	21	22	21	$94

Middletown | 8836 Hollow Rd. | 301-371-0000 | www.marylandnational.com | 6811/4844; 73.1/68.3; 137/120

"Worth the drive" to "the middle of nowhere" in central Maryland, this "awesome" Arthur Hills design serves up "loads of fun" on its "immaculate fairways"; expect "heavy slanting", "long carries" over wetlands and "elevation changes to make you dizzy" on a "rolling" layout that some duffers deem an "unfair test" – "there isn't a flat lie anywhere"; nevertheless, all agree that the "splendid views" of the Catoctin Mountains help to make it a "hidden gem."

P.B. Dye

	22	21	21	18	$89

Ijamsville | 9526 Doctor Perry Rd. | 301-607-4653 | www.pbdyegolf.com | 7036/4900; 74.2/68.3; 140/123

With enough "typical Pete Dye railroad ties" that "you expect the engine to come around the corner at any moment", this "imaginative" P.B. Dye design begs the question – "like father, like son?"; it's a "fun" hillside frolic near Frederick, but the architect's "diabolical", "bowling-alley-fast greens" and what some say are "too many blind shots" have a few duffers dubbing it "gimmicky" and "close to unfair"; nevertheless, with "replay only $20" and "bargain twilight rates", you may find it "worth the pain."

Whiskey Creek ♨

	25	23	22	19	$97

Ijamsville | 4804 Whiskey Ct. | 301-694-2900 | 888-883-1174 | www.whiskeycreekgolf.com | 7001/5296; 74.5/70.5; 137/121

"Truly an out-of-the-way experience" "nestled at the foot" of the Catoctin Mountains near Frederick, this "magnificent" "local gem" is "tough but fair": "thoughtfully designed" by architect J. Michael Poellot and consultant Ernie Els, it "rewards good play and punishes errant shots"; it also provides players with "marvelous vistas" plus "one of the most memorable finishing holes anywhere" (a par-5 18th with "charming" "whiskey shed ruins splitting the fairway"); meanwhile, a "modern clubhouse" and "attentive service" add up to a "country-club atmosphere."

	COURSE	FACIL.	SERVICE	VALUE	COST

Worthington Manor

	23	18	19	22	$79

Urbana | 8329 Fingerboard Rd. | 301-874-5400 |
www.worthingtonmanor.com | 7034/5206; 74.4/70.1; 144/116

"The slickest greens around" characterize this site of the 2006 U.S.
Open Qualifier that's "beautifully laid out in the hills near Frederick";
"well worth the drive north from DC", the "challenging" "mix of holes"
"alternately requires precision and power" and is "a bit open" with its
"sloping fairways" and "lovely vistas"; though the facilities seem to
some to be "merely a place to pay", the fees themselves make it one
of the "best values" on the I-270 corridor.

Ocean City

Eagle's Landing

	23	17	18	22	$90

Berlin | 12367 Eagles Nest Rd. | 410-213-7277 | 800-283-3846 |
www.eagleslandinggolf.com | 7003/4896; 73.6/67.9; 126/112

"While you're at the beach", head to this "favorite near Ocean City", a
"beautifully manicured" muni that offers "challenges" as it "winds
through" wetlands and natural grasses; "the marsh holes are some of
the most memorable anywhere" and this "very scenic" spread has
"beautiful vistas" of Assateague Island and Sinepuxent Bay to match;
although the "lack of a driving range hurts", it's "still a great value."

☑ Links at Lighthouse Sound 🏌

	28	25	25	19	$169

Bishopville | 12723 St. Martins Neck Rd. | 410-352-5767 |
www.lighthousesound.com | 7031/4553; 73.3/67.1; 144/107

"One of the best in the region", "hands down", this "picturesque"
"bayside beauty" from Arthur Hills is "as scenic as coastal golf gets"
courtesy of a "windy" front nine with "incredible views" of Assawoman
Bay and the Ocean City skyline; while the wooded, wetland-laced back
is "plain" in comparison, it is just as "wonderfully manicured" and features "long boardwalks over the marsh"; regular fees can be "pricey",
but twilight rates are "a real value at $50."

Ocean City Golf Club, Newport Bay

	20	20	19	21	$105

Berlin | 11401 Country Club Dr. | 410-641-1779 | 800-442-3570 |
www.ocgolfandyacht.com | 6657/5205; 71/71.5; 126/119

A "classic course updated nicely" in 1998, this "pleasurable golfing
experience" just west of Ocean City is now a "nice", "not so long" layout with a few "very interesting holes"; although the entire spread is
kept in "great shape", the back nine is "breathtaking" as it rambles
along the Sinepuxent Bay with "beautiful views" of the water; just
"don't forget the bug spray" – the facility is "not too crowded" with
people, but "the mosquitos will eat you alive."

River Run

	20	16	19	19	$92

Berlin | 11605 Masters Ln. | 410-641-7200 | 800-733-7786 |
www.riverrungolf.com | 6705/4818; 72.1/69.5; 136/124

This "scenic" Gary Player design "fits its name" with a routing along
the St. Martin's River near Ocean City and "lots of water" on its "beautifully landscaped" grounds; with "tight greens" and a "unique style"
that's loaded with links-style mounding on the front and marshes and
pine trees on the back, it's an "interesting layout" that will "make you
think" but is "not too difficult"; P.S. it's a "great value" at twilight.

| | COURSE | FACIL. | SERVICE | VALUE | COST |

Rum Pointe

`25` `21` `22` `21` `$129`

Berlin | 7000 Rum Pointe Ln. | 410-629-1414 | 888-809-4653 |
www.rumpointe.com | 7001/5276; 72.6/70.3; 122/120

"Bring lots of golf balls" to this Pete and P.B. Dye "masterpiece" near
Ocean City, as "old Blackbeard the pirate will gobble them up" on the
many "outstanding bayside holes" that offer "awesome views" of the
Sinepuxent; the "fantastic" wide-open links layout is "challenging
without being tricked-up", although its "beauty can be a distraction"
and "when the wind blows, it's a bear"; "comfortable facilities" and an
"accommodating" staff are two more reasons it's a "must-play."

Massachusetts

TOP COURSES IN STATE

`28` Taconic | *Berkshires*

Crumpin-Fox | *Berkshires*

`27` Ranch | *Springfield*

Pinehills, Nicklaus | *Boston*

`26` Blackstone Nat'l | *Worcester*

Berkshires

☒ Crumpin-Fox

`28` `21` `24` `24` `$71`

Bernardston | Parmenter Rd. | 413-648-9101 | 800-943-1901 |
www.golfthefox.com | 7007/5432; 73.8/71.5; 141/131

"Why did they put one of the country's great courses in the middle of
nowhere?" ask aficionados of this "hidden gem" nestled in "the beautiful Berkshires foothills" "near the Vermont border"; with a "tremendous routing" through rolling, "forested terrain", this "monster of a
course" offers an "unusual" "mix of holes" that includes "carries
across water" and a par-5 8th that "will make or break your round";
P.S. "sate all of your appetites" with their "excellently priced" golf
and dinner package.

☒ Taconic ⊙

`28` `19` `21` `21` `$145`

Williamstown | 19 Meacham St. | 413-458-3997 | www.taconicgolf.com |
6640/5202; 72.5/70.2; 129/121

"A crisp fall day at Taconic is about as good as it gets" aver admirers
of this "beautiful, old-style New England" layout – built in 1896 –
where "real golf is played"; voted Massachusetts' top-rated Course,
this "gem of the Berkshires" is "a pleasure through and through" courtesy of its "magnificent setting", "fabulous views", "pristine fairways"
and "lightning-fast greens"; sure, it can be "tough to get a tee time, but
it's worth the effort"; N.B. Williams College students, alumni and staff
receive deep discounts.

Boston

Atlantic Country Club

`21` `18` `19` `22` `$58`

Plymouth | 450 Little Sandy Pond Rd. | 508-759-6644 |
www.atlanticcountryclub.com | 6728/4918; 73/68.3; 131/116

"Worth the twisting ride" south from Boston, this "solid" "test" in historic Plymouth is "not as glamorous as other area courses" (read:

Pinehills), but you'll "usually leave [here] with a good feeling" – although minus "a few lost golf balls"; some thrill-seekers say it's "boring", but the layout's tight, hilly fairways are kept "in pretty good shape" and pilgrims praise it as one of "the best values" around.

Granite Links at Quarry Hills 🏞⏱   22 | 20 | 18 | 14 | $120

Quincy | 100 Quarry Hills Dr. | 617-689-1900 | www.granitelinksgolfclub.com | 6818/5001; 73.4/70.6; 141/124

The "best thing" about this "unique" course "designed around an old quarry" is "its proximity to Boston", so expect "stunning views of the city skyline" from its "open", "links-style" holes; to some, it seems "tricked-up" and "way too windy", but most consider the granite-laced layout to be a "fun", "fair test"; either way, "you'll pay through the nose", although swingers say the "twilight golf is a steal"; N.B. there are three nines, with Granite and Milton open to the public and Quincy remaining members-only until May 2007.

Olde Scotland Links   ▽ 21 | 11 | 16 | 24 | $48

Bridgewater | 695 Pine St. | 508-279-3344 | www.oldescotlandlinks.com | 6790/4949; 72.6/68.4; 126/111

"It's not Olde and it's not in Scotland" but "bring your kilt and your driver" anyway, because this town-owned track 30 miles south of Boston "is links golf at its most fun" with windy, wide-open fairways and sloping greens that are "always a challenge"; although the "facilities are not nice at all", "don't let that fool you" – "the course is a treat", offering "plenty of surprises" and a "greens fee that's hard to beat."

Pinehills, Jones   25 | 26 | 23 | 19 | $100

Plymouth | 54 Clubhouse Dr. | 508-209-3000 | 866-855-4653 | www.pinehillsgolf.com | 7175/5380; 73.8/71.2; 135/125

Head to this glacially carved Rees Jones design to see just "what an Ice Age can do for a golf course"; the "high-end" layout is "a guaranteed good time" "from tee to green", but players should brace themselves for "blind shots, uneven lies" and fairways that are "narrower than on the Nicklaus course"; some say it's "simply too unforgiving", but given its "phenomenal practice facilities", most agree it's "worth the steep prices" and 40-mile "haul [south] from Boston."

Pinehills, Nicklaus   27 | 26 | 24 | 21 | $100

Plymouth | 54 Clubhouse Dr. | 508-209-3000 | 866-855-4653 | www.pinehillsgolf.com | 7243/5185; 74.3/69.4; 135/123

It was actually "designed by Jack's son", but "the name [still] says it all" at this "incredible" if "expensive" course that's considered "prettier and more player-friendly than its sister, Jones"; the jacked-up layout "flows nicely" through white pines and wetlands and proves an "excellent challenge" for all levels – just be sure to "keep the ball straight" if you hope to reach the "awesome greens"; better yet, there's a "great clubhouse" and "amazing practice area" to make it even more of "a pleasure."

Poquoy Brook   23 | 17 | 20 | 25 | $48

Lakeville | 20 Leonard St. | 508-947-5261 | www.poquoybrook.com | 6762/5415; 72.4/71; 128/114

"The trees and the hills make for fabulous views" on this "solid" "old course" (built in 1962) located "an hour [south] of Boston"; "other than the 3rd tee being four feet from the road", it's a "pretty", "well-maintained" layout with "wide" fairways, large greens and "some difficult finishing holes"; it's also "reasonably priced", but "watch out for the blackflies" – there are "more bugs [here] than at Watergate."

Cape Cod

Ballymeade 🖳 ⊙

19 | 21 | 19 | 17 | $75

North Falmouth | 125 Falmouth Woods Rd. | 508-540-4005 | www.ballymeade.com | 6928/4871; 74.7/69.6; 140/123

"Keep it on the fairway or kiss your score and your balls goodbye" on this "short but quite demanding" layout whose "tight", "hilly" holes are "lined with scrub pine"; some find this 1989 Jim Fazio/Chi Chi Rodriguez redesign to be "tricked-up" and "confusing" – "countless blind shots" make it "frustrating to play" – but it's nevertheless a "gorgeous course" sprinkled with "scenic" Cape Cod vistas; P.S. "summer rates make this no bargain."

Brookside

20 | 20 | 22 | 22 | $65

Bourne | 11 Brigadoon Rd. | 508-743-4653 | www.thebrooksideclub.com | 6400/5130; 71.1/69.6; 126/118

"Bring your mountain climbing gear", as this "hilly" 1996 redesign located just over the Bourne Bridge has few flat lies, thick rough and "some blind shots" that will have you scanning the sky "for flying balls"; golfers gripe that "housing construction" is diminishing this "beautiful", "well-maintained" layout, but there appear to be no complaints about the "friendly staff" or a clubhouse that provides panoramic views of the Cape Cod Canal.

Captains, Port

21 | 18 | 18 | 23 | $62

Brewster | 1000 Freemans Way | 508-896-1716 | 877-843-9081 | www.captainsgolfcourse.com | 6724/5282; 73.5/71.1; 130/119

"A good way to spend the day", this "classic Cape Cod" layout – "along with its Starboard companion" – is one of "the nicest town-owned courses" around, boasting a newly installed irrigation system on its "tremendous variety of holes"; the "pretty, challenging" spread is "fair" and "player-friendly", but both the 573-yard par-5 8th and "summer crowds" may just "make you cry"; P.S. for an even better "value", "take advantage of the twilight specials."

Captains, Starboard

22 | 19 | 19 | 23 | $62

Brewster | 1000 Freemans Way | 508-896-1716 | 877-843-9081 | www.captainsgolfcourse.com | 6776/5359; 72.6/71.2; 130/116

"Among the best public courses the Cape has to offer", this "nice" woodlander is part of a "superb 36-hole facility" in Brewster; vacationers vouch for the "nice variety of challenges" on this "well-maintained" layout that's as "great as its sister, Port", if slightly longer and with "very friendly greens"; though "especially crowded in the summer" and "slow on weekends", it's an overall "fun" experience.

Cranberry Valley

24 | 18 | 18 | 23 | $60

Harwich | 183 Oak St. | 508-430-5234 | www.cranberrygolfcourse.com | 6482/5568; 71.6/72.2; 127/124

One of the "best use of tax dollars on the Cape" is this "relaxing 18" in Harwich that's "not too tough" but "can challenge from the back tees";

although "plagued by slow play" "in summer" – "book an early tee time" – the "solid public course" is always "well-manicured" (with "lots of green foliage") and has recently redone its bunkers and added new practice facilities; P.S. it's "perfect for a family foursome", especially at such "an excellent price."

Dennis Pines

| 22 | 17 | 18 | 22 | $55 |

East Dennis | 50 Golf Course Rd. | 508-385-8347 | www.dennisgolf.com | 7000/5567; 74.4/73.1; 135/133

"Set amid the pines of Cape Cod", this "well-run municipal course" is "worth the trip" to East Dennis for "a challenge" that "starts easy and gets tougher as you go"; the "beautiful" 1965 layout is "hilly" and "tight" with "narrow fairways", several of which "slope sideways toward a central lake"; "despite lots of play" "during the busy summer months", it's generally "in great condition" – "much improved over past years" – and always "an excellent value."

Olde Barnstable Fairgrounds

| 23 | 17 | 19 | 21 | $60 |

Marstons Mills | 1460 Rte. 149 | 508-420-1141 | www.obfgolf.com | 6479/5122; 71.4/69.1; 128/119

"A good bet when visiting Cape Cod", this "varied" Mark Mungeam design doles out "sufficient challenge" while proving "not impossible for the average player"; although surveyors say that the facilities and service lag behind at this municipal layout, "that is secondary" to the course's conditions (it's "always in shape") and its "great location" in Marstons Mills with "no homes along the fairways to detract from the experience."

Martha's Vineyard

Farm Neck

| 26 | 21 | 21 | 20 | $145 |

Oak Bluffs | 1 Farm Neck Way | 508-693-3057 | 6815/4987; 72.8/68.4; 135/121

"Any place Bill Clinton plays is good enough for me" fawn fans of this "memorable" Martha's Vineyard layout where "the front nine is wooded with pines" and the back nine "moves out toward the salt ponds and ocean", providing "spectacular water views" and "a more-than-adequate test when the sea breeze is up"; though detractors describe it as "pricey" and "tough to get on in summer", it's "well worth" the trouble; P.S. be sure to "stay for lunch" at the "hidden gem" of a clubhouse restaurant.

Nantucket

Miacomet

| 21 | 17 | 18 | 18 | $95 |

Nantucket | 12 W. Miacomet Rd. | 508-325-0333 | www.miacometgolf.com | 6831/5159; 73/69.6; 123/118

"Expanded from nine to 18 holes" in 2003, this "terrific" daily fee offers the only "opportunity to play great golf on Nantucket without being the friend of a billionaire"; although it now feels "like two different courses" (with wider fairways and larger greens on the new front), it still sports the same "beautiful water views" to take the edge off the "overpriced" fees; N.B. the older nine is currently being renovated and will reopen in fall 2007.

Springfield

Ranch, The
27 | 26 | 24 | 20 | $110

Southwick | 65 Sunnyside Rd. | 413-569-9315 | 866-790-9333 |
www.theranchgolfclub.com | 7171/4983; 74.1/69.7; 140/122

"One of New England's best", this "exceptional" links layout holds "a special place" in the hearts of those who appreciate its "very hilly but playable" Pioneer Valley terrain – especially on the "wild 9th"; given its "excellent conditioning" and a "friendly staff" that "prides itself" on the service it provides at the "great clubhouse" and "first-rate practice facilities", it's "well worth the drive [west] from Boston"; P.S. the "pricey" fees include "carts with helpful GPS."

Worcester

Blackstone National
26 | 19 | 20 | 18 | $79

Sutton | 227 Putnam Hill Rd. | 508-865-2111 | www.bngc.net |
6909/5203; 73.5/70; 132/122

Though "a wee bit hard to get to" in the Blackstone Valley near Worcester, this "surprisingly nice" Rees Jones design represents "golf as it should be": "deep in the woods", "free of road noise and houses"; make sure to "get a cart", however, as it's a "long", "hilly" walk between each of the "distinct holes" and "elevation changes are a factor"; although some find the experience "kind of pricey for central Massachusetts", most agree you're getting "a great value for the $$$."

Cyprian Keyes
24 | 22 | 23 | 20 | $64

Boylston | 284 E. Temple St. | 508-869-9900 | www.cypriankeyes.com |
6871/5029; 74.4/71.2; 136/126

"Bring your A-game" but "leave your driver at home" to play this "woodsy" layout that's "worth the ride to central Massachusetts" for "target golf at its best": the "quirky", "memorable" Mark Mungeam design has "lots of elevation changes" with "little room for wayward shots" – "miss the fairway or rough and good luck finding your ball in the trees"; plus, "everyone is treated like a VIP" and there's a "family-friendly par-3 course on-site."

Red Tail
26 | 15 | 19 | 19 | $95

Devens | 15 Bulge Rd. | 978-772-3273 | www.redtailgolf.net |
7006/5049; 73.9/69.4; 138/120

A "hidden jewel in the middle of nowhere" north of Worcester, this "challenging" course "makes you think a bit about" your "target shots" via "interesting illusions" (e.g. "lots of sand that doesn't necessarily come into play"); the tight, tree-lined track also features "fun" remnants from its days as a "former military base" – the 17th has both "a huge waste bunker *and* an [old] artillery bunker" – and they've just completed work on a "nice" new clubhouse.

Shaker Hills
24 | 22 | 19 | 19 | $85

Harvard | 146 Shaker Rd. | 978-772-2227 | www.shakerhills.com |
6850/4999; 74/69.8; 137/122

"Is there a prettier course to play in October?" muse those who "love" this "scenic" spread northeast of Worcester that "makes great use of the natural landscape" on each of its "distinct holes" – think "long fair-

	COURSE	FACIL.	SERVICE	VALUE	COST

ways" with "lots of rock outcroppings", pine trees and "elevation changes"; all in all, though some shake their heads at the "uptight" service, the layout itself is "clean", "well-manicured" and "very fair for players of all abilities" – "a rarity."

Stow Acres, North
20 | 17 | 16 | 19 | $60

Stow | 58 Randall Rd. | 978-568-8690 | www.stowacres.com | 7035/5936; 74.2/74.4; 131/132

Though "a bit of a drive [west] from Boston", the "more difficult of the two" courses at Stow Acres is "worth the trip" for a "fun and challenging" day of golf on an "open", "tree-lined" layout that may not be "especially imaginative" but is nevertheless "always reliable"; still, the "solid public facility" can get "played to death" "on the weekends", which prompts critics to claim this "classic" "needs a face-lift" "to compete with the newer daily fees."

Wachusett
▽ 20 | 18 | 18 | 22 | $40

West Boylston | 187 Prospect St. | 508-835-2264 | www.wachusettcc.com | 6567/5573; 71.7/74.6; 124/121

One of the "best values in central Massachusetts" may just be this 1927 Donald Ross design that boasts "beautiful vistas" of Mount Wachusett and the nearby reservoir; family-owned and -operated for almost 70 years, this "fine" "test" is "always a good time" – especially when you're sipping some of the "coldest draft beer anywhere" on the outdoor deck; it "looks tired" to some fussy foozlers, but the majority considers it a "bang for the buck."

Michigan

TOP COURSES IN STATE

Bay City

Lakewood Shores, Gailes
▽ 28 | 18 | 19 | 23 | $63

Oscoda | 7751 Cedar Lake Rd. | 989-739-2073 | 800-882-2493 | www.lakewoodshores.com | 6954/5246; 75/72.2; 138/122

"This is pretty darn close to playing in Scotland" insist swingers who appreciate this "true links experience" nestled in a "very out-of-the-way location" next to Lake Huron nearly two hours north of Bay City; the longest and oldest of three resort courses, this "very difficult" design can get windy and features deep, sod-faced bunkers, thick rough and tall fescue; P.S. grab one of the "great" off-season deals.

Red Hawk
▽ 27 | 23 | 25 | 25 | $89

East Tawas | 350 W. Davison Rd. | 989-362-0800 | www.redhawkgolf.net | 6589/4883; 71.6/69; 139/120

A "must-play any time you're in Michigan", this "lush", "beautiful" woodlander is "worth the trip" 90 minutes north of Bay City; the short Arthur Hills design traverses ridgetops, valleys and wetlands, so expect varied terrain and plenty of elevation as well as "great greens" that allow you to "shoot at the pins"; before you head home, stop at the Red Hawk Grill, which overlooks the 1st, 10th and 18th holes.

Detroit

Majestic at Lake Walden ⌂
23 | 17 | 16 | 18 | $69

Hartland | 9600 Crouse Rd. | 810-632-5235 | 800-762-3280 | www.majesticgolf.com
10/27 | 6904/4896; 72/67.6; 136/109
1/18 | 7009/5081; 73.8/68.7; 132/111
19/9 | 6749/5033; 71.6/67.9; 134/113

"Play the original 18 for the best experience" on this "fabulous", "scenic", "very serene" 27-holer where the first two sections encircle Lake Walden and you "must take a boat ride in between nines"; its "interesting" setup notwithstanding, the layout is located midway between Detroit and East Lansing and "gets a lot of play", which has naysayers noting "it's a two-day trip: one to get there" and another to play a round "so slow you could time it with a sundial."

Orchards, The
25 | 22 | 23 | 19 | $80

Washington | 62900 Campground Rd. | 586-786-7200 | www.orchards.com | 7036/5158; 74.5/70.3; 136/123

"A true golfers' course", this "spectacular" "metro Detroit gem" is a "well-maintained" Robert Trent Jones Jr. design that you "must play to appreciate"; the woodsy front and links-style back are both "fun", but you'll "have to do well to score" on a spread that's "challenging enough to have hosted" the 2002 U.S. Amateur Public Links Championship; still, with a "great overall feel", "nice clubhouse" and city views, expect it to get "crowded on weekends."

☒ Shepherd's Hollow
28 | 25 | 24 | 21 | $85

Clarkston | 9085 Big Lake Rd. | 248-922-0300 | www.shepherdshollow.com
10/19 | 7235/4982; 76.1/70.4; 144/120
1/10 | 7236/4906; 76.1/69.7; 147/120
19/1 | 7169/4960; 75.5/69.7; 143/120

"Quite simply the best course in the Detroit area", this Arthur Hills 27-holer "plays like a Pinehurst" with its "beautiful" routing through a hardwood forest and "immaculate conditions"; it's "not the cheapest" around, but "rolling terrain" with lots of elevation changes and "a northern Michigan feel" plus "many risk/reward holes" make it a "must-visit at least once a year"; even better, it offers "great facilities" and "exceptional service" that make it "worth getting lost" on the 30-minute ride north from the city.

Gaylord

Black Lake
▽ 28 | 24 | 23 | 24 | $85

Onaway | 2800 Maxon Rd. | 989-733-4653 | www.blacklakegolf.com | 7046/5058; 74.4/70.1; 138/120

"Owned by the UAW (hey, you're in Michigan)" and set on the "beautiful" grounds of the auto workers' family education center, this "solid" spread is "worth the trip" an hour northeast of Gaylord for a classic, "meticulously kept", "typical Rees Jones" design that "uses the natural terrain well" as it sweeps over forests and wetlands; plus, if you don't want to drive home after your round, you can always "stay at the lodge" – "just make sure your car is American made."

Elk Ridge

| 27 | 24 | 25 | 25 | $75 |

Atlanta | 9400 Rouse Rd. | 989-785-2275 | 800-626-4355 | www.elkridgegolf.com | 7072/5261; 75.8/74.2; 145/133

"If you can find" this "strong layout" "buried deep in forestland" in "remote" Atlanta, you'll discover "one of Michigan's best courses" "offering solitude, beauty" and "lots of wildlife"; "fair" and "worth playing", this "beautiful" woodlander features rolling terrain, plenty of "left-to-right doglegs" and carries over wetlands and water; plus, they "never overbook", have a "wonderful clubhouse" and serve the "best sandwiches" – after all, they're "owned by the HoneyBaked Ham people."

Treetops, Rick Smith Signature

| 26 | 25 | 24 | 22 | $120 |

Gaylord | 3962 Wilkinson Rd. | 989-732-6711 | 888-873-3867 | www.treetops.com | 6653/4604; 72.8/67; 140/123

Taking "golf back to its roots", this signature spread is a "beautiful, classic-style course" that's sometimes "underrated compared to" its Treetops siblings but is nevertheless "better than it gets credit for" and "worth playing"; "easily the most scenic" of the four resort layouts, this "crowded" northern Michigan course is "not for novices" (although "great for women") – that is, unless beginners plan a pre-game visit to the architect's Rick Smith Golf Academy.

Treetops,
Robert Trent Jones Masterpiece

| 26 | 25 | 24 | 23 | $120 |

Gaylord | 3962 Wilkinson Rd. | 989-732-6711 | 888-873-3867 | www.treetops.com | 7060/4972; 75.5/70; 144/123

"The name says it all" about this "outstanding" design "from one of the masters" that's "what traditional golf is all about" as it courses through the "beautiful" northern Michigan mountains; "the toughest at Treetops" is "like sparring with Mike Tyson" given its "narrow greens", "elevation changes and blind tee shots", but if you "pick the right tees, you'll have a fair test"; plus, it's all part of a "great resort" with recently remodeled lodging and a variety of packages.

Treetops, Tom Fazio Premier

| 26 | 25 | 25 | 24 | $120 |

Gaylord | 3962 Wilkinson Rd. | 989-732-6711 | 888-873-3867 | www.treetops.com | 6832/5039; 73.6/69.8; 134/122

"A bit easier than the Smith and the Jones", this "very Fazio" foray is a "great course from start to finish"; both "pretty and challenging", the mountain "gem" gets "easier to play on the second or third visit after you get to know" its narrow fairways, "tricky greens" and dramatic elevation changes; the "only problem" is that the "great resort" offers only "one driving range for four courses – get there early or you may have to wait."

Grand Rapids

NEW Mines

| - | - | - | - | $39 |

Grand Rapids | 330 Covell Ave. SW | 616-791-7544 | www.minesgolfcourse.com | 6701/5438; 72.7/65.9; 137/108

Conveniently located just five minutes from Downtown Grand Rapids, this Mike DeVries design takes its name from the abandoned gypsum mines over which it is built; set on rolling, wooded terrain just west of I-196, the layout features fairways flanked by trees and laced with over 30 bunkers and even a few dune formations; N.B. the facility expects to open a nine-hole par-3 course in spring 2007.

Pilgrim's Run
▽ 28 | 25 | 25 | 28 | $65

Pierson | 11401 Newcosta Ave. | 888-533-7742 | www.pilgrimsrun.com | 7093/4863; 74.1/67.7; 138/114

Pilgrims run to this "beautiful course" laid out over densely wooded terrain "in the middle of nowhere" 30 minutes north of Grand Rapids; kept in "impeccable" shape ("great", bunker-guarded greens, wide "fairways like carpets"), the "value"-priced spread is a "wonderful, scenic" destination to which players "love to return"; P.S. expect a low-key 19th hole, as there is no alcohol sold or permitted.

St. Ives Resort, St. Ives
▽ 26 | 25 | 24 | 22 | $99

Stanwood | 9900 St. Ives Dr. | 231-972-4837 | 800-972-4837 | www.stivesgolf.com | 6702/4821; 73.3/68.7; 140/120

There's "lots of character" at this "fantastic golf course" that's "challenging without being gimmicky" and "worth the drive" 45 minutes north of Grand Rapids; a "scenic", "pretty place to play", the spread sports "holes framed by large trees" and carries over wetlands but is nevertheless a "playable" and "enjoyable" option; in fact, given the nearby casino and charming inn accommodations, your vacation here can be "fun for the whole family."

St. Ives Resort, Tullymore
▽ 27 | 17 | 24 | 23 | $99

Stanwood | 11969 Tullymore Dr. | 231-972-4837 | 800-972-4837 | www.stivesgolf.com | 7148/4668; 74.9/68.8; 148/115

"Don't miss" this "wonderful" layout "that should be played when visiting" the Lake Mecosta region north of Grand Rapids; considered "more difficult than its sister" spread, this Jim Engh design is "challenging for even the most skilled golfer" with its "great green speed" and long par 5s; the resort's amenities and service have some saying they "love every inch of this place", although unlike its St. Ives sibling, the course "does not have a clubhouse" on-site.

Lansing

Forest Akers MSU, East
▽ 14 | 15 | 19 | 21 | $27

East Lansing | Harrison Rd. | 517-355-1635 | www.golf.msu.edu | 6559/5111; 70.3/67.8; 114/110

A "fun, sporty course" designed by Michigan State alum Arthur Hills, this "reasonably priced" home to the MSU Spartans is conveniently located midway between Detroit and Grand Rapids; the gently rolling, user-friendly layout boasts a "great driving range" and "good service" and is a particularly nice "value" for students, staff and alumni; N.B. the on-site Golf Center offers classes and clinics.

Forest Akers MSU, West
▽ 22 | 18 | 20 | 22 | $44

East Lansing | 3535 Forest Rd. | 517-355-1635 | www.golf.msu.edu | 7013/5278; 74/70.3; 136/123

Thanks to a student-developed Environmental Stewardship Program, this university layout is "an exemplar of turf and grounds management", boasting "well-manicured" conditions that make this truly a "green course" for a "green school"; the older of the two MSU offerings, this 1958 classic was redesigned and lengthened by Arthur Hills in 1992, so watch out for the "long par 3s" – and for the many students taking advantage of the "value" pricing.

Hawk Hollow ⛳

▽ 22 | 24 | 17 | 18 | $65

Bath | 15101 Chandler Rd. | 517-641-4295 | 888-411-4295 | www.hawkhollow.com
10/19 | 6693/4962; 72.8/70; 134/120
1/10 | 6974/5078; 73.7/69.7; 136/120
19/1 | 6487/4934; 71.7/69.1; 129/117

Part of a golf complex just north of Lansing, this "very good" trio of "challenging" woodland nines offers plenty of variety and shot options on its risk/reward holes; though players are perplexed about the course's conditions ("good" vs. "hit-or-miss"), they find no fault at all with facilities that include a "nice clubhouse", a golf academy and an extensive practice area armed with an 18-hole putting track and two driving ranges.

Pohlcat

▽ 21 | 18 | 19 | 19 | $75

Mt. Pleasant | 6595 E. Airport Rd. | 989-773-4221 | 800-292-8891 | www.pohlcat.net | 6889/5140; 74.2/69; 140/127

Players purr over this layout located just an hour from Lansing and a few hours north of Detroit, saying it's a "nice" diversion "in between gambling" at the nearby Soaring Eagles casino and taking in a race at the Mt. Pleasant Meadows horse track; "not bad for the Midwest", the local "favorite" was designed by Champions Tour veteran and area native Dan Pohl and comes complete with a recently constructed log cabin-style clubhouse.

Muskegon

Double JJ Ranch, Thoroughbred ⛳

23 | 20 | 20 | 20 | $79

Rothbury | 6886 Water Rd. | 231-894-4444 | www.doublejj.com | 6773/4879; 73.6/68.3; 146/121

"Bring your A-game to ride" this "fun, challenging" Arthur Hills design that's "part of a dude ranch" ("mechanical bull and all") in "out-of-the-way Rothbury" north of Muskegon; although they are currently "concentrating all of their efforts on a new water park" and condos, expect to find a "great family setup" where the "kids can be entertained while the parents" tackle a true "test of golf" that starts it off right with "a 475-yard par 4 – need I say more?"

Petoskey

Bay Harbor ⛳

26 | 27 | 24 | 19 | $199

Bay Harbor | 3600 Village Harbor Dr. | 231-439-4028 | 800-462-6963 | www.bayharborgolf.com
Links/Quarry | 6780/4151; 73/67.4; 145/117
Preserve/Links | 6810/4087; 72.9/65.5; 142/113
Quarry/Preserve | 6726/3906; 73.4/65.1; 146/116

"Nestled among the pines and dunes of northern Michigan", this "ultrachallenging", "visually stunning" Arthur Hills design offers "great variety on its three nines": the Links plays along the lakeside cliffs and shoreline, the Quarry "intimidates" with "granite walls" and gorges and the "impressive" Preserve provides a parkland experience; add in "impeccable conditions" and top facilities and it's "a must-play" – as long as you "play on someone else's dime."

Boyne Highlands, Arthur Hills 🏔

| 26 | 23 | 23 | 23 | $134 |

Harbor Springs | 600 Highland Dr. | 231-526-3028 | 800-462-6963 | www.boynehighlands.com | 7312/4834; 76.4/68.5; 144/117

"A word to the wise: bring your A+-game" to the "most memorable" and "best of the four at Boyne Highlands" just north of Petoskey; an "Arthur Hills special" with "wide", "challenging fairways", difficult water hazards, huge waste areas and "impossible greens", this resort course is one you may "not want to play every day" but is nevertheless "fun for the traveling golfer"; a "friendly staff" and "breathtaking scenery" are just two more reasons why "this course is a treat."

Boyne Highlands, Donald Ross Memorial 🏔

| 26 | 24 | 23 | 22 | $109 |

Harbor Springs | 600 Highland Dr. | 231-526-3029 | 800-462-6963 | www.boynehighlands.com | 6814/4929; 74.5/68.7; 136/122

"Mr. Ross would be proud" of this "very cool", "one-of-a-kind" design where "18 of his best holes" from sites like Aronimink, Oakland Hills and Pinehurst are not only "replicated in one place" but are also "pretty close to the originals"; one of four courses at Boyne Highlands – "the mecca of northern Michigan golf" – this "tough", "eclectic test" comes "highly recommended" by those who appreciate hilly layouts "with lots of water."

Boyne Highlands, Heather

| 24 | 23 | 22 | 21 | $134 |

Harbor Springs | 600 Highland Dr. | 231-526-3029 | 800-462-6963 | www.boynehighlands.com | 6890/4845; 74.8/70.5; 141/118

Rambling through woods and blueberry bogs with "water on the majority of its holes", this "classic" RTJ Sr. "purist's delight" "still plays great" after 30 years; though perhaps "not as scenic as the other" Boyne Highlands layouts, this "challenging test of golf" has been "restored to its glory days" via a "beautiful" bunker renovation and will be adding championship tee boxes for the 2007 season; P.S. take advantage of fall's "great rates and eye-popping colors."

Boyne Highlands, Moor

| 20 | 20 | 21 | 20 | $79 |

Harbor Springs | 600 Highland Dr. | 231-526-3029 | 800-462-6963 | www.boynehighlands.com | 6850/5100; 74.6/72; 135/122

"The most forgiving of the four Highlands courses", this "oldie but goodie" is a "quiet and challenging" alternative featuring "a few doglegs, some wetlands" and lots of water but "no real surprises" or "gimmicks"; considering the nearby competition, pros propose there's "no need to bother with this one", but it's "fun to play" and ideal "for beginners or families", as "you can still score even if you don't hit it long."

Dunmaglas 🏔

| 21 | 12 | 15 | 18 | $89 |

Charlevoix | 9031 Boyne City Rd. | 231-547-1022 | www.dunmaglas.com | 6901/5175; 73.5/69.8; 139/123

"Don't miss" "one the best twilight values" in the area, this "very scenic" spread sporting vistas of Lake Michigan and Charlevoix; "worth playing" (especially "in the fall"), this "great course" features a links-style back and a rolling, parkland front on which "the first holes require distance and accuracy", so "make sure you warm up" first; meanwhile, duffers who decry the "unassuming" facilities will be pleased by recent renovations to the clubhouse and practice areas that may outdate the above Facilities score.

Traverse City

☒ Arcadia Bluffs   29 | 27 | 25 | 21 | $180

Arcadia | 14710 Northwood Hwy. | 231-889-3001 | 800-494-8666 | www.arcadiabluffs.com | 7300/5107; 75.4/70.1; 147/121

"As close to Scotland as you will get this side of the pond", the state's top-rated Course is "visually unbeatable and plays just as well", a bit of "unexpected brilliance" located "on the eastern shore of Lake Michigan" southwest of Traverse City; the "price is a little high", but you'll find the links experience "spectacular in every regard", from the "fast, tricky greens" and "many risk/reward" situations to the "amazing views" "from every hole" and the "wonderful facilities and service."

Grand Traverse, The Bear 🏨   24 | 23 | 21 | 19 | $140

Acme | 100 Grand Traverse Blvd. | 231-938-1620 | 800-236-1577 | www.grandtraverseresort.com | 7065/5281; 76.8/73.1; 146/137

Try to "tame this wild beast for 18 holes" and you'll see why swingers say Jack Nicklaus' linksy resort "gem" in Acme is "correctly named"; as you play through this "extremely difficult" "test" featuring terraced fairways, difficult carries, "slick greens" and "sand traps that will take you to the extreme and back again", "just remember that the 19th hole awaits with its breathtaking views" of Grand Traverse Bay; nonetheless, for some it all comes at an "un-bear-able cost."

High Pointe   ▽ 20 | 16 | 19 | 23 | $51

Williamsburg | 5555 Arnold Rd. | 231-267-9900 | 800-753-7888 | www.highpointegolf.com | 6890/4974; 73.3/68.7; 136/120

"Be prepared for two completely opposite nines" on this "surprisingly good" "combination of links and woodland" just east of Traverse City, as the "front offers a links-style test while the back is a more traditional – and difficult – tree-lined setting"; a "fairly unassuming" offering from star course designer and state resident Tom Doak, it's a "terrific" "deal for the money", especially during the months when "twilight rates start at 2 PM."

Shanty Creek, Cedar River   ▽ 24 | 24 | 24 | 22 | $99

Bellaire | 1 Shanty Creek Rd. | 231-533-8621 | 800-678-4111 | www.shantycreek.com | 6989/5315; 73.6/70.5; 144/128

"Great fun to play", this "can't-miss" design from Tom Weiskopf is a "beautiful track" that's "quiet and secluded" as it rambles over rolling, wooded terrain an hour northeast of Traverse City; some snip it's "nice but not in the top tier", but others insist "you'll love it" for its family-friendly resort amenities (including five restaurants and a spa) and greens fees that have "come way down to where they should be."

Shanty Creek, The Legend   25 | 23 | 22 | 19 | $99

Bellaire | 1 Shanty Creek Rd. | 231-533-8621 | 800-678-4111 | www.shantycreek.com | 6764/4953; 73.6/69.6; 137/124

"More interesting than a Grisham novel, more fun than a barrel of monkeys", this "awesome" Arnold Palmer effort is a "tough" resort layout – "score well here and be proud of yourself"; the "beautiful" course travels from hill to valley with "total seclusion on every hole" and "scenic views" of Lake Bellaire that "you'll remember for a long time", so "play it in the fall to enjoy the color change"; sure, it's a smidge "pricey, but it's well worth the expense."

Upper Peninsula

NEW Marquette, Greywalls | - | - | - | - | $125 |

Marquette | 1075 Grove St. | 906-225-0721 | 866-678-7171 | www.marquettegolfclub.com | 6828/4577; 73/66.7; 144/120

Set on over 200 acres of a wooded valley with views of Lake Superior in the distance, this Upper Peninsula layout designed by Mike DeVries is a ways away from mainland Michigan, but rewards long-haulers with a picturesque and walkable golf experience; named for its numerous exposed-granite walls and outcroppings, the track features massive elevation changes as well as tee shots over ravines and wetlands.

TimberStone 🏞 | ▽ 25 | 14 | 22 | 26 | $68 |

Iron Mountain | 1 TimberStone Dr. | 906-776-0111 | www.timberstonegolf.com | 6937/5077; 75.2/72; 144/131

Towering trees and native stone characterize this "gorgeous course" that's linked to northern Michigan's Pine Mountain resort and laced with scenic holes like the 17th (with a 100-ft. vertical drop from tee to green); it also offers a "friendly, excellent staff", but although acolytes admit Upper Peninsula's "yoopers know their golf", a few feel they may still need to learn "how to build a clubhouse."

Minnesota

Brainerd

Grand View Lodge, Deacon's Lodge | 27 | 25 | 25 | 23 | $106 |

Pequot Lakes | Breezy Point, 9348 Arnold Palmer Dr. | 218-562-6262 | 888-437-4637 | www.deaconslodge.com | 6964/4766; 73.8/68.6; 146/1198

"Named after [designer] Arnold Palmer's father", this "breathtaking" "test of golf" will make you "feel like you're in the Colorado mountains" courtesy of a "scenic" location "in the woods" near northern Minnesota's Pelican Lake; "the best of the courses at the Grand View Lodge" is a "tough" "must-play" that "can prove fun and challenging for novices or advanced players" alike – so "get ready to relax and enjoy the whole ambiance."

Grand View Lodge, Pines | ▽ 22 | 24 | 23 | 21 | $96 |

Nisswa | 23521 Nokomis Ave. | 218-963-0001 | 888-437-4637 | www.grandviewlodge.com
Lakes/Woods | 6874/5134; 74.1/70.7; 144/128
Marsh/Lakes | 6837/5112; 74.2/71; 145/131
Woods/Marsh | 6883/5210; 74.3/71.5; 145/128

"Use your brains" on this "wonderful" if "typical Northwoods resort course" that serves up "a great variety" of "clever" holes on its three distinct, aptly named nines; with a "scenic" routing through woods and over gently rolling hills, the "tight" track adds up to a "very enjoyable" day of "fun, no-pressure golf"; N.B. play-and-stay packages include rounds at Deacon's Lodge, Preserve and the nine-hole Garden.

Grand View Lodge, Preserve

▽ 25 | 23 | 26 | 24 | $96

Nisswa | 5506 Preserve Blvd. | 218-568-4944 | 888-437-4637 | www.grandviewlodge.com | 6601/4816; 72.8/69.4; 140/126

"An up-and-comer" that's "usually in the shadow of the Brainerd-area giants", this "sleeper" of a course is "a treat to play" given its "many tight little pitches on long par 4s" and "baffling elevated shots"; considered "better than the Pines" among the "wonderful Grand View Lodge trio", the "scenic" spread sports both a "friendly staff" and "great" clubhouse views of the rolling, wooded terrain.

☑ Madden's on Gull Lake, Classic

28 | 24 | 26 | 23 | $109

Brainerd | 11266 Pine Beach Peninsula | 218-829-2811 | 800-642-5363 | www.maddens.com | 7102/4859; 75/69.4; 143/124

This "player's dream" rolls through red oaks and around Bass Lake, a "fantastic" "resort layout in the land of 10,000 courses" that has "no brand-name architect" (it was designed by its golf superintendent, Scott Hoffman), but is "the best in the Brainerd area" courtesy of "immaculate conditioning", dramatic elevation and lots of water; though "expensive" and over "two hours from the Twin Cities", this "visual gem" with a "Northwoods feel" just "shouldn't be missed."

Duluth

Giants Ridge, Legend

– | – | – | – | $85

Biwabik | County Rd. 138 | 218-865-3001 | 800-688-7669 | www.giantsridge.com | 6930/5084; 74.3/70.3; 138/124

"Check it out" chime those charmed by this Jeff Brauer design that's "a great course" and a picturesque play near the Superior National Forest an hour north of Duluth; although walking isn't permitted at this resort layout, you'll nevertheless enjoy a scenic spread sprinkled with lakes, wetlands, boulders and towering trees; plus, you can top it all with a stay at the upscale Giants Ridge lodge.

Giants Ridge, Quarry

▽ 29 | 19 | 22 | 26 | $85

Biwabik | County Rd. 138 | 218-865-3088 | 800-688-7669 | www.giantsridge.com | 7201/5119; 75.6/70.8; 146/125

A "big, bold, natural setting" characterizes this "very unique" "Jeff Brauer course built on an old quarry" north of Duluth; offering 18 "breathtaking" holes routed through woods and over wetlands, this "fabulous" foray features open mine pits, deep bunkers and steep drop-offs to make it "difficult for the average golfer"; still, most masochists "would be happy to play it again and again", as it's undeniably "beautiful golf!"

Wilderness at Fortune Bay

– | – | – | – | $86

Tower | 1450 Bois Forte Rd. | 218-753-8917 | 800-992-4680 | www.thewildernessgolf.com | 7207/5324; 75.3/71.9; 144/127

"Well worth the cost and the drive" 90 miles north of Duluth, this "exceptional" Jeff Brauer design stretches 7,207 yards from the tips on a long track that offers expansive views of Lake Vermilion; whether the tree-lined layout – bolstered by boulders, ridges and rock outcroppings – is "better than" or "just a bit behind" the nearby Giants Ridge courses, it's undeniably a "beautiful" resort option.

	COURSE	FACIL.	SERVICE	VALUE	COST

Minneapolis

Baker National
20 | 16 | 17 | 27 | $36

Medina | 2935 Parkview Dr. | 763-694-7670 | www.bakernational.com | 6762/5313; 73.9/72.7; 135/128

"Don't be fooled by the quaint red farmhouse off the first green", as this "challenging" muni just west of Minneapolis "packs a subtle yet crafty punch" with its wide-open front and "particularly worthy" back; add in a "quiet, serene" setting "in the middle of a regional park" with views of Lake Spurzem and "no houses", and you have an "enjoyable, unique course" that's "arguably the best value" around.

Chaska Town
26 | 21 | 22 | 25 | $55

Chaska | 3000 Town Course Dr. | 952-443-3748 | www.chaskatowncourse.com | 6817/4853; 73.8/69.4; 140/119

"An Arthur Hills muni that has the design and maintenance of a private club", this "outstanding", "value"-priced public may be situated southwest of Minneapolis but it's also very "close" to a "golf heaven on earth"; the "front nine is a little easier than the back" at this co-host of the 2006 U.S. Amateur Championship, but both halves boast a "natural landscape" that's "beautiful all year, but off the charts in fall."

Edinburgh USA ⅟
23 | 23 | 21 | 22 | $49

Brooklyn Park | 8700 Edinbrook Crossing | 763-315-8550 | www.edinburghusa.org | 6888/5319; 74.2/71.5; 149/133

For "a pleasant round with some challenging holes", this "solid" muni "close to Downtown" Minneapolis is "a spot to consider"; "much harder than it appears", the RTJ Jr. design "requires accuracy and patience" – it "doesn't allow you to bang away with your driver off the tee" – on a "well-kept" layout loaded with "tricky bunkers and water everywhere"; a "nice, fairly new short-game practice area" is another reason it's a "value."

Legends Club
26 | 26 | 25 | 20 | $75

Prior Lake | 8670 Credit River Blvd. | 952-226-4777 | www.legendsgc.com | 7058/5297; 74/71.1; 144/126

"Even the holes you think aren't much from the tee end up being fantastic" on this "solid" spread offering "18 great holes" that "you'll want to keep playing and playing"; considered one of the "best public courses in the Twin Cities area", it "has everything": facilities that are "like [at] a private club" and a "well-maintained" layout with "beautifully manicured greens", lakes, trees, marshes and, unfortunately, "some homes" – although they're "never in play."

Les Bolstad
▽ 16 | 11 | 13 | 26 | $33

University of Minnesota Golf Course

St. Paul | 2275 Larpenteur Ave. W. | 612-627-4000 | www.uofmgolf.com | 6278/5478; 70.2/71.8; 123/122

"An annual treat" to tackle "in the fall when the oaks are blazing in color", this "old, park-style course" may "play short for low handicaps" but its "small, elevated greens and quirky fairways" make it seem "just like Watergate" to some: "one bad lie after another"; nevertheless, neither the "challenging" holes nor the "minimal" facilities can dissuade Golden Gopher fans from this "great value" – especially given the special "discounts for alums."

	COURSE	FACIL.	SERVICE	VALUE	COST

NEW Meadows at Mystic Lake 🏌

– | **–** | **–** | **–** | **$85**

Prior Lake | 2400 Mystic Lake Blvd. | 952-233-5533 |
www.shakopeedakota.org/meadows | 7144/5293; 74.2/71.4; 142/128

Part of the Shakopee Mdewakanton Sioux Community just 30 minutes southwest of Minneapolis, this linksy layout features fairways lined with flowers and fescue, creeks and ponds that bring water into play on over half of the course and views of the surrounding hills and wetlands; the Prior Lake area, meanwhile, is also home to the Twin Cities' only casino hotel, which shares the same ownership and no-alcohol policy as the golf club.

Rush Creek

22 | **21** | **21** | **16** | **$99**

Maple Grove | 7801 County Rd. 101 | 763-494-8844 | www.rushcreek.com |
7125/5422; 74.8/72; 144/131

This "beautiful course" 20 minutes northwest of Minneapolis was "built on marshes" and sports "some memorable holes" (e.g. elevated tees on the 12th, 14th and 18th that provide scenic vistas) on its "very nice" layout; although this former host of the 2004 U.S. Amateur Public Links Championship and several '90s-era LPGA events is "well-manicured and in solid shape", some detractors declare "there are many better values to be had in the Twin Cities" area.

StoneRidge

25 | **23** | **24** | **21** | **$79**

Stillwater | 13600 Hudson Blvd. N. | 651-436-4653 | www.stoneridgegc.com |
6992/5247; 74.2/71.3; 140/131

"Like Ireland and Scotland without the ocean", this "heathland" links design by Bobby Weed is "an absolute joy to play" with "some interesting holes and elevation changes" and a location "just far enough away" (east of Minneapolis near the Wisconsin border) "not to be overrun by Twin Cities citizens"; it's kept "in top-notch shape" – it's "like playing a private course" – but comes with "pricey" greens fees, so try to "get one of the discount coupons."

Wilds, The

24 | **22** | **20** | **16** | **$99**

Prior Lake | 3151 Wilds Ridge Ct., NW | 952-445-3500 |
www.golfthewilds.com | 7025/5095; 74.5/71.1; 152/132

Sodden swingers suspect that "at least half of the lakes in the state are on" this Weiskopf/Morrish "challenge" just south of Minneapolis that "grows on you the more you play" its "lush, beautiful, well-maintained fairways and greens"; "autumn is a real treat" since "the round costs the temperature" (otherwise, it's "pricey"), but some semanticists suggest "the name is entirely deceiving", as the course is "cramped by oversized homes" that require "endless out-of-bounds markers."

Willingers

26 | **20** | **23** | **25** | **$44**

Northfield | 6900 Canby Trail | 952-652-2500 | www.willingersgc.com |
6775/5166; 74.4/71.8; 150/135

"True golfers will appreciate the design and layout, the smooth, accurate greens and the pristine scenery" at this "escape from reality" that proves "an excellent value if you're willing to drive an hour [south] from the Twin Cities"; you'll find "some interesting holes" on a "front that winds around marshes and a back that cuts through trees", but you can also "get into trouble here, so bring your A-game" to tackle the "tough tee shots" and "elevation changes."

Mississippi

Gulfport

NEW Beau Rivage Resort, Fallen Oak

- | - | - | - | $200

Biloxi | 24400 Highway 15 N. | 228-386-7015 | 877-805-4657 | www.fallenoak.com | 7487/5362

Construction on this 2006 layout was delayed due to Hurricane Katrina, but now nature comes alive in a different way at Tom Fazio's Biloxi-area design: with numerous elevation changes and a few long drives over wetlands, the track winds through tall trees, streams and lakes; of course, you'll need to be a guest at the Beau Rivage Resort to play, but that may be a bonus given its recent half-billion-dollar renovation and spacious casino; N.B. it has not yet been rated by the USGA.

Bridges at Hollywood Casino

- | - | - | - | $95

Bay Saint Louis | 711 Hollywood Casino Blvd. | 228-467-9257 | www.hollywoodcasinobsl.com | 6841/5108; 73.5/70.1; 138/126

Over the bridges (21 in all) and through the wetlands (17 lakes and 14 acres of marsh) comes the reincarnation of this Katrina-damaged Arnold Palmer design; the Gulfport-area resort course recently re-opened after renovations to repair hurricane damage: the yardage is the same, but they've replaced the turf, improved drainage and built a new clubhouse; after a round, test your luck at the updated Hollywood Casino; N.B. they will receive updated USGA ratings in March 2007.

Grand Biloxi, Grand Bear

▽ 26 | 24 | 23 | 23 | $65

Saucier | 12040 Grand Way Blvd. | 228-604-7100 | 888-524-5695 | www.golfgrandbear.com | 7204/4802; 75.5/68.4; 143/120

Purchased by Harrah's and reopened in November 2006, this "awesome", "well-maintained" Katrina survivor snakes its way inland through the pines and wetlands of the "beautiful" DeSoto National Forest north of Gulfport; not only have fees "gone down since the hurricane" (making the Jack Nicklaus design "much more affordable"), you no longer need to be a guest of the resort to play – so now even more duffers will have the chance to declare they "love it."

Oaks, The

▽ 20 | 19 | 21 | 22 | $90

Pass Christian | 24384 Club House Dr. | 228-452-0909 | www.theoaksgolfclub.com | 6885/4691; 72.5/66.4; 131/107

Located "on a nice piece of land" just west of Gulfport, this "good course" "has always been a favorite" of players who appreciate the tight woodlander's "many trees", native wetlands and strategic bunkering; though a few feel it's "ok at best", the hardy "value" is conveniently located in a gated Gulf Coast community near I-10.

Jackson

Dancing Rabbit, Azaleas

26 | 24 | 22 | 25 | $109

Choctaw | 1 Choctaw Trail | 601-663-0011 | 866-447-3275 | www.dancingrabbitgolf.com | 7128/4909; 74.4/68.6; 135/115

"Everything golf should be", this "great" layout designed by Tom Fazio and Jerry Pate winds through wetlands and woodlands northwest of

Jackson and features a notable 465-yard par-4 8th; part of the "under-rated" Pearl River Resort; you can expect to have a "fantastic week-end" here – but after you "look for John Daly at the craps table", be sure to "leave the casino and get to the course."

Dancing Rabbit, Oaks
▽ 28 | 25 | 22 | 26 | $109

Choctaw | 1 Choctaw Trail | 601-663-0011 | 866-447-3275 | www.dancingrabbitgolf.com | 7076/5097; 74.6/69; 139/123

Far from being "an ugly stepsister to the older Azaleas course", this 1999 layout designed by the same architects (Tom Fazio and Jerry Pate) delivers "primo golf" on a slightly shorter track that features roll-ing fairways, rock formations and two meandering creeks plus memo-rable views from holes like the 444-yard par-4 12th; even better, the affiliated resort and casino makes it "great for group outings."

Pascagoula

Shell Landing 🖾
▽ 25 | 24 | 23 | 22 | $65

Gautier | 3499 Shell Landing Blvd. | 228-497-5683 | 866-851-0541 | www.shelllanding.com | 7024/5047; 73.2/68.6; 128/112

"Davis Love III designs very good golf courses" and this woodsy "winner" – nestled midway between Biloxi and Pascagoula – is a "huge course with many psych-out shots" that "look dangerous but are very forgiving" and are followed up with "lots of fun on the greens"; as it is "picturesque and never crowded" with a "great practice area" and "im-proved staff attitude", "all is well" at this nice "value" – except, per-haps, for the fact that "the mosquitos own it."

Missouri

Kansas City

Tiffany Greens
▽ 24 | 21 | 22 | 21 | $66

Kansas City | 6100 NW Tiffany Springs Pkwy. | 816-880-9600 | www.tiffanygreensgolf.com | 6977/5391; 74.4/71.3; 136/121

"Excellent conditions" prevail at this Robert Trent Jones Jr. design that sits atop the rolling hills northwest of Kansas City; while the tree-lined layout has "multiple tee boxes" that allow for all levels of play, it also offers "lots of interesting shots" to keep it challenging and force "good decision-making"; extensive practice facilities and a 26,000-sq.-ft. clubhouse make the "very reasonable prices" seem even better.

Lake of the Ozarks

Lodge of Four Seasons, Seasons Ridge 🖾
▽ 24 | 21 | 21 | 22 | $79

Lake Ozark | Horseshoe Bend Pkwy. | 573-365-8544 | 800-843-5253 | www.4seasonsresort.com | 6447/4617; 71.4/67.2; 130/115

"You may feel like a mountain goat" at the younger of the two layouts at the Lodge of Four Seasons, "but a fun time" can be had playing this "beautiful course on the Lake of the Ozarks" that's characterized by "tight fairways" and "rolling, wooded hills"; it's "pricey", but swingers say the "lovely course" offers "great twilight rates" and packages to "help its value"; N.B. the resort also has a nine-hole short game course.

MISSOURI

	COURSE	FACIL.	SERVICE	VALUE	COST

Lodge of Four Seasons, Witch's Cove ⛳

▽ 25 | 23 | 24 | 23 | $85

Lake Ozark | Horseshoe Bend Pkwy. | 573-365-8544 | 800-843-5253 | www.4seasonsresort.com | 6557/5238; 71/70.8; 133/124

A "beautiful course" located at the Lake of the Ozarks, this "fun" 1971 Robert Trent Jones Sr. design is "still a challenging layout" with its 65 bunkers and numerous water hazards; it's also a "good value" that's made even better by its association with the luxe Lodge of Four Seasons, where players can take advantage of three restaurants, a posh spa and a full-service marina – just make sure to "choose your seasons well because it can get hot in the summer."

�Z Old Kinderhook ⛳

29 | 24 | 23 | 24 | $89

Camdenton | 20 Eagle Ridge Rd. | 573-346-4444 | 888-346-4949 | www.oldkinderhook.com | 6855/4962; 72.8/69.5; 137/123

"An opportunity that should not be passed up", this "extremely well-maintained" Tom Weiskopf design is "very challenging for the intermediate player" but nevertheless "enjoyable"; flowing over rugged, "wooded property" with "beautiful panoramas" of the Lake of the Ozarks region, this "modern" spread sports "fast greens that roll true" and "spectacular elevation changes" – which means walking is discouraged; in short: it's a "high-caliber course" at "an excellent value."

Osage National ⛳

▽ 26 | 23 | 20 | 23 | $72

Lake Ozark | 400 Osage Hills Rd. | 573-365-1950 | 866-365-1950 | www.osagenational.com
Links/River | 7103/5026; 74.6/69.1; 141/120
Mountain/Links | 7165/5076; 74.7/69.9; 139/121
River/Mountain | 7150/5016; 75.6/69.2; 145/119

There's "tremendous variety" at this "hidden" Lake Ozark "gem" that's one of the "most difficult" courses around courtesy of three distinct nines that are kept "in good condition"; in particular, swingers say the Arnold Palmer–designed River and Mountain "have to be played due to their majestic beauty and interesting layouts": the former is "flat" but "pretty" and "on the Osage River", while the latter is "hilly, wacky and fun" with "some hellacious blind shots."

Tan-Tar-A, The Oaks

▽ 19 | 21 | 20 | 18 | $75

Osage Beach | State Rd. KK | 573-348-8521 | 800-826-8272 | www.tan-tar-a.com | 6432/3931; 72.1/62.5; 143/103

This resort course is "great and has been for years" fawn fans who favor the "short" – it's just 6,432 yards long – but "very tight" track offering 18 "hilly holes" (11 with water), lots of trees and "great scenery" as it plays along the Lake of the Ozarks; plus, this Bruce Devlin and Robert von Hagge design is just one part of a family-friendly "vacation golf experience" that also includes a luxurious spa and an indoor waterpark.

Springfield

�Z Branson Creek

28 | 15 | 22 | 25 | $94

Hollister | 144 Maple St. | 417-339-4653 | www.bransoncreekgolf.com | 7036/5032; 73/68.6; 133/113

"Anybody will enjoy the challenge" of this "wonderful", "interesting" Tom Fazio design that bounds over "very hilly terrain" "not far from

Branson" and is considered by some to be "one of the best tracks in Missouri"; although the mountain "must-play" offers plenty of elevation changes and "magnificent views" of the surrounding Ozarks, swingers say it's simply "a shame they can't get a clubhouse built."

St. Louis

Missouri Bluffs ⊙

| 25 | 22 | 21 | 19 | $95 |

St. Charles | 18 Research Park Circle | 636-939-6494 | 800-939-6760 | www.mobluffs.com | 7047/5191; 73.2/69.2; 131/115

You may find yourself "interrupted by deer crossing" the "challenging holes" at this "long, hilly" Tom Fazio design that's cut out of a "pleasant" forest northwest of St. Louis; it's a "beautiful" if "pricey" experience offering "scenic vistas" and "good grass and greens" that are "always in excellent shape", which is what you might expect from a "prestigious public course" that's "trying to go private" – so play it before the "members feel" requires a membership.

Pevely Farms

| 23 | 22 | 20 | 21 | $69 |

Eureka | 400 Lewis Rd. | 636-938-7000 | www.pevelyfarms.com | 7115/5249; 74.6/70.7; 138/117

"Plan to climb hills" on this "tricky and challenging" Arthur Hills design where "there's a fair amount of walking" on a "remote yet pricey course" that "requires accuracy and a long shot off the tee to score well"; you'll also need to navigate "contoured", tree-lined fairways and "long rough" on this former dairy farm southwest of St. Louis, although you'll get to see "wonderful wildlife" and "beautiful views" "along the way."

Montana

Butte

Old Works

| ▽ 23 | 21 | 24 | 26 | $44 |

Anaconda | 1205 Pizzini Way | 406-563-5989 | 888-229-4833 | www.oldworks.org | 7705/5348; 75.8/65; 135/103

Playing this lengthy Jack Nicklaus layout built over an old copper smelting site west of Butte "sure beats fishing"; although the back is "a little less" inspiring than the "tremendous front", both halves feature the same dramatic links-style design dotted with historical relics (e.g. the huge stone fireplaces that line the 3rd fairway) and "awesome black slag bunkers" that "can be hot" to handle – just like this "difficult course."

Kalispell

Big Mountain

| - | - | - | - | $51 |

Kalispell | 3230 Hwy. 93 N. | 406-751-1950 | 800-255-5641 | www.golfmt.com | 7015/5421; 72.4/69.2; 126/114

Expect "amazing mountain views" at this aptly named Flathead Valley track (formerly known as Northern Pines) that features a linksy, "wide-open front" and a "tighter", tree-lined back that snakes along the Stillwater River in Kalispell; a "nice course for the money", this "beautiful" Andy North and Roger Packard design is kept "in amazing condition with rich fairways, true greens and tough rough"; P.S. it can prove "a real challenge when the wind is blowing."

	COURSE	FACIL.	SERVICE	VALUE	COST

Eagle Bend, Championship 🏃

	-	-	-	-	$90

Bigfork | 279 Eagle Bend Dr. | 406-837-7310 | 800-255-5641 | www.golfmt.com | 6711/5075; 71/68.1; 124/117

"If you're in Bigfork, you're already in heaven" sigh swingers who say this 6,711-yard semi-private on Flathead Lake is nearly as "nice" as its "very pleasant" environs; although a few foozlers feel it "has a couple of funky holes", it's an overall "awesome place to play" with scenic views of the surrounding mountains and an elegant, spacious clubhouse; N.B. a Nicklaus-designed nine-holer completes the picture.

Whitefish Lake, North

	-	-	-	-	$46

Whitefish | Hwy. 93 N. | 406-862-4000 | www.golfwhitefish.com | 6703/5520; 70.7/70.9; 128/128

"Anyone who loves golf and and hasn't [yet] played in northwestern Montana is missing one of the best treats around" insist surveyors who swear this "reasonably priced" layout is "like taking a walk in the woods" complete with "nice views of Whitefish Lake and the nearby mountains"; when you've had your fill of "fun" on the tree-lined fairways, head to the clubhouse for "wonderful service" and upscale eats.

Whitefish Lake, South

	-	-	-	-	$46

Whitefish | Hwy. 93 N. | 406-862-4000 | www.golfwhitefish.com | 6551/5361; 71.6/71.2; 131/126

Elevation-savvy swingers are "not kidding" when they suggest that "golfers adjust for the thinner air" at this Whitefish layout that "plays way above sea level" and seems a lot like "two golf courses" to some: a "lovely middle nine along the banks of a lake" that's sandwiched by a "start and finish that wind among houses"; the "sloped fairways can be challenging" (as can the numerous water hazards), but you'll find your frustration offset by the soothing, scenic setting.

Nebraska

North Platte

Wild Horse

	▽ 29	20	24	29	$38

Gothenburg | 40950 Rd. 768 | 308-537-7700 | www.playwildhorse.com | 6955/4688; 73.6/67.5; 134/109

Like going to "Scotland without the flight", this "poor man's Sand Hills" is "worth the detour off I-80" near Gothenburg as "nothing" quite "beats a links layout in the middle of Nebraska"; lots of "wind posts a strong defense to scoring" on this "fantastic" track that also features over 60 bunkers, ample mounding and views over the Platte River Valley; in short: "if cornfields were a tourist destination, this would be a $250 course" – but as it stands, "it's a bargain."

Omaha

Quarry Oaks

	▽ 27	25	25	26	$72

Ashland | 16600 Quarry Oaks Dr. | 402-944-6000 | 888-944-6001 | www.quarryoaks.com | 7010/5068; 75.1/72.3; 143/124

"One of Nebraska's most scenic courses", this "fantastic" design delivers "amazing scenery as you play along the Platte River"; "spectacular setting" aside, the tree-lined layout is also loaded with "lots of challenges for your game" (including several water hazards), prompting one golfer to gush this "could be the best I have ever played"; a spacious clubhouse and the nearby Big Basin Prairie Preserve help to make this "worth the drive from Lincoln or Omaha."

Nevada

TOP COURSES IN STATE

Las Vegas

Angel Park, Mountain 🏌

| 19 | 18 | 19 | 21 | $130 |

Las Vegas | 100 S. Rampart Blvd. | 702-254-4653 | 888-629-3929 | www.angelpark.com | 6722/5150; 71.1/69.1; 130/114

"One of the busiest courses in Vegas for a reason", this often "overcrowded" Arnold Palmer/Ed Seay design is "beautiful, challenging and fun to play" with a "friendly staff" and "beautiful views" of the valley to deter critics who claim it's merely "ordinary"; a few feel there are "better [options] in the area", but perhaps not at such "bargain" prices – "you won't need a high-rolling bank account to play here."

Angel Park, Palm 🏌

| 18 | 21 | 21 | 19 | $130 |

Las Vegas | 100 S. Rampart Blvd. | 702-254-4653 | 888-629-3929 | www.angelpark.com | 6525/4570; 70.9/66.2; 129/111

"Not for the low-handicapper", this "interesting", "decent" design offers just enough challenge – "lots of water, some forced carries and big, undulating greens" – to make it "great for a fun outing with friends" and "very woman-friendly"; the "scenic" spread is enhanced by "beautiful desert landscaping", a "nice pro shop" and a "friendly staff", but some suggest "you get what you pay for in Vegas" – which in this case, may be an "unmemorable" experience.

Bali Hai 🏌

| 22 | 22 | 23 | 13 | $325 |

Las Vegas | 5160 Las Vegas Blvd. S. | 702-450-8000 | 888-427-6678 | www.balihaigolfclub.com | 7002/5535; 73/71.5; 130/121

The "exotic beaches, marvelous palms", "water hazards" and black volcanic rock are all "nice touches" at this "South Pacific–themed" spread that's "forgiving" due to "generous", "funnel-shaped fairways" and "loud" courtesy of a "convenient location" "next to McCarran Airport"; though it's also "pricey" for a place with "no driving range", it has an "excellent pro shop" and, besides, "it could charge $400 and people would still pay because of its proximity to the Strip."

Bear's Best Las Vegas 🏌

| 25 | 24 | 24 | 18 | $245 |

Las Vegas | 11111 W. Flamingo Rd. | 702-804-8500 | 866-385-8500 | www.bearsbest.com | 7194/5043; 74/68.7; 147/116

Bringing together "Jack's best holes" from his "greatest Western hits", this "impressive" "collection" is "a lot of fun" but can be "tricky", so "you'll need and want" the "required forecaddy" "despite what you might think"; plus, it's "only beginning to be developed", although "as houses are added", the "spectacular views of the skyline and red rock landscape" may "be less inviting"; the only downside for now: "all of the courses in Vegas are overpriced – and this is no exception."

☑ Cascata 大 ⚬

| 29 | 29 | 29 | 17 | $500 |

Boulder City | 1 Cascata Dr. | 702-294-2000 | www.golfcascata.com | 7137/5591; 74.6/67.2; 143/117

"Vegas tourists must play this course at least twice in their life", as Rees Jones' "absolutely amazing" resort spread southeast of Henderson is "every bit the experience of Shadow Creek" – and is also Nevada's top-rated Course; while the "immaculately maintained greens" and "stunning scenery" "wow" club-wielders, it's the "world-class clubhouse" (where "a running waterfall welcomes you") and "fantastic service" that make this "rare treat" worth its "hefty fees": "they treat you very well – but for that kind of money, they ought to."

Falls at Lake Las Vegas Resort 🚐

| 27 | 24 | 25 | 20 | $285 |

Henderson | 101 Via Vin Santo | 702-740-5258 | 877-698-4653 | www.lakelasvegas.com | 7243/5300; 74.7/68.3; 136/118

"Extremely tough but worth the whupping", this "desert oasis" winds "through the mountains" near Henderson with "significant elevation changes", particularly on a "spectacular back nine" that has some swingers saying you'll "need a caddy the first time"; although the "expensive" resort design delivers "dramatic views of Downtown Vegas", the "challenging" layout has already caught "the disease that many nice courses get" – "condo-itis" – so while you should be sure to "play it, try not to pay full price."

Las Vegas Paiute Resort, Snow Mountain 🚐

| 25 | 24 | 24 | 22 | $169 |

Las Vegas | 10325 Nu Wav Kaiv Blvd. | 702-658-1400 | 866-284-2833 | www.lvpaiutegolf.com | 7146/5341; 73.3/71.4; 125/117

Golfers "can't go wrong with any of the three courses" at the Paiute Resort, so head "north by northwest to the reservation" to play the facility's "outstanding" original design, this "beautiful" Pete Dye piece that's "always in pristine condition"; offering mountain views plus "quality and service that continue to set the standard", the "fun", "reasonably priced" option proves "well worth the 25-minute" "trip from the Strip" – "now if only they could turn down that wind."

Las Vegas Paiute Resort, Sun Mountain 🚐

| 26 | 24 | 23 | 21 | $169 |

Las Vegas | 10325 Nu Wav Kaiv Blvd. | 702-658-1400 | 866-284-2833 | www.lvpaiutegolf.com | 7112/5465; 73.3/71.4; 134/125

"You won't believe this oasis could exist" "just a short drive from the Strip", but this "beautifully kept" resort course "pops out of the desert to provide an incredible experience for the avid golfer" on a "tough" but "playable" Pete Dye design that remains "faithful to the local topography" – meaning it can "get very windy in the PM"; although some find it "pricey", most "love" the "quality course" for its "amazing mountain views", grass driving range and "courteous, friendly staff."

	COURSE	FACIL.	SERVICE	VALUE	COST

Las Vegas Paiute Resort, Wolf ⛳

| 27 | 24 | 23 | 23 | $219 |

Las Vegas | 10325 Nu Wav Kaiv Blvd. | 702-658-1400 | 866-284-2833 | www.lvpaiutegolf.com | 7604/5910; 76.3/64.1; 149/119

"Fall asleep for a second and the Wolf will bite you in the butt" bemoan boosters of "the hardest of the Paiute courses", this "tough but fair" Pete Dye creation that's an "utterly superb" "long ball hitter's delight" delivering "incredible views of the desert and mountains"; "get out early to beat the breezes", but "rest assured" that the AM tee time and "drive is worth it" for a "top-notch" experience that can be summed up in four simple words: "golf, clubhouse, nature, period."

Legacy, The ⛳

| 20 | 20 | 21 | 19 | $155 |

Henderson | 130 Par Excellence Dr. | 702-897-2187 | 888-446-5358 | www.thelegacygc.com | 7233/5340; 74.5/71; 137/120

Proving you "don't need to break the piggy bank to play a decent course" "in the land of the casinos", this "solid" Arthur Hills design is "great fun" and a "good selection for your day of departure", as it's "close to the airport" in Henderson; although some say the "older course" "needs to spruce things up a bit", most maintain it's "a cut above a muni" and downright "wonderful when it's in shape."

NEW Oasis, Canyons ⛳

| - | - | - | - | $110 |

Mesquite | 100 Palmer Ln. | 702-346-7820 | www.theoasisgolfclub.com | 6408/4739; 71.3/67.3; 129/112

An expansion of Oasis' existing nine-holer, this shorter and less expensive sister to the Palmer layout boasts endless vistas of the desert and mountain landscape near Mesquite plus ball-eating ravines and vibrant green fairways flanked by canyon walls; even with plenty of room off the tee, the 434-yard par-4 opener proves to be a challenging start – although players will find the finish is easy: a 29,000-sq.-ft. clubhouse sanctuary.

Oasis, Palmer ⛳

| 21 | 19 | 18 | 20 | $129 |

Mesquite | 100 Palmer Ln. | 702-346-7820 | www.theoasisgolfclub.com | 6633/4227; 71.5/64.2; 133/106

"Arnie did a great job on this track" tucked away an hour northeast of Las Vegas, designing a "hidden, unexpected gem" with "lots of elevations changes" and "a few exceptionally dramatic holes" to "keep you coming back for more"; the canyon-carved course can be "windy and hot, except in the winter when it's windy and cold" – but no matter the season, you may discover that "housing development distracts" from the layout's panoramic desert views.

Primm Valley, Desert ⛳

| 24 | 21 | 23 | 23 | $175 |

Primm | 31900 Las Vegas Blvd. S. | 702-679-5510 | 800-386-7837 | www.primmvalleyresorts.com | 7131/5397; 74.6/71.6; 138/129

"A true hidden gem" "located on the California-Nevada border 45 minutes south of the Strip", this "serious golfer's paradise" is "rather challenging" thanks to "some water and lots of sand" (waste bunkers line seven of its holes); with "postcard views from every tee box", "beautiful" desert landscaping and reduced fees for MGM Mirage guests, it's no wonder swingers say this Tom Fazio resort design is a "great value"; P.S. "watch the forecast to avoid the wind."

	COURSE	FACIL.	SERVICE	VALUE	COST

Primm Valley, Lakes 🏌

25	21	21	23	$175

Primm | 31900 Las Vegas Blvd. S. | 702-679-5510 | 800-386-7837 | www.primmvalleyresorts.com | 6945/4842; 74/68.5; 134/121

"As you drive down the highway from Vegas, the course appears in the distance like a mirage", a "picturesque" resort layout with "hundreds of trees and lots of lakes in the middle of the desert"; the "clever" Tom Fazio design is "a bit tamer" and "more user-friendly than its Desert sibling", but it's "still a fantastic golf course", so "play both" and you'll have "a day you won't forget" – especially if you go "in the summer" when the "110-degree days are brutal."

Reflection Bay at Lake Las Vegas Resort

27	25	24	17	$295

Henderson | 75 Montelago Blvd. | 702-740-4653 | 877-698-4653 | www.lakelasvegas.com | 7261/5166; 74.8/70; 138/127

Is this "feast for the eyes" "really in Nevada?" ask swingers surprised to find "mountains, desert and water all in one" "beautiful course" routed "along Lake Las Vegas" in Henderson; though "fairly flat", the "fantastic" Jack Nicklaus resort design features "a few really tough holes", especially on the "more difficult back"; be sure, however, to "watch out for the coyotes", "bad rattlesnakes" and "freakishly expensive" fees – "forgive me Jack", for though "the lakeside holes are great, they don't justify the price."

Revere, Concord

23	24	23	21	$195

Henderson | 2600 Hampton Rd. | 702-259-4653 | 877-273-8373 | www.reveregolf.com | 7034/5306; 72.8/70; 126/119

"Take your mind off the casino tables" at this "forgiving, forgiving, forgiving" layout that's the newer of the two tracks at this Paul Revere-themed facility in Henderson; "a mid-handicapper's delight", the "wide-open" "mountain course" offers "amazing terrain changes", "huge greens" and "rough that slopes back to the fairway"; "gorgeous scenery" and a location "within 20 minutes of the Strip" are two more reasons it's a "secret jewel."

Revere, Lexington 🏌

24	23	21	20	$235

Henderson | 2600 Hampton Rd. | 702-259-4653 | 877-273-8373 | www.reveregolf.com | 7143/5305; 73.6/69.9; 139/116

"You'll need to play it a couple of times" or "bring your A-game" to this "tough" track that serves up "sloped lies", "small greens", "blind shots" and "lots of hills" on a "tight" layout that, "unlike the Concord, doesn't funnel wayward shots back to the fairway"; all in all, the "magnificent" "mountain course" is "really nifty" with "some great views and awesome lighting at dusk", but given a "beautiful" location so near to Vegas, "it tends to get crowded."

Rio Secco

27	23	21	18	$350

Henderson | 2851 Grand Hills Dr. | 702-889-2400 | 888-867-3226 | www.riosecco.net | 7332/5778; 75.7/70; 142/127

It's "hard to believe such a rustic course is 20 minutes from the craps tables", but this "long, challenging" Rees Jones design is nestled in the Vegas foothills; "play the back tees" only "if you have masochistic tendencies", as the desert track "runs through canyons" and valleys with "forced carries" and "heavy winds"; still, though "faithful to the terrain", the layout is "surrounded by million-dollar homes" – with "expensive" greens fees to match; N.B. it's home to the Butch Harmon School of Golf.

Royal Links 충

22 | 21 | 23 | 16 | $239

Las Vegas | 5995 Vegas Valley Dr. | 702-450-8123 | 888-427-6682 | www.waltersgolf.com | 7029/5142; 73.7/69.8; 135/115

"If you can't get to the U.K.", head to this collection of "the best holes from the great British Open courses" that's "wonderfully fun" with its "huge pot bunkers", "unusual rough" and "traditionally garbed caddies"; though the "enjoyable experience" comes with a castlelike clubhouse and English tavern, a few commoners claim you "can't get a real links feel without an ocean", which makes this the type of "faux reality" you find "only in Vegas."

⊿ Shadow Creek 충 ०↝

29 | 28 | 28 | 20 | $500

North Las Vegas | 3 Shadow Creek Dr. | 702-791-7161 | 866-260-0069 | www.shadowcreek.com | 7239/6701

"Somehow, they managed to build a North Carolina course in the middle of Vegas", so enjoy a "top-shelf day" at this "insanely beautiful" "feat of engineering" that pairs its "amazing" stream-filled setting with "to-die-for views" and "superlative service"; "you might well bump into Tiger" or get a "locker next to Michael Jordan's" at this "expensive, exclusive" MGM Mirage retreat, so though you'd "never guess you were in the desert", you'll know you're getting "a once-in-a-lifetime opportunity"; N.B. it remains unrated by the USGA.

Siena 🏞

22 | 21 | 22 | 22 | $179

Las Vegas | 10575 Siena Monte Ave. | 702-341-9200 | 888-689-6469 | www.sienagolfclub.com | 6843/4978; 71.5/68; 129/112

"Traps, traps, traps" make it "tough to avoid the beach at this sporty" track that's "worth the drive from the Strip" to "the outskirts of Vegas"; a "nice course" "all the way around" with its "breathtaking vistas of the desert and mountain terrain", "great clubhouse", "good upkeep" and greens fees that are "not prohibitively expensive", this "beautiful" "hidden gem" "sure beats four hours at the craps table."

⊿ Wolf Creek 🏞

29 | 22 | 24 | 25 | $185

Mesquite | 403 Paradise Pkwy. | 702-346-9026 | 866-252-4653 | www.golfwolfcreek.com | 6923/4169; 75.4/61; 154/106

"Every hole is a picture postcard" on this "surreal" "must-play" where "immaculate" "emerald pathways" wind "through cliffs, mountains and valleys" an hour northeast of Vegas; it "will beat you down" with its "massive elevation changes", "but you'll have fun while it's happening" – as long as you "bring an extra bag of balls or a snake bite kit [for when] you hit out of bounds"; facilities may be "limited", but an "accommodating staff" adds to the "awesome" experience.

Wynn Las Vegas 충 ०↝

25 | 25 | 26 | 12 | $500

Las Vegas | 3131 Las Vegas Blvd. S. | 702-770-3575 | 888-320-9966 | www.wynnlasvegas.com | 7042/6464

"Like being taken to a golf oasis in the middle of a slot-machine desert", this guests-only Tom Fazio/Steve Wynn "wonder" "has the advantage of a fabulous location" on the Strip; while "well-manicured conditions" and "the best service available" make it "a helluva place to play", some say the "decent" design is "not nearly as challenging" as the "ridiculously priced" greens fees and the "shockingly snooty" vibe; N.B. the layout has not yet been rated by the USGA.

Reno

Edgewood Tahoe 🏌️

| 25 | 25 | 23 | 16 | $200 |

Lake Tahoe | 180 Lake Pkwy. | 775-588-3566 | 888-881-8659 | www.edgewood-tahoe.com | 7445/5567; 75.5/71.3; 144/136

"More beautiful than Julia Roberts" with a "gorgeous" location on the shores of Lake Tahoe, this George Fazio design delivers "spectacular views" on its "many lakeside holes", including a finish that "makes the entire course"; while "hitting a ball at 7,500 feet is a good feeling" as is relaxing in a "clubhouse with flat-screens everywhere", some say this resort host of the annual Celebrity Golf Championship charges "stiff greens fees" that are about "$100 too much."

New Hampshire

Colebrook

Balsams, Panorama ⏱

| 25 | 21 | 23 | 23 | $70 |

Dixville Notch | Rte. 26 | 603-255-4961 | 800-255-0600 | www.thebalsams.com | 6804/4978; 72.8/67.8; 130/115

"Heavenly views of the rolling hills to the north" "make the name appropriate" at this 1912 Donald Ross design tucked into the "remote [northeast] part of the state"; though "a challenge to stop staring at the scenery", try "to focus on the shot", as the "terrific" but "tricky" "mountain course" offers "no flat lies" and greens that "are near impossible to read"; whether or not the round feels "frustrating", however, you can relax and enjoy a "first-class resort experience."

Concord

Canterbury Woods

| ▽ 21 | 18 | 21 | 20 | $44 |

Canterbury | 15 West Rd. | 603-783-9400 | www.canterburywoodscc.com | 6644/4482; 71.7/62.1; 136/100

"Bordering a real farm" just north of Concord, with "views of cows as you finish the first hole", this "fun layout" "has a rural feel – as a New Hampshire course should"; "very hilly" with "a variety of challenges", this "up-and-down" design "can't be walked comfortably", although the "isolated holes (no hitting into other fairways here)" are worth it; after your round, "lunch on the deck" served by the "accommodating staff" is a "casual and perfect ending."

Keene

Bretwood, North

| ▽ 24 | 15 | 18 | 28 | $40 |

Keene | 365 E. Surry Rd. | 603-352-7626 | www.bretwoodgolf.com | 6976/5140; 73.7/69.8; 136/120

With "great details like stone walls, covered bridges" and the clubhouse's "lovely wraparound porch", this "fun" frolic feels like "the ultimate New England course", one that's "not tremendously challenging" but offers plenty of water via "a river that snakes throughout"; "friendly service" and "play-all-day" deals are just two more reasons it's "worth

	COURSE	FACIL.	SERVICE	VALUE	COST

the trip" to the southwest corner of the state; N.B. it does not accept reservations on weekdays.

Portsmouth

Breakfast Hill ⏱

| | − | − | − | − | $54 |

Greenland | 339 Breakfast Hill Rd. | 603-436-5001 | www.breakfasthill.com | 6500/5000; 70.8/64.7; 134/108

"A wonderful romp through the woods" just south of Portsmouth near New Hampshire's seacoast, this "hidden gem" set on 250-year-old former farm land offers a "pleasant, low-key, customer-oriented" experience; though short (at only 6,500 yards) and "nothing fabulous", the rolling, tree-lined semi-private course is nevertheless "well-maintained", "easy to access" and a "value for the $$$."

Portsmouth Country Club ⏱

| | ▽ 27 | 23 | 23 | 21 | $80 |

Greenland | 80 Country Club Ln. | 603-436-9719 | www.portsmouthcc.net | 7072/5134; 73.6/64.8; 123/108

"What a gem" pronounce putters about this "old-school" course with a "great location on the water" an hour north of Boston; boasting "beautiful views" of the adjacent Great Bay plus a layout that's "flat, nicely contoured and fun to play", this Robert Trent Jones Sr. semi-private "accommodates any handicap" – although it can be tricky "when the wind blows"; also note that it's a local favorite, so it may be "tough to get on at a decent hour."

New Jersey

TOP COURSES IN STATE

27 Pine Hill | *Camden*
    Crystal Springs, Ballyowen | *NYC Metro*
26 Hominy Hill | *Freehold*
    Charleston Springs, North | *Freehold*
    Atlantic City Country Club | *Atlantic City*

Atlantic City

Atlantic City Country Club 🏌

| | 26 | 24 | 22 | 19 | $202 |

Northfield | 1 Leo Fraser Dr. | 609-236-4400 | www.accountryclub.com | 6577/5349; 72/71.4; 128/125

Retaining the "air of an exclusive club" – and matching prices – this "wonderful" 100+-year-old baysider west of Atlantic City recently switched from private to public, so now even "non-high rollers" can play on a course boasting a "great range and short-game areas"; "excellent" service and "fantastic" views are part of the package, and "entering the clubhouse is like stepping into history"; P.S. "the term 'birdie' was coined here."

Blue Heron Pines, West

| | 23 | 20 | 20 | 18 | $90 |

Cologne | 550 W. Country Club Dr. | 609-965-4653 | 888-478-2746 | www.blueheronpines.com | 6805/5053; 72.8/69.2; 135/120

Although "newer courses" have supplanted it as one of the best daily-fee options around, this "flat", "beautifully treed" track holds its own, with most maintaining you "can have a nice round" here; "helpful" service helps heal the sting of somewhat high prices, while savvy South Jersey swingers par-take of the "exceptional value in the off-season."

Harbor Pines ⚑   22 | 20 | 20 | 17 | $115

Egg Harbor Township | 500 St. Andrews Dr. | 609-927-0006 | www.harborpines.com | 6827/5099; 72.3/68.8; 129/118

Located a few minutes south of Atlantic City, this "terrific" daily fee is "great for an outing" but "can get crowded in summer", so try to "play it in the off-season"; the "pleasant routing" is suitable "for almost any level", with "sleeping bunkers" to make it "challenging" and wide, "plush fairways" that "allow you to score well"; though a few claim it's just "not worth the money" to play "holes you'll forget in two days", it's nevertheless a "consistently" "well-maintained" option.

McCullough's Emerald Golf Links   17 | 14 | 17 | 20 | $80

Egg Harbor Township | 3016 Ocean Heights Ave. | 609-926-3900 | www.mcculloughsgolf.com | 6535/4962; 71.7/67.2; 130/118

"If you can't afford the pilgrimage to a real links" course, check out this British Isles "copycat track" just west of Atlantic City; a "challenging" muni built on "what used to be a dump", it offers "a lot of fun" "for the money" via "interesting elevation changes", "risk/reward holes" and "numerous blind shots", but warm up before you arrive as it "lacks a practice facility."

Sea Oaks ⊙   23 | 23 | 21 | 19 | $105

Little Egg Harbor Township | 99 Golf View Dr. | 609-296-2656 | www.seaoaksgolf.com | 6950/5150; 72.4/68.9; 129/119

This Little Egg Harbor layout sports "great risk/reward" holes that are manageable "for all skill levels" and a "pleasure to play", partly due to their "superb condition"; a "huge clubhouse", "excellent staff" and commendable food add to the enjoyment, and if peak-time fees are "pricey", there are "good deals" at twilight – though that's when it morphs into "mosquitoville."

Seaview Marriott, Bay   22 | 23 | 23 | 18 | $129

Absecon | 401 S. New York Rd. | 609-748-7680 | 800-932-8000 | www.seaviewgolf.com | 6247/5017; 70.7/68.4; 122/114

Just "wait until you try to drive into the Absecon Bay breeze" at this 1914 "Donald Ross classic", a "short but challenging" course accessorized with an "on-site Faldo Golf Institute" and "tremendous history" (Sam Snead won the 1942 PGA Championship here); but despite its heritage, the "wide-open, links-style layout" with its "turtle-shell greens" "won't leave you scratching your head" – although the "brutal flies" just might.

⛶ Seaview Marriott, Pines   23 | 24 | 24 | 19 | $129

Absecon | 401 S. New York Rd. | 609-748-7680 | 800-932-8000 | www.seaviewgolf.com | 6731/5276; 71.7/69.8; 128/119

Although this younger "inland" sibling to the Bay course is perhaps "not as popular" to visitors, locals laud it as the "superior" setup, offering "traditional" holes that prove "more challenging" thanks to "longer, narrower", "tree-lined" fairways and "small greens"; given two layouts so "totally opposite", "you won't believe you're at the same resort", except that the duo shares a "required cart and forecaddie" policy and a clubhouse so "old-world" that "argyles, knickers and a necktie" seem fitting.

	COURSE	FACIL.	SERVICE	VALUE	COST

Shore Gate

	24	17	20	19	$99

Ocean View | 35 School House Ln. | 609-624-8337 |
www.shoregategolfclub.com | 7227/5284; 74.9/71.1; 136/126

"Bring your A-game" to Ocean View and "one of the toughest courses at
the Shore", a layout that's "still growing in" and promising to become
even more "brutally difficult" with time; there's "no residential development to spoil the aesthetic value" of its towering trees, "miles of waste
bunkers and sand", "well-defined" holes and "well-protected greens",
but some lament that the rates seem to be "getting higher every year."

⛳ Twisted Dune

	24	16	19	20	$105

Egg Harbor Township | 2101 Ocean Heights Ave. | 609-653-8019 |
www.twisteddune.com | 7329/5166; 75.2/69; 132/120

"Pass the haggis" say fans of this "links-style" "bit of Scotland" in Egg
Harbor Township, a "visually intimidating" course where "enormous
dunes", "fast fairways" and fescue make it "unlike any other" "at the
Jersey Shore" and a "great value"; "high-handicappers beware", for
while the "driver-friendly" holes are "wide", "if it's out of the fairway,
it's probably gone", and that's no laughing matter – unlike the spartan
clubhouse, which is "a joke for a course of this caliber."

Vineyard Golf at Renault

	20	17	19	19	$89

Egg Harbor | 72 N. Bremen Ave. | 609-965-2111 | www.renaultwinery.com |
7213/5176; 75.3/68.8; 132/117

Though it's somewhat "close to Philly", fans liken this Egg Harbor
course to a leisurely "trip to Napa" where you "hit over Chardonnay
vines" on to "beautiful" and "interesting holes" laid out amid "acres of
vineyards" that provide just "enough challenge without being impossible"; however, like some of the pressings from the "winery on-site",
this 2004 vintage "needs maturity", as well as a practice area to go
with its "great" "adjoining hotel and restaurant."

Bridgewater

Neshanic Valley

	25	23	20	25	$75

Neshanic Station | 2301 S. Branch Rd. | 908-369-8200 |
www.somersetcountyparks.org
Lake/Meadow | 7069/5096; 73.8/69.4; 130/119
Meadow/Ridge | 7079/5050; 73.7/69.1; 130/118
Ridge/Lake | 7065/5061; 73.7/64.5; 128/110

"A value even for non-residents" of Somerset County, this "challenging
but fair" 27-holer boasts a long, treeless expanse "kept in immaculate
condition" plus "state-of-the-art" facilities including "a two-sided
driving range, putting greens and practice holes" as well as an "enjoyable executive course" and "on-site Callaway demo center"; all in all,
it goes "way beyond what you expect" for a muni.

Royce Brook, East

	22	22	21	19	$105

Hillsborough | 201 Hamilton Rd. | 908-904-4786 | 888-434-3673 |
www.roycebrook.com | 6946/5062; 73.9/69.6; 135/121

"One of the few high-end courses without housing" abutting its holes,
this "well-maintained" Hillsborough parklander is "like a links course"
with its "wide-open" fairways ("beware the wind"), "plentiful bunkers" and "multi-tiered greens"; other assets include "one of the best

practice facilities" in the state, a "nice clubhouse" and a staff that "treats you like a member" of "the private West course" – an effect enhanced by the "expensive" fees.

Camden

☑ Pine Hill ⏱

27	25	23	20	$100

Pine Hill | 500 W. Branch Ave. | 856-435-3100 | 877-450-8866 | www.golfpinehill.com | 6969/4922; 74.2/68.4; 144/121

Though some surveyors nickname this the "poor man's Pine Valley", this "tough" Tom Fazio design is "pricey" just like its private "next-door" neighbor; nevertheless, the majority maintains it's "worth the money" to "test your skills" on New Jersey's top-rated Course, a "beautiful" but "unforgiving" layout marked by "first-rate grooming", "elevation not usually seen" in these parts and "views of the Philly skyline" to the northwest; you'll "remember every hole", but "hurry" – it's "soon to go private."

Scotland Run

24	22	20	18	$105

Williamstown | 2626 Fries Mill Rd. | 856-863-3737 | www.scotlandrun.com | 6810/5010; 73.3/69.5; 134/120

"No, it's not Scotland", but this "impeccably manicured" track in Williamstown is still "linksy without the water" and supplies abundant "drama" via "rolling, rumpled" fairways and "long carries", not to mention a view of "skydivers" thanks to the nearby airport ("if a parachutist lands on your head, what's the ruling?"); it's "pricey", but an "accommodating" staff and "terrific 19th hole" help to make it "the paradigm for the country-club-for-a-day" experience.

Cape May

Cape May National

19	15	16	16	$85

Cape May | Florence Ave. at Rte. 9 | 609-884-1563 | www.cmngc.com | 6905/4711; 73.4/66.7; 136/116

It's nicknamed 'The Natural', and this Cape May course "tries hard to keep it that way", so be sure to "bring your bug spray" to play a "beautiful" layout that includes a 50-acre bird sanctuary; although some say the wetland-strewn "course could stand better maintenance", purists enjoy "a mix of links and standard holes" that provide "risk/reward shots" and just "enough variation"; sure, you'll pay "Jersey Shore prices", but it's a "nice escape" when "on vacation with the family."

Sand Barrens

23	19	20	19	$115

Swainton | 1765 Rte. 9 N. | 609-465-3555 | 800-465-3122 | www.sandbarrensgolf.com
North/South | 6969/4946; 72.7/68; 133/120
South/West | 6895/4971; 71.7/68.3; 130/119
West/North | 7092/4951; 70.4/67.9; 129/119

There "must be 1,000 traps" strewn among the "interesting" three nines of this "aptly named" layout (bring a "bucket to build sand castles"), but where there is turf, it's generally in "fantastic" condition, with "wide fairways" that only cause trouble "if you miss them"; given its proximity to Cape May, it's "crowded" come summer, thus some putters plea "hey, spread out the tee times a little!"

	COURSE	FACIL.	SERVICE	VALUE	COST

Freehold

Charleston Springs, North

26	20	19	25	$72

Millstone | 101 Woodville Rd. | 732-409-7227 |
www.monmouthcountyparks.com | 7011/5071; 73.4/69.7; 126/117
"You would think you were at a Carolinas resort course" playing this
Monmouth County muni, as the "well-kept", links-style holes are
adorned with "lots of fescue" and the primary rough can grow to
"three or four inches high"; the undulating, well-bunkered layout
comes complete with a "helpful" staff and "beautiful facilities" (including a "grass driving range and practice area"), making it – along
with its younger sibling – one of the "best values in New Jersey."

Charleston Springs, South ⏰

25	20	18	27	$72

Millstone | 101 Woodville Rd. | 732-409-7227 |
www.monmouthcountyparks.com | 6953/5153; 73.2/69.7; 125/118
Whether or not this Mark Mungeam design is "a shade below" its sibling, North, the hilly parkland muni is still considered "one of the very
best in New Jersey", boasting "solid, true" greens kept in "perfect condition", plenty of bunkers and fescue to "make it tough" and "extensive
practice facilities"; in fact, clubbers who "can't believe it's a county-
run" layout laud it as a "great course at a great value."

Eagle Ridge 🏨

21	19	19	20	$97

Lakewood | 2 Augusta Blvd. | 732-901-4900 | www.eagleridgegolf.com |
6607/4792; 72.4/68.3; 132/125
"Tight, entertaining" and "surprisingly hilly", this Ault/Clark design in
Lakewood is a "solid course near the Jersey Shore", where "you need
all the shots" to navigate its "interesting structure"; though critics are
underwhelmed by the sight of "tract homes" on the front nine, the
"renovated clubhouse is gorgeous" and the "restaurant is excellent",
"scoring a double eagle with its panoramic views of the 10th and 18th."

Hominy Hill

26	16	16	24	$80

Colts Neck | 92 Mercer Rd. | 732-462-9223 |
www.monmouthcountyparks.com | 7049/5793; 74.2/73.6; 131/129
A "jewel in the Monmouth County system", this "Robert Trent
Jones Sr.-designed" muni in "beautiful" "horse country" is "what others should aspire to be": a "real challenge" that "requires all the shots"
and is "a screaming deal" (though "nonresident fees" elicit an "ouch");
maybe the facilities "don't match the course" (ditto the service), but
its popularity is such that "getting a tee time" can be tough and you
may face a "slow go on weekends."

Howell Park

20	14	15	23	$56

Farmingdale | Preventorium Rd. | 732-938-4771 |
www.monmouthcountyparks.com | 6964/5698; 73/72.5; 126/125
"Monmouth County residents rejoice" over the "bang for the buck" delivered by this muni with "true rolling greens" and a "nice mix" of
"challenging" and "go-for-it" holes; despite some complaints – there's
"no snack bar or cart service", staffers "could use lessons in courtesy"
and course conditions "have gone downhill in recent years" – most
deem it a "very playable" "value"; P.S. hydrophobes suggest you "can-
cel your tee time if it rains."

NYC Metro

☑ Architects

25 | 16 | 20 | 20 | $100

Phillipsburg | 700 Strykers Rd. | 908-213-3080 | www.thearchitectsclub.com | 6863/5233; 73.3/71.1; 130/123

"History abounds" at this tribute to golf's "great architects", a "diverse" course 70 miles from NYC that incorporates styles from legendary designers in an "incredible layout" that "flows" well and is "fair for all levels"; even better, it offers "spectacular views of the countryside"; P.S. the Facilities score may not reflect the addition of a new clubhouse, which makes this "pricey" proposition one step closer to being "a country club without the initiation fee."

Berkshire Valley ☉

22 | 14 | 16 | 22 | $75

Oak Ridge | 28 Cozy Lake Rd. | 973-208-0018 | www.morrisparks.net | 6810/4647; 73.1/66.9; 133/115

"Hit it straight" then "hang on for your life" during the first few holes perched atop a steep ridge (the "long drop-offs" are "unforgiving") at this "pricey" Morris County muni, a "challenging public track" where "carts are a must"; thankfully, "the rest of the course plays in a valley" and has such "scenic views" that you'll forget any initial headaches.

☑ Crystal Springs, Ballyowen 🏌

27 | 25 | 24 | 19 | $140

Hamburg | 105-137 Wheatsworth Rd. | 973-827-5996 | www.crystalgolfresort.com | 7094/4903; 73.6/66.9; 131/106

There's "no need to go to Europe" when you can "BYOK (bring your own kilt)" to this "shockingly nice links-style layout" in Hamburg that's like "a Scottish moor" thanks to "rolling fairways", wandering sheep and "the sound of bagpipes" "to cap off the day"; "fast greens" and "unforgiving" fescue make it "tough", but "every hole is distinctive and in great condition", so ignore the "high greens fees" and be rewarded with a "really unique experience."

Crystal Springs, Black Bear 🏌

19 | 18 | 18 | 18 | $82

Hamburg | 138 State Rte. 23 N. | 973-827-5996 | www.crystalgolfresort.com | 6673/4785; 72.2/67.7; 130/116

Crystal Springs' "secluded" "bear of a course" is "cheaper than its brothers, but no less sweet", a slightly different animal that's "fun", "forgiving" and "great for novice to intermediate" players (facilities include the on-site David Glenz Golf Academy); expect "blind shots", elevation changes and other "challenges" – "decision-making is key" – but it's "worth the effort" for the "magnificent mountain views" alone.

Crystal Springs, Crystal Springs Course 🏌

19 | 22 | 21 | 16 | $95

Hamburg | 1 Wild Turkey Way | 973-827-5996 | www.crystalgolfresort.com | 6808/5111; 74.1/70.5; 137/123

"If you can play well here, you can play well anywhere" say proponents of this "pricey" mountain parcel that offers one of the "best collections of par 3s" around (including a "majestic 11th with an 80-ft. drop from tee to green") plus "beautiful facilities"; but the "scenic" course "weaves in and out of housing developments", and some find the "narrow" track "gimmicky", citing "awkward lies" that "punish good shots" and "so many moguls you could ski the course."

	COURSE	FACIL.	SERVICE	VALUE	COST

Crystal Springs, Wild Turkey 🏌

| | 24 | 24 | 22 | 20 | $119 |

Hamburg | 1 Wild Turkey Way | 973-827-5996 | www.crystalgolfresort.com |
7202/5024; 74.8/69; 131/118

"Always in prime shape", this "slice of golfing heaven" (the youngest
of the Crystal Springs' flock) offers "a little bit of everything": "magnificent mountain views", a lodge-style clubhouse, "varied elevations"
and "breathtaking holes" like the "tough par-3 7th over a water-filled
rock quarry"; birdie-hunters are advised to "bring your A-game, your
wallet" and some patience, as this "close second" to sister Ballyowen
is "expensive" and "crowded."

Crystal Springs, Great Gorge 🏌

| | 21 | 15 | 16 | 18 | $89 |

McAfee | State Rte. 517 | 973-827-7603 | www.crystalgolfresort.com
Lakeside/Quarryside | 6710/5354; 72.7/66.6; 133/119
Quarryside/Railside | 6758/5502; 72.9/66.8; 129/115
Railside/Lakeside | 6852/5518; 73.3/67.2; 132/117

Now drawing a different sort of swinger, this McAfee facility adjacent
to an "old Playboy Club" in New Jersey's "boonies" offers three "beautiful, diverse" nines; the courses' "challenging" but "fun" holes make
for "a good outing" featuring "stunning scenery" that includes
"unique" rock cliffs, railroad artifacts and "lots of water"; sure, it's
"not always in the best shape", but drivers deem it "a better value than
the other" Crystal Springs courses.

Flanders Valley, Red/Gold

| | 21 | 10 | 13 | 23 | $51 |

Flanders | 81 Pleasant Hill Rd. | 973-584-5382 | www.morrisparks.org |
6770/5540; 72.3/72.8; 130/127

Morris County clubbers can see their "property taxes at work" at this
"wonderful muni" that offers both "scenic beauty" and "challenge" –
"you need to be half-mountain goat, half-woodpecker to survive the
hills and trees"; although it draws criticism for its "poor maintenance"
(the "once-premier public" "desperately needs a driving range"),
putters proclaim it "fun to play" and "overall" "a great value."

Flanders Valley, White/Blue

| | 21 | 12 | 13 | 25 | $51 |

Flanders | 81 Pleasant Hill Rd. | 973-584-5382 | www.morrisparks.org |
6765/5534; 72.5/72.6; 129/127

"A value for residents" of Morris County, the flatter of the Flanders
Valley munis is a narrow, tree-lined track that's "a pleasure to play",
"fun to walk" and "nearly as challenging as" its Red/Gold sibling; but
though it "compares very well to New Jersey's [other] public courses",
you should nevertheless expect conditions that "have not been well-
maintained" and "grumpy old starters" that for at least one well-
wisher "add to the charm."

High Bridge Hills

| | 20 | 12 | 15 | 21 | $75 |

High Bridge | 203 Cregar Rd. | 908-638-5055 | www.highbridgehills.com |
6640/4928; 72/68.9; 130/116

"Don't make dinner plans" unless you factor in a "five-and-a-half-hour
round" on weekends, as this "beautiful", "links-style" Hunterdon
County "hidden gem" is "not so secret anymore", attracting "too many
hackers who can't handle the wind", the "thick fescue" or "blind
shots"; "fantastic views" help atone for "severely lacking" facilities,
and if some say service has "slipped a bit", at least the staff is "nice."

	COURSE	FACIL.	SERVICE	VALUE	COST

Sunset Valley — 19 | 10 | 11 | 21 | $49

Pompton Plains | 47 W. Sunset Rd. | 973-835-1515 | www.morrisparks.net | 6483/5274; 76.9/71; 136/122

No wonder it's "hard to get a tee time" at this "short" but "scenic" course, a "good value in Morris County" where "extremely hilly" terrain and "challenging", speedy greens "can eat your lunch"; while the "mature trees" give it "more than a hint of country-club flavor", "barebones" facilities and a "grumpy" staff "remind you that this is a muni."

New Mexico

Albuquerque

☑ Paa-Ko Ridge — 28 | 23 | 23 | 26 | $71

Sandia Park | 1 Clubhouse Dr. | 505-281-6000 | 866-898-5987 | www.paakoridge.com
Back Nine/New Nine | 7667/5846; 75.8/71.9; 139/134
Front Nine/Back Nine | 7562/5702; 75.2/71.7; 137/134
New Nine/Front Nine | 7579/5896; 75.6/72.2; 137/134

This course "should be on your must-play list" because "all three nines" are draped across the "mountainous countryside" outside Albuquerque, offering "elevation changes galore" amid "scenery that takes your breath away" with "plenty of trees" and wildlife; the "superb design" offsets the "generous fairway width" by "penalizing stray shots severely", making it "great for all levels", not to mention an "amazing value" for all wallets.

NEW Sandia — ▽ 23 | 23 | 21 | 21 | $75

Albuquerque | 30 Rainbow Rd. NE | 505-798-3990 | www.sandiagolf.com | 7772/5112; 75.1/67; 125/113

Architect Scott Miller of Coeur d'Alene fame designed this "great new course" in Albuquerque that's "right next to one of the best casinos" around and boasts "nice views of the Sandia Mountains"; it's "enjoyable" and "very forgiving", with "long downhill and short uphill holes", and fans predict with "another year to mature" it "will only get better" and fully complement the "excellent" resort facilities.

Santa Ana Golf Course — ▽ 19 | 21 | 18 | 21 | $55

Bernalillo | 288 Prarie Star Rd. | 505-867-9464 | www.santaanagolf.com
Cheena/Star | 7145/5060; 73/68.3; 135/118
Star/Tamaya | 7187/4936; 73.1/72.9; 134/133
Tamaya/Cheena | 7298/7034; 74.1/68.2; 133/122

Given its "other-worldly terrain" "overlooking the Rio Grande" and the Sandia Mountains, this is "one of the prettiest courses in New Mexico", a linksy Albuquerque-area layout where all three nine-hole tracks are "well laid out" and provide a "good value"; for many, the "friendly starters" are worth the price of admission alone, as is the adobe-styled Prairie Star restaurant, which offers an eclectic Southwestern menu.

Twin Warriors — 25 | 24 | 22 | 20 | $145

Santa Ana Pueblo | 1301 Tuyuna Trail | 505-771-6155 | www.twinwarriorsgolf.com | 7736/5843; 75/69.6; 130/125

"Santa Ana's upscale cousin" is one of the "most expensive" courses in the area, but when desert duffers declare "there are no cheap pars here", most are referring to the "difficult", "target-golf" design with "arroyos everywhere" and "some nasty canyons" that "call for strategic play"; situated an hour north of Albuquerque, the layout also sports a "superb" staff, a primo practice area and the "fabulous" Hyatt Regency nearby.

University of New Mexico Championship Golf Course

24 | 16 | 17 | 27 | $67

Albuquerque | 3601 University Blvd. SE | 505-277-4546 | 7272/5451; 74.6/69.1; 133/128

Like college (i.e. "fun and demanding"), this U. of New Mexico track "tests all areas of one's game" through its "great variety" of "deceptively challenging" holes designed with "approach shots to elevated greens" that are "fast" and "tricky"; even though the 40-year-old course "has an old muni feel to it" and some say it "needs TLC", the track is a valedictorian in the value category – it's a "great course for the money."

Farmington

Piñon Hills

▽ 25 | 20 | 19 | 28 | $40

Farmington | 2101 Sunrise Pkwy. | 505-326-6066 | www.farmington.nm.us | 7198/5428; 73.9/70.6; 139/125

Arguably one of the "best values in the country", this "beautiful", "challenging" track in "out-of-the-way" Farmington is "one of the best you'll ever play" attest aficionados; given the terrain, with its sandstone canyons and arroyos, it's no surprise there are a "couple of funky holes", but it's a "solid design" overall and, when "combined with a fishing trip on the San Juan River", it adds up to a "perfect weekend."

Santa Fe

Black Mesa

24 | 15 | 18 | 22 | $64

La Mesilla | 115 State Rd. 399 | 505-747-8946 | www.blackmesagolfclub.com | 7307/5162; 73.9/71.2; 141/125

"Bring your camera" (and "plenty of balls") to this "gorgeous", "hilly" La Mesilla course "carved into the mesas", where "every hole has its own challenges", including "funky greens" and "many blind shots" that could wind up in "rattlesnake habitats" because there is "no out of bounds"; it can be "difficult for average golfers", but many still enjoy this "desert oasis" where you "feel like you're the only one there."

New York

TOP COURSES IN STATE

	COURSE	FACIL.	SERVICE	VALUE	COST

Adirondacks

Lake Placid Resort, Links

▽ **25** | **18** | **18** | **20** | **$69**

Lake Placid | 1 Morningside Dr. | 518-523-2556 | 800-874-1980 | 6936/5021; 73.6/71; 138/125

"Regardless of your handicap", you'll have "fun", since there's "not too much trouble for well-struck shots" when playing this links-style Adirondacks track boasting "consistently well-maintained" holes; given the "amazing views" of the surrounding mountains, it's no surprise that some claim the course "should be walked" – and others say the "outstanding" resort setting is perfect for "post-round libations" on the clubhouse deck.

Lake Placid Resort, Mountain

▽ **20** | **19** | **18** | **22** | **$45**

Lake Placid | 1 Morningside Dr. | 518-523-2556 | 800-874-1980 | 6294/4985; 71.6/72; 127/120

This "nice mix of holes" in the Adirondacks "doesn't rely on length to be challenging", but instead employs "very hilly" terrain that can "make level lies a rarity" – "billy goats are the ones who should be playing this course" – and "blind shots" commonplace; the "spectacular views of the mountains" and "unbeatable prices" help atone for the "sinful lack of yardage markers."

Sagamore, The

24 | **22** | **22** | **19** | **$125**

Bolton Landing | Frank Cameron Rd. | 518-644-9400 | www.thesagamore.com | 6821/5176; 73.8/73; 137/122

You'll "step back in time" when you step onto this "classic Donald Ross track" in the Adirondacks, a "hard" yet "fun" "shot-maker's course" offering "superb views" of Lake George and the mountains, "varied elevations", "wooded terrain" and the architect's "signature greens with false fronts"; be advised, however, that both the "cart-path-only" rule and the "steep prices" are strictly 21st century.

Whiteface

▽ **22** | **20** | **21** | **19** | **$55**

Lake Placid | Whiteface Inn Rd. | 518-523-2551 | 800-422-6757 | www.whitefaceclubresort.com | 6451/5305; 71.1/72; 123/126

"Whiteface Mountain is a stunning backdrop" for this "mature" "forest" course producing a mix of "easy" and "challenging" holes, particularly those that are "tight", "tree-lined" and have trouble spots off the fairway "where the sun doesn't shine"; aside from "occasional greenskeeping" lapses that can sometimes leave the "9th green as bald as Bruce Willis", this "attractive" Adirondacks layout is "not to be missed."

Albany

Leatherstocking

24 | **22** | **24** | **20** | **$95**

Cooperstown | 60 Lake St. | 607-547-9931 | 800-348-6222 | www.otesaga.com | 6401/5180; 70.8/70.2; 135/122

One reason "so many Hall of Famers return for Cooperstown's induction weekend every summer" is to hit this "thinking player's" course, a "sporty and fun" layout along the shores of Lake Otesaga with "beautiful views" of the water plus "short, tight, rolling fairways", "small", "elevated greens" and a "closing hole that resembles [the one at] Pebble Beach"; P.S. the track is also hitched to a "first-class" resort.

	COURSE	FACIL.	SERVICE	VALUE	COST

NEW YORK

Saratoga National 🏌

| 25 | 24 | 24 | 20 | $175 |

Saratoga Springs | 458 Union Ave. | 518-583-4653 |
www.golfsaratoga.com | 7265/4954; 75.7/69.3; 147/121
A public course with a "country-club feel", this "beautiful" and "very challenging" track features "well-maintained" peninsula tees, fairways and greens that are complemented by a "great clubhouse" with "spectacular food" and a "friendly staff"; the "only downside is that it's so expensive", but "it helps when a pony comes out a winner for you" at the Saratoga Race Track "only three miles away."

Saratoga Spa, Championship 🏌

| – | – | – | – | $32 |

Saratoga Springs | 60 Roosevelt Dr. | 518-584-2006 |
www.saratogaspagolf.com | 7141/5567; 74.4/71.1; 130/119
Nestled in Saratoga Spa State Park just south of Saratoga Springs, this value-priced public is known for the towering pine trees that flank its generous fairways, offering players a sense of seclusion from other golfers; the self-proclaimed 'home of the four-and-a-half-hour round' is also home to a golf school, nine-hole executive course, grass driving range and the casual Catherine's in the Park restaurant.

Catskills

Concord Resort, Monster

| 24 | 14 | 15 | 19 | $95 |

Kiamesha Lake | 91 Chalet Rd. | 845-794-4000 | 888-448-9686 |
www.concordresort.com | 7650/5442; 76.8/70.6; 137/125
This Catskills course is aptly named for the "monumental test" it administers over "rolling hills", "long, long, long" holes with "lots of water" and "large greens" with "subtle breaks"; a new resort is being built to replace the "limited", "drab" facilities and the course will undergo a "badly needed face-lift" in 2007, so expect a return to what "was once a mecca of vacationing"; N.B. the International course will remain open during the Monster's renovation.

Grossinger, Big G

| 25 | 14 | 16 | 21 | $85 |

Liberty | 127 Grossinger Rd. | 845-292-9000 | www.grossingergolf.net |
7004/5730; 73.5/72.3; 133/127
Located at what was once a thriving Borscht Belt resort, this track is "the best in the Catskills", a "lovely", "championship-caliber" mountain course with "valley holes" that offer "wide fairways" and "rolling greens", the latter being a "nightmare" to read at times; despite the layout's "poor facilities" ("it deserves better care and attention"), it's still "first-rate" and an "excellent value" too.

Nevele Grande

| 17 | 14 | 16 | 17 | $75 |

Ellenville | 1 Nevele Rd. | 845-647-6000 | 800-647-6000 | www.nevele.com
Blue/Red | 6823/5145; 73.5/69.8; 126/118
Red/White | 6532/4570; 71.8/66.6; 126/113
White/Blue | 6573/4881; 71.7/68; 124/116
While the Catskills may be passé, these 27 holes are "surprisingly good" (the Blue nine was designed by Robert Trent Jones Jr.) and lots of "fun", "especially when you leave the kids in the Nevele camp and play unrushed"; nevertheless, critics complain of "lackluster" service and maintenance, and urge management to "invest" in "renovating" a course that they say still boasts a "great layout."

Windham

19 | 16 | 18 | 21 | $60

Windham | 36 South St. | 518-734-9910 | www.windhamcountryclub.com | 6091/4733; 70.4/69.2; 120/112

At just over "6,000 yards", this "fun mountain course" "isn't terribly long" but it is prized as a "tough" track with "great views", "fast greens" and the type of "scenic" rolling terrain where "you'll be hiking up and down hills, even with a cart"; what's more, it's "one of the best-manicured spots in the Catskills."

Finger Lakes

Bristol Harbour ⛳

▽ 23 | 22 | 20 | 24 | $69

Canandaigua | 5410 Seneca Point Rd. | 585-396-2460 | 800-288-8248 | www.bristolharbour.com | 6662/5482; 73.4/72.5; 136/132

Though both nines at this "well-conditioned", "challenging" course in the Finger Lakes region were designed by RTJ Sr. and afford "great views of Lake Canandaigua", they are "very different" in terms of terrain: the front is level while the back is hilly with holes like the 14th, which "drops off the face of the earth into a gorge"; regulars also compliment a 19th hole where you can "sit in a chair and take in the views of the lake."

Chenango Valley State Park

▽ 16 | 13 | 16 | 25 | $24

Chenango Forks | 153 State Park Rd. | 607-648-9804 | www.nysparks.com | 6406/5282; 70.4/69.3; 125/120

Just 15 minutes north of Binghamton, this state-owned, "old-style" public is "very well-kept" and "fun to play", with "some interesting holes" (as well as "some dogs") plus "tree-lined fairways" that can be "challenging"; the atmosphere is "comfortable" and "good senior rates" add to its "super value."

Conklin Players Club

27 | 19 | 20 | 26 | $62

Conklin | 1520 Conklin Rd. | 607-775-3042 | www.conklinplayers.com | 6772/4699; 72.5/67.8; 127/116

The "scenic views" almost equal the "fantastic conditions" at this "natural course" just southeast of Binghamton, where the "tough but still fun" "design follows the landscape"; the "par 3s are relatively short" and some grouse the "par 4s lack imagination", but with "greens that roll like carpets", an "accommodating" staff and GPS-equipped carts, many feel it's one of the "best values in upstate New York."

Greystone

- | - | - | - | $45

Walworth | 1400 Atlantic Ave. | 315-524-0022 | 800-810-2325 | www.234golf.com | 7215/5277; 74.3/70.4; 128/118

Locals long for this "lovely" links layout just south of Lake Ontario, where there are "no bum holes", only "real beauties" that include the "great" 429-yard par-4 closer with a do-or-die carry over a green-guarding pond; after a round, fans can repair to the warmly decorated Stoney's Pub, where they'll watch other whiffers take whacks at the 9th and 18th's gargantuan shared green.

Links at Hiawatha Landing

▽ 24 | 21 | 24 | 24 | $65

Apalachin | 2350 Marshland Rd. | 607-687-6952 | 800-304-6533 | www.hiawathalinks.com | 7150/5101; 74.4/69.8; 133/118

"Fescue abounds" at this "well-maintained" "links-style" layout that's "one of the best" in the Binghamton area thanks to a design that "makes you use every club in the bag"; a "helpful" staff and "great" facilities bolster the course's "good-value" status.

Ravenwood   23 | 20 | 19 | 22 | $57

Victor | 929 Lynaugh Rd. | 585-924-5100 | www.ravenwoodgolf.com | 7026/4906; 73.7/68.7; 138/118

This 2002 Robin Nelson layout has "come into its own" and matured into a "true golf course" where you can expect "good conditioning" and "great holes" (plus a couple of "quirky" ones) that are "playable" given the "five tee box choices"; overall, they must be doing something right at this Victor venue, as the "pace of play is excellent."

Seven Oaks ⏱   ▽ 24 | 15 | 16 | 26 | $65

Hamilton | 13 Oak Dr. | 315-824-1432 | www.sevenoaksgolf.com | 6915/5252; 74.4/72.1; 144/125

Even "if you aren't smart enough" to attend Colgate, playing its "Robert Trent Jones Sr. original" is a no-brainer, thanks to the "genius architect" who created a "long, demanding" course in a "pastoral" setting with "great views of the campus"; though the "facilities are spartan", it's still a "great deal if you're a student or alumnus" and "pretty cheap" for everyone else; N.B. no non-member tee times before 1 PM on weekends.

Turning Stone, Atunyote   ▽ 28 | 28 | 28 | 18 | $200

Verona | 5218 Patrick Rd. | 315-829-3867 | 800-771-7711 | www.turning-stone.com | 7315/5120; 75.6/69.8; 140/120

Stretching more than "7,300 yards from the tips", the "best of the Turning Stone courses" "plays long but fair" and is considered "deserving" of a "PGA Tour stop"; located 40 minutes east of Syracuse, the layout is "pricey" but "spectacular in every way", from the "immaculate conditions" and "great facilities" to a staff that "treats you like a member" and amenities like a complimentary "sleeve of Pro Vs, lunch or breakfast and on-course refreshments."

Turning Stone, Kaluhyat 🏌   ▽ 27 | 28 | 27 | 22 | $125

Verona | 5218 Patrick Rd. | 315-361-8518 | 800-771-7711 | www.turning-stone.com | 7105/5293; 75.1/71.5; 146/134

Those swingers who "can't pronounce the name" (ga-LU-yut) still find this Robert Trent Jones Jr. design to be "another outstanding course at Turning Stone" and an "excellent alternative" to Atunyote; while "not as hard" as its "pricier big brother", it's "not for beginners" either, for a number of "long carries" mean there's "not an easy hole" in the bunch; it's in "great condition" and usually "not crowded", making it "worth the trip" even for those who live "far away."

Turning Stone, Shenendoah   27 | 26 | 25 | 21 | $130

Verona | 5218 Patrick Rd. | 315-361-8518 | 800-771-7711 | www.turning-stone.com | 7129/5185; 74.1/71.6; 142/120

"The first of the three" courses built at the Oneida Indian Nation's Turning Stone resort is also "the busiest", likely because it boasts the "widest of fairways" as well as a "variety of holes" that "mix parkland with links-style" and can "accommodate any skill level"; there's also a "great practice range" and facilities, a "helpful staff" and carts that are "equipped with GPS and maps", but if you want to crack a cold one, remember that it's "BYOB."

	COURSE	FACIL.	SERVICE	VALUE	COST

Hudson Valley

Garrison Golf Club

| 21 | 15 | 17 | 20 | $90 |

Garrison | 2015 Rte. 9 | 845-424-4747 | www.garrisongolfclub.com | 6497/4902; 71.7/69.6; 132/123

Located "on the Hudson River opposite West Point", this circa-1960s Dick Wilson design offers "woodsy", "rolling hills" with "many elevation changes", "tough tee shots over deep ravines", "sidehill lies" and "challenging greens" with "lots of false fronts"; it's "much less crowded than city courses" plus a "much better value" for many, and while some grouse about the "claustrophobic" facilities, golfergourmands praise the "great restaurant and 19th hole."

Links at Union Vale

| 23 | 20 | 21 | 23 | $65 |

LaGrangeville | 153 N. Parliman Rd. | 845-223-1000 | www.thelinksatunionvale.com | 6954/5198; 73.8/72; 136/126

"Irish charm and hospitality" (the staff "couldn't be nicer") turn up in the Hudson Valley at this "beautifully maintained", bona fide links-style course that challenges with "few trees and lots of rough"; in all, the "scenic" views, "good value" and "amazing beer offerings" in the pub make you "feel like you're playing in Ireland."

Tennanah Lake Golf & Tennis Club

∇ | 16 | 14 | 18 | 22 | $50 |

Roscoe | 100 Fairway View Dr. | 607-498-5000 | 888-561-3935 | www.tennanah.com | 6546/5164; 72.1/70.1; 128/120

Early risers can "tee off with a beautiful view of morning fog in the valleys" and "deer prancing" at this Catskills course designed by Sam Snead, but critics find the track "flat, straight and uninteresting" and some even wish the Slammer had "stuck to golfing"; still, given the "attentive" staff, "recently renovated" clubhouse and "plans afoot to update the hotel", optimists feel the experience only "promises to get better."

Town of Wallkill Golf Club

| 20 | 15 | 15 | 23 | $48 |

Middletown | 40 Sands Rd. | 845-361-1022 | www.townofwallkill.com | 6470/5125; 72.5/70.7; 125/118

There is "a lot of variety" in the "scenic and well-maintained" layout of this Orange County muni, including several "doglegs" and "blind shots", and with its "narrow fairways" "you better throw darts" off the tee and onto the "big greens"; though it "fills up fast", it "plays fast" too, and you "can't complain about the price", "especially if you live in the county."

Long Island

☑ Bethpage, Black 朮

| 29 | 19 | 18 | 28 | $102 |

Farmingdale | 99 Quaker Meeting House Rd. | 516-249-0700 | www.nysparks.com | 7297/6223; 76.6/78.9; 148/146

It "can take months" to secure a slot, so "be prepared to sleep in your car to get a tee time" at A.W. Tillinghast's Farmingdale "masterpiece", the 2002 (and future 2009) U.S. Open host that's also New York's top-rated Course; despite "slow rounds", this "monster" is "worth the effort" on account of the "priceless beating it gives you" – every hole seems like it's either "uphill" or a sharp dogleg, and the rough is so "thick and deep" that even slightly "misplaced tee shots leave bogey at best"; N.B. it's walking-only.

Bethpage, Blue 🏌

22 | 19 | 17 | 26 | $36

Farmingdale | 99 Quaker Meeting House Rd. | 516-249-0700 | www.nysparks.com | 6638/6158; 71.7/74.7; 124/129

Although it "doesn't get the attention the Black and Red do", the "third best" at Bethpage offers a "great variety" of holes that are kept in "top condition", especially the "inverted bowl-shaped greens" that "repel all but the best shots"; the front side's a "bear", so "when you round the 9th you feel like you've played 18", but that's due in part to the un-marshaled, "brutally long rounds"; remember, "you don't go here for service or facilities", "just great golf at a great price."

Bethpage, Green 🏌

20 | 19 | 16 | 26 | $36

Farmingdale | 99 Quaker Meeting House Rd. | 516-249-0700 | www.nysparks.com | 6378/5826; 70.6/73.7; 126/125

For a "user-friendly" "taste of the Black", Bethpage's original course is a "much shorter" and "far less penal" alternative, with "wide-open fairways", "less rough and far, far fewer bunkers"; still, it's no push-over, offering "nice elevation changes", "small greens that emphasize precision" and "some interesting dipsy doodles" that make "you feel like you're walking back through time" – unfortunately, the "six-hour weekend rounds" make some feel stuck in it too.

☑ Bethpage, Red 🏌

26 | 19 | 17 | 28 | $82

Farmingdale | 99 Quaker Meeting House Rd. | 516-249-0700 | www.nysparks.com | 7014/6206; 73/75.2; 128/130

The "Black course for the rest of us" is how some describe this Bethpage "bargain" that's "a little less punishing" than its noir coun-terpart but is still a "world-class track" that's kept in "great shape"; just keep in mind that the "long, tight" layout with doglegs, "fast greens and tall, thick rough" can make for equally "long rounds", es-pecially on weekends when play "slows to a crawl"; P.S. "you can ride in a cart", but "don't expect a lot of [other] amenities."

☑ Harbor Links

21 | 18 | 18 | 16 | $106

Port Washington | 1 Fairway Dr. | 516-767-4807 | www.harborlinks.com | 6927/5465; 73.4/69.1; 129/121

"Finally, a real clubhouse was built" to complement this "well-manicured" muni located 45 minutes from Manhattan, a links-style layout where "good decision-making is essential" given the "rolling hills", "deep grasses" and "split fairways"; "now, if they can just work on getting a grass range" and solving the "way-too-slow" pace of play – then it will be an even nicer "value for residents."

Island's End

18 | 15 | 17 | 20 | $54

Greenport | Rte. 25 | 631-477-0777 | www.islandsendgolf.com | 6655/5017; 71.5/69.6; 123/117

Some say the "religious experience you'll have on the 16th" (a par 3 that plays along the cliffs of the Long Island Sound) makes it "worth the drive" to the tip of the North Fork for this "clubby" public course; while the turf "could be better maintained" and the facilities may "need an upgrade", the track's "not a bad" option, especially since the "price is right."

Long Island National

23 | 20 | 20 | 18 | $129

Riverhead | 1793 Northville Tpke. | 631-727-4653 |
www.longislandnationalgc.com | 6838/5006; 73.6/65.3; 132/114

This "tough" Robert Trent Jones Jr. links design known for its open layout and "deep rough" could be nicknamed "Long Drive" National, because not only is it "far from New York City" in Riverhead, but there's also often "a club or two wind" thwarting players' tee shots; putters pronounce it "pricey" and say the pacing can be "slow on the weekends" on account of "people hunting for balls" in the tall, ever-present fescue.

⊠ Montauk Downs

26 | 18 | 18 | 27 | $82

Montauk | 50 S. Fairview Ave. | 631-668-1100 |
6874/5787; 74.7/75.5; 141/137

It's a real "schlep" to the "tip of Long Island", but this "well-run" state course is an "invigorating" experience, where you can "smell the ocean air" and "wipe the salt spray off your ball"; the "wonderful, old-school layout" has been "made even better by recent refinements by Rees Jones", offering a "varied terrain" and "hidden challenges", with the wind "adding another dimension"; the "driving range is a disappointment" and the "food concession could use improvement", but for most it's still "the bargain of the century."

Oyster Bay Town Golf Course

21 | 16 | 17 | 20 | $65

Woodbury | Southwoods Rd. | 516-677-5980 |
6376/5101; 71.5/70.4; 131/126

"One of the few Fazio courses in the region", this muni is a "short" but "narrow" track with many "elevation changes" and "undulating greens" that "make local knowledge much needed"; it's a "fantastic value if you live in Oyster Bay", although some "non-residents" find it "expensive", especially given the "very small range" and facilities that "need updating."

Rock Hill

20 | 14 | 16 | 19 | $69

Manorville | 105 Clancy Rd. | 631-878-2250 | www.rockhillgolf.com |
7050/5390; 73.4/71.4; 136/121

While it "doesn't compare to more dramatic courses nearby", this "hilly" hot spot has "one of Long Island's best front nines" courtesy of a few "challenging par 4s"; though the "front and back are like two different courses", the flatter second half is "long" and "aesthetically pleasing" – and worthy of a few whacks before you head further east to the Hamptons.

Smithtown Landing ⊙

19 | 16 | 18 | 23 | $35

Smithtown | 495 Landing Ave. | 631-979-6534 | www.mikehebron.com |
6114/5263; 69.3/69.8; 127/121

Fans are glad "one of the top teachers in the U.S.", Mike Hebron, is the pro at this "beautifully maintained" town-owned track "on the north shore of Long Island", for there's "never a flat lie" on its "undulating fairways", offering a "nice challenge" to both "mid-handicappers" and those "playing from the tips"; after the "two beautiful finishing holes", many opt for off-course eats, as the "facilities are just ok"; N.B. only residents or guests accompanied by two residents can play on weekends.

	COURSE	FACIL.	SERVICE	VALUE	COST

Swan Lake

20 | 15 | 16 | 21 | $70

Manorville | 388 River Rd. | 631-369-1818 | 7011/5245; 73.2/69; 125/112

"Yes, there are swans", but those may be the only birdies you'll see at this otherwise "flat" and "forgiving" track where the "extremely large greens" make "three-putts the norm"; though the facilities aren't much more than a "dinky, overpriced coffee shop", fans are simply glad they can "just walk on" a course "on the east end" of Long Island and play "without the crowds."

NYC Metro

Blue Hill

20 | 14 | 16 | 22 | $50

Pearl River | 285 Blue Hill Rd. | 845-735-2094 | www.orangetown.com
Lakeside/Pines | 6500/5500; 70.8/69.8; 128/119
Pines/Woodland | 6400/5200; 70.8/69.8; 128/119
Woodland/Lakeside | 6400/5100; 70.8/69.8; 128/119

The "groundskeeper should be knighted" for how "well-maintained" this "town-owned" 27-holer is, despite the number of rounds played by "Rockland County natives" and city slickers who drive "35-40 minutes" for the "great value"; you might don armor, too, to deflect "wayward shots from nearby holes" (many are "short par-4 doglegs"), but leave your high horse at home and "be real nice" to the staff "to get a tee time."

☒ Centennial

23 | 23 | 21 | 17 | $125

Carmel | 185 Simpson Rd. | 845-225-5700 | 877-783-5700 |
www.centennialgolf.com
Fairways/Meadows | 7050/5208; 74.2/70.6; 137/123
Lakes/Fairways | 7133/5208; 75.3/70.5; 145/126
Lakes/Meadows | 7115/5208; 74.7/70.3; 136/126

This Carmel public provides "three distinct nine-hole courses" that are "as good as advertised", with "breathtaking" views, "dramatic elevation changes" and "challenges" that include "more doglegs than the local shelter"; you'll pay "a lot of money" and "weekend rounds can be long", but that's par for any course "within an hour of NYC", and the "fantastic practice facility", "ESPN and Dave Pelz schools" and "accommodating" staff help to make it a "rewarding" experience.

Hudson Hills

20 | 15 | 17 | 19 | $115

Ossining | 400 Croton Dam Rd. | 914-864-3000 | www.hudsonhillsgolf.com |
6935/5102; 73.3/64.3; 129/110

"Stretch out the hamstrings", because despite being "beautiful to look at" and offering "stunning views", this Westchester County course is a "demanding layout" with "severe elevation changes" and "very high" rough; some, however, say there are "too many trick and blind tee shots" and "dangerous parallel fairways" for an "expensive" muni that "lacks a driving range" on which to warm up.

Mansion Ridge ⛳

23 | 20 | 20 | 17 | $139

Monroe | 1292 Orange Tpke. | 845-782-7888 | www.mansionridge.com |
6889/4785; 73.7/67.9; 142/121

"If you're not long off the tee, bring a lot of balls" to this Jack Nicklaus-designed "challenge" an hour from NYC with "lots of long forced carries" and holes favoring "players who like to fade the ball" or who can "control their slice"; for some, it's "too pricey for what it is" ("GPS in the carts would be nice") and may be best for those on "corporate outings."

Spook Rock

| | 21 | 15 | 15 | 21 | $65 |

Suffern | 233 Spook Rock Rd. | 845-357-6466 | www.ramapo.org | 6806/4880; 72.9/68.3; 136/121

Located "about 40 miles from NYC", this "wonderful" muni "has it all", including "doglegs, water, tricky par 3s" and a design that lives up to its name, especially the greens where you should "play for less break" than the craggy surroundings suggest; it can be "pricey" for non-residents, and getting a tee time can be "impossible", even though there's "not much in the form of practice facilities" and the rangers "do nothing" to alleviate the "very slow play."

North Carolina

TOP COURSES IN STATE

28 Pinehurst, No. 2 | *Pinehurst*
   Pinehurst, No. 8 | *Pinehurst*
26 Pine Needles Lodge, Pine Needles | *Pinehurst*
   Ocean Ridge, Tiger's Eye | *Myrtle Beach Area*
   Oyster Bay | *Myrtle Beach Area*
25 Rivers Edge | *Myrtle Beach Area*
   Pinehurst, No. 7 | *Pinehurst*
   Duke University | *Raleigh-Durham*
   Tobacco Road | *Pinehurst*
   Pinehurst, No. 4 | *Pinehurst*

Asheville

Linville ⚲

| ▽ | 27 | 23 | 24 | 23 | $125 |

Linville | 83 Roseboro Rd. | 828-733-4363 | www.eseeola.com | 6959/4948; 72.7/69.1; 139/122

"Lots of elevation changes" are key to the "fun" at this Donald Ross "mountain" design that attracts aces to its "remote" locale 90 minutes northeast of Asheville with a "beautiful" layout and "great" grooming; despite "tight fairways", some say "it's relatively easy to score here", and all agree the food in the restaurant makes it "worth the visit."

Mt. Mitchell

| | - | - | - | - | $79 |

Burnsville | 11484 Hwy. 80 S. | 828-675-5454 | www.mountmitchellgolfresort.com | 6495/5455; 70/69.5; 121/117

This Toe River Valley course is named more for its spectacular views of the mountains than for its terrain, which proves practically flat and very conducive to walking; indeed, after trekking around this track (whose holes hop the river's southern branch), you can put your feet up at the club's Hawtree's Pub or check into one of the on-site accommodations.

Charlotte

Highland Creek 🏌

| ▽ | 18 | 18 | 15 | 17 | $65 |

Charlotte | 7001 Highland Creek Pkwy. | 704-875-9000 | www.highlandcreekgolfclub.com | 7043/5080; 73.9/70.1; 138/125

Swingers are undecided about this creekside course in Charlotte: while acolytes aver it's a "great" track (especially if you like "lots of water"), purists say it's an "average", "overdeveloped" layout with "houses everywhere"; nevertheless, the parkland design is a "fun-to-play" challenge that places a premium on precise pokes from the tee.

Greensboro

Bryan Park Golf, Champions 🏌

| – | – | – | – | $57 |

Greensboro | 6275 Bryan Park Rd. | 336-375-2200 | www.bryanpark.com | 7155/5395; 74.5/71; 135/121

Set in a 1,500-acre park just north of Greensboro, this 1990 Rees Jones design is a long, picturesque layout that's scheduled to host the U.S. Amateur Public Links Championship in 2010; while the seven holes playing along Lake Townsend and the nearly 100 bunkers should offer participants a steady challenge, a 27-acre practice facility and golf school will help to get regular Joes raring to go.

Tot Hill Farm 🏌

| ▽ 26 | 19 | 21 | 27 | $59 |

Asheboro | 3185 Tot Hill Farm Rd. | 336-857-4455 | 800-868-4455 | www.tothillfarm.com | 6543/4556; 72.5/67.9; 138/118

While this "superb" "Mike Strantz course" with "superior conditioning" is "a lot like Tobacco Road" (i.e. "golf on steroids"), it's a "different experience aesthetically"; aficionados advise "if you're looking for a pretty clubhouse and a spa, go elsewhere", but "if you want fantastic golf" and a "very good value", this Asheboro option "is your place."

Myrtle Beach Area

Bald Head Island

| 22 | 20 | 21 | 18 | $110 |

Bald Head Island | 301 S. Baldhead Wind | 910-457-7310 | 866-657-7311 | www.bhigolf.com | 6804/4847; 73.8/69.1; 137/113

"Those who are up to the challenge of getting there" ("you have to take a ferry") are treated to a "lovely" links-style course that "fits the Lowcountry land nicely as it winds through the forest" and past freshwater lagoons in which there "may be a gator or two"; true, the design may be "dated", but "let's face it, if you're on Bald Head Island and you're a golfer, you're going to play here."

Carolina National 🏌

| 25 | 22 | 22 | 24 | $97 |

Bolivia | 1643 Goley Hewett Rd. SE | 910-755-5200 | 888-200-6455 | www.carolinanationalgolf.com
Egret/Heron | 7017/4738; 74.4/67.3; 138/104
Heron/Ibis | 6961/4675; 72.5/66.8; 140/109
Ibis/Egret | 6944/4737; 72.3/67.3; 136/100

"All three nines are wonderful" at this Fred Couples design that's set along Lockwood Folly River in Bolivia and "winds its way through wetlands and Carolina pines"; the "beautiful" setting makes for "nice aesthetics on each approach" shot, while "ample room off the tee" and "tricky putting surfaces" "keep you thinking"; and though there are "homes on the course", they "don't crowd it", which is yet another reason it's "worth a visit while on vacation."

Ocean Ridge Plantation, Lion's Paw 🏌

| 19 | 22 | 20 | 20 | $71 |

Ocean Isle Beach | 351 Ocean Ridge Pkwy. | 910-287-1703 | www.big-cats.com | 7003/5363; 75/70.3; 137/129

It may just be "good, not great" and somewhat "lacking in character", but this marshy layout located an hour up the coast from Myrtle Beach does offer "challenging holes", "fast", "well-kept" greens and "great service" from the staff; N.B. a fourth course, Leopard's Chase, will open in February 2007, while a fifth, Jaguar's Lair, is under construction and could open as early as 2008.

Ocean Ridge Plantation, Panther's Run 🏌

23 | 22 | 24 | 21 | $78

Ocean Isle Beach | 351 Ocean Ridge Pkwy. | 910-287-1703 | www.big-cats.com | 7089/5023; 75.2/70; 148/123

You'll stroke through a varied parkland paradise with wide-open fairways and water on almost every hole of this "top-notch" Ocean Ridge Plantation track; if you can't tame this cat, then you can always sharpen your claws (and skills) at the plantation's golf academy – or better yet, seek solace in the deluxe pro shop.

Ocean Ridge Plantation, Tiger's Eye

26 | 23 | 24 | 22 | $113

Ocean Isle Beach | 351 Ocean Ridge Pkwy. | 910-287-7228 | www.big-cats.com | 7014/4502; 73.5/66.6; 144/108

"If you can only play one" of the Ocean Ridge courses, "play this one" insist pros who call this "the best of the three current cats", a "beautiful" shot-maker's layout featuring elevation changes that are rare for the Myrtle Beach region as well as an abundance of marshes and natural waste areas; P.S. the pride of the pack is also a "great value."

Oyster Bay 🏌

26 | 19 | 20 | 23 | $113

Sunset Beach | 614 Lakeshore Dr. | 910-579-3528 | 800-552-2660 | www.legendsgolf.com | 6685/4665; 71.6/68; 134/118

Oyster shells lie in sand traps and surround the "island greens" at this "pearl" of a "peaceful" course situated on intercoastal wetlands; while the "facilities need an upgrade", the track's "interesting holes" (a "spectacular back") and "value" are "as good as anything in Myrtle Beach" – and its location an hour up the shore comes "without the traffic."

Porters Neck Plantation 🏌

▽ 22 | 20 | 18 | 18 | $110

Wilmington | 8403 Vintage Club Circle | 910-686-1177 | 800-947-8177 | www.porters-neck.com | 7112/5145; 75.3/70.5; 136/121

Yes, this Tom Fazio design may suffer from "lack of elevation" as it "threads its way through a residential community" in Wilmington, but its "rolling fairways and greens" and "interesting holes" trump any of its drawbacks; all in all, "moderate and advanced" players can expect a "challenge", and the "nice practice facilities" add extra value.

Rivers Edge 🏌

25 | 19 | 20 | 21 | $120

Shallotte | 2000 Arnold Palmer Dr. | 910-755-3434 | 877-748-3718 | www.river18.com | 6909/4692; 74.7/68.2; 149/119

The "beautiful scenery" is par-ticularly pleasing at Arnold Palmer's "river-side gem" an hour north of Myrtle Beach, where the layout is as "challenging" as it is "fun" and the "attentive" service makes it a "great course for the money"; the consensus: fans "wish that all Palmer layouts were this good"; P.S. the "closing holes are fantastic."

Sea Trail, Dan Maples 🏌

▽ 23 | 22 | 22 | 23 | $95

Sunset Beach | 210 Clubhouse Rd. | 910-287-1150 | 800-546-5748 | www.seatrail.com | 6797/5110; 71.3/71.9; 135/129

Multi-day stays may be inevitable after a visit to this Dan Maples "value" of a resort course where the "fantastic" staff "treats everyone like family"; situated an hour north of Myrtle Beach, the layout draws praise for its "fine facilities", but the track's 18 "interesting holes" (some routed along Calabash Creek amid oaks and pines) are also hard to ignore.

Sea Trail, Rees Jones ⚐ ▽ 25 | 21 | 22 | 21 | $105

Sunset Beach | 75 Clubhouse Rd. SW | 910-287-1150 | 800-546-5748 | www.seatrail.com | 6761/4912; 72.8/68.9; 132/119

"Put it on your list if you're going to Myrtle Beach" say fans of this "championship" track featuring "terrific views", forgiving fairways, bountiful bunkers and a wealth of water hazards on 11 of 18 holes; throw in a "great restaurant and conference center" and you easily end up with the "best of the Sea Trail courses."

Sea Trail, Willard Byrd ⚐ ▽ 21 | 23 | 23 | 21 | $85

Sunset Beach | 75 Clubhouse Rd. SW | 910-287-1150 | 800-546-5748 | www.seatrail.com | 6750/4697; 72.6/68.3; 132/109

"Salt breezes blow across the well-maintained fairways" at this "beautiful course" near the coast, a "difficult but fair" test that's likely to "make you think before reaching for your club" – and before you try to retrieve any balls from the alligator-prone hazards; experts insist that this "good value" is in the "best shape" of its life.

St. James Plantation, Players Club ⚐ ▽ 22 | 23 | 20 | 22 | $80

Southport | 3640 Players Club Dr. | 910-457-0049 | 800-281-6626 | www.stjamesplantation.com | 6940/4463; 74.6/66.6; 150/113

Local boy Tim Cate "continues to produce exciting, challenging and interesting designs", and this "fair", "well-maintained" layout 90 minutes north of Myrtle Beach is no exception with its narrow fairways, marshy areas and waste bunkers; it's "perfect for recreational golfers and low-handicappers", and since rangers "enforce the pace of play" by "using timers in the carts", it's ideal for anyone who wants to wrap up a round in "four hours and change."

Outer Banks

Currituck 22 | 20 | 21 | 16 | $165

Corolla | 620 Currituck Clubhouse Dr. | 252-453-9400 | 888-453-9400 | www.thecurrituckgolfclub.com | 6885/4766; 74/68.5; 136/120

You're in for a "wild and windy" ride at this "beautiful" links-style layout that's considered the "best on the Outer Banks"; "high up" with "great views" of the ocean and Sound, this "challenging-yet-scoreable" Rees Jones design winds its way through diverse coastal terrain with "plenty of sand"; though they make a very "devoted attempt to separate golfers from their money" with the "steep fees", the "good service and amenities soften the sting."

Nags Head 21 | 17 | 19 | 21 | $115

Nags Head | 5615 S. Seachase Dr. | 252-441-8073 | 800-851-9404 | www.nagsheadgolflinks.com | 6126/4415; 71.2/68.5; 138/117

It feels like the "world's longest short course when the wind is blowing" say those who've been "beaten up" by this "scenic" layout near Roanoke Sound that can create "havoc" considering its "hilly terrain" and "ample water and dunes"; overall, though, it's a "favorite" that adds up to "a good value given the limited choices on the Outer Banks."

Pinehurst

Carolina Club 🏌

23 | 18 | 21 | 22 | $84

Pinehurst | 277 Ave. of the Carolina | 910-949-2811 | 888-725-6372 | www.thecarolina.com | 6928/4828; 73.2/68.6; 142/117

"Undiscovered by North Carolina's visitors", this "Palmer challenge" is nevertheless an "interesting", "wide-open", "well-maintained" course that cuts through wetlands and pine trees near the Moore County Airport and features greens so "huge" and "undulating" that you may suspect there are "hidden elephants" beneath them; the facilities are "sparse" (a clubhouse is in the planning stages), but surveyors conclude it's "a great track" that's also "affordable."

Legacy 🏌

24 | 20 | 20 | 25 | $99

Aberdeen | 12615 Hwy. 15/501 S. | 910-944-8825 | 800-344-8825 | www.legacypinehurst.com | 7018/4923; 73.2/68.3; 132/120

Papa Nicklaus and "Jack Jr. should be proud" of the latter's "picturesque" Pinehurst design, a "fantastic" and "fun" mix of holes that will "challenge your mental game as well as your physical game", especially on the "risk/reward 18th"; even better, the "pretty" "getaway" "isn't surrounded by houses" – it's set amid the seclusion of the Sand Hills forest near Aberdeen – and "isn't a lot of $$$" either.

Little River

▽ 16 | 16 | 15 | 20 | $95

Carthage | 500 Little River Farm Blvd. | 910-949-4600 | 888-766-6538 | www.littleriver.com | 6939/4998; 73.4/68.7; 135/122

This "short", hilly parcel (originally conceived by Dan Maples) is "worth a trip" 20 minutes north of Pinehurst for a front nine links that's a challenge and a wooded back that "makes you think", as it "won't give you many chances to hit the driver"; N.B. new owners have added an expansive clubhouse and two-bedroom condos with high-speed Internet access.

Mid Pines Inn 🏨 ⚐

23 | 23 | 23 | 20 | $180

Southern Pines | 1010 Midland Rd. | 910-692-2114 | 800-323-2114 | www.pineneedles-midpines.com | 6528/4921; 71/68.8; 126/119

"Southern charm" is in store for those who check out this Donald Ross "classic" that's like "playing in the old days" (e.g. walkers taking caddies) and "isn't tricked-up" (everything's "right in front of you") unlike other short, "challenging" layouts; the "nice" facilities and "pleasant" staffers make the course a "must if you're in the Pinehurst area."

Pinehurst Resort, No. 1 🏨 ⚐

20 | 28 | 27 | 21 | $160

Pinehurst | 1 Carolina Vista Dr. | 910-295-6811 | 800-795-4653 | www.pinehurst.com | 6128/5297; 69.4/70.5; 116/117

First built in 1898 and subsequently redesigned by Donald Ross, this "trip back in time" provides "various challenges" for players with a "variety of skills"; be aware that the "old-school" layout is "shorter" than other Pinehurst courses and perhaps "not the most interesting", but the majority maintains it's a "deal" given that it benefits from the resort's "top-tier" service and facilities; N.B. upcoming renovations will close the layout from summer 2007 to spring 2008.

☑ Pinehurst Resort, No. 2 🏨 ⛳

| 28 | 27 | 26 | 19 | $375 |

Pinehurst | 1 Carolina Vista Dr. | 910-295-6811 | 800-795-4653 |
www.pinehurst.com | 7305/5045; 75.9/69.1; 138/124

"There aren't enough superlatives" to describe this former U.S. Open
venue (1999, 2005) showcasing "Donald Ross at his best" – or sneak-
iest, since the "wide", "friendly fairways" lead to "slick", "domed" and
"undulating" putting surfaces on which "balls roll right off"; while admission into the state's top-rated Course is "ridiculously expensive", if
you're looking for the "ultimate golf experience" complete with "dynamite caddies", "first-class service" and "great history", this is it;
N.B. they're celebrating their 100th anniversary with package deals.

Pinehurst Resort, No. 3 🏨 ⛳

| 19 | 27 | 26 | 20 | $160 |

Pinehurst | 1 Carolina Vista Dr. | 910-295-6811 | 800-795-4653 |
www.pinehurst.com | 5682/5232; 67.3/70.2; 115/116

If "staying at Pinehurst is a requirement to make your life complete",
pros propose playing this "short, fun" 1910 track as a rite of passage;
while somewhat "overlooked", its Donald Ross–designed holes featuring "intricate greens" "still provide a great test" and offer a "tune-up
for the other seven courses" – "for less money" to boot.

Pinehurst Resort, No. 4 🏨 ⛳

| 25 | 28 | 26 | 21 | $250 |

Pinehurst | 1 Carolina Vista Dr. | 910-295-6811 | 800-795-4653 |
www.pinehurst.com | 7117/5217; 74.5/70.6; 136/123

Tom Fazio's "redesigned homage to Pinehurst" "will test your iron
and short-game skills" over a "variety" of par 3s, long par 4s and
"risk/reward par 5s", all with the "crowned greens" and "heavy bunkering" for which its first architect, Donald Ross, is known; though some say
it's "a half-step behind No. 2", backers believe it's "as satisfying."

☑ Pinehurst Resort, No. 5 🏨 ⛳

| 24 | 29 | 27 | 22 | $160 |

Pinehurst | 1 Carolina Vista Dr. | 910-295-6811 | 800-795-4653 |
www.pinehurst.com | 6848/5248; 72.6/70; 132/114

"Nothing beats the Pinehurst experience", but if the Pinehurst experience is beating you, downshift and play "where the locals play": on
this "traditional" parkland layout (designed by Ellis Maples and redesigned by Robert Trent Jones Sr.) featuring more water hazards and
variety than the other courses; P.S. "unless your ego needs No. 2", this
is a "great alternative."

Pinehurst Resort, No. 6 🏨 ⛳

| 23 | 24 | 26 | 21 | $250 |

Pinehurst | 1 Carolina Vista Dr. | 910-295-6811 | 800-795-4653 |
www.pinehurst.com | 6990/5001; 74.4/70; 139/121

"When you're tired of getting beaten up on No. 2 or No. 4", ease into
this "remodeled" George and Tom Fazio routing that runs through rolling hills and is "forgiving if you're having a bad day"; unfortunately, it
also "runs through a housing development", but while it's perhaps "not
the best of Pinehurst", it's often "in the best shape", and when you factor
in the "friendly staff", it might be the biggest "secret at the resort."

Pinehurst Resort, No. 7 🏨 ⛳

| 25 | 25 | 26 | 20 | $250 |

Pinehurst | 1 Carolina Vista Dr. | 910-295-6811 | 800-795-4653 |
www.pinehurst.com | 7216/5183; 75.5/71.7; 149/127

Rees Jones' 1986 effort is "not your typical Pinehurst" in that it's
"long", "hilly" and has "lots of trees" and wetlands, but like its

"cousins", it "offers history and great golf"; the original architect followed up with a relatively recent renovation that may have made it "even more difficult", but aces attest the course "couldn't be in better shape" now.

☑ Pinehurst Resort, No. 8 🏌 ⚓

| 28 | 27 | 27 | 21 | $250 |

Pinehurst | 1 Carolina Vista Dr. | 910-295-6811 | 800-795-4653 | www.pinehurst.com | 7092/5177; 74.2/69.8; 135/122

"Perhaps the most beautiful" layout in the family of eight, this "immaculate" Tom Fazio track treks through a "pristine environment" of wetlands and pines, and features "generous landing areas" and "forgiving greens" that are ideal "for amateurs" who enjoy a "challenge", albeit a "realistic" one; the "most playable of the Pinehurst layouts" comes with a "nice clubhouse", encouraging some to say the course offers the "best dollar value" of its brethren.

Pine Needles Lodge, Pine Needles 🏌

| 26 | 23 | 24 | 23 | $235 |

Southern Pines | 1005 Midland Rd. | 910-692-8611 | 800-747-7272 | www.pineneedles-midpines.com | 7015/4936; 73.5/68.6; 135/119

Donald Ross' "timeless classic" is in "perfect condition" and "tests you with long par 3s and par 4s" and the designer's trademark "mounded greens", all in a "natural and fair" layout located just southeast of Pinehurst; it's "a must-play and a must-stay" on account of its "great value", "old-style", "heavenly" ambiance, "helpful" service and "outstanding golf school"; N.B. in 2007, the club will host its third U.S. Women's Open Championship.

Pinewild, Holly 🏌

| ∇ 21 | 21 | 22 | 22 | $135 |

Pinehurst | 801 Linden Rd. | 910-295-5145 | 800-523-1499 | www.pinewildcc.com | 7021/5968; 73.3/68.7; 138/123

Although this Gary Player design "isn't played a lot", admirers insist it "should be", as it's a "good" Pinehurst option set amid "beautiful sand traps and pine trees"; what's more, the "huge range and three-hole practice course" are "perfect for warming up"; N.B. the club also features a second 18-hole course along with a nine-hole, par-3 track called Azalea.

Pit Golf Links, The

| 19 | 18 | 18 | 19 | $109 |

Aberdeen | 110 Pit Links Ln. | 910-944-1600 | 800-574-4653 | www.pitgolf.com | 7018/4751; 74/67.8; 139/109

"Bring your A-game" or risk being "eaten alive" because "not in your wildest dreams – or nightmares" – could you imagine so many challenging, "quirky" holes than there are at this Aberdeen course in a reclaimed sand quarry; while some talk of "too many tricked-up holes", aces applaud it for forcing you to "think about your shots."

Talamore 🏌

| 21 | 19 | 21 | 21 | $125 |

Southern Pines | 48 Talamore Dr. | 910-692-5884 | 800-552-6292 | www.talamore.com | 6840/4993; 73.2/68.7; 140/120

Some courses "make you want to play well", and this Rees Jones junket just southeast of Pinehurst is one of them given that its strategic, shot-maker's layout is "in great shape" and the pace of play is "good"; though some "don't understand the need for the llama gimmick" (they're available to carry clubs), it's an overall "fair" and worthy test.

	COURSE	FACIL.	SERVICE	VALUE	COST

Tobacco Road

	25	19	21	23	$115

Sanford | 442 Tobacco Rd. | 919-775-1940 | www.tobaccoroadgolf.com | 6554/5094; 73.2/66.1; 150/115

Forget tobacco, this "shot-maker's course" by the late Mike Strantz is "golf on LSD", a "roller-coaster ride" with "twists and turns" and "blind shots galore" "amongst sand dunes" 40 minutes north of Pinehurst; visually "intimidating from the tee", it's "not for everyone" and even aficionados "wouldn't want to play here every day", but the "quirky" "thrill ride" is nevertheless "playable" and "certainly not boring."

Raleigh-Durham

Duke University Golf Club

	25	23	20	22	$90

Durham | 3001 Cameron Blvd. | 919-681-2288 | www.washingtondukeinn.com | 7105/5474; 73.9/72.2; 141/126

Blue Devil boosters "don't know how the students manage not to flunk out" of school with this "great Robert Trent Jones Sr. design" ("later revised by [his son] Rees").located "right off the Duke campus" on the grounds of the Washington Duke Hotel; its "hilly" but "walkable" "tree-lined" holes and "over-the-top greens" make it "similar to the great courses of the Northeast", and the hotel offers "lovely overnight facilities", a "fabulous" pub and a "great restaurant."

Winston-Salem

Tanglewood Park, Championship

	24	16	18	23	$46

Clemmons | 4061 Clemmons Rd. | 336-778-6300 | www.tanglewoodpark.org | 7101/5119; 75.4/69.8; 142/126

There aren't too many places where you can "play a major course for less than $50", so this 1974 PGA Championship venue just southwest of Winston-Salem "may be the best course for the money in the Carolinas"; just be sure to "bring a shovel to get out of the myriad bunkers" and remember that this is a muni, so while the course is a "thrill", the "facilities can appear a little rustic if you're unprepared."

Tanglewood Park, Reynolds

	▽ 22	17	20	24	$19

Clemmons | 4061 Clemmons Rd. | 336-778-6300 | www.tanglewoodpark.org | 6537/4709; 72.5/68; 136/116

Thank philanthropist William Neal Reynolds (of the RJ Reynolds company) for this 6,500-yard RTJ Sr. design that's the companion to Tanglewood Park's Championship layout; the parklander features narrow, tree-lined fairways and water hazards on five of its holes, and is part of a municipal facility that also includes an 18-hole, par-3 course.

North Dakota

Bismarck

NEW Bully Pulpit

	-	-	-	-	$50

Medora | 3731 Bible Camp Rd. | 701-623-4653 | 800-633-6721 | www.medora.com | 7166/4750; 75.4/68.3; 133/113

Owned by the restored Wild West town that was once home to Teddy Roosevelt, this minimalist muni designed by Michael Hurdzan is built on the rippled banks of the Little Missouri River in the Badlands section of western North Dakota; its holes are situated amid dunes, creeks, sandstone canyons and plateaus, with some featuring 200-ft. drops from tee to fairway.

Hawktree

– | – | – | – | $63

Bismarck | 3400 Burnt Creek Loop | 701-355-0995 | 888-465-4295 | www.hawktree.com | 7085/4868; 75.2/69.7; 137/116

Fans feel it's "worth the trip" to Bismarck just to play this "terrific", "long, links-type" Jim Engh design that's "built into the land, not on it"; the 18 holes "roll up and down valleys" and feature "signature black coal slag in the bunkers", which "makes your ball easy to find" and doesn't blow out like regular sand, a plus because "wind is king here."

Williston

Links of North Dakota

– | – | – | – | $50

Williston | Hwy. 1804 E. | 701-568-2600 | 866-733-6453 | www.linksnd.com | 7092/5249; 75.1/71.6; 128/122

Admirers "envy any golfer who lives in this area" in the northwestern part of North Dakota where what they call "North America's best course that's near nothing" is located; overlooking Lake Sakakawea, the wind-whipped Stephen Kay design features over 80 bunkers and plenty of punishing prairie-grass roughs, but the layout nevertheless seems "like heaven" to fans and also more than makes up for the basic clubhouse fare.

Ohio

Akron

NEW Blue Heron, Highlands/Lakes

– | – | – | – | $69

Medina | 3225 Blue Heron Trace | 330-722-0227 | 888-876-6687 | www.golfblueheron.com | 6932/5031; 74.7/70.1; 144/125

Winding its way through the rugged forestland west of Akron, this 27-hole course currently has only two of its distinct nines open: while the River is scheduled to debut in June 2007, the Lakes already dodges water on seven of its holes and the Highlands is characterized by dramatic elevation changes and deep ravines; the facility's clubhouse is posh and spacious with a versatile grill, so be sure to check it out.

Windmill Lakes

22 | 20 | 20 | 24 | $54

Ravenna | 6544 State Rte. 14 | 330-297-0440 | www.windmill-lakes-golf.com | 6936/5368; 73.8/70.4; 128/115

"Get off the Ohio Turnpike and play here!" wail those who "would love to have this as a home course" – as the golf teams at nearby Kent State do – for the challenge of a layout whose "holes look straightforward, but somehow get their way over you" with their water-laced routes and large, undulating greens; a "super-friendly staff" adds to the "value", although the "great pro shop" may just "scarf up the cash you saved on green fees."

	COURSE	FACIL.	SERVICE	VALUE	COST

Cincinnati

Shaker Run 🏌

| 25 | 23 | 21 | 21 | $78 |

Lebanon | 4361 Greentree Rd. | 513-727-0007 | www.shakerrungolfclub.com
Lakeside/Meadows | 6991/5046; 73.7/68.4; 136/118
Meadows/Woodlands | 7092/5161; 74.1/69.6; 134/119
Woodlands/Lakeside | 6953/5075; 74/68.8; 138/121

"Stunning woods surround the entire course", making this former private club in Lebanon a "memorable" option; perhaps "too many outings" have caused conditions to "slip" and become somewhat "variable", but that likely wasn't the case when "Michelle Wie played here" in 2005 as the first woman to ever advance to the men's U.S. Amateur Public Links Championship; N.B. the Meadows nine is the newest of the three.

Vineyard, The

| 23 | 17 | 20 | 25 | $45 |

Cincinnati | 600 Nordyke Rd. | 513-474-3007 | www.greatparks.org |
6789/4747; 72.8/67.9; 132/114

"It's amazing it's a public course" acknowledge experts who've played this "good test of golf" in Cincinnati, a "well-maintained" municipal "gem" featuring "narrow", "slanted" holes; if the facilities "need updating", the track's "down-to-earth" staff and overall "tremendous value" more than make up for any shortcomings.

Cleveland

Avalon Lakes

| ▽ 24 | 21 | 21 | 19 | $135 |

Warren | 1 American Way NE | 330-856-8800 | www.avalonlakes.com |
7551/4904; 76.9/68.5; 143/119

Located "in the Pittsburgh to Cleveland corridor", this "absolutely beautiful" "example of a parkland course" was remodeled in 2000 by original architect Pete Dye, who brought more water into play, widened the corridors, added elevation to formerly flat fairways and expanded the practice range; while some feel it's "not his best", it's one "the average player can enjoy without relying on luck."

Fowler's Mill

| 25 | 19 | 18 | 23 | $64 |

Chesterland | 13095 Rockhaven Rd. | 440-729-7569 |
www.fowlersmillgc.com
Lake/Maple | 6595/5828; 72.1/72.3; 128/120
Maple/River | 6385/5712; 70.7/71.1; 125/119
River/Lake | 7002/5950; 74.7/71.8; 136/118

In designing these three "long", "no-nonsense" nines, architect Pete Dye "considered where most of us hacks tend to miss", so "hit it where it's designed to be played" or it will "kick your butt"; "plenty of challenges, sand" and "Dye signatures" abound, including the Lake's "pretty" 4th hole, so "if you score well, you've earned it", by beating "a local gem" with lots of "character."

Little Mountain ⏰

| 26 | 22 | 24 | 23 | $57 |

Concord | 7667 Hermitage Rd. | 440-358-7888 | www.lmccgolf.com |
6615/4980; 73.1/68.6; 131/119

"One of the best courses in northeast Ohio", this hilly, "picturesque" Hurdzan/Fry design sports "a great collection of holes", with "long and short challenges and everything in between" – so "bring your sand

game", as you'll encounter "some of the most difficult bunkers" anywhere; meanwhile, a "super staff" won't be able to help with your
score, but at least "their kindness makes up for" a frustrating round.

Reserve at Thunder Hill

▽ 24 | 19 | 19 | 24 | $64

Madison | 7050 Griswold Rd. | 440-298-3474 | www.thunderhillgolf.com |
7504/4769; 78.5/68.5; 152/121

Despite an on-site pro who "goes out of his way to make people
happy", duffers deem this "diabolical" northeast Ohio layout a "beautiful" but ultra-challenging track with water hazards on every hole that
seem "designed to eat golf balls" and "can be torture from the back
tees" – especially "if you don't hit it straight"; yes, it "may be the
hardest course" in the area, but those golfers who like it that way
have "found mecca."

Sawmill Creek

▽ 20 | 22 | 19 | 17 | $63

Huron | 300 Sawmill Creek | 419-433-3789 | 800-729-6455 |
www.sawmillcreek.com | 6702/5074; 72.3/69.4; 128/115

"Some of the holes back up to Lake Erie, providing beautiful views" for
swingers at this Tom Fazio resort course (his first in Ohio) that
"doesn't seem to get too much play"; though there are "some funky
holes due to a rerouting" for condo construction, it's "worth the trip"
to this Huron "value", if not for the scenery alone.

StoneWater

25 | 24 | 21 | 17 | $99

Highland Heights | 1 Club Dr. | 440-461-4653 | www.stonewatergolf.com |
7020/4952; 74.8/69.2; 138/123

"Even though it winds through a housing development" 20 miles
northeast of Cleveland, this Hurdzan/Fry design "built into the land,
not out of it" "doesn't feel pinched", unless water hazards cramp your
style, in which case you'll find "tough holes from the get-go" (you can
always warm up at the "great practice facility" or enjoy post-putting
drinks at the bar); one thing you won't pinch are pennies – the fees
here are "expensive."

Columbus

Cooks Creek

25 | 17 | 20 | 23 | $50

Ashville | 16405 US Hwy. 23 | 740-983-3636 | www.cookscreek.com |
7071/5095; 73.7/68.2; 131/120

PGA Tour player John Cook and architects Michael Hurdzan and Dana
Fry have cooked up this "fabulous layout" in Ashville featuring a "nice
selection of holes" that are "beautiful and challenging" and "reward
good shots"; greens that are "always in primo condition", a "nice practice facility" and "views of the main house from the fairways" add to
its appeal and make it one of the "best values in the state."

Eaglesticks

25 | 19 | 19 | 25 | $50

Zanesville | 2655 Maysville Pike | 740-454-4900 | 800-782-4493 |
www.eaglesticks.com | 6508/4233; 70.7/63.7; 123/107

"Short but challenging", this "hilly" "target course" just south of
Zanesville has "a lot of open areas and trouble mixed nicely together"
plus greens that "can be killer, but roll superbly"; it's "always in top-
notch condition" and the "staff is very friendly", making it "enjoyable
every time" and a "great value for the money."

OHIO

	COURSE	FACIL.	SERVICE	VALUE	COST

Granville

▽ 24 | 14 | 16 | 24 | $39

Granville | 555 Newark Rd. | 740-587-0843 | www.granvillegolf.com | 6559/5197; 71.3/69.6; 128/123

Originally built in 1924 as part of the Granville Inn and located 35 miles east of Columbus, this "classic Donald Ross layout" is a "must-play" for those who appreciate "straightforward golf" on a track in "excellent condition"; there's "nothing fancy here" (save for the "new houses on the back nine"), just "lovely, rolling hills" and "spectacular views", particularly from the 18th tee, which is elevated 125 feet above the fairway.

☑ Longaberger

29 | 27 | 26 | 20 | $125

Nashport | 1 Long Dr. | 740-763-1100 | www.longabergergolfclub.com | 7243/4985; 75.2/68.9; 138/122

"Reserve a tee time well in advance" for this Arthur Hills offering that's "super in every way", with a "gorgeous yet difficult" layout showcasing a "great mix of holes" abetted by "first-rate" facilities; playing this "out-of-the-way" wonder an hour east of Columbus may be "as expensive as its gets" in these parts, but wicker worshipers insist it "doesn't get any better than this."

Dayton

Heatherwoode

▽ 21 | 20 | 19 | 22 | $59

Springboro | 88 Heatherwoode Blvd. | 937-748-3222 | 800-231-4049 | 6730/5069; 72.2/70.1; 134/123

This "well-maintained" Denis Griffiths course located 25 minutes south of Dayton on the way to Cincinnati is "a challenge from either set of tees"; a "great municipal" parklander with plenty of water, it's a somewhat overlooked player that insiders nevertheless prize for offering "one of the very best values" around.

Yankee Trace, Championship

▽ 21 | 18 | 18 | 18 | $47

Centerville | 10000 Yankee St. | 937-438-4653 | www.yankeetrace.org | 7139/5204; 74.1/70.6; 136/121

Located in Centerville "between Cincinnati and Dayton", this "very enjoyable" muni meanders across 550 acres of relatively flat farmland dotted with mature trees; nitpickers find the "greens fees hard to justify" – especially "on weekends" – but others judge the Gene Bates design "a good value" given its "nice facilities", which include a country club–style clubhouse with indoor practice area; N.B. there's also a separate nine-hole course.

Toledo

Maumee Bay

▽ 21 | 16 | 17 | 25 | $28

Oregon | 1750 Park Rd. | 419-836-9009 | www.maumeebayresort.com | 6941/5221; 73.5/70.4; 131/120

Expect to be confronted by "challenging" conditions when the wind "blows off Lake Erie" at this "value" of a "links-style" resort layout that's located in a 1,850-acre state park just across the Maumee River from Toledo; it's "pure golf", something the state's U.S. Open qualifying tournament participants can certainly attest to after playing rounds here.

Red Hawk Run
| | | | | $58 |

Findlay | 18441 US Rte. 224 E. | 419-894-4653 | 877-484-3429 | www.redhawkrun.com | 7155/4997; 74/67.9; 132/116

Yet "another Arthur Hills gem", this expansive layout routed through a housing community 45 minutes south of Toledo has a "good variety of holes" (six of which contend with the Eagle and Red Hawk Lakes) that require carries over an ever-present creek; good thing, then, that there's an eight-acre practice range and a 10,000-sq.-ft. putting green.

Oklahoma

Durant

Chickasaw Pointe
| | | | | $45 |

Kingston | Hwy. 70 E. | 580-564-2581 | 866-602-4653 | www.oklahomagolf.com | 7085/5285; 74.5/72.2; 125/126

"Don't let the first two holes put you to sleep" because "the rest of" this "long, challenging" state-owned "surprise" in southern Oklahoma will require "all of your skills", particularly given "the wind" and "elevation changes"; with 15 holes on Lake Texoma, it's a "great combo of golf and views" that also provides putting greens and a practice range.

Oklahoma City

Jimmie Austin
University of Oklahoma Golf Course
| | | | | $40 |

Norman | 1 Par Dr. | 405-325-6716 | www.ou.edu/admin/jaougc | 7197/5310; 74.9/71.6; 134/119

Home of the U. of Oklahoma Sooners, this traditional 1996 Bob Cupp redesign is being made over for the 2009 U.S. Amateur Public Links Championship; the already "excellent practice facilities" are now matched by a restaurant, and it plans to "completely redo the greens"; the patio will remain the same, however, with its views of the 18th hole.

Stillwater

Karsten Creek 🏌
| ▽ 27 | 25 | 24 | 16 | $250 |

Stillwater | 1800 S. Memorial Dr. | 405-743-1658 | www.karstencreek.net | 7285/4906; 74.8/70.1; 142/127

With this "extraordinary" but "hard" Tom Fazio design serving as "home to Oklahoma State's golf team", it's no wonder the Cowboys are "10-time NCAA champions"; set "in the middle of nowhere" on Lake Louise, the "beautiful" Stillwater layout features undulating, tree-lined fairways that "are as good as at Augusta" and "fast, rolling greens"; it's "way too expensive", but the "amazing" spread may be difficult to resist.

Tulsa

Forest Ridge
| | | | | $60 |

Broken Arrow | 7501 E. Kenosha St. | 918-357-2443 | www.forestridge.com | 7012/5341; 74.8/73.3; 137/132

For "real golf with real people", head to this Randy Heckenkemper design located in a planned residential community just east of

	COURSE	FACIL.	SERVICE	VALUE	COST

Downtown Tulsa; memberships and annual discount cards moderate the "pricey" fees, but "anyone can play" this "great" 7,012-yard woodlander that features lakes and creeks on 12 of its holes and also offers upscale amenities.

Oregon

TOP COURSES IN STATE

Bend

Black Butte Ranch, Big Meadow | 24 | 20 | 23 | 25 | $69 |

Black Butte | 13020 Hawks Beard | 541-595-1500 | 800-399-2322 | www.blackbutteranch.com | 7002/5485; 71.6/70.1; 125/126

There are few better ways to spend "lazy summer days" than at this central Oregon course surrounded by "gorgeous" mountain scenery (think "blue skies and tall trees") and supported by a "friendly", "helpful" staff; given "new bunkering", aces can now expect more of a "challenge" – there's "more sand here than on some Southern California beaches."

Black Butte Ranch, Glaze Meadow ▽ | 21 | 23 | 24 | 25 | $65 |

Black Butte | 13020 Hawks Beard | 541-595-1500 | 800-399-2322 | www.blackbutteranch.com | 6574/5545; 70.8/70.9; 122/125

"Black Butte looms" over this "user-friendly" yet still "challenging" layout, a petite parklander designed by Gene 'Bunny' Mason amid "beautiful country" that's highlighted by "tall trees and mountain backdrops"; N.B. tee times can be still be secured at this seasonal sanctuary until the snow settles, and there are numerous accommodations on-site, as well as three restaurants.

NEW Juniper | - | - | - | - | $65 |

Redmond | 1938 SW Elkhorn Ave. | 541-548-3121 | 800-600-3121 | www.junipergolf.com | 7186/5500; 73.8/70.5; 133/128

Although the club has been around since 1951, a Redmond highway project forced it to replace its existing course with a new layout two miles south; the resulting 2005 John Harbottle design has already been chosen as a U.S. Amateur Championship qualifying site courtesy of its punishing fescue grasses, rock ridges and contoured greens; thankfully, there's an extensive practice facility (featuring a double-ended range) as well as a brand-new clubhouse.

Sunriver, Crosswater ⚬⟞ | 27 | 26 | 24 | 22 | $160 |

Sunriver | 17600 Canoe Camp Dr. | 541-593-1221 | 800-547-3922 | www.sunriver-resort.com | 7683/5359; 76.5/71.1; 153/133

"Get away", get a room and get ready for this "amazing test" in a "great big valley" 20 miles south of Bend – "you must stay to play" the "breathtaking" Bob Cupp/John Fought design, where you "need to think" your way around "long, difficult" holes with "tight fairways, lots of water" and "huge greens", and not be distracted by "looking at the scenery"; decorum doyens warn if you try to "play it from the tips", you may find yourself "cursing like a sailor."

Sunriver, Meadows

20 | 23 | 23 | 19 | $125

Sunriver | 1 Center Dr. | 541-593-1221 | 800-547-3922 | www.sunriver-resort.com | 7012/5287; 72.9/70.4; 131/125

"Medium- to high-handicappers" endorse the "well-kept" conditions of this tree-lined track skirting the Sun River, a John Fought design that pays homage to famous American courses of the 1920s and 1930s; a nine-hole putting course and on-site Academy of Golf are two more reasons this is truly a "delightful resort layout."

Sunriver, Woodlands

▽ 18 | 19 | 22 | 18 | $125

Sunriver | 1 Center Dr. | 541-593-1221 | 800-547-3922 | www.sunriver-resort.com | 6946/5446; 72.7/71.2; 134/132

While some feel this Robert Trent Jones Jr. jaunt (a former host of the Oregon Open) "suffers by comparison to [siblings] Meadows and Crosswater", most agree playing its "very narrow fairways" pinched by trees, meadows, water hazards and rock outcroppings is "worth the experience"; regulars recommend you "purchase the package" of all three courses for a "good value" and "pack for cool nights and mornings" – after all, this is the "high desert."

Central Coast

Salishan

20 | 20 | 21 | 20 | $119

Gleneden Beach | 7760 Hwy. 101 N. | 541-764-2371 | 800-890-0387 | www.salishan.com | 6470/5237; 72.2/71.3; 134/128

A "great redesign" by PGA Tour pro Peter Jacobsen has made this "resort course" "on the ocean" a "much better test of golf" than before; it's "pricey", and while some "would not go out of their way to play" here, the "lovely setting", "good hotel" and "great restaurant" together make for an "excellent stop" "on the way down from Portland to Bandon Dunes" – especially "if you have a crystal ball that lets you plan a day with no rain."

Coos Bay

☑ Bandon Dunes, Bandon Dunes Course ⚡

29 | 27 | 29 | 26 | $240

Bandon | 57744 Round Lake Dr. | 541-347-4380 | 888-345-6008 | www.bandondunesgolf.com | 6745/5087; 73.9/71; 142/120

"Everything you hear is true" about this "astonishingly beautiful" links layout "right on the ocean" in southern Oregon: it offers "pure golf" "through the dunes" and not only "looks like Scotland, it plays like Scotland" – complete with a walking-only policy, "knowledgeable" caddies and "wild weather"; expect an "epic experience", but one that's "low-key" and "without the American decadence" found at others in its class; N.B. look for a fourth, Tom Doak–designed course in 2010.

☑ Bandon Dunes, Bandon Trails ⚡

26 | 27 | 28 | 25 | $240

Bandon | 57744 Round Lake Dr. | 541-347-4380 | 888-345-6008 | www.bandondunesgolf.com | 6765/5064; 73.4/70.6; 130/120

"Holding its own" in stellar company, this "inland" links sidekick (courtesy of Bill Coore and Ben Crenshaw) "winds its way from the coast" into the "towering trees" then "back to the coast", offering along the way "wide fairways", "big elevation changes", the "best collection of par 3s on the planet" and some occasional "relief" from the wind; like its relatives, it shares "first-class service and facilities" and a "great clubhouse restaurant"; N.B. walking-only.

☑ Bandon Dunes, Pacific Dunes 🏌

	COURSE	FACIL.	SERVICE	VALUE	COST
	30	27	28	27	$240

Bandon | 57744 Round Lake Dr. | 541-347-4380 | 888-345-6008 | www.bandondunesgolf.com | 6633/5088; 72.6/69.3; 138/128

"Sorry, Pebble Beach", the "best of the Bandon Dunes" options is also "the best anywhere" – it's the top-rated Course in both the state and the country in this year's Survey – thanks to "knock-your-socks-off holes", "breathtaking views along the ocean" and "memorable challenges" along a "true sand links" that "tests your skill and imagination" – expect "glory" if you manage your shots, "agony" if you don't; "helpful caddies" (it's walking-only), a "huge practice facility" and "excellent lodging" are all part of the "amazing" package.

Eugene

Sandpines

	COURSE	FACIL.	SERVICE	VALUE	COST
	24	14	19	23	$95

Florence | 1201 35th St. | 541-997-1940 | www.sandpines.com | 7190/5345; 76/65.8; 131/111

Rees Jones designed this "hidden gem on the Oregon coast", a "well-maintained", "linkslike" "walking" course with "plenty of sand, on and off the fairways", and wind that's "always a factor", making it "four to five strokes more difficult"; still, it's a "great ego booster after playing nearby Bandon Dunes", and the facility "will benefit from the new clubhouse" and restaurant, which is sure to boost its already "super value" while outdating the above Facilities score.

Tokatee

	COURSE	FACIL.	SERVICE	VALUE	COST
	▽ 22	17	17	21	$40

Blue River | 54947 McKenzie Hwy. | 541-822-3220 | 800-452-6376 | www.tokatee.com | 6806/5018; 72.4/67.8; 127/109

"Shhh!" – surveyors hope word doesn't get out about this "terrific value", a "too good to be true" Ted Robinson design that's "off the beaten path" in the Cascades but nevertheless "worth the trek" for a "fun and challenging" round; living up to its name (meaning 'a place of restful beauty'), the easily walkable, straightforward spread is set in the "beautiful" McKenzie River Valley and offers a "gorgeous" "backdrop of timbered mountains."

Klamath Falls

Running Y Ranch

	COURSE	FACIL.	SERVICE	VALUE	COST
	-	-	-	-	$90

Klamath Falls | 5790 Coopers Hawk Rd. | 541-850-5580 | 888-850-0261 | www.runningy.com | 7133/4842; 73.2/66.4; 131/120

"All levels of players can enjoy" Arnold Palmer's only Oregon design, a "beautiful" course in a "lovely setting" just north of the California border, with "great views" of woodlands and restored wetlands on the front and Payne Canyon on the back; insiders warn "the mosquitoes will eat you alive", so bring bug spray or take cover in the 83-room, timber-ceilinged Lodge and Ranch House Restaurant; N.B. there's also an 18-hole, all-grass putting course.

OREGON

COURSE
FACIL.
SERVICE
VALUE
COST

Portland

Heron Lakes, Great Blue
22 | 12 | 14 | 24 | $40

Portland | 3500 N. Victory Blvd. | 503-289-1818 | www.heronlakesgolf.com | 6902/5258; 73.2/70.7; 140/127

"Portland has many great public courses", and this Robert Trent Jones Jr. design is one of its best "bang-for-your-buck" bargains, a bit "nicer than the Greenback" course according to some who favor its "linkslike" layout that "plays tough but is not overwhelming", unlike the "noise" from the "nearby raceway and airport"; "tons of rounds keep it in mediocre shape" and the "clubhouse and snack bar are weak", but it's "still a great value" for most.

Heron Lakes, Greenback
▽ 19 | 14 | 15 | 27 | $30

Portland | 3500 N. Victory Blvd. | 503-289-1818 | www.heronlakesgolf.com | 6615/5240; 71.4/69.1; 124/122

This "popular" Portland parklander works in "great tandem with [sibling] Great Blue", and though "several holes feel the same", many say this is the more "fun" and "playable" track given its "great river setting", "wide fairways, smooth greens" and six ponds that are "home to all kinds of wildlife"; like it's bolder, bigger brother, it's also a "great bang for the buck."

Langdon Farms
24 | 23 | 23 | 22 | $90

Aurora | 24377 NE Airport Rd. | 503-678-4653 | www.langdonfarms.com | 6931/5246; 73.5/70.7; 125/124

Located "right off the interstate" (though "you'd never know it") in Aurora, this "beautiful and natural links-style" track is "not your usual" design, with "many different" holes that are "tough" but "rewarding"; there's a "big red barn" that "can be seen from all over the course" and serves as "a great reference point for judging the wind", and though "the value here depends on the time of day" you play, the "great service and nice facilities" are constant.

OGA Golf Course
▽ 22 | 20 | 21 | 25 | $50

Woodburn | 2850 Hazlenut Dr. | 503-981-6105 | www.ogagolfcourse.com | 6650/5498; 71.7/71.8; 132/128

"One of the best values in the Portland metro area" (especially if you're "a member" of the Oregon Golf Association), this track does "everything the big boys do without the delusions of grandeur"; it's "a little hard to find" but "not that far out of town" and worth the drive for its flat, straightforward holes featuring "good greens" and views of Mt. Hood; in short, it's a "great course for the money."

⊿ Pumpkin Ridge, Ghost Creek
28 | 25 | 24 | 23 | $135

North Plains | 12930 Old Pumpkin Ridge Rd. | 503-647-9977 | 888-594-4653 | www.pumpkinridge.com | 6839/5111; 74/70.7; 145/128

The "fairways are so lush" at this "pristine" parklander just west of Portland that you may feel like you're "playing on velvet", but watch out, since "accuracy is [at a] premium" on this tricky track that offers "plenty of challenges", like the "sneaky creek that comes into play" when you least expect it; the "pricey" fees seem a pittance once you remember you're on what's "widely considered the best public course in the area."

	COURSE	FACIL.	SERVICE	VALUE	COST

Reserve Vineyards, North
▽ **25** | **27** | **24** | **19** | **$88**

Aloha | 4805 SW 229th Ave. | 503-649-8191 | www.reservegolf.com | 6845/5278; 73.5/70.9; 135/132

For a "chance to play where Champions Tour professionals do" (at the JELD-WEN Tradition), check out "one of Oregon's best" layouts, this "linksy" Aloha track that's the handiwork of designer Bob Cupp; aces suggest looking out for "online discounts", but don't skimp on the "fantastic food" in the restaurant; N.B. the course is reserved for members and guests only during the first half of each month.

Reserve Vineyards, South
▽ **24** | **28** | **24** | **20** | **$88**

Aloha | 4805 SW 229th Ave. | 503-649-8191 | www.reservegolf.com | 7172/5189; 74.7/70.1; 132/125

Players "have a whole new appreciation for the pros" after tackling this Willamette Valley track at a time when the "rough is at Tour height" or even when it's just the "many interesting holes", "snow-white" "sand traps everywhere" and a few "shared fairways and greens" that are a challenge; most find it much easier dining in the "nice" clubhouse's Vintage Room, where fans attest you'll make an "excellent choice" no matter what you order.

Pennsylvania

TOP COURSES IN STATE

<u>27</u> Olde Stonewall | *Pittsburgh*
      Golf Course at Glen Mills | *Philadelphia*
<u>26</u> Nemacolin Woodlands, Mystic Rock | *Pittsburgh*
<u>25</u> Hershey, West | *Harrisburg*
      Wyncote | *Lancaster*

Allentown

Center Valley Club
23 | **19** | **21** | **19** | **$85**

Center Valley | 3300 Center Valley Pkwy. | 610-791-5580 | www.centervalleyclubgolf.com | 6916/4925; 73.7/68.6; 138/116

Presenting players with "two very different nines" – a "links-style" front and a "beautiful" woodland back – this "fun" Geoffrey Cornish design features "interesting, challenging holes" that "place a premium on well-thought-out shot-making"; although it's "on the expensive side" and "facilities are sparse" ("build a clubhouse!"), the course is "well-maintained" and the staff is viewed as one of "the best and friendliest in the Lehigh Valley."

NEW Club at Morgan Hill
22 | **21** | **21** | **21** | **$79**

Easton | 100 Clubhouse Dr. | 610-923-8480 | www.theclubatmorganhill.com | 6749/5166; 72.8/70.9; 135/125

"Talk about a different design!" – "incredible elevation changes", split fairways, "blind shots" and "undulating greens" mean you'll have to play this "great new course" from Kelly Blake Moran "more than once to reveal its secrets"; but although it's "worth the drive" to the PA-NJ border for this mountain layout's "unbelievable" Delaware River views, swingers say the facility "needs to put in a real driving range" to go with its "great clubhouse" and "top-notch restaurant."

	COURSE	FACIL.	SERVICE	VALUE	COST

Olde Homestead
22 **17** **19** **22** **$60**

New Tripoli | 6598 Rte. 309 | 610-298-4653 |
www.oldehomesteadgolfclub.com |
6800/4953; 73.2/68.2; 137/116

Located "out in the boonies" west of Allentown, this "fun track" is "playable for all levels" but offers "enough changes in elevation, contours and traps" to make traversing its "wide fairways" "interesting"; and since the "price is right too", it's "well worth the hike" to this former potato farm to take in its "spectacular" mountain views; N.B. the practice facilities include a nine-hole, par-3 course.

Whitetail
18 **15** **17** **23** **$56**

Bath | 2679 Klein Rd. | 610-837-9626 | www.whitetailgolfclub.com |
6432/5152; 70.6/65.3; 128/113

"Very reasonable greens fees" and a "challenging" Jim Blaukovitch design that's "always in good shape" make this "local favorite" near Bath dear to the hearts of those who appreciate "good, solid" golf "without the nonsense frills"; it's a little "off the beaten path" in the Lehigh Valley, but it's the kind of "great value" of which "we need more."

Gettysburg

Bridges, The
24 **19** **19** **24** **$57**

Abbottstown | 6729 York Rd. | 717-624-9551 | www.bridgesgc.com |
6713/5134; 71.7/69.6; 132/113

Those who have done battle on this "nice little track" near Gettysburg advise you "be prepared" for the "windy" conditions that come with its Pennsylvania Dutch country terrain; the links and mountain combo is "friendly to women" and to its surroundings – 10 wooden bridges protect both wetlands and woodlands – and it also offers a restaurant in which war-weary soldiers can relax post-round.

Carroll Valley, Carroll Valley Course
∇ **19** **16** **17** **22** **$56**

Fairfield | 121 Sanders Rd. | 717-642-8211 | 800-548-8504 |
www.carrollvalley.com | 6688/5022; 72.3/68.8; 128/116

Situated "in the middle of nowhere" just southwest of Gettysburg, this resort course combines its "great views" of the Catoctin Mountains with "value" pricing and a generally "easy", "woman-friendly" layout complicated only by a meandering creek and two large lakes; one naysayer notes "you get what you pay for" here – "dated facilities" and "scarce service" – but it's been "greatly improved" and now touts a newly redone grill and lounge.

Links at Gettysburg
22 **20** **20** **21** **$80**

Gettysburg | 601 Mason-Dixon Rd. | 717-359-8000 |
888-793-9498 | www.thelinksatgettysburg.com |
7031/4861; 73.9/68.8; 140/120

"It doesn't get much better" than "golf and war history", so prepare to clash with this "spectacular" spread situated south of the Civil War battlefield amid the "scenery" of the Blue Ridge Mountains and red rock cliffs; the "interesting mix of holes" is "a blast to play" with its ample "water and man-made rolling hills", but it "will not break your spirit" – unlike the "new" "homes around the course"; nevertheless, it offers a "beautiful clubhouse" and "good food."

	COURSE	FACIL.	SERVICE	VALUE	COST

Penn National, Founders

▽ 25 | 24 | 25 | 24 | $72

Fayetteville | 3720 Club House Dr. | 717-352-3000 | 800-221-7366 | www.penngolf.com | 6972/5378; 73.9/71.4; 139/123

Be sure to bring your camera, because this traditional "park-type" track laid out by Ed Ault in 1968 is "spectacular in the fall" courtesy of fairways lined with oaks, pines and hardwoods; the "neat course" also features a lake and large, well-bunkered greens, and it's all nestled in a setting 20 miles west of Gettysburg that's so bucolic, you may just wish you'd booked a room in one of the adjacent cottages.

Penn National, Iron Forge

- | - | - | - | $72

Fayetteville | 3720 Club House Dr. | 717-352-3000 | 800-221-7366 | www.penngolf.com | 7009/5246; 73.8/70.3; 133/120

Situated west of Gettysburg on land that once supported iron production (thus the name), this "real nice" Bill Love layout is quite different from its woodsy sibling – which is older by 30 years – in that its modern "links-type" design is virtually treeless; the sculpted fairways do, however, offer views of the Michaux State Forest as well as South Mountain, and there's even an 1800s-era lime kiln behind the eighth green to provide a sense of the area's history.

Harrisburg

Hershey, East 🚶‍♂️ o─

24 | 24 | 23 | 22 | $99

Hershey | 1000 E. Derry Rd. | 717-533-2464 | 800-437-7439 | www.hersheypa.com | 7061/5645; 74.5/73.6; 136/128

"Don't expect a chocolate kiss" from this "classic", "beautifully maintained" George Fazio course which is "fair and fun" but can be "difficult for average golfers" with its "rolling terrain", "uphill and downhill approach shots" and 100-plus bunkers; the "unbelievable smell" of the famous confections will whet your "appetite for post-game dessert", as will the extra walking, since there's "no transportation" between the Hershey Lodge and the clubhouse.

Hershey, West 🚶‍♂️ o─

25 | 23 | 23 | 21 | $99

Hershey | 1000 E. Derry Rd. | 717-533-2464 | 800-437-7439 | www.hersheypa.com | 6860/5598; 72.6/72.6; 130/129

Since this "classic", "hilly" course was "good enough for Ben Hogan", the 1940 PGA Championship and the LPGA's Lady Keystone Open for 20 years, fans attest "it's good enough for us" – especially those who've "spent a grand" trying to stay out of the rough with its wide, "open fairways"; besides the "enjoyable layout", you "can smell the chocolate while you play."

Lancaster

Pilgrim's Oak

22 | 15 | 19 | 26 | $59

Peach Bottom | 1107 Pilgrim's Pathway | 717-548-3011 | www.pilgrimsoak.com | 6766/5063; 73.4/70.9; 146/123

Pilgrims proclaim this Peach Bottom parcel "a terrific place to play" and well "worth the trip" to southern Lancaster County; you'll need to "bring a gyroscope to find a level lie" on this "links-style" layout whose "tough and tricky" routing – "devilish greens", tall rough, turf so tight "you can putt from the fairways" – offers "wide-open vistas"; a few

| | COURSE | FACIL. | SERVICE | VALUE | COST |

feel the "facilities are lacking", but the "midpriced public" provides "a fun round" at an "outstanding value."

Reading Country Club
— | — | — | — | $50

Reading | 5311 Perkiomen Ave. | 610-779-1000 |
www.readingcountryclub.com | 6162/5131; 69.4/70.2; 128/121

It's hard to believe that this former private course - designed by architect Alex Findlay in the 1920s, home to golf pro Byron Nelson in the late '30s and host to such greats as Sam Snead, Cary Middlecoff and Lloyd Mangrum - is now open to the public, but Exeter Township took the reins in 2006; this newly minted muni is a step back in time, from the moment you enter the castle-style clubhouse to the second you finish a round on the short, tight, tree-lined layout.

Wyncote
25 | 22 | 20 | 21 | $78

Oxford | 50 Wyncote Dr. | 610-932-8900 | www.wyncote.com |
7148/5454; 74/71.6; 130/126

This "wonderful farm-to-links conversion" in "rolling Chester County" has "no trees" "but a lot of wind" whipping across its "interesting" holes, which "brings the fescue-lined rough into play" on any given shot; although it's a "bit of a trip" to get here, the "excellent" layout and facilities are "worth the drive", especially the "cool" Ball & Thistle pub in the clubhouse, where many go to "recover after a round."

Philadelphia

Downingtown
19 | 19 | 19 | 18 | $69

Downingtown | 85 Country Club Dr. | 610-269-2000 |
www.golfdowningtown.com | 6642/5092; 72.3/69.6; 129/122

An "old-line beauty" situated 45 minutes east of Philadelphia, this "classically designed" 1965 George Fazio woodlander "isn't long" but it offers "plenty of challenge", so "be prepared to hit a long iron into uphill greens" that allow for "few straight putts"; it "lacks a practice range and short-game area" and "course upkeep could be better", but "decent facilities" and a "service-oriented staff" add to its "value."

Z Golf Course at Glen Mills
27 | 21 | 23 | 23 | $90

Glen Mills | 221 Glen Mills Rd. | 610-558-2142 | www.glenmillsgolf.com |
6641/4703; 72.3/67.3; 138/116

Fans tout this "fair but formidable" "Bobby Weed design" as "the best public course in the Philadelphia area" thanks to its unique "blend of links" and "wooded" holes, with "wonderful elevation changes" and "some of the best views in the country"; it's "beautifully maintained" by "disadvantaged youths" "learning course management and maintenance" at the Glen Mills School, and though "there's no food or drink service of note", the "hospitality is as good as any five-star resort" and "knowing the course helps children is great for the soul."

Hickory Valley, Presidential
20 | 15 | 17 | 23 | $57

Gilbertsville | 1921 Ludwig Rd. | 610-754-9862 | www.hickoryvalley.com |
6676/5271; 72.8/71.2; 133/128

For "no-frills golf in the boonies", enthusiasts elect this "great value" northwest of Philadelphia with a "split personality": the "newer", "interesting" front nine is large and wide compared to the "very narrow" "back nine reminiscent of Tillinghast"; despite the executive name, "don't expect much more" than basic amenities, while the "staff leaves something to be desired."

NEW Lederach
20 | 21 | 21 | 20 | $75

Harleysville | 900 Clubhouse Dr. | 215-513-3034 | www.lederachgolfclub.com | 7023/5034; 73.9/64.3; 137/110

You can play this "brand-new" Kelly Blake Moran design "again and again and not be bored", as the "imaginative" layout features "lots of elevation changes", "risk/reward opportunities", "hidden fairway bunkers" and "contoured greens"; the "challenging course" should "only get better with time" – "just wait until the rough grows in" – but its already "very good clubhouse" and "friendly service" make it well worth the drive north of Philadelphia.

NEW Raven's Claw
17 | 17 | 18 | 18 | $75

Pottstown | 120 Masters Dr. | 610-495-4710 | www.ravensclawgolfclub.com | 6740/4834; 71/67.1; 130/112

"Just a year old", this fledgling's fairways may be "a bit thin", but clubbers are "confident" that the 2005 design "will be a very nice course once it grows in a little more"; sporting a "tough", old-style layout "carved into the hills" and woods of west Montgomery County, this "promising" track offers holes that are "sometimes quirky" but "keep your interest" via strategic bunkering and several risk/reward shots; P.S. be sure to stop in at the "fantastic" restaurant.

Turtle Creek
20 | 12 | 17 | 22 | $60

Limerick | 303 W. Ridge Pike | 610-489-5133 | www.turtlecreekgolf.com | 6702/5131; 72.1/68.6; 127/115

Because its owners "also own a turf farm", this "wide-open", "links-style" layout 30 miles from Philly is in "consistently excellent condition" and offers "many challenges", including a "real creek", "penal rough" and "finishing holes as good as any in Pennsylvania"; the place exudes "more of a mom-and-pop" feel, and some grouse that the "driving range is not on-site" and service is "limited", but the addition of a "new clubhouse" may mean things are "getting better."

Pittsburgh

Hidden Valley ⌂
18 | 12 | 17 | 20 | $45

Hidden Valley | 1 Craighead Dr. | 814-443-8444 | 800-458-0175 | www.hiddenvalleyresort.com | 6589/5027; 73.1/70.3; 142/127

A "hidden pleasure" in western Pennsylvania, this "long, challenging" layout is a "mountain"-style "shot-makers' course" with "wonderful views"; skeptics shrug it's "ok, if you're there for other reasons", but most agree the "friendly, personable staff in the clubhouse and restaurant" help to make it a "good value."

Nemacolin Woodlands, Mystic Rock ⌂
26 | 27 | 24 | 18 | $185

Farmington | 1001 Lafayette Dr. | 724-329-8555 | 800-422-2736 | www.nemacolin.com | 7397/4803; 77.5/68.8; 150/126

"Difficult but exciting", this "terrific" Pete Dye design 90 minutes south of "the Iron City" "will test your game" with its boulders, bunkers and bumpy greens that belie its "beautiful surroundings" and are "even tougher after" the annual 84 Lumber Classic; as you would expect of an "expensive" bastion of "elegance in the Alleghenies",

	COURSE	FACIL.	SERVICE	VALUE	COST

"forecaddies are provided" and there are "lavish, luxurious" facilities; P.S. it's a "great resort for the whole family."

Nemacolin Woodlands, The Links
| 20 | 24 | 25 | 21 | $84 |

Farmington | 1001 Lafayette Dr. | 724-329-8555 | 800-422-2736 | www.nemacolin.com | 6661/4709; 73/67.3; 131/115

While it's "obviously not as grand as its sister course", this "much easier" links-style original is nonetheless a "well-kept and exciting" layout with "some memorable holes", especially on a "fun back nine" that offers views of the Alleghenies as it rambles over rocky, wooded terrain; if nothing else, it can be a "good warm-up for Mystic Rock", with which it shares an "excellent halfway house" and "high-end resort" amenities.

Olde Stonewall
| 27 | 25 | 24 | 17 | $160 |

Ellwood City | 1495 Mercer Rd. | 724-752-4653 | www.oldestonewall.com | 7052/5203; 73.8/69.4; 144/125

Knights with shining Tommy Armours "can't say enough good things" about this "beautiful layout" located 45 minutes north of Pittsburgh; kept in "excellent condition", Pennsylvania's top-rated Course is a "challenge for every level of player", with "hills and stone walls" and a "mountainous back nine" to "cap off the round memorably"; the medieval motif and "pricey" fees may be too much for some swingers, but the "pleasant personnel" are just right.

Quicksilver
| ▽ 21 | 19 | 20 | 21 | $70 |

Midway | 2000 Quicksilver Rd. | 724-796-1594 | www.quicksilvergolf.com | 7083/5069; 75.7/68.6; 145/115

Though still "a real test of a course" with its long, "hilly" routing and super-"slick greens", this former host of Nationwide Tour and Senior PGA events "has gone downhill" in the last few years; however, recent course and clubhouse renovations (courtesy of a 2002 ownership change) have the potential to make this "once-great facility" once again worth the drive west of Pittsburgh.

Seven Springs Mountain 🏌
| ▽ 18 | 18 | 18 | 20 | $72 |

Champion | 777 Waterwheel Dr. | 814-352-7777 | 800-452-2223 | www.7springs.com | 6454/4934; 71.7/68.9; 131/119

"Ski in winter, golf in summer" on this "beautiful course in the Laurel Mountains", a "scenic and enjoyable" experience thanks to the nice mix of sloped and level holes and "fair tee time management"; the track is "well-kept", but cynics sniff that it looks "like a throwback to the '70s" (it was built in 1969), and the "clubhouse and resort need a lot of work."

Tom's Run at Chestnut Ridge
| ▽ 25 | 22 | 22 | 23 | $75 |

Blairsville | 1762 Old William Penn Hwy. | 724-459-7188 | 6812/5363; 73/71; 135/126

Named for the creek that weaves through the front nine, this "enjoyable" course located about 45 miles east of Pittsburgh runs "up and down and all around" tree-lined canyons and rolling hills; swingers insist the "well-conditioned" layout is the "best course for the price" in the area, especially considering its "fantastic greens"; N.B. after your round, try the buffet lunch or one of the other great specials at Goombah's restaurant.

Poconos

Hideaway Hills

| 22 | 17 | 19 | 23 | $59 |

Kresgeville | 5590 Carney Rd. | 610-681-6000 | www.hideawaygolf.com | 6933/5047; 72.7/68.4; 127/116

This "scenic" mountain layout may "not be the best in the Poconos, but it's one of the most interesting" and "fun to play" as it offers four lakes, an island green and "lots of elevation changes" to make it a "fatiguing" foray; though some snipe about "bare-bones service", you "can't beat it for the price", especially if you opt for a stay-and-play package.

Shawnee Inn

| 17 | 15 | 15 | 18 | $70. |

Shawnee-On-Delaware | 1 River Rd. | 570-424-4000 | 800-742-9633 | www.shawneeinn.com
Blue/Red | 6800/5650; 72.8/72.5; 129/123
Blue/White | 6665/5398; 72.4/71.1; 131/121
Red/White | 6589/5424; 72.2/71.4; 132/121

A.W. Tillinghast's first golf course design is a "traditional" 27-hole layout sitting on a peninsula "alongside the Delaware" with "fast greens" and "fun" shots "over the river", but given its 100-year history, which includes the 1938 PGA Championship, 1938 NCAA Championship and the ghosts of "Tillie, Snead and Gleason", you'd think the "course would be nicer"; complaints about "lack of maintenance" and "poor" service lead some to wonder if "management doesn't know how to manage."

State College

Toftrees

| 22 | 23 | 22 | 21 | $98 |

State College | 1 Country Club Ln. | 814-234-8000 | 800-252-3551 | www.toftrees.com | 7018/5555; 74.3/72.2; 138/125

"Located in a heavenly place" in "golf-starved central Pennsylvania", this "strong course" is a great place to "play when visiting for a PSU football game", with tree-lined holes that "wind through" the "beautiful landscape" and "excellent bentgrass greens"; plus, it's probably easier to score a tee time than a Nittany Lions ticket, so "stay at the resort for the total experience", including the "A+" facilities.

Puerto Rico

Dorado

Dorado Beach Resort, East

| 25 | 21 | 22 | 18 | $195 |

Dorado | Hwy. 693 | 787-796-8961 | 7005/5735; 75.7/75.4; 140/135

"If you are in Puerto Rico to play golf, you have to play this" "classic course" by Robert Trent Jones Sr. "set in an old palm tree plantation", with holes that "zigzag" through the trees and offer many "risk/reward possibilities"; the facilities have an "old-school vibe", though some find it merely "old and tired", but since "Hyatt decided to leave", many expect it'll get a lift from the new management and planned hotel.

Dorado Beach Resort, West

| 23 | 23 | 21 | 18 | $195 |

Dorado | Hwy. 693 | 787-796-8961 | 6975/5730; 74.5/75.2; 132/132

A "great resort course" that's "challenging but soothing at the same time" is rare, but this "beautiful waterfront" Robert Trent Jones Sr. design (renovated in 2002 by Raymond Floyd) offers an appealing mix of "interesting winds" and "tough oceanside holes" with "wide fairways" and serene views; its "price makes it a questionable value", but roundsmen reveal "it's worth playing" both on vacation or on someone else's dime.

Dorado Del Mar 🏌

21 | 21 | 21 | 20 | $102

Dorado | 200 Dorado Del Mar | 787-796-3070 |
www.embassysuitesdorado.com | 6940/5245; 75.2/71.9; 138/125
Designed by native son Chi Chi Rodriguez, this "pleasant" resort course boasting "simply beautiful" ocean and mountain views is one of the "best price/value combos in Puerto Rico" according to fans, which is why it's often "crowded", leaving claustrophobes feeling "a little squeezed"; the driving range (open weekends until 10 PM), the Oregano Italian Grill & Bar and the Embassy Suites hotel's Blue Seahorse both offer some refuge.

Las Croabas

El Conquistador Resort 🏌

25 | 24 | 24 | 18 | $190

Las Croabas | 1000 El Conquistador Ave. | 787-863-6784 |
www.luxuryresorts.com | 6746/4939; 72.5/70.1; 131/120
"Appropriately hilly", this Arthur Hills course at the Luxury Resorts (formerly Wyndham) Los Croabas resort and spa is "breathtakingly beautiful" and "not for beginners", with most of its tee boxes "elevated substantially above the fairways and greens"; errant shots "disappear in a tropical forest" and there are ocean views galore, as well as the occasional "five-ft. lizard" lying on the "lush" turf; though there may be "more challenging courses on the island", for many the "picturesque layout is what makes the round enjoyable."

Rio Grande

Westin Rio Mar, Ocean 🏌

22 | 22 | 21 | 18 | $190

Rio Grande | 6000 Rio Mar Blvd. | 787-888-6000 | 888-627-8556 |
www.westinriomar.com | 6782/5450; 73.8/72.6; 132/126
Ok, so it's "not really an ocean course" as "only one hole is on the ocean", but this Fazio formulation in Rio Grande is still "one of the better tracks in the Caribbean", with "some great holes", "beautiful views" and lots of "wildlife, especially iguanas"; beware "hot and humid" conditions, and note that playing post-"rain storm" can mar the experience (think "rice paddy").

Westin Rio Mar, River 🏌

22 | 22 | 21 | 18 | $190

Rio Grande | 6000 Rio Mar Blvd. | 787-888-6000 | 888-627-8556 |
www.westinriomar.com | 6931/5088; 74.5/69.8; 135/120
Considered to be "more of a challenge" compared to its Ocean sibling, this Greg Norman resort course has "no dramatic or memorable" moments, but it does offer "one well-laid-out, tough hole after another" to "test your accuracy"; situated along the Mameyes River, the long, tight track has a "different, inland feel" with carries over wetlands and water plus views of the surrounding moutains; sure, it's "pricey", but the rates include zoolike views of "friendly iguanas" "as big as alligators."

	COURSE	FACIL.	SERVICE	VALUE	COST

Rhode Island

Newport

Newport National, Orchard ⚐

| 25 | 14 | 19 | 18 | $150 |

Middletown | 324 Mitchell's Ln. | 401-848-9690 |
www.newportnational.com | 7244/5217; 74.4/68.8; 138/119

Given its "excellent condition", "beautiful" routing and views of the Atlantic Ocean and Sakonnet Passage, "it's hard to believe" this "superb" 2002 design "is a public course", but anyone and "any handicap" can play Arthur Hills' "very long", "links-style" layout laden with four-ft.-tall fescue and undulating, bunker-guarded greens; prices at this Newport-area newcomer are "a bit high" "for the shape it's in" – there's "no clubhouse or practice facility" – but Rhode Islanders can expect to "save on greens fees."

Providence

Triggs Memorial

| ▽ 23 | 17 | 16 | 25 | $51 |

Providence | 1533 Chalkstone Ave. | 401-521-8460 | www.triggs.us |
6522/5392; 71.5/70.5; 129/126

An "all-around good" muni situated on Providence's upper west side, this short but "tough" 1932 Donald Ross design features a relatively flat front, gentle elevation on the back and lots of strategic bunkering throughout; although it offers few amenities beyond its clubhouse, it's become a regular host of corporate outings and "tournaments Friday-Sunday", so be sure to book your tee time early.

South Carolina

TOP COURSES IN STATE

29 Kiawah Island, Ocean | *Charleston*
   Caledonia Golf & Fish Club | *Pawleys Island*
27 Tidewater | *Myrtle Beach*
   Sea Pines, Harbour Town | *Hilton Head*
   Wild Dunes, Links | *Charleston*
   Dunes Golf & Beach Club | *Myrtle Beach*
   Glen Dornoch Waterway | *Myrtle Beach*
   TPC Myrtle Beach | *Myrtle Beach*
   Barefoot, Fazio | *Myrtle Beach*
26 Heritage Club | *Pawleys Island*

Charleston

Charleston National ⚐

| 22 | 18 | 18 | 21 | $65 |

Mt. Pleasant | 1360 National Dr. | 843-884-4653 |
www.charlestonnationalgolf.com | 7064/5086; 75.1/70.8; 142/126

You can thank Hurricane Hugo for this "scenic layout" just outside of Charleston, as the "nice" Rees Jones design went from private to public shortly after the storm swept through in 1989; the playable spread is situated along the Intracoastal – "bring bug spray" – with 14 water holes and several forced carries over protected marshland; N.B. they recently opened a new practice facility.

	COURSE	FACIL.	SERVICE	VALUE	COST

Dunes West ⚐

▽ 21 | 20 | 21 | 20 | $89

Mt. Pleasant | 3535 Wando Plantation Way | 843-856-9000 | www.duneswestgolfclub.com | 6859/5208; 73.7/69.2; 139/118

Arthur Hills designed this "challenging yet not unreasonable" test on the site of the former Lexington Plantation northeast of Charleston; the "well-maintained" course is a "great value" and "worth a stop during your Southern campaign", but aficionados advise you "watch out for the rough" and 200-year-old trees, "make sure you know where the 18th green is" and always play at "off-peak times" – otherwise, a round could take "five-plus hours."

Kiawah Island, Cougar Point 🏌

22 | 20 | 23 | 19 | $215

Kiawah Island | 1 Sanctuary Beach Dr. | 843-768-2121 | 800-576-1570 | www.kiawahgolf.com | 6875/4776; 74/67.6; 138/118

It may be the "oldest gem on Kiawah" Island, but thanks to a 1997 Gary Player redesign, this "ocean to swamp" romp is both "surprisingly good" and "playable" "for beginners"; its "memorable par 3s" are routed "along a tidal marsh" ("don't step on any alligators"), and the traditional track offers "spectacular river views" plus all the upscale amenities of its siblings – "fabulous conditions", "Southern hospitality" and a "spectacular hotel."

☑ Kiawah Island, Ocean 🏌

29 | 25 | 26 | 21 | $320

Kiawah Island | 1000 Ocean Course Dr. | 843-768-2121 | 800-576-1570 | www.kiawahgolf.com | 7356/5327; 77.2/72.7; 144/124

"Every serious golfer should experience" South Carolina's top-rated Course, this "brutally demanding", links-style Pete Dye design that will treat you to a "gorgeous ocean backdrop" as it tests you with "high winds", "long forced carries" and "greens that break with tenacity"; the greens fees are "astronomical", but a "grand oceanside clubhouse" – to be completed in time for the 2007 Senior PGA Championship – "will only add to what is already" "one of the best in the world"; P.S. it's walking-only before noon, so grab one of the "excellent caddies."

Kiawah Island, Osprey Point 🏌

23 | 25 | 25 | 21 | $215

Kiawah Island | 700 Governors Dr. | 843-768-2121 | 800-576-1570 | www.kiawahgolf.com | 6932/5023; 73.3/70; 135/121

Probably "the fairest test of golf on Kiawah" Island, Tom Fazio's "gorgeous, natural course" is routed through lakes, wetlands and maritime forest, offering a "variety" of holes with "lots of water"and "outstanding marsh views" – just "don't look too long" for errant shots as the "beautiful wildlife" includes some of the "biggest alligators ever seen"; if you make it back to the "great clubhouse", you can expect to find "charming facilities" and "outstanding service."

Kiawah Island, Turtle Point 🏌

23 | 24 | 25 | 20 | $215

Kiawah Island | 1 Turtle Point Ln. | 843-768-2121 | 800-576-1570 | www.kiawahgolf.com | 7061/5210; 74.2/71.5; 141/126

The three "interesting holes along the ocean" are "the highlight" of this "challenging" Jack Nicklaus design that's "long and tight" with a "small margin for error"; nevertheless, it's "not as hard as the neighboring Ocean course" and "plays very well" "for the average golfer" ("love the front tees for the ladies"); it also offers "great practice facilities" and a "new clubhouse" as well as the "top-notch conditions" and "excellent service" for which the resort is known.

Links at Stono Ferry

▽ 21 | 18 | 21 | 24 | $75

Hollywood | 4812 Stono Links Dr. | 843-763-1817 | www.stonoferrygolf.com | 6700/4946; 72/69.7; 136/114

The "owners have done a great job improving" this once-"ignored" property, and now it's hard to overlook this "beautiful" links layout located on the site of a Revolutionary War battle 15 miles west of Charleston; though "the back is nicer than the front" with three "pretty holes" along the Intracoastal Waterway, the entire course is "a pleasure for golfers of varying abilities"; N.B. they will be redoing the driving range and practice facility in 2007, which may outdate the above Facilities score.

Wild Dunes, Harbor 🔎

22 | 20 | 20 | 20 | $110

Isle of Palms | 5757 Palm Blvd. | 843-886-2180 | 800-845-8880 | www.wilddunes.com | 6709/4907; 73.1/70.4; 132/120

"Be ready for a challenge" because Tom Fazio doesn't design easy golf courses, and this 1985 effort an hour up the coast from Kiawah Island "plays longer" than its scorecard indicates and has water on almost every hole, including the "final two along the ocean", which provide "a great ending"; P.S. "you'd never know that Hurricane Hugo left sofas and chairs on the 18th green."

Wild Dunes, Links 🔎

27 | 23 | 22 | 21 | $160

Isle of Palms | 5757 Palm Blvd. | 843-886-2180 | 800-845-8880 | www.wilddunes.com | 6709/4907; 73.1/70.4; 132/120

It's "always a thrill" to play this "classic links course in an unexpected location" east of Charleston, since it's "fun" to "figure out how to play certain holes" on Tom Fazio's first solo design, a "short but challenging" charge through massive sand dunes with "spectacular elevation changes and ocean views on the finishing holes"; that it's routinely "in excellent shape" means it's more than "worth the expense."

Hilton Head

Country Club of Hilton Head 🔎 ⏱

23 | 22 | 22 | 21 | $112

Hilton Head Island | 70 Skull Creek Dr. | 843-681-4653 | www.hiltonheadclub.com | 6919/5658; 74/71.3; 138/123

"When the surge hits", head to the "high point of Hilton Head Island on No. 12" on this "exceptionally conditioned" "Rees Jones masterpiece" where you'll also get "amazing views of Skull Creek" and the lagoons; though some say it's "not as attractive as other island courses", it's nevertheless "perfect for all levels of players", and "even if you're not a member", the staff will take "great care" of you.

Daufuskie Island, Bloody Point

23 | 22 | 23 | 21 | $109

Hilton Head Island | 1 Seabrook Dr. | 843-341-4875 | 888-909-4653 | www.daufuskieresort.com | 6900/5220; 72.7/69.7; 132/126

"Bloody beautiful", this "Gullah gem", which "can only be reached by ferry from Hilton Head" or Savannah, is a "refreshing and challenging remote experience" with "great views of the Atlantic Ocean and historic Daufuskie Island"; while it makes "a great day trip", aficionados advise "play early" or "bring bug spray", or else "you'll be the one who's bloody" from all the mosquitos that even the wonderful "hospitality" can't squash.

Daufuskie Island, Melrose

| 25 | 23 | 22 | 21 | $129 |

Hilton Head Island | 1 Seabrook Dr. | 843-341-4810 | 888-909-4653 | www.daufuskieresort.com | 7081/5575; 74.2/72.3; 138/126

Taking a "boat ride" from Hilton Head to play this "Jack Nicklaus design" is "an all-day affair", but seafarers swoon over its "isolation", as well as the "great split fairways", the "excellent" finishing holes (including the 18th, a par 5 that "juts out into the water") and the "views of the ocean" that "make it tough to keep your head down"; it's "expensive", but most agree "it just has to be done, at least once."

Golden Bear At Indigo Run ⌖

| 22 | 22 | 22 | 21 | $115 |

Hilton Head Island | 72 Golden Bear Way | 843-689-2200 | www.goldenbear-indigorun.com | 7014/5259; 73.7/66.4; 132/115

Bullish boosters "avoid the time-share sales pitch" and stick to playing this "great Nicklaus design" on Hilton Head Island that's "fair, but makes you think" by mixing "open fairways" with "lots of water" and certain spots where you must "bend your drives"; the course is "very well-marked" and there's "GPS on the carts", two more reasons one of the island's "best-kept courses" is also "one of the best values."

Hilton Head National ⌖

| 24 | 21 | 21 | 23 | $75 |

Bluffton | 60 Hilton Head National Dr. | 843-842-5900 | 888-955-1234 | www.scratch-golf.com
National/Player | 6659/4563; 72.8/66.2; 135/106
Player/Weed | 6655/4631; 72.7/66; 135/111
Weed/National | 6718/4682; 72.7/66; 131/108

"Make sure you have time to play all 27 holes" of this Gary Player/Bobby Weed design that's "right over the bridge" from Hilton Head, for they're "as good as any on the island" and "better than some better-known" layouts, offering more "variety" and "immaculate" conditioning; the facilities are "minimal" but most find it a "pleasant surprise" and "one of the best values in the area."

May River at Palmetto Bluff ⛳ ⌖

| ▽ 27 | 23 | 27 | 20 | $240 |

Bluffton | 476 Mount Pelia Rd. | 843-706-6580 | www.palmettobluffresort.com | 7171/5223; 75.4/70.4; 140/118

If you think it's "hard to get on" now, give this young but "perfectly conditioned" Jack Nicklaus Signature spread in Bluffton "a couple of years" until the amenities catch up to the caddies-required course, which is already "one of the best" around, commanding fees that are "at the top end in the Lowcountry"; the "lovely people" add to a "classy" setup, notwithstanding some "growing pains in the dining room."

Old South ⌖

| 19 | 17 | 19 | 21 | $95 |

Bluffton | 50 Buckingham Plantation Dr. | 843-785-5353 | 800-257-8997 | www.oldsouthgolf.com | 6772/4776; 73.3/68.2; 141/116

You can "leave your big sticks in the bag on some par 4s" at this 1991 Clyde Johnston design set in a "serene" Bluffton locale, for it's a "placement-style course" on which you "hit to areas" rather than grip and rip; you can leave the high-limit plastic behind, as well, because this "well-maintained" track with basic facilities comes "without the sky-high Hilton Head greens fees."

	COURSE	FACIL.	SERVICE	VALUE	COST

Oyster Reef

	21	19	18	21	$125

Hilton Head Island | 155 High Bluff Rd. | 843-681-1750 | 800-234-6318 | www.heritagegolfgroup.com | 7018/5288; 74.7/71.1; 137/120

With a "pretty" "signature 6th" on Port Royal Sound that "makes you want to stay all day" plus "many doglegs to give it length", this "fair and challenging" Rees Jones design on Hilton Head Island "lives up to the lofty expectations set by his father"; it's the "favorite course" of many "frequent" visitors, but newbies "of all skill levels" can also appreciate its "cooperative" staff and "excellent value compared to other Island courses."

Palmetto Dunes, Arthur Hills

	24	21	21	19	$139

Hilton Head Island | 2 Leamington Ln. | 843-785-1140 | 800-827-3006 | www.palmettodunes.com | 6651/4999; 72.9/69.2; 129/119

Fans "tip their hats" to Arthur Hills for this "enjoyable layout" on Hilton Head Island that's in "perfect condition" "every year", offering "many interesting holes", "marvelous views" and water (along with the accompanying "gators"), complemented by service from a "friendly, guest-oriented" staff; though it's "walkable", there are Segways and air-conditioned carts to carry your clubs, and while it can be "pricey", it's a "great value if you're staying" at the resort.

Palmetto Dunes, George Fazio

	21	21	20	20	$115

Hilton Head Island | 2 Carnoustie Rd. | 843-785-1130 | 800-827-3006 | www.palmettodunes.com | 6873/5273; 73.9/70.8; 135/127

"Bring your long game" and "lots of balls" to this "longer" Palmetto Dunes track, for if designer "George Fazio and his timbers" don't shorten your shots, there's "lots of water" and "many sand traps" to pick up the slack; there are several "interesting holes" with "great scenery" but there's "still no practice range" and it can be quite pricey on its own, although "the package to play all the [resort's] courses makes it a great deal."

Palmetto Dunes, Robert Trent Jones 🏌

	23	21	21	20	$139

Hilton Head Island | 7 Trent Jones Ln. | 843-785-1136 | 800-827-3006 | www.palmettodunes.com | 7005/5035; 74.3/64.6; 138/109

Use your doubloons to play the Robert Trent Jones Sr.-designed "signature course at Palmetto Dunes", which is "much improved since its renovation", "curving along lagoons" and boasting even better "ocean views" just before and after the turn; although the "front nine is a little noisy because of the highway" and purists consider "no grass driving range" to be a "shame", it's an "enjoyable" layout complete with "kid-friendly tees" and "Segway golf transporters."

Palmetto Hall, Arthur Hills

	22	20	19	19	$95

Hilton Head Island | 108 Fort Howell Rd. | 843-681-7717 | 800-234-6318 | www.palmettohallclub.com | 6918/5006; 73.7/70.6; 136/123

Holes lined with towering pines and glistening lakes make for a "beautiful setting" and "some intimidating driving" at this "challenging but fair" Hilton Head Island layout that has "a lot of character for a resort course"; it's seen "significant improvements" recently, so though a few find it "not very memorable", it's "better than not playing" on the island at all, so pick a day when it's open to the public (it alternates as private with its sibling course, Robert Cupp).

	COURSE	FACIL.	SERVICE	VALUE	COST

⚡ Sea Pines, Harbour Town Golf Links | 27 | 25 | 24 | 17 | $270

Hilton Head Island | 11 Lighthouse Ln. | 843-363-4485 | www.seapines.com |
6973/5208; 75.2/70.7; 146/124

"If you want to play a PGA Tour stop, you could do a whole lot worse"
than this "Pete Dye gem" with its "narrow fairways", "microscopic
greens" and Hilton Head "island ambiance"; though it's an all-around
"amazing course", "the last three holes are what you'll remember", especially "the beautiful 18th with the lighthouse" and "great views of
the Atlantic"; it's "best to play before or after" the Verizon Heritage,
however, when the "gorgeous conditioning" makes it worth the
"whoppingly expensive" greens fee.

Sea Pines, Ocean | 22 | 22 | 21 | 19 | $140

Hilton Head Island | 100 N. Sea Pines Dr. | 843-842-8484 | 800-955-8337 |
www.seapines.com | 6906/5325; 73.4/71.1; 142/124

"Calling a course with only one ocean view the 'Ocean' is a bit of a
stretch", but there's no denying that this "challenging but fair" 1995
redesign is both "beautiful" and "fun to play"; "winding through" the
resort, its "nicely designed holes" feature "wide fairways", "not-too-
monstrous greens" and lots of lagoons, so "watch out for the alligators"; it's "a bit expensive", but it's a "great way to play Sea Pines without the Harbour Town cost."

Myrtle Beach

Arrowhead 🏌 | 25 | 21 | 22 | 22 | $115

Myrtle Beach | 1201 Burcale Rd. | 843-236-3243 | 800-236-3243 |
www.arrowheadcc.com
Cypress/Lakes | 6668/4812; 71.4/69.1; 141/124
Lakes/Waterway | 6614/4698; 71.6/68.1; 140/118
Waterway/Cypress | 6644/4624; 71.6/69.1; 141/121

This pre-plane pit stop near the Myrtle Beach airport is a "great track,
especially if you want to play 27" holes with "beautiful landscaping"
and "well-manicured greens" to facilitate "accurate putt reads";
routed over "challenging terrain" along the Intracoastal Waterway, the
layout's "very different" nines "will allow you to hit it hard, but you'll
have to keep it on the fairway", as most of the holes have water in play.

Barefoot Resort, Dye | 24 | 23 | 23 | 20 | $170

North Myrtle Beach | 2700 Pete Dye Dr. | 843-399-7238 | 877-237-3767 |
www.barefootgolf.com | 7343/5021; 73.3/69.1; 149/119

Even if this is "not the best Barefoot Resort course", "don't overlook"
this North Myrtle Beach track because its holes are "dead ringers for
those great Pete Dye [designs] you've seen on TV"; although the layout can be "punitive" with its "innumerable bunkers" and mounding,
it's actually "very playable" and comes with "excellent service" and
"comfortable facilities" that include its own clubhouse; N.B. the resort
just added a 27-acre practice facility.

Barefoot Resort, Fazio 🏌 | 27 | 26 | 23 | 22 | $170

North Myrtle Beach | 4980 Barefoot Resort Bridge Rd. | 843-390-3200 |
877-237-3767 | www.barefootgolf.com | 6834/4820; 73.7/68; 139/115

Strap on your spikes and play "the best of the Barefoots", this "truly
exceptional" "textbook Fazio" design providing the "perfect mix of

	COURSE	FACIL.	SERVICE	VALUE	COST

challenge and fun" courtesy of "great driving holes" and "plenty of thinking opportunities" on a "beautiful" Lowcountry layout that "looks natural" as it "rolls with the countryside"; though "pricey", the "first-class" experience is "worth it" given the "excellent" course conditioning, "beautiful facilities" and "very friendly staff."

Barefoot Resort, Love 🏖

| 26 | 25 | 24 | 21 | $170 |

North Myrtle Beach | 4980 Barefoot Resort Bridge Rd. | 843-390-3200 | 877-237-3767 | www.barefootgolf.com | 7047/5346; 75.1/70.9; 138/118
Like a true "Southern belle", this Davis Love III design is both "visually intoxicating" and "immaculately maintained", offering "lots of drama" via "memorable holes" that play amid the re-created "old ruins" of a plantation house ("very cool" to some, "a bit hokey" to others); the "wonderful layout" is "exciting for all handicaps" and comes complete with a "beautiful clubhouse" and the resort's "nice accommodations."

Barefoot Resort, Norman 🏖

| 21 | 22 | 22 | 17 | $170 |

North Myrtle Beach | 4980 Barefoot Resort Bridge Rd. | 843-390-3200 | 877-237-3767 | www.barefootgolf.com | 7035/4953; 73.9/68.6; 136/112
This "classic Greg Norman design" may be the "least attractive and interesting of the Barefoot courses", but it's nevertheless quite "playable" and offers "some nice holes" bordering the Intracoastal Waterway plus creek carries, zoysia rough and sod wall bunkering; it has the same "comfortable facilities" as its siblings, but that doesn't prevent putters from pondering "how they can charge this much" for something that "can not compare."

Blackmoor 🏖

| 23 | 19 | 21 | 22 | $94 |

Murrells Inlet | 6100 Longwood Rd. | 843-650-5555 | 866-952-5555 | www.blackmoor.com | 6614/4807; 71.1/67.9; 126/115
"Challenging for the average golfer", this "classic" Gary Player design "makes you think" as you tackle its "predominantly dogleg" holes that are loaded up with "long carries" and "lots of elevation changes"; even Lowcountry laymen will "love" this "old beauty", however, as its woodland front and linksy back offer "rewards for the adventurous"; although some feel the "facilities need updating", it's considered one of the "best values" in the Myrtle Beach area.

Dunes Golf & Beach Club ⛳

| 27 | 23 | 24 | 22 | $170 |

Myrtle Beach | 9000 N. Ocean Blvd. | 843-449-5914 | 866-386-3722 | www.dunesgolfandbeachclub.com | 7195/5345; 75.7/71.4; 144/131
It's "difficult" and "expensive" to get on this 1948 Robert Trent Jones Sr. "classic" "just a few hundred yards from the beach", but most agree the "old-school" design is worth the effort and cost; there's "lots of Lowcountry history" here, including "many [Senior] PGA events", and the course is "traditional, vs. most of the others in the Myrtle area", while "great facilities" and "great service" add to its "country-club ambiance."

Glen Dornoch Waterway 🏖

| 27 | 23 | 23 | 23 | $136 |

Little River | Hwy. 17 N. | 843-249-2541 | 800-717-8784 | www.glendornoch.com | 6890/5002; 73.1/69.8; 145/129
This "interesting" layout located a mile from the North Carolina border boasts "beautiful" holes that "challenge" "without being impossible for the high-handicapper", although cognoscenti call the three

"grand" finishing holes the "hardest in the area"; conditions are "excellent" and the views of the Intracoastal Waterway are "awesome", but a few wish they could play for "less money."

Grande Dunes 🏌

| 25 | 25 | 24 | 19 | $199 |

Myrtle Beach | 8700 Golf Village Ln. | 843-449-7070 | 888-886-8877 | www.grandedunes.com | 7618/5353; 77.3/71.2; 142/123

The "interesting and challenging" holes are "always in top shape" and the views are "beautiful" at this "amazing" Myrtle Beach layout designed by Roger Rulewich that runs "along and above the Intracoastal Waterway"; built in 2001, it "will only get better with age", but the amenities are already "first-class" and you can really "feel the luxury" in the "short-game practice area" and "great service and grill" – not to mention the "high" fees.

Heather Glen 🏌

| 24 | 20 | 21 | 24 | $102 |

Little River | Hwy. 17 N. | 843-249-9000 | 800-868-4536 |
www.heatherglen.com
Blue/Red | 6783/5101; 72.4/69.3; 134/117
Red/White | 6771/5053; 72.4/69.3; 134/117
White/Blue | 6822/5082; 72.4/69.3; 137/117

An "old-style" "gem in a sea of new and gimmicky designs", this "solid 27-hole facility" north of Myrtle Beach offers "lots of variety" on its "well-forested" layout that incorporates plenty of elevation changes and water; while some feel it's "getting a little long in the tooth" and the conditioning "could be better", the "friendly, helpful" staff "treats you like you're the only one here", leading some to say this "value" is a "great" course "for the money."

Legends, Heathland 🏌

| 24 | 24 | 22 | 23 | $113 |

Myrtle Beach | 1500 Legends Dr. | 843-236-9318 | 800-552-2660 |
www.legendsgolf.com | 6785/5115; 72.3/71; 127/121

It's hard to choose from the "many courses to play in Myrtle", but don't overlook this "underrated gem" that channels "Scotland in South Carolina"; yet "another excellent Legends course", the "links-style" spread is "fun for all levels", a "wide-open" layout with "no houses" and "no trees" to mar your view; even better, it's part of "a great complex" that's "legend for its fine conditioning", lighted practice facility and "on-course condo" accommodations.

Legends, Moorland 🏌

| 24 | 24 | 23 | 23 | $113 |

Myrtle Beach | 1500 Legends Dr. | 843-236-9318 | 800-552-2660 |
www.legendsgolf.com | 6799/4905; 73/72.8; 134/118

"One of the more unusual courses" in the area and "a big favorite" among Legends' legions, this "scenic and interesting" P.B. Dye design represents "target golf at its best"; it's either "fairways or bunkers" on this "well-maintained" "shot-maker's course" where only "the mounding stands out" – you'll find there are "no houses in sight"; though "challenging", it's "always a treat" and "a must-play on every Myrtle Beach trip!"

Legends, Parkland 🏌

| 22 | 24 | 22 | 23 | $113 |

Myrtle Beach | 1500 Legends Dr. | 843-236-9318 | 800-552-2660 |
www.legendsgolf.com | 7170/5518; 74.9/71; 136/125

Perhaps the most "traditional" of Legends' "very nice courses", this "surprisingly difficult" parklander is definitely "not a walk in the park":

despite its "wide fairways", the "tree-lined" track features deep bunkers, multi-tiered greens and can at times seem "long for the sake of being long"; nevertheless, it's "in great condition" and has the same upscale amenities as its siblings, so expect to have a "pleasant day."

Long Bay

24 | 22 | 21 | 21 | $122

Longs | 350 Foxtail Dr. | 843-399-2222 | 800-344-5590 | www.mbn.com | 7025/4944; 74.3/69.2; 140/115

"Bring your 'Jack' game" and your "beach towel, pail and shovel" to this Golden Bear gauntlet, where aside from "huge bunkers everywhere" are "a few holes where you have to decide to play smart or go for it" to traverse the traps; though "a bit off the beaten path" north of Myrtle Beach, this inland design delivers "a fun round that can be improved by knowing the course" – one reason why adventurous types "keep returning."

Myrtle Beach National, King's North

26 | 23 | 20 | 21 | $160

Myrtle Beach | 4900 National Dr. | 843-448-2308 | 800-344-5590 | www.mbn.com | 7017/4816; 72.6/67.4; 136/113

Arnold Palmer designed this track to be "playable" and "fun, no matter what your handicap is", providing "plenty of strategically placed hazards" that you can either conquer or concede to, such as the famous island fairway on the "Gambler hole" 6th that "makes the round"; though it's the "most expensive of the three at Myrtle Beach National", people "go back year after year", mainly for the "entertaining layout", "nice facilities" and "A-1 service", but also because you "need to play this course twice to figure it out."

Myrtle Beach National, SouthCreek

20 | 25 | 22 | 23 | $99

Myrtle Beach | 4900 National Dr. | 843-448-2308 | 800-344-5590 | www.mbn.com | 6416/4723; 71/68; 128/117

Winding through wetlands and forests, this Myrtle Beach "locals' favorite" is "a great alternative to the North course" because it's "less expensive" and "not too difficult", but still "lots of fun"; while it's the "shortest of the Myrtle Beach National courses", it still "requires the most accuracy", although errant shots sometimes get a locals' bounce from "helpful" "homeowners along the course" who "may kick your ball back into play."

Tidewater

27 | 21 | 23 | 20 | $189

North Myrtle Beach | 1400 Tidewater Dr. | 843-249-3829 | 800-446-5363 | www.tide-water.com | 7078/4615; 74.8/67.1; 144/115

"One of Myrtle's best tracks" is this "fascinating" and "memorable" "gem" designed by South Carolina native Ken Tomlinson and laid out "along the Intracoastal Waterway" with acres of pine trees and "scenic" "tidal flats in the background"; the "well-groomed layout" features 15 "water holes" and some "really tough par 3s", but all in all, it's "just straightforward golf" with "no tricks" and a staff that may be "the friendliest and most helpful" around.

TPC Myrtle Beach

27 | 25 | 23 | 20 | $185

Murrells Inlet | 1199 TPC Blvd. | 843-357-3399 | 888-742-8721 | www.tpc.com | 6950/5118; 74.2/70.3; 145/125

Requiring "your A-driving game", your "long game" and some extra golf balls, this "tough" host of the 2000 Senior Tour Championship is an "impossibly tight" layout loaded with "long forced carries over swamp and lakes"; "what you see is what you get", however, so although service receives a mixed response ("accommodating" vs. "unfriendly"), there's nothing tricky about this "wonderful" course near Myrtle Beach; in fact, "except for the price, this is a gem!"

Wachesaw Plantation East 🔊 | 22 | 19 | 19 | 20 | $103 |

Murrells Inlet | 911 Riverwood Dr. | 843-357-2090 | 888-922-0027 | www.wachesaweast.com | 6933/4995; 73.6/68.8; 132/117

"Narrow, tree-lined" fairways, "large, fast greens" and many water hazards make Clyde Johnston's ode to Scotland on a former rice plantation near Myrtle Beach "a tough course at times"; still, from the right tees, this former LPGA host is "women-friendly" and it's a "super layout for anyone" (even "novices will feel·like golfers"), so those who find it "could be maintained better" are overruled by a vocal majority that maintains it's well "worth the money."

Wild Wing Plantation, Avocet 🔊 | 22 | 22 | 19 | 19 | $130 |

Myrtle Beach | 1000 Wild Wing Blvd. | 843-347-9464 | 800-736-9464 | www.wildwing.com | 7127/5298; 74.6/70.4; 133/118

When it "was part of a four-course facility", this Larry Nelson design with "strategic mounding" and risk/reward opportunities "used to be one of the favorites" in Myrtle Beach, but since "they did away with the other courses for housing", "it's the only one" left, and the conditions have "really slipped"; still, a staff that "treats you like a PGA professional" and a massive clubhouse with lots of goodies inside make it a "good place to play" for stalwarts.

Witch, The 🔊 | 23 | 18 | 20 | 23 | $99 |

Conway | 1900 Hwy. 544 | 843-448-1300 | www.mysticalgolf.com | 6796/4812; 71.2/69; 133/109

Those looking for a course that's "different from the other 99+ near Myrtle Beach" are bewitched by this inland Dan Maples design that feels like it's in "another world" as it "winds through woodlands" and "wetlands" with "lots of elevation changes", some of which are bridges over the "many hazards" inhabited by "gators and snakes"; it's an "incredible value", but landlubbers warn it can be "very wet."

Wizard, The 🔊 | 20 | 20 | 20 | 21 | $89 |

Myrtle Beach | 4601 Leeshire Blvd. | 843-236-9393 | www.mysticalgolf.com | 6721/4972; 72/71.2; 125/121

With "wide fairways" and "no trouble lurking", this Myrtle Beach track is a "nice course for high-handicappers and couples" and a nice ego booster because you "can really score", especially "if you stay out of the water" "on the 17th and 18th"; it's also a "volume play", however, "lacking in service and amenities" as well as a good rationale for the "illogical" "equine theme" and "hokey faux-castle clubhouse."

Pawleys Island

🅩 Caledonia Golf & Fish Club | 29 | 25 | 26 | 24 | $185 |

Pawleys Island | 369 Caledonia Dr. | 843-237-3675 | 800-483-6800 | www.fishclub.com | 6526/4957; 72.1/68.7; 140/122

"Rest in peace, Mike Strantz", knowing your "elegant test" "set beautifully amongst the marshes" of Pawleys Island represents "Southern golf at its finest": "tough in a civilized way", with "well-protected greens", "lots of sand and water", "impeccable conditioning" and an "antebellum feel"; it's "costly", but you'll receive "pampering service" as you sit on the veranda at the "awesome old clubhouse" watching "duffers dunk their balls in the pond" fronting the "knee-knocking 18th."

Heritage Club 🏌

| 26 | 23 | 22 | 21 | $123 |

Pawleys Island | 478 Heritage Dr. | 843-237-3424 | 800-552-2660 | www.legendsgolf.com | 7005/5250; 74.8/67.4; 144/119

Located on a former plantation in Pawleys Island, this "beautiful" course pleases purists with its "challenging routing" of "great marsh and inland holes" that makes "position more important than length", while offering some "birdie opportunities for just about any golfer"; the practice facilities are "nice", and though the clubhouse and "impressive" avenue of "huge old trees" remind some of *Gone With the Wind*, the "friendly" staff "keeps things light."

Pawleys Plantation 🏌

| 25 | 23 | 23 | 21 | $135 |

Pawleys Island | 70 Tanglewood Dr. | 843-237-6200 | 800-367-9959 | www.pawleysplantation.com | 7026/5017; 75.3/70.5; 146/124

"Even though you're less than a mile from the ocean", "don't expect links golf" at this "memorable" "salt marsh-and-lowlands" Pawleys Island layout where "Jack Nicklaus makes you hit high shots" to "signature" island greens that "challenge even the most steel-nerved player"; it's "well-conditioned" and "woman-friendly", although anyone can lose shots playing while "awestruck by the scenery" and "distracted by the wildlife."

Tradition Club, The 🏌

| 21 | 20 | 19 | 21 | $115 |

Pawleys Island | 1027 Willbrook Blvd. | 843-237-5041 | 877-599-0888 | www.traditiongolfclub.com | 6875/4106; 72.6/64.4; 132/104

"A fixture in south Myrtle Beach" since it opened in 1995, this Ron Garl design is located on the site of an old plantation in Pawleys Island; "in contrast to the outstanding courses" in the area, it can be somewhat "boring" (save for a couple of island greens), but the wood- and water-laced layout is "great" if you like to swing with abandon off the tee, as its wide fairways offer an equally wide margin of error.

True Blue

| 25 | 22 | 22 | 20 | $150 |

Pawleys Island | 900 Blue Stem Dr. | 843-235-0900 | 888-483-6801 | www.truebluegolf.com | 7062/4995; 74.3/65.4; 145/109

"Mike Strantz did some great work" at this "thoughtfully designed" Carolina course (and relative of Caledonia) that employs "huge waste areas", "undulating greens" and "unusual changes in elevation for a beach course"; there's "lots of trouble to get into", so expect a "test of skills and patience", as this Pawleys Island journey "to hell and back" will be "memorable" and "worth every lost ball."

Willbrook Plantation 🏌

| 24 | 22 | 23 | 24 | $105 |

Pawleys Island | Millbrook Blvd. | 843-237-4900 | 800-344-5590 | www.mbn.com | 6722/4956; 72.6/67.7; 133/118

New "Bermuda greens" and other "recent changes" have helped this "visually appealing" Dan Maples design at "the southern end of Myrtle Beach" in Pawleys Island "move up the list of the area's best"; it still provides "surprises around every corner", including "forced carries over marsh", while "terrific" service, "attention to detail" and a "nice, antebellum clubhouse" add to the allure.

South Dakota

Vermillion

Bluffs, The

`- - - - | $26`

Vermillion | 2021 E. Main St. | 605-677-7058 | www.bluffsinfo.com | 6684/4926; 72.4/68.5; 123/113

Playing through a residential housing development in the southeast section of the state, this affordably priced public is a "good course with some elevation changes": four of its holes play through the Missouri River Valley and the remainder over prairie highlands; the host of the South Dakota Open, this links-style layout is laced with wetlands and lakes and features a stunning 13th with a tee set 80 feet above the fairway; in short, swingers say it's a "value."

Tennessee

Chattanooga

Bear Trace At Harrison Bay

`- - - - | $49`

Harrison | 8919 Harrison Bay Rd. | 423-326-0885 | 877-611-2327 | www.beartrace.com | 7313/5292; 74.9/70.3; 136/118

Located just about 20 minutes north of Chattanooga, this second of five "state-owned and state-run" golf courses in the Bear Trace family may be hemmed in by water and trees but it's decidedly playable, with wide fairways and open-front greens; though a few feel it "could stand some manicuring" to be a true golden bear, all in all, there's "value here."

Knoxville

Stonehenge at Fairfield Glade

`▽ 27 | 24 | 24 | 25 | $79`

Fairfield Glade | 222 Fairfield Blvd. | 931-484-3731 | www.stonehengegolf.com | 6549/5000; 71.8/69.6; 135/124

The Cumberland Mountains provide "lots of elevation changes", rugged rock outcroppings and "challenging holes, especially the par 3s" at this course "hidden in the middle of the state" in Fairfield Glade; granted, it seems "wet all the time", but the "layout and scenery can make you forget your wet pants cuffs" and the "great value" makes it "worth the trip from Nashville or Knoxville."

Nashville

Bear Trace At Ross Creek Landing

`- - - - | $49`

Clifton | 110 Airport Rd. | 931-676-3174 | 866-770-2327 | www.beartrace.com | 7131/5504; 74.7/71.6; 197/123

This "friendly layout in a resort area" is the latest of Jack Nicklaus' Tennessee titans, a "scenic and challenging" "gem" riding the banks of a river two hours southwest of Nashville; it offers a combination of tree-lined and wide-open holes with a heavy water

	COURSE	FACIL.	SERVICE	VALUE	COST

presence, which has pros predicting this "great value" "could end up being a great course."

Gaylord Springs, Springhouse ⛳ ▽ 22 | 22 | 21 | 16 | $90

Nashville | 18 Springhouse Ln. | 615-458-1730 | www.gaylordsprings.com | 6842/5040; 74/70.2; 133/118

Larry Nelson's 1990 links-style design along the Cumberland River is "not tough if you're hitting it straight, but there are double bogies" to be had on its "interesting holes" that wind through limestone outcroppings and wetlands; it "gets plenty of play because of its association with the Opryland Resort", and while fans marvel at the staff and facilities, they're less enthused by the "overpriced" fees.

Hermitage, General's Retreat ▽ 25 | 20 | 22 | 20 | $57

Old Hickory | 3939 Old Hickory Blvd. | 615-847-4001 | www.hermitagegolf.com | 6773/5437; 72.3/70.8; 129/120

If you want to golf "a stone's throw from President Andrew Jackson's home", play this former site of the LPGA's Sara Lee Classic, a track along the Cumberland River northeast of Nashville; it's "in great condition" and features a par-5 11th that's notable for two reasons: it stretches to 600 yards and hops water hazards on both the tee shot and the approach.

Hermitage, President's Reserve ▽ 25 | 21 | 21 | 22 | $67

Old Hickory | 3939 Old Hickory Blvd. | 615-847-4001 | www.hermitagegolf.com | 7157/5138; 74.2/69; 134/115

Though perhaps "not as scenic as the General's Retreat", this 2000 Denis Griffiths design still offers "terrific shots of the Cumberland River" and is actually a "bump up" in challenge thanks to "very long holes" that bring water into play; one thing, though: it's relatively "expensive compared to local courses."

Tennessean, The - | - | - | - | $42

Paris | 900 Olde Tennessee Trail | 731-642-7271 | 866-710-4653 | www.tennesseangolfclub.com | 7183/5633; 74.6/67.5; 136/121

Located in Paris, TN, this design by lesser-known but highly respected architect Keith Foster has elevation changes galore and roller-coaster holes that are "enjoyed by low-handicappers"; thankfully, however, the "forward tees allow mutual enjoyment by higher-handicappers", although they may be less enthused with the "iffy conditioning" - of course, it's hard to grow grass on such rugged terrain.

Texas

TOP COURSES IN STATE

Austin

Barton Creek, Crenshaw Cliffside 👥 ⚲ ⏱
| 23 | 26 | 24 | 18 | $165 |

Austin | 8212 Barton Club Dr. | 512-329-4653 | 800-336-6158 |
www.bartoncreek.com | 6630/4726; 72.3/67.2; 132/110

It may "not be the most interesting layout" in the Barton Creek resort family, but this Austin course "always looks great", is "good for the money" and has the same upscale service and facilities as its siblings; the greens, which "make or break the course depending on how you putt", can be "challenging" for high-handicappers.

☑ Barton Creek, Fazio Canyons 👥 ⚲ ⏱
| 28 | 26 | 26 | 21 | $240 |

Austin | 8212 Barton Club Dr. | 512-329-4653 | 800-336-6158 |
www.bartoncreek.com | 7153/5098; 75.4/70.6; 138/121

"Tough but gorgeous", this Tom Fazio effort "in a remote, wooded area" of the resort is Texas' top-rated Course and "commands great respect from amateur golfers" for being "as hard as management wants to make it and as different as the selected tees and weather allow"; plus, the "long", tree-lined lanes are laid out across "rolling hills" with plenty of "risk/reward" strategy needed; N.B. caddies required.

Barton Creek, Fazio Foothills 👥 ⚲ ⏱
| 27 | 27 | 26 | 22 | $205 |

Austin | 8212 Barton Club Dr. | 512-329-4653 | 800-336-6158 |
www.bartoncreek.com | 7125/5185; 74.2/69.4; 135/115

"Some people prefer this to the Canyons, and they would have a good argument" attest acolytes of this "Hill Country" Fazio design, a "favorite" of those who like to "use all their clubs" and who admire "excellent" conditioning; all in all, it's "worth playing" – and paying for – especially given a "wonderfully accommodating staff"; N.B. caddies required.

Barton Creek, Palmer Lakeside 👥 ⚲ ⏱
| 22 | 21 | 22 | 21 | $125 |

Austin | 8212 Barton Club Dr. | 512-329-4653 | 800-336-6158 |
www.bartoncreek.com | 6645/5107; 72.3/70; 135/124

What can seem like "an afterthought" may be "worth the drive" (especially if you're an "Arnie fan") say backers of this layout known for its wide, tee-ball tempting fairways and views of Lake Travis; if some "would rather play the other courses at Barton Creek", this one is good for a rapid round since it's "not as backed up" as the others.

Forest Creek
| ▽ 22 | 13 | 16 | 20 | $59 |

Round Rock | 99 Twin Ridge Pkwy. | 512-388-2874 | www.forestcreek.com |
7147/5394; 73.8/71.9; 136/124

Just north of Austin, this "playable" track – host of the Central Texas Amateur Championship – is kept "in shape", but "can be gusty", making the "hilly" holes and "blind shots" downright "challenging" (good thing there's a three-tiered practice range on which to warm up); P.S. "check out their Internet specials" for the best price.

Horseshoe Bay Resort, Applerock 🏌 ⚲
| ▽ 27 | 22 | 25 | 21 | $166 |

Horseshoe Bay | 1 Horseshoe Bay Blvd. | 830-598-6561 | 800-252-9363 |
www.hsbresort.com | 6999/5536; 74/73; 139/128

After 20 years, this "great" Hill Country course, the resort's third, is still a challenge thanks to masterful architect Robert Trent Jones Sr.

and the rocky terrain high above Lake LBJ; if you have your own plane, you can fly in using the property's private airport – as long as you can land within 6,000 feet.

Horseshoe Bay Resort, Ram Rock 🏌 ⛳

▽ 28 | 25 | 25 | 23 | $166

Horseshoe Bay | 1 Horseshoe Bay Blvd. | 830-598-6561 | 800-252-9363 | www.hsbresort.com | 6926/5306; 74.5/72.5; 140/129

"This old bird'll still hunt", and "from the back tees, it is one of the toughest in Texas" marvel aces who appreciate this "extremely challenging" but "fantastic" foray through narrow fairways, over and along creeks and in between rock gardens; it's also one of the state's "most beautiful courses" but, in the end, you're likely to hear many murmur "man, is it hard."

Horseshoe Bay Resort, Slick Rock 🏌 ⛳

▽ 24 | 23 | 25 | 19 | $166

Horseshoe Bay | 1 Horseshoe Bay Blvd. | 830-598-2561 | 800-252-9363 | www.hsbresort.com | 6834/5438; 72.6/72.1; 127/127

Opened in 1971, the first and "easiest of the three Rocks" is a fan "favorite" for its "great design" (featuring a tree-lined front and an open, rolling back) and "scenic" views; a visit here proves "Horseshoe Bay still knows how to take care of its courses and guests"; N.B. visit the Slick Rock Bar & Grill after your round for one of the Austin area's highly touted burgers.

NEW Wolfdancer 🏌

– | – | – | – | $145

Lost Pines | 575 Hyatt Lost Pines Rd. | 512-308-9653 | www.lostpines.hyatt.com | 7205/4953; 76.1/69.1; 137/118

Named for a ritual dance performed by the indigenous Tonkawa Indians, this dramatic new layout from Arthur Hills and design partner Christopher Wilczynski weaves together three diverse topographies: open prairie, tree-lined ridge and river valley; situated just 25 miles southeast of Austin, it's part of the upscale Hyatt Regency Lost Pines, which also offers a spa and riding stables; N.B. caddies available.

Dallas

Buffalo Creek 🏌

▽ 23 | 16 | 17 | 23 | $59

Heath | 624 Country Club Dr. | 972-771-4003 | www.americangolf.com | 7018/5209; 73.8/67; 133/113

Though it's a half-hour from Downtown Dallas, this "well-tended" Weiskopf/Morrish design rolls past water hazards on 11 holes; it's both a "pleasure" and a "test of skills", "especially from the back tees", which stretch to more than 7,000 yards; don't expect luxe, though – the facilities are merely "decent."

Cliffs, The 🏌

▽ 24 | 19 | 20 | 24 | $85

Graford | 160 Cliffs Dr. | 940-779-4520 | 888-843-2543 | www.thecliffsresort.com | 6808/4876; 73.9/68.4; 143/124

Robert von Hagge teamed up with touring pro Bruce Devlin to create this "stunning course" nestled in a "beautiful area" overlooking Possum Kingdom Lake two hours west of Dallas; if you miss the wide fairways bordered by rock outcroppings, cedar groves and tall grasses, "don't look in the rough for balls" – you may just "find snakes" instead; N.B. don't miss having a bite on the outdoor patio at the Chaparral Grille and Spurs bar.

Cowboys 🏌

26	25	26	20	$160

Grapevine | 1600 Fairway Dr. | 817-481-7277 | www.cowboysgolfclub.com | 7017/4702; 74.2/68.9; 140/114

"If you love the Dallas Cowboys", you'll be roped in by "the huge star in the middle of a fairway", "golf carts with images of ex-football players on the side" and "team history on every tee" at this "fun" Grapevine track also worshipped for its "dramatic elevations" and "super-friendly staff"; yes, it's "pricey", but it turns into a "great value" since "you pay once" and you "can get around twice" and "pig out" on the "good food."

Four Seasons at Las Colinas, TPC ⟲

24	27	26	17	$165

Irving | 4150 N. MacArthur Blvd. | 972-717-2500 | www.thesportsclubfourseasons.com | 7009/5340; 75.1/73.3; 140/134

Although it's "never as pretty as it looks on TV" during the PGA Tour's EDS Byron Nelson Championship, this Jay Morrish design in Irving is an "incredible course when it's in shape" and has "some great holes, including the 17th and 18th"; add in "top-notch training facilities", "great caddies" and the "Four Seasons' service and amenities" and you've got a facility that's "first-class all the way"; N.B. it's scheduled to close for renovations in May 2007 and will reopen in early 2008.

Pine Dunes

▽ 28	16	19	25	$79

Frankston | 159 Private Rd. 7019 | 903-876-4336 | www.pinedunes.com | 7117/5150; 74.4/71.3; 131/126

"Pure golf in the middle of nowhere" in Frankston keeps aces over-joyed and the greens "uncrowded" at this "heavenly" site where "there's not much breeze blowin'", though you can be sure that the "attentive staff will keep you cool with lots of ice water"; the price is "great", and all in all, it's "like being at Pinehurst", even if there's "not much of a service area."

Tangle Ridge

▽ 22	16	21	20	$50

Grand Prairie | 818 Tangle Ridge Dr. | 972-299-6837 | www.tangleridge.com | 6835/5187; 72.2/70.2; 129/117

In a "surprising setting" near Joe Pool Lake (midway between Dallas and Ft. Worth), this "secret course" is one of the "hilliest in the metroplex" but also affords "great" water views; "wide", "liberal land-ing areas off the tee" and "fair, bentgrass greens" mean the track is a "pleasure to play" even in the summer.

Texas Star

24	19	18	22	$77

Euless | 1400 Texas Star Pkwy. | 817-685-7888 | 888-839-7827 | www.texasstargolf.com | 6936/4962; 73.6/69.7; 135/124

Located between Dallas and Ft. Worth, this "awesome" Keith Foster-designed muni is often "underestimated" but is "tough" given the "surprising up-and-down layout" where you "need to hit it straight" or risk having "lots of golf balls eaten up"; backers can't believe how this "hidden gem" is "always in perfect shape" and looks so bucolic in such "urban" environs.

	COURSE	FACIL.	SERVICE	VALUE	COST

Tour 18 Dallas ⛳

Flower Mound | 8718 Amen Corner | 817-430-2000 | 800-946-5310 | www.tour18-dallas.com | 7033/5493; 74.3/66.3; 138/119

20 | 18 | 17 | 17 | $89

If you like "the idea of playing the best holes from other courses", try the "gorgeous, challenging" reproductions at this Flower Mound track that offers examples of the layouts on which the pros play; it's certainly "fun" for fans, but a few frazzled foozlers say that you can replicate holes, but "you can't replicate ambiance."

Tribute ⛳

The Colony | 1000 Boyd Rd. | 972-370-5465 | www.thetributegolflinks.com | 7002/5352; 73.2/65.6; 128/111

26 | 23 | 22 | 22 | $125

Architect Tripp Davis "got it right" when he copied "famous holes from links-style courses in the United Kingdom" (including St. Andrews' 1st, 17th and 18th) that play like the real thing, especially when battling the "wind off Lake Lewisville"; if the track's "a little pricey", the holes are "in pristine shape" and, overall, the "value is great", especially since you don't have to travel more than 30 miles north of Dallas to "experience Scotland."

Westin Stonebriar, Fazio ⛳

Frisco | 1549 Legacy Dr. | 972-668-8748 | www.westinstonebriar.com | 7021/5208; 73.8/72.4; 133/105

22 | 24 | 22 | 19 | $116

Although it "isn't one of Tom Fazio's strongest designs", this Westin course is part of a "beautiful landscape" about a half hour north of Dallas and offers a "number of risk/reward holes" that can create "a few extra moments of thought" and "fun" once you "know where to take your chances"; thanks to the hotel, expect plenty of guest amenities, not to mention "excellent service."

El Paso

Painted Dunes Desert •

El Paso | 12000 McCombs St. | 915-821-2122 | www.painteddunes.com
East/West | 6925/4781; 72.7/63.2; 134/114
North/East | 6904/4934; 72.3/63.5; 128/110
West/North | 6941/4917; 72.6/63.4; 131/114

▽ 21 | 15 | 18 | 27 | $43

Playing this "well-maintained" El Paso course "feels like you're in Tucson or Phoenix with desert target golf" topography throughout its 27 holes; even better, there's the "phenomenally low price" to consider, along with "great views" courtesy of the course's location in the Chihuahuan Desert at the base of the Franklin Mountains.

Houston

Augusta Pines ⏲

Spring | 18 Augusta Pines Dr. | 832-381-1010 | www.tour18.com | 7041/5007; 73.6/68.5; 125/112

25 | 23 | 21 | 21 | $85

"Immaculately maintained" is the middle name of this Texas track where the degree of challenge "depends on the tees selected"; though the tight fairway and island green on "the 18th is a killer", you can always take comfort in the "excellent facilities and staff" and its convenient location just 30 minutes north of Houston.

BlackHorse, North

22 | 21 | 21 | 19 | $89

Cypress | 12205 Fry Rd. | 281-304-1747 | www.blackhorsegolfclub.com |
7301/5065; 75/69.8; 130/119

There's no horsing around at this Jim Hardy/Peter Jacobsen design
that's a "challenge on every hole", with lakes, wetlands and a seemingly ever-present creek to contend with (at times, it can feel "harder
than the South" course); if "overpriced", it's also only 30 minutes
northwest of Houston and "always in great shape."

BlackHorse, South

▽ 23 | 22 | 23 | 22 | $89

Cypress | 12205 Fry Rd. | 281-304-1747 | www.blackhorsegolfclub.com |
7191/4839; 74.7/68.5; 138/123

Bring "guile to survive" the "better of the two" BlackHorse layouts, and
don't be lulled into complacency, since the first half is "easy", with
"merely entertaining, flatland golf", while "the back nine encom-
passes a former gravel quarry" where "dry ground is a rarity rather
than the norm" and the "highly tempting carry options" often "lead to
ruin"; P.S. "the 15th–17th holes are as good as it gets."

Cypresswood, Tradition

21 | 16 | 15 | 19 | $65

Spring | 21602 Cypresswood Dr. | 281-821-6300 | www.cypresswood.com |
7220/4785; 74.7/68.1; 136/116

Players posit this "good" Keith Foster design delivers a "typical
Houston-area public experience": an "average course that could be
excellent" if not for "poor service" and maintenance ("conditioning in
the area's heat leaves something to be desired"); still, it offers a scenic
routing over rolling, wooded terrain and is crisscrossed by two creeks,
leading optimists to argue it's "worth playing."

Falls, The

▽ 27 | 19 | 21 | 24 | $70

New Ulm | 1750 N. Falls Dr. | 979-992-3123 | www.thefallsresort.com |
6765/5348; 72.5/70; 135/123

If you're looking for "some elevation close to Houston", head to this resort layout in New Ulm to play its "unique fairways and greens" that are
often protected by water; though it may be "tough to find", it's a "wonderful experience" and a "great value", especially because you can "cook
out in one of the cabins" that are rentable for a "weekend getaway."

Meadowbrook Farms

▽ 20 | 20 | 21 | 19 | $75

Katy | 9595 S. Fry Rd. | 281-693-4653 | www.meadowbrookfarms.com |
7100/5000; 74.2/68; 137/108

"Bravo, Greg" (as in Norman) for this "day-use course" just 30 minutes west of Houston, a layout laced with "interesting" holes that
wend their way past lakes, streams and wetlands, and whose greens
are protected by sod-walled bunkers and tall grasses; granted, it's
"pricey", so it's a good idea to look for "specials."

Memorial Park

20 | 17 | 16 | 24 | $37

Houston | 1001 E. Memorial Loop | 713-862-4033 |
www.memorialparkgolf.com | 7305/5459; 73/70.7; 122/114

"The lucky ones that get on" to this "crowded" Houston park layout attest to the track's "playable" holes set amid "majestic pines and oaks";
no, it's "certainly not an elite course" anymore, but it does offer "fine
conditioning (especially for a muni)" on a "solid" spread sporting
"amazingly affordable" prices; N.B. closed Tuesdays.

	COURSE	FACIL.	SERVICE	VALUE	COST

NEW Redstone, Tournament

	-	-	-	-	$125

Humble | 5860 Wilson Rd. | 281-459-7800 | www.redstonegolfclub.com | 7422/5926; 75.8/70.1; 138/115

This new Rees Jones–designed home of the Shell Houston Open is just that: it's one of only 10 non-resort PGA Tour venues that are open to the public; veteran player David Toms consulted on the layout, which is situated only 20 minutes from Downtown Houston but nevertheless retains a secluded feel due to its lack of surrounding houses; refreshingly, the setup emphasizes precision over power on some of its holes.

Tour 18 Houston

	21	18	19	19	$89

Humble | 3102 FM 1960 Rd. E. | 281-540-1818 | 800-856-8687 | www.tour18golf.com | 6782/5380; 72.7/71.3; 129/129

"Let your golf fantasies come true" at this "popular tour-ist stop" where "reproductions of America's finest" holes – like "Augusta's Amen Corner" and the "wraparound par 5 from Bay Hill" – stand out; though other sections of the course "don't quite pull it off" and general "overuse" leads to turf that "isn't well kept up", the Humble track's "worth" a visit, especially if you score one of their "great meal deals."

Lubbock

Rawls Course at Texas Tech University

	-	-	-	-	$42

Lubbock | 3720 Fourth St. | 806-742-4653 | www.texastechgolf.ttu.edu | 7308/5373; 73.2/64.9; 126/112

It took more than Texas Tech alum Jerry Rawls' money to move over a million cubic yards of earth at this former pancake-flat site that's now rife with unique, canyonlike landforms, contoured fairways and large, wide greens that are fortified by deep, fingerlike bunkers; while the public can use the clubhouse restaurant and driving range, the indoor hitting stations and 3-hole practice course are for Red Raider team members only.

San Antonio

Canyon Springs

	24	20	20	19	$100

San Antonio | 24400 Wilderness Oak Rd. | 210-497-1770 | www.canyonspringsgc.com | 7077/5234; 72.8/70; 130/115

Its loyalists call it the "best public course in the San Antonio area", and this "Hill Country" option is indeed "beautiful and challenging" with a "great finishing hole"; still, the staff and policies can be "goofy": you're on your own to find the "proper practice range" (not the "one just for members") and they'll "charge you extra for using the GPS on the carts."

Hyatt Hill Country

	21	25	23	16	$125

San Antonio | 9800 Hyatt Resort Dr. | 210-520-4040 | 888-901-4653 | www.hyatt.com
Creeks/Oaks | 6867/4825; 73.3/68.2; 131/119
Lakes/Creeks | 6931/4939; 73.7/69.2; 132/118
Lakes/Oaks | 6940/4778; 73.7/67.8; 136/118

Although Arthur Hills' 27-hole San Antonio spread "is kind of strange" in that the "newer part is a little tricked-up compared to the original 18", it's still "kept in top condition" and overseen by an "impeccable" staff; the little extras – "state of Texas range balls", GPS in every cart and a serene "patio for after-golf drinks" – all add up, as does the expense (it's "pricey if you don't get in on the special deals").

La Cantera, Palmer

27 | 27 | 26 | 20 | $140

San Antonio | 16641 La Cantera Pkwy. | 210-558-2365 | 800-446-5387 | www.lacanteragolfclub.com | 6926/5066; 74.2/65.3; 142/116

"What the Hill Country is all about", this "pricey" San Antonio resort "beauty" boasts "spectacular views", "opportunities to get up close and personal with native wildlife" and the chance to hit many "heroic shots" – and "many blind" ones – down "tight fairways" kept in "great shape"; meanwhile, an "extremely nice staff" and clubhouse also keep hitters happy.

La Cantera, Resort

26 | 27 | 26 | 21 | $140

San Antonio | 16641 La Cantera Pkwy. | 210-558-4653 | 800-446-5387 | www.lacanteragolfclub.com | 7021/4940; 72.5/67.1; 134/108

Although "teeing off right next to roller coasters" while beholding "stunning views of San Antonio" make this "memorable" track "a real hoot", the home of the PGA Tour's Valero Texas Open is no laughing matter: "the 1st is 665 yards long" and followed by an "awesome variety" of holes, some that "test your nerves", some with "lots of elevation changes" and others that "reward target golf"; "cordial, professional" service and "nice facilities" are also pluses.

Pecan Valley

21 | 16 | 17 | 24 | $59

San Antonio | 4700 Pecan Valley Dr. | 210-333-9018 | www.pecanvalleygc.com | 7047/5310; 74.4/65.9; 132/118

"The grand old lady of San Antonio" (and host of the 1968 PGA Championship) is known for "narrow", "tree-lined" fairways, "elevated greens" and Salado Creek, which runs alongside the layout; if "questionable conditioning" leaves the track "a bit rough around the edges", some say this "value" is still an "enjoyable" experience.

Quarry

24 | 21 | 21 | 21 | $90

San Antonio | 444 E. Basse Rd. | 210-824-4500 | 800-347-7759 | www.quarrygolf.com | 6740/4897; 72.4/67.4; 128/115

Keith Foster designed "completely different front and back nines" at this San Antonio spread, and while the former is "links style" and "rather nondescript", the back nine is decidedly "awesome" as it "plays in a circle around the quarry ridge" so that swingers' "slices bounce off the walls and back into play"; P.S. "don't bother playing if you hit a hook" because it's "so blasted hot in that hole" you could get "heat stroke."

SilverHorn

23 | 18 | 20 | 23 | $72

San Antonio | 1100 W. Bitters Rd. | 210-545-5300 | www.silverhorngolfclub.com | 6922/5271; 73.4/71.8; 138/132

You may want to "wear earplugs as the planes fly right above you" at this "tight", "tree-lined" track in San Antonio where there's plenty of water and the greens are "usually excellent", if a bit on the "slow" side; the "value" makes it worth a visit – just wear quick-drying duds, because it gets "hot" when there's "no breeze."

	COURSE	FACIL.	SERVICE	VALUE	COST

U.S. Virgin Islands

St. Croix

Carambola
22	19	18	16	$70

Kingshill | 72 Estate River | 340-778-5638 | www.carambolabeach.com |
6865/5425; 74.3/71.7; 135/128

Built in 1966 by Laurance Rockefeller, this "mature" Robert Trent
Jones Sr. design is considered by some to be the "best course in the
Virgin Islands" and, therefore, the "best course on St. Croix"; "inconsistent conditions", however, are part of the package, and note that
though it's "lush", there are "no water views" – except during the
"rainouts" that come with its location "on the wet side of the island."

St. Thomas

Mahogany Run ⚐
19	16	18	14	$150

St. Thomas | 1 Mahogany Run Rd. N. | 340-777-6250 | 800-253-7103 |
www.mahoganyrungolf.com | 6008/4873; 70.5/70.9; 133/134

The "Devil's Triangle" holes (the 13th–15th) are "among the most
beautiful on earth", with "breathtaking" water views and "200-ft.
drops" from cliffs that are alone "worth the price of admission" to this
George and Tom Fazio track; the "rest is mediocre", but realists add
that this St. Thomas spread is "the only game in town."

Utah

Salt Lake City

NEW Soldier Hollow, Gold ⚐
▽	26	20	19	26	$39

Midway | 1370 W. Soldier Hollow Ln. | 435-654-7442 |
www.stateparkgolf.utah.gov | 7598/5658; 74.4/70.1; 131/119

Gene Bates transformed "the 2002 Olympic ski trails" above Midway
into this "exciting" state-owned course showcasing elevation changes
and "beautiful" views of the Heber Valley and the Wasatch Mountains;
true, it "must be played twice" to figure out "the mountainside holes",
but given that it's "still young" and hitched to a "soaring glass" clubhouse, most say they "couldn't have dreamed up an experience" like this.

NEW Soldier Hollow, Silver
▽	21	21	20	26	$39

Midway | 1370 W. Soldier Hollow Ln. | 435-654-7442 |
www.stateparkgolf.utah.gov | 7355/5532; 73.2/68.3; 131/111

"Not as hilly as the Gold course", and perhaps "easier" considering "five
of the par 3s are the same length" and its fairways are shorter and wider,
Gene Bates' silver sister is still "excellent" and kept in "top condition
for a public course"; it also shares "stunning mountain" vistas and the
"best clubhouse in the West", a "beautiful" building featuring floor-to-
ceiling windows ideal for viewing the Heber Valley's pastoral fields.

Thanksgiving Point ⚐
▽	28	26	25	21	$79

Lehi | 3300 W. Clubhouse Dr. | 801-768-7400 | www.thanksgivingpoint.com |
7714/5838; 76.2/72.8; 140/134

It's "worth the detour" to play this "hidden gem" a half hour south of
Salt Lake City where "Johnny Miller turned dirt into gold" by trans-

forming a whopping 7,728 yards of soil into 18 "challenging, almost diabolical" holes; the consensus: play here at all costs, because although it's an "expensive course for Utah", it would be a "good value" anywhere else.

Valley View   ▽ 25 | 17 | 18 | 29 | $26

Layton | 2501 E. Gentile St. | 801-546-1630 | www.golfingutah.com | 7147/5679; 73.5/71.1; 123/125

Visitors can watch the "air shows at the nearby Air Force base", but it's the dramatic "speed and slope" of the "challenging" greens at this "outstanding" layout that really entices Salt Lake City residents to make the 30-minute drive north; meanwhile, its "reasonable rates" help to turn "one of the better public courses in Utah" into a "fantastic" bang for the buck.

Wasatch Mountain, Lakes   ▽ 21 | 17 | 22 | 25 | $39

Midway | 975 W. Golf Course Dr. | 435-654-0532 | www.stateparkgolf.utah.gov | 6942/5573; 72/71.5; 128/123

Whatever you do, "don't let the beautiful mountain views" and "abundant flora and fauna" distract you from your game at this "gorgeous" Midway-area track where a "river runs through many of the tree-lined holes"; pros say the course's 5,500-ft. elevation means it's "good for hot weather", plus the "relatively flat" fairways make walking easy.

Wasatch Mountain, Mountain 🏌 ▽ 23 | 16 | 20 | 26 | $39

Midway | 975 W. Golf Course Dr. | 435-654-0532 | www.stateparkgolf.utah.gov | 6459/5009; 70.4/67.2; 125/119

Although it's a bit "tougher than the Lakes course" (there are "lots of elevation changes" and uphill, downhill and sidehill lies), this "top public course" in Utah boasts a mountain setting "as scenic as it gets"; yes, it's a "great value", but frankly, some would "pay just to enjoy the views" and the varied wildlife.

St. George

Coral Canyon   26 | 22 | 24 | 24 | $98

Washington | 1925 Canyon Greens Dr. | 435-688-1700 | www.suncorgolf.com | 7029/4125; 73/69.1; 137/122

Budget some time "on the way to Zion National Park" to stop in the St. George area and admire the "jaw-dropping beauty" of this "lush, green oasis surrounded by red rock"; voters vouch for the "tremendous value" at this "tough yet fair" Keith Foster layout that's "playable for all levels", especially when you factor in the course's "great condition" and GPS-equipped carts.

Entrada at Snow Canyon 🏌   '25 | 21 | 21 | 20 | $120

St. George | 2511 Entrada Trail | 435-674-7500 | www.golfentrada.com | 7059/5200; 73.6/68.7; 131/115

The "contrasting colors" and "natural beauty" of "black lava against red rock and green fairways" make it "hard to concentrate" at this "magical course in the high desert region of southwestern Utah"; Johnny Miller designed the "challenging" layout with a "great back nine", but alas, the entire course is now private – although booking a room at St. George's Inn at Entrada ensures access.

Vermont

Northern Vermont

Sugarbush 🏌

 ▽ 22 | 15 | 19 | 22 | $60

Warren | 1091 Golf Course Rd. | 802-583-6725 | 800-537-8427 |
www.sugarbush.com | 6464/5231; 71.7/70.5; 128/129

"One of the most beautiful mountain courses anywhere" is this "classic" Robert Trent Jones Sr. site set in the hills above the Mad River Valley in Northern Vermont – expect "outstanding views" but "no flat lies"; the "owners continue to invest and rebuild" the facility, including enlarging the deck off Hogan's Pub where they serve locally brewed ale.

Southern Vermont

Gleneagles at The Equinox

21 | 19 | 22 | 17 | $99

Manchester | 108 Union St. | 802-362-3223 | 800-362-4747 |
www.equinox.rockresorts.com | 6423/5082; 70.8/74.6; 129/132

"Every hole is memorable" on this "hilly", "historic" track, a showcase for "classic Walter Travis design features" (think "church pew bunkers") and for "breathtaking foliage in the fall"; although "pretty expensive" for having "no driving range", "welcoming" service and an abundance of "things to do in the area" (including shopping "in the village of Manchester") help you forget about the fees.

Green Mountain National

25 | 19 | 21 | 23 | $89

Killington | Barrows Towne Rd. | 802-422-4653 | 888-483-4653 |
www.greenmountainnational.com | 6589/4740; 72.1/63.9; 138/118

"Tee off for position, not distance" at this "target" mountain course in central Vermont where the "fairways are tight", "the rough is woodsy" and the conditions are "always in top shape" since it's "cart-path only 100 percent of the time"; bring a camera to record the "gorgeous views", and save some snaps for the clubhouse too, because the "friendly, down-to-earth staffers" seem always ready to smile.

Okemo Valley

24 | 24 | 23 | 21 | $75

Ludlow | 89 Fox Ln. | 802-228-1396 | www.okemo.com |
6400/5105; 71.1/70.1; 130/125

"Huge elevation changes" are no surprise at this "interesting" resort layout "built on a side of a mountain" in central Vermont and offering "visual treats on nearly every hole" plus "immaculately groomed" conditions throughout; "they allow you to walk the course", but first "eat a hearty breakfast" at Willie Dunn's Grille to fortify yourself before the romp through the "rolling terrain."

Stratton Mountain

22 | 21 | 20 | 20 | $99

Stratton Mountain | Stratton Mountain Rd. | 802-297-2200 | 800-787-2886 |
www.stratton.com
Forest/Lake | 6526/5153; 71.2/69.8; 125/123
Lake/Mountain | 6602/5410; 72/71.1; 125/124
Mountain/Forest | 6478/5163; 71.2/69.9; 126/123

"Slope rating takes on a new meaning" at these three "terrific" nine-hole courses, because even though they're "set at the base of Stratton Mountain", they feature "lots of elevation changes" that make "walking tough"; yes, the challenge of "many hidden greens" means "making par here is like hitting a home run", but with the "spectacular scenery", on-site golf school and "attentive staff", some say it's worth all the pain – playing here is "better than skiing."

Woodstock Country Club
19 | **19** | **22** | **18** | **$85**

Woodstock | 14 The Green | 802-457-6674 | www.woodstockinn.com | 6052/4924; 69.7/69; 123/113

Although the name of its first designer is a mystery (it was built in 1895), Robert Trent Jones Sr. restored it years later, and this "small", "hilly" course in central Vermont provides "fun" in the form of Kedron Brook, which "crosses several holes twice" and seems as if it's "in front of almost every green"; P.S. "bring your ball retriever, as it will be the best thing in your bag."

Virginia

TOP COURSES IN STATE

28 Homestead, Cascades | *Roanoke*
Golden Horseshoe, Gold | *Williamsburg*
26 Stonewall | *Leesburg*
Kingsmill, River | *Williamsburg*
Wintergreen, Stoney Creek | *Charlottesville*

Charlottesville

Birdwood
22 | **17** | **17** | **22** | **$60**

Charlottesville | 410 Golf Course Dr. | 434-293-4653 | 800-476-1988 | www.boarsheadinn.com | 6865/5041; 74.4/69.4; 141/122

Yes, the "front side is easy", but aces assert the back nine at this UVA course (the handiwork of Lindsay Ervin) is "one of the best in the state", as it features "billy-goat" hills, an island green on the 14th and a "doozy" of a dogleg par-5 15th; it's "not the longest" track around, but it is the "ultimate value" – "especially if you're associated with the school."

Keswick Club ⚬
▽ **21** | **24** | **24** | **18** | **$130**

Keswick | 701 Club Dr. | 434-923-4363 | www.keswick.com | 6325/4925; 70.6/68.5; 129/113

Given its "sloped greens" and its "dramatic, elevated tees" from which you "can see forever", this "well-maintained" Arnold Palmer redesign situated just east of Charlottesville supplies solid "fun"; all in all, it's a "great" getaway, since you have the Orient Express-owned Keswick Hall's facilities (and "good food") at your disposal.

Wintergreen, Devil's Knob
22 | **21** | **22** | **21** | **$110**

Wintergreen | Rte. 664 | 434-325-8250 | 800-926-3723 | www.wintergreenresort.com | 6382/4392; 72.2/66.7; 138/128

Purportedly the highest course in Virginia (at an elevation of 3,850 feet) with temperatures that are "generally cooler" than the plains, this "underrated" Wintergreen course "moves along the high, narrow ridges of the Blue Ridge Mountains", providing "great variety in elevations" and "wonderful views"; "accuracy, not power, is the key" to scoring on this "short, tight" track where "wild shots fall off the mountain" and poor putts roll off the "glass-tabletop" greens.

	COURSE	FACIL.	SERVICE	VALUE	COST

Wintergreen, Stoney Creek

	26	20	20	20	$110

Wintergreen | Rte. 664 | 434-325-8250 | 800-926-3723 |
www.wintergreenresort.com
Monocan/Shamokin | 7005/5500; 74.2/71.8; 137/127
Shamokin/Tuckahoe | 6998/5594; 74.1/72.4; 135/128
Tuckahoe/Monocan | 6951/5462; 73.8/71.6; 136/129

This "Rees Jones design" is "open year-round", so you can ski in the
morning and "play golf in the afternoon", though you'll have to choose
between "27 great holes"; each nine has "a different feel": the Tuckahoe
offers "variation in elevation and is very long", the Monocan features
"water challenges" and the Shamokin rambles through "woods and
rough terrain"; all share "improving" service and "fantastic views"
"framed by the Blue Ridge Mountains."

DC Metro Area

Augustine

	25	21	20	22	$69

Stafford | 76 Monument Dr. | 540-659-0566 | www.augustinegolf.com |
6817/4838; 74.3/68; 142/117

"Shot-making is required" at this "test of skill", a Rick Jacobsen design
composed of 18 "very good" holes, including a "great opener" with a
"split fairway", followed by "a par-4 [2nd] over water to a narrow"
landing area; "try to play on a weekday", since the pace of play can
be "slow" on weekends (the course is just south "of the overcrowded
DC metro area").

Gauntlet

	21	18	20	21	$50

Fredericksburg | 18 Fairway Dr. | 540-752-0963 | 888-755-7888 |
www.golfgauntlet.com | 6857/4955; 73.4/69.6; 139/119

With "rarely anyone else on the course", "you can take your time" pondering your shots on these "tight", "challenging" and "tricky"
P.B. Dye-designed holes laced with "blind tee shots", "tough carries"
over water and "crowned greens"; even better, "play multiple times to
figure out club selection", a hassle-free assignment given that it's "always easy to get a tee time", perhaps because it's situated just over an
hour south of the DC metro area.

Westfields

	24	22	23	19	$104

Clifton | 13940 Balmoral Greens Ave. | 703-631-3300 |
www.westfieldsgolf.com | 6897/4597; 72.7/65.9; 136/114

Designed by "Boom Boom" (aka Fred Couples), this "challenging but
very playable" Clifton course "isn't a driver off every tee, so it makes
for a thinking round" with "not too much water"; it's "pricey", but in
such "great shape" "you can eat off the fairways", while the clubhouse
is "beautiful" and the "friendly staff" provides service that's "as close
to a private club as you can get."

Leesburg

Bull Run

	20	19	18	18	$90

Haymarket | 3520 James Madison Hwy. | 703-753-7777 | 866-285-5786 |
www.bullrungolfclub.com | 7009/5069; 73.1/68.3; 134/110

Admire the "beautiful" scenery south of Leesburg as you enjoy the
"wide-open fairways" of this Rick Jacobsen layout that's a "value" for

fans and accommodating to players of "all calibers"; while some say it has "rebounded over the past year", others object and add "it's a nice layout and a good weekend course, nothing more."

NEW Lansdowne Resort, Norman 🏨 ⛳
| 22 | 24 | 23 | 17 | $145 |

Lansdowne | 44050 Woodridge Pkwy. | 703-729-4071 | 800-541-4801 | www.lansdowneresort.com | 7032/5371; 75.4/70.2; 147/128

Although this Greg Norman design is "still young" and will be even more of a "treat" "when it matures", it's "a real shark" now (the Shark himself has dubbed the last four holes the hardest mile in golf); it's just a 10-minute drive from Leesburg with "fantastic views of the Potomac River" and "excellent new facilities" (e.g. a "great clubhouse") that assuage those who pout the price is "a little steep for a course that hasn't grown in yet."

Raspberry Falls
| 25 | 22 | 21 | 19 | $98 |

Leesburg | 41601 Raspberry Dr. | 703-779-2555 | www.raspberryfalls.com | 7191/4854; 74.3/68; 134/115

Acolytes aver it "doesn't get much better" than this "wonderful Gary Player design" "in the foothills of the Shenandoahs" with "lots of elevation changes", "stacked sod-walled bunkers", "tricky greens" and wildlife sightings; still, for some critics, the "spotty conditions", "overpriced" fees and "new home construction encroaching on the beauty of the course" "take away from the experience."

Stonewall
| 26 | 24 | 23 | 20 | $115 |

Gainesville | 15601 Turtle Point Dr. | 703-753-5101 | www.stonewallgolfclub.com | 7002/4889; 74.1/67.9; 142/114

"If you can't get on Robert Trent Jones Golf Club" ("where they play the Presidents Cup"), fans recommend this "superb layout" "right across the lake" as the "best alternative" and, indeed, "one of the best in northern Virginia"; it also has some of the "area's most expensive" fees, and though the price includes cart, range balls and a "good GPS" system, as well as a "great facility" and "friendly" service, some question whether it's "worth fighting traffic to get there from DC."

Virginia National
| ▽ 21 | 18 | 19 | 21 | $75 |

Bluemont | 1400 Parker Ln. | 540-955-2966 | 888-283-4653 | www.virginianational.com | 6789/4981; 73.3/68.3; 137/116

The "surrounding scenery is special" at this Shenandoah Valley course boasting "two differing nines", a "flat, narrow" front that "runs along the river" and a back that "meanders up and down the [foot]hills" of the Blue Ridge Mountains, with "lots of elevation change"; though the course is relatively young, the property is full of history, with the manor house of Judge Richard E. Parker, who presided over the hanging trial of John Brown, overlooking the 18th green.

Richmond

NEW King Carter
| - | - | - | - | $49 |

Irvington | 480 Old Saint Johns Rd. | 804-435-7842 | www.kingcartergolfclub.com | 6818/4911; 73.8/69; 135/121

Named for a local 18th-century tobacco baron, this relatively new design is part of a housing development situated on the peninsula where the Rappahannock River meets the Chesapeake Bay; while its open front (with ponds and gentle mounding) contrasts with its more rugged, wooded back, both halves of the layout feature free-form bunkers à la famed architect Alister MacKenzie; N.B. a clubhouse is planned for fall 2007.

Roanoke

Draper Valley

| | | | | $48 |

Draper | 2800 Big Valley Dr. | 540-980-4653 | 866-980-4653 | www.drapervalleygolf.com | 7070/4683; 73.5/65.3; 127/113

Harold Louthen, a highway engineer, may not be well-known in golf architecture circles, but he cleverly combined "wide-open" holes with others that are "a little tight", making for "good variety" and "lots of fun" along the rolling terrain of southwest Virginia; note that there's only a basic clubhouse, so "plan on changing your clothes" elsewhere.

☒ Homestead, Cascades 🏌

| 28 | 24 | 25 | 21 | $260 |

Hot Springs | Homestead Hotel, Rte. 220 | 540-839-7994 | 800-838-1766 | www.thehomestead.com | 6256/4967; 70.8/70.3; 131/124

There "aren't many times you'd put down this much money to get beaten and enjoy it", but you will at this "amazing mountain" layout that's the top-rated Course in Virginia; nestled 90 minutes north of Roanoke, this "classic" 1923 William Flynn design is kept "in great condition" and made "memorable" with "lots of hanging lies and hills", making it "worth the price" to play what some say is "Homestead's best", i.e. "one of the best in the country."

Homestead, Lower Cascades 🏌

| 24 | 19 | 22 | 18 | $140 |

Hot Springs | Homestead Hotel, Rte. 220 | 540-839-7995 | 800-838-1766 | www.thehomestead.com | 6295/4710; 69.8/66.2; 129/110

This Robert Trent Jones Sr. alternative to the "famed" Cascades course is "a fine test of mountain golf", so "expect a lot of sidehill lies" and even "some fairways that slope so much they are very difficult to hold"; still, though "less expensive" than its counterpart, it's also a "lesser experience", with pros picking apart conditioning "in need of repair" and "facilities that need effort put into them."

Homestead, Old 🏌

| 22 | 24 | 27 | 19 | $160 |

Hot Springs | Homestead Hotel, Rte. 220 | 540-839-7739 | 800-838-1766 | www.thehomestead.com | 5816/4877; 66.9/67.7; 125/116

The former site of many USGA events, this historic Homestead course dates back to 1892 and has undergone updates from William Flynn, Donald Ross and Rees Jones, masters who have molded it into a "wide-open" track featuring "Ross' turtle-back greens"; "you have to play an excellent game to score well", but even if you don't, the staff is so "nice and helpful" that they make this "oldie" "loads of fun for all."

Pete Dye River Course of Virginia Tech

| | | | | $70 |

Radford | 8400 River Course Dr. | 540-633-6732 | 888-738-3393 | www.rivercoursegolf.vt.edu | 6495/5142; 71.7/69.5; 130/120

Thanks to both the largesse of Virginia Tech alumnus Bill Goodwin and the renovation expertise of Pete Dye, "no other area course even comes close" to this new home of the Hokies, an "awesome" layout marked by "blind tee shots", nines that are divided by a 70-ft. cliff and eight holes that run along the New River; with "two years to mature" and a new clubhouse scheduled for 2007, this "fantastic" track may just become "a destination course."

Virginia Beach

Bay Creek, Arnold Palmer 🏌
— | — | — | — | $95

Cape Charles | 1 Clubhouse Way | 757-331-9000 | www.baycreek.net | 7250/5195; 75.2/69.8; 142/119

Situated near the historic town of Cape Charles, this remote layout on the Virginia shoreline features holes on either the Chesapeake Bay or Old Plantation Creek; "great respect is given to nature" on this "beautiful" Arnold Palmer "gem", but book a tee time soon, as it plans to go private within a year.

NEW Bay Creek, Jack Nicklaus
— | — | — | — | $100

Cape Charles | 1 Clubhouse Way | 757-331-8620 | 800-501-7141 | www.baycreek.net | 7417/5244; 76.7/68.7; 144/124

Like its Arnold Palmer sibling, this Cape Charles design offers holes that dance along the Chesapeake Bay and Old Plantation Creek, but while Arnie has stamped his layout with his signature beach bunkers, the sandy depressions on this Jack Nicklaus course take the form of huge waste areas and traditional, round-style challenges – more than 100 of them; N.B. both tracks intend to go private in the near future.

Williamsburg

Z Golden Horseshoe, Gold
28 | 26 | 25 | 21 | $155

Williamsburg | 401 S. England St. | 757-220-7696 | 800-648-6653 | www.goldenhorseshoegolf.com | 6817/5168; 73.8/65.6; 144/124

"Simply magnificent" sums up this RTJ Sr. "golden experience", "one of the true classics in the Mid-Atlantic", whose claim to fame is not only the "beautiful" Williamsburg-area landscaping (like a "botanical garden") but also the "standout" par 3s: the "rush" of a 7th and a 16th that is said to have the country's first island green; overall, it's "worth the extra money", especially considering the fees for the Green course are reduced if you play it the same day.

Golden Horseshoe, Green
25 | 23 | 25 | 23 | $99

Williamsburg | 401 S. England St. | 757-220-7696 | 800-648-6653 | www.goldenhorseshoegolf.com | 7120/5348; 75.1/66.3; 138/118

Rees Jones followed up his father's golden formula with an "incredible course" of his own, a "more subtle challenge" only "slightly behind the Gold"; expect a "fairy-tale setting" of "picturesque views, rolling hills and wooden bridges over ponds" plus "surprises hiding around every corner" (like some of the "smallest and toughest greens in the U.S."); like its relative, it boasts the same "great amenities."

Kingsmill, Plantation 🏌
24 | 26 | 26 | 19 | $115

Williamsburg | 1010 Kingsmill Rd. | 757-253-3906 | 800-832-5665 | www.kingsmill.com | 6060/4880; 69.8/69.2; 123/122

Opened in 1975 but still "in good shape", this River course relative is "fit for a king", as Arnold Palmer's design firm has expertly crafted holes that are forgiving off the tee but "challenging" enough on approach to be "compelling"; greens fees are "pricey" at this Williamsburg option, but you'd be wise to factor in the "excellent facilities" and dining options (e.g. Eagles, which features the resort's trademarked smoked meats).

Kingsmill, River ⛳

| 26 | 27 | 25 | 21 | $175 |

Williamsburg | 1010 Kingsmill Rd. | 757-253-3906 | 800-832-5665 | www.kingsmill.com | 6853/4646; 67.1/65.3; 137/113

If you could use "a day away from Colonial Williamsburg", point your wagon toward this "revamped" and "beautifully well-manicured" Pete Dye design along the James River where "challenges await"; that it used to host a PGA Tour event and now hosts an event on the LPGA Tour should be the tip-off that its "difficulty could make a saint curse"; nevertheless, "forgiveness exists" in the form of an "extremely helpful staff" and a "brewery right around the corner."

Kingsmill, Woods ⛳

| 24 | 23 | 24 | 21 | $125 |

Williamsburg | 1010 Kingsmill Rd. | 757-253-3906 | 800-832-5665 | www.kingsmill.com | 6784/5140; 72.7/68.7; 131/120

Tucked "away from it all" near Williamsburg, this "kid-friendly" Curtis Strange layout is full of "character", rambling "through the woods" and leaving you "in constant awe" of its beauty; "despite the River course getting all the attention", some think this one is "the real gem" and perhaps "the most interesting at Kingsmill."

Kiskiack

| ▽ 23 | 21 | 18 | 25 | $85 |

Williamsburg | 8104 Club Dr. | 757-566-2200 | www.traditionalclubs.com | 6405/4902; 70.8/67.8; 131/112

Located on Williamsburg-area land once occupied by the Chickiack Indians, this "great course" boasts an "excellent design" that's "a blast to play" for "the average golfer" because its forgiving front nine "can make an amateur feel like a pro"; note that the back is "not a walk in the park" and better players will find a real "challenge from the tips."

Royal New Kent

| 25 | 23 | 20 | 22 | $99 |

Providence Forge | 10100 Kentland Trail | 804-966-7023 | 800-253-4363 | www.traditionalclubs.com | 6965/4971; 74.9/72; 144/130

It's like taking a "step across the pond" to Ireland at this "fun, links-style" design near Richmond, a Mike Strantz "monster" with some "daunting blind shots" and green inclines that "make you think about your game" and curb the urge to "grip it and rip it"; "be prepared to lose lots of balls", for it "will abuse you", although proponents promise "you'll enjoy the beating so much, you'll want another."

Tradition at Stonehouse ⛳

| ▽ 23 | 21 | 21 | 21 | $99 |

Toano | 9700 Mill Pond Run | 757-566-1138 | 888-825-3436 | www.traditionalclubs.com | 6963/5013; 75/69.1; 140/121

"One of the best" courses in the area according to fans, this "incredible" but "wickedly tough" layout just outside Williamsburg "must be played to be fully appreciated", presenting "many blind shots" and some holes that critics grouse are "too tricked-up"; even if you don't shoot your record round here, it's "as pretty a course as you will play in Virginia" and the "conditioning is getting better all the time."

Washington

Bremerton

Gold Mountain, Cascade

▽ 25 | 23 | 22 | 28 | $35

Bremerton | 7263 W. Belfair Valley Rd. | 360-415-5432 | www.goldmt.com | 6707/5306; 72.1/70.3; 120/117

"A far cry from the typical municipal course", this "beautiful" Bremerton layout just north of the airport is "well-groomed and well-maintained" with a "very accommodating staff" and "quality carts"; you'll also be "pleasantly surprised" to discover that the tree-lined track is "almost as good" and only "a little more forgiving" than "its more praised sister", Olympic, while perhaps being an even better "value" – so prepare yourself, as a round on this spread constitutes "a grand golf experience."

☑ Gold Mountain, Olympic

26 | 21 | 20 | 28 | $55

Bremerton | 7263 W. Belfair Valley Rd. | 360-415-5432 | www.goldmt.com | 7104/5220; 74.1/70.2; 135/122

"Home of the 2006 U.S. Amateur Public Links Championship", this "spectacular" "example of a Pacific Northwest course" combines "wonderful" "views of the Olympic Mountains" with a "very tough but fair test of golf" that plays longer than its sibling and "demands your best game", especially on its "perfect greens"; even better, little extras like the "grass practice range and chipping area" help to make this "first-class" muni an "incredible value" and well "worth the ferry ride [west] from Seattle."

McCormick Woods

25 | 21 | 21 | 23 | $59

Port Orchard | 5155 McCormick Woods Dr. SW | 360-895-0130 | 800-323-0130 | www.mccormickwoodsgolf.com | 7040/5299; 74.3/71.6; 134/127

You should "hope you get paired with someone who's played here before" because this "tough" and "quirky" course "requires local knowledge" to navigate its tree-lined fairways and "difficult greens"; kept "in great condition" and located in a picturesque setting at the foot of Mt. Rainier near Port Orchard, this layout is "hard to get to" but a "find for out-of-state travelers" as it tends to be "uncrowded" and "easy to get a tee time"; "superb service" makes it even more of a "great value."

Port Ludlow

▽ 25 | 14 | 19 | 22 | $57

Port Ludlow | 751 Highland Dr. | 360-437-0272 | 800-455-0272 | www.portludlowresort.com
Tide/Timber | 6241/5482; 72/72.1; 125/125
Timber/Trail | 6324/5231; 69.8/70.8; 128/125
Trail/Tide | 6179/5086; 70.6/70.5; 132/123

For "gorgeous Northwest golf" in a "wonderful setting" less than 30 miles west of Downtown Seattle, head to this Robert Muir Graves creation that offers three distinct nines: the Tide with its many water hazards, the Timber with its fir-lined fairways and the scenic and challenging Trail with its views of Ludlow Bay; all in all, the 27-hole layout "keeps getting better with age" and it's part of a resort complex that includes an inn, marina and beach.

	COURSE	FACIL.	SERVICE	VALUE	COST

Trophy Lake

	25	22	21	22	$79

Port Orchard | 3900 SW Lake Flora Rd. | 360-874-8337 |
www.trophylakegolf.com | 7206/5342; 74.5/65.4; 135/118

Situated "more than an hour [west of] Seattle", this "beautiful" lake-side destination is the "place to go if you want to fish and golf" in a "rarely crowded" "resort atmosphere"; the "interesting" course appeals to "all levels" with a "challenging" but "fair" layout that's laced with "pot bunkers" and "fast greens"; factor in "good service and a nice area to eat after a round" – the appropriately named Dry Fly Cafe – and most critics consider this to be "a great value."

Seattle

Apple Tree

	▽ 23	20	18	20	$60

Yakima | 8804 Occidental Ave. | 509-966-5877 | www.appletreeresort.com |
6981/5428; 73.5/71.5; 135/127

"Winding its way through apple orchards" in the Yakima Valley wine country, this "interesting", "fun-to-play" layout is, as you might expect, "most gorgeous" when the eponymous trees "are in bloom"; all in all, the sometimes "windy" spread "has great potential", although some swingers wish that "the whole course were as dramatic" as the "big finish": an "enormous apple-shaped island green on the 17th" followed by a "huge carry over water off the 18th tee."

Druids Glen

	23	18	19	22	$48

Covington | 29925 207th Ave. SE | 253-638-1200 | www.druidsglengolf.com |
7146/5354; 75.2/70.7; 140/129

Sporting "spectacular views of Mt. Rainier" that are as "humbling" as Keith Foster's design, this "challenging" layout 40 minutes south of Seattle "specializes in visual intimidation", requiring you to "think on every tee" as you tackle "water, sand, wetlands, encroaching trees and steep slopes"; given that the "greens can be slicker than Phil Mickelson's hair" and the "rough gnarlier than Bobby Clampett's", this "value" caters to those who "play golf for the adrenaline rush."

☒ Golf Club at Newcastle, China Creek

	22	28	25	16	$110

Newcastle | 15500 Six Penny Ln. | 425-793-5566 | www.newcastlegolf.com |
6632/4782; 72.3/67.4; 129/115

Although "cheaper than its sister, Coal Creek" (in part due to a lack of Seattle skyline views), some say this Bob Cupp/Fred Couples design is still "a little overpriced", as the "nice course" simply "does not match" the rest of the Newcastle venue's "absolutely top-notch service and facilities"; nevertheless, the layout is "well-maintained", "busy" and just one part of a "country club" setup that includes a heated driving range and 18-hole putting track.

☒ Golf Club at Newcastle, Coal Creek

	23	28	26	16	$160

Newcastle | 15500 Six Penny Ln. | 425-793-5566 | www.newcastlegolf.com |
7024/5153; 74.7/71; 142/123

"Exquisite" "views of the mountains and Seattle's" skyline will "keep you coming back" to "the better of the two" Newcastle courses, this "challenging but rewarding" Bob Cupp/Fred Couples collaboration that features "lightning-fast greens" and 300 feet of elevation change; although a "magnificent 44,000-sq.-ft. clubhouse" and "great service" up the ante, some say the track "is not being kept in the condition befitting $160 greens fees" – it's "nice, but not three figures nice."

Harbour Pointe

| 20 | 17 | 19 | 19 | $55 |

Mukilteo | 11817 Harbour Pointe Blvd. | 425-355-6060 | 800-233-3128 | www.harbourpointegolf.com | 6878/4836; 73.3/69.1; 140/119

"Leave your driver in the bag or buy [extra] balls" because there's "water on the first 10 holes" of this "fine" Arthur Hills layout located north of Seattle; while the front may be "better and tougher" than the hilly, "woodlands" back, the entire course offers some of the "best greens in the area" – "hard" and true, but capable of bouncing "what you think is a perfect shot into the rough"; the catch: there are "too many homes close" to the already "narrow fairways."

NEW Suncadia Inn, Prospector

| – | – | – | – | $100 |

Roslyn Cle Elum | 3320 Suncadia Trail | 509-649-6000 | 866-715-5050 | www.suncadia.com | 7112/6159; 73.4/74.8; 135/135

Set amid majestic firs and pines overlooking the Cle Elum River, this Arnold Palmer design provides stunning views of the Cascades on holes like the signature 10th, a 411-yard par 4 with a 150-ft. drop from tee to fairway; affiliated with the new Suncadia Inn just 90 minutes east of Seattle, the course will be joined by a sibling spread in spring 2008; N.B. the Inn is part of an upcoming lodge and village complex.

Tacoma

Classic Golf Club

▽ | 21 | 13 | 21 | 23 | $42 |

Spanaway | 4908 208th St. E. | 253-847-4440 | www.classicgolfclub.net | 6917/5656; 73.2/67; 134/122

It should come as no surprise that the "old-school" "course that [PGA Tour player] Ryan Moore grew up on" "provides challenges for every skill level" but is particularly suited to "better golfers" given its "very narrow", tree-lined fairways, "fast greens" and copious amounts "of water"; although sparse facilities and "surrounding houses" are "downsides", this "out-of-the-way" layout just south of Tacoma compensates with its "very friendly" service.

Washington National

| 25 | 20 | 21 | 20 | $94 |

Auburn | 14330 SE Husky Way | 253-333-5000 | www.washingtonnationalgolfclub.com | 7304/5117; 75.5/65.2; 143/113

"If you're a Washington State Cougar fan", be aware that this east-of-Tacoma home of the UW golf team "is all Huskies, all the time"; the "long, hard" course is also "a real test" that displays a "serious addiction to sand and waste areas" and features "greens that slope and swell"; plus, although there are "great views of Mt. Rainier" from the "flat front" and the "moderately hilly back", the "shabby clubhouse" means it's "not a full package" for the price.

Vancouver Area

Resort Semiahmoo, Loomis Trail ⏱

▽ | 28 | 27 | 26 | 25 | $75 |

Blaine | 8720 Semiahmoo Pkwy. | 360-332-1725 | www.semiahmoo.com | 7137/5399; 75.1/71.9; 145/125

Noted Canadian architect Graham Cooke designed this "gorgeous" but "reasonably priced" resort course highlighted by a series of canals and

COURSE FACIL. SERVICE VALUE COST

lakes that bring water into play on every hole; a "lovely clubhouse" also helps to make the "great" links layout "worth a round or two" if you're near the Canadian border, especially if you stay at the luxe oceanside hotel and spa; N.B. it is open to the public on even days of the month.

Resort Semiahmoo, Semiahmoo Course ⏱

▽ 25 | 25 | 22 | 21 | $75

Blaine | 8720 Semiahmoo Pkwy. | 360-371-7005 | www.semiahmoo.com | 7005/5288; 73.9/70.6; 137/124

Although perhaps "not as good as Loomis Trail" (and "not one for which you need a low handicap"), this Arnold Palmer Signature course is nevertheless a "beautiful" and "very natural" tree-lined track on which you can "expect to see wildlife" that includes "plentiful deer, rabbits and birds"; it also possesses a few "challenging holes", so it may still be worth a quick visit to the club's Jeff Coston Golf Academy; N.B. it is open to the public on odd days of the month.

Wenatchee

Desert Canyon 🚗

▽ 23 | 13 | 16 | 18 | $79

Orondo | 1201 Desert Canyon Blvd. | 509-784-1111 | 800-258-4173 | www.desertcanyon.com | 7285/5200; 75.3/70.2; 138/123

With "spectacular views of the Columbia River Gorge", this "big, brawny" desert design in Orondo can be "challenging, especially when the wind blows"; though "the bare bones" of the place remain "beautiful" and "prices have been lowered", recent financial issues have meant that the formerly well-kept layout "is now suffering from conditioning problems" that some surveyors say "it needs to get past"; N.B. there is also an 18-hole putting course.

West Virginia

Elkins

Raven at Snowshoe Mountain

- | - | - | - | $79

Snowshoe | 10 Snowshoe Dr. | 304-572-1000 | www.snowshoemtn.com | 7045/4363; 75.5/65.3; 142/120

This "must-play" mountain resort course in Pocohontas County may be "a royal pain to get to", but slicers say "it's five-star all the way once you do"; and with its "spectacular scenery and elevation changes", the "fantastic" Gary Player–designed layout proves "challenging for the competitive golfer, but fair to the novice" and "enjoyable" to boot.

Weston

Stonewall Resort, Palmer

- | - | - | - | $85

Roanoke | 940 Resort Dr. | 304-269-8885 | www.stonewallresort.com | 7149/4921; 75.4/69.6; 143/127

A "hidden gem" nestled two hours south of Pittsburgh, this relatively new Arnold Palmer layout is designed to be challenging but playable by all levels (there are six sets of tees); situated amid lush, rolling hills on Stonewall Jackson Lake, the "incredible course" makes for "a perfect day of golf" – if your idea of perfect is thick fescue, numerous water hazards and a forced 92-yard carry over wetlands.

	COURSE	FACIL.	SERVICE	VALUE	COST

White Sulphur Springs

☑ Greenbrier, Greenbrier Course 🏌

| 28 | 29 | 29 | 22 | $185 |

White Sulphur Springs | 300 W. Main St. | 304-536-1110 | 800-624-6070 | www.greenbrier.com | 6675/5095; 73.1/69; 135/120

"A true must-play" that's "hosted both the Ryder Cup and the Solheim Cup", this "absolutely fantastic", "challenging" "but fair" layout in White Sulphur Springs receives high praise for its "knowledgeable caddies" – it ranks No. 1 for Service in this year's Survey – and "excellent conditions" ("the best greens I've putted"); a few bemoan the "McMansions scattered around", but most agree "if you can afford the resort", you'll have "a memorable experience."

☑ Greenbrier, Meadows 🏌

| 22 | 29 | 28 | 22 | $185 |

White Sulphur Springs | 300 W. Main St. | 304-536-1110 | 800-624-6070 | www.greenbrier.com | 6795/4979; 72.8/68.2; 129/114

"Where else can you catch a trout if the play is slow" than at this "picture-perfect" course "set in West Virginia's rolling foothills" and boasting "superb greens and fairways" and a "babbling creek" that keeps play "deceptively difficult" – so "keep a fly rod in your bag" as you traverse this "wide-open but challenging layout"; even better, the "resort luxury" evident at its 19th hole has helped it snag the top rating for Facilities in this year's Survey.

☑ Greenbrier, Old White 🏌

| 26 | 28 | 27 | 21 | $185 |

White Sulphur Springs | 300 W. Main St. | 304-536-1110 | 800-624-6070 | www.greenbrier.com | 6826/5813; 73.7/69.3; 137/130

"A classic made even more classic", this "wonderful" 1914 layout has recently been "restored to its original condition" courtesy of a multiyear renovation; it remains "a joy to play" with "lots of variety", "interesting holes" and "worth-the-trip" "challenges" such as the "unique dragon's teeth bunkers"; "it's expensive", but expect "pure luxury and service."

Wisconsin

TOP COURSES IN STATE

30 Whistling Straits, Straits | *Kohler*
28 Blackwolf Run, River | *Kohler*
27 University Ridge | *Madison*
  Whistling Straits, Irish | *Kohler*
  Lawsonia, Woodlands | *Madison*

Kohler

☑ Blackwolf Run, Meadow Valleys 🏌

| 25 | 28 | 27 | 20 | $141 |

Kohler | 1111 W. Riverside Dr. | 920-457-4446 | 800-618-5535 | www.blackwolfrun.com | 7142/5065; 74.6/70.2; 144/117

Some say this "more forgiving" Kohler course "suffers by comparison to its siblings", but you "better bring your A-game" to handle its "beautiful but challenging" and "hilly" layout that's pitted with pot bunkers and topped off with an "excellent finishing hole" bisected by the Sheboygan River; the "fees are high", but players "love the experience", which includes "great" conditioning, "amazing facilities" and service that "makes you feel like a king for a day."

	COURSE	FACIL.	SERVICE	VALUE	COST

☒ Blackwolf Run, River 🏌 ⊕ | 28 | 28 | 27 | 22 | $189 |

Kohler | 1111 W. Riverside Dr. | 920-457-4446 | 800-618-5535 |
www.blackwolfrun.com | 6991/5115; 74.4/70.1; 148/124
For "championship-level golf in a perfect atmosphere", try this "diabolical", "deceptively challenging" Pete Dye design that "gives Whistling
Straits a run for its money" via "memorable" "risk-and-reward holes"
that feature "a tremendous use of angles and undulations" as they
skirt the Sheboygan ("caddies are a must"); even better, as part of
"the Kohler golf mecca", it offers a "terrific restaurant", "outstanding
service", a "gorgeous clubhouse" and "world-class accommodations"
at the American Club.

Bull at Pinehurst Farms, The | 24 | 23 | 22 | 20 | $155 |

Sheboygan | 1 Long Dr. | 920-467-1500 | 800-584-3285 |
www.golfthebull.com | 7332/5087; 76.4/70.9; 146/127
This Jack Nicklaus "gem" is "somewhat ignored because of Blackwolf
Run and Whistling Straits", but Sheboygan's "excellent" 2003
parkland/woodland mix "is a much better value"; so "if you're in the
area", take advantage of one of its "many specials" to play a "solid",
"nicely kept course" that makes "tremendous use of its terrain"
(dense forests, wetlands, ponds and ravines) "to create a challenging
but fair venue" with "a great finishing stretch."

☒ Whistling Straits, Irish 🏌 | 27 | 28 | 28 | 22 | $141 |

Sheboygan | N8501 County Rd. LS | 920-565-6050 | 800-618-5535 |
www.destinationkohler.com | 7201/5109; 75.6/65.6; 146/122
"If you make the pilgrimage" to the Kohler area, don't miss this linksy
"test of skill and endurance" where "playing poorly is like being
spurned by a beautiful woman – all you can think of is trying again";
"more forgiving" than the Straits "while plenty difficult", this inland
Pete Dye design features "unusual moonlike topography" that's punc-
tuated by sand dunes, "lots of bunkers" and four meandering streams;
it's "expensive but worth it for the experience", which includes "unbeatable facilities" and "the best of service."

☒ Whistling Straits, Straits 🏌 ⊕ | 30 | 28 | 28 | 22 | $270 |

Sheboygan | N8501 County Rd. LS | 920-565-6050 | 800-618-5535 |
www.destinationkohler.com | 7362/5396; 76.7/72.2; 151/132
"It's hard to believe this course is in Wisconsin and not Scotland" (especially when a "sheep wanders by"), but this "real links" layout from
Pete Dye is the top-rated Course in the state and one of the "finest in
the U.S.", a "windy, complex" spread whose "seemingly endless hazards" include Lake Michigan; "walking is required" at this host of the
2004 PGA Championship, "but you wouldn't want it any other way"
given the "top-notch caddies" and "breathtaking scenery"; all in all,
it's just "one of those places you have to play regardless of its cost."

Lake Geneva

Geneva National, Gary Player 🏠 ⊕ | 24 | 24 | 22 | 19 | $125 |

Lake Geneva | 1221 Geneva National Ave. S. | 262-245-7000 |
www.genevanationalresort.com | 7018/4823; 74.3/68.4; 141/120
Experienced hands recommend you "don't go off the fairway" on this
rolling, wooded Gary Player–designed track that offers "many fun

holes" made "challenging" by ever-present bunkers and water hazards; perhaps the "best of the three" at this Lake Geneva venue, the "classic" layout also boasts "great views" of Lake Como, making it a "very enjoyable" course that's also a "value" during early-bird and twilight hours.

Geneva National, Palmer 🏌⏱

| 24 | 24 | 21 | 20 | $115 |

Lake Geneva | 1221 Geneva National Ave. S. | 262-245-7000 | www.genevanationalresort.com | 7171/4904; 74.7/68.5; 140/122

Winding over hilly woodlands dotted with creeks and ponds, this Arnold Palmer design is a "very beautiful course", sporting steeply sloped greens and a heavily wooded back nine that can make it "very challenging" indeed; meanwhile, its "outstanding views" of Lake Como on the 16th and 17th are only part of the reason one swinger swears this is one of the "best around."

Geneva National, Trevino 🏌⏱

| ▽ 23 | 25 | 23 | 19 | $115 |

Lake Geneva | 1221 Geneva National Ave. S. | 262-245-7000 | www.genevanationalresort.com | 7120/5193; 74.3/70.2; 136/124

With a forgiving woodlands design suitable for all players, this Lee Trevino track features wide fairways lined with old oaks, hickories and walnuts; the course has plenty of water in play, including a creek that guards the green on the signature par-5 5th; and though the layout's "tucked in among condos", you can always get your dose of Lake Como views at Geneva National's upscale Hunt Club restaurant.

Grand Geneva, Brute 🏌

| 24 | 22 | 23 | 21 | $145 |

Lake Geneva | 7036 Grand Geneva Way | 262-248-2556 | 800-558-3417 | www.grandgeneva.com | 7085/5244; 73.8/70; 136/129

This "beautiful" Lake Geneva course certainly "lives up to its name" – "it is a brute"; "difficult for the average player", it's a particularly "long" track that features tree- and water-lined fairways, "huge greens" ("can you say 'three-putt'?") and some "nice final holes", including a huge par-5 15th that's cut in half by a river; but even more "excellent" than the play are the resort's lavish facilities.

Grand Geneva, Highlands 🏌

| 23 | 23 | 23 | 19 | $125 |

Lake Geneva | 7036 Grand Geneva Way | 262-248-2556 | 800-558-3417 | www.grandgeneva.com | 6633/5038; 71.5/68.3; 125/115

"A very pleasant change of pace", this older sibling to the Brute proves "more player-friendly", a "short, fun track" that was originally designed by Jack Nicklaus and Pete Dye in 1968 and renovated by Bob Cupp in 1996; though "hilly and challenging", the "beautiful course" is "mid-handicapper-friendly" with "fascinating holes", "well-manicured" terrain and "excellent facilities"; N.B. a redo added bunkering on three holes.

Madison

Lawsonia, Links

| 26 | 19 | 20 | 27 | $76 |

Green Lake | W2615 S. Valley View Dr. | 920-294-3320 | 800-529-4453 | www.lawsonia.com | 7000/5078; 72.8/65.2; 130/115

It's "worth" driving to "the middle of America's dairyland" 80 miles north of Madison to play this "hidden gem" "for serious golfers", a "links-style course like no other" featuring rolling, mostly treeless terrain laced with some 90 "grass bunkers that add to" the layout's "unique look"; although "most holes are generous on the tee shot",

	COURSE	FACIL.	SERVICE	VALUE	COST

"the real challenge lies" in conquering the "elevated greens" – they're "some of the biggest and toughest anywhere."

Lawsonia, Woodlands ⌂

| 27 | 20 | 19 | 24 | $76 |

Green Lake | W2615 S. Valley View Dr. | 920-294-3320 | 800-529-4453 | www.lawsonia.com | 6618/5106; 72.7/69.6; 132/125

It's "either forest or fairway" at this "beautiful" layout that's "as challenging" but "the complete opposite of" its links-style sibling; it's "fun to play", but be sure to "bring your A-game" to this shot-maker's course where the "greens are true but tricky" – a quarry separates the fairway from the green on the par-4 2nd – and the "dense [woods] and shrub" have one whacker wondering "if I hit all the trees in the forest, would anyone hear it?"

NEW Northern Bay

| - | - | - | - | $95 |

Arkdale | 1844 20th Ave. | 608-339-2090 | 800-350-0049 | www.northernbayresort.com | 7223/5197; 74.4/69.7; 131/123

Nestled on the northwest corner of Castle Rock Lake just north of the Wisconsin Dells is this kaleidoscope of unforgettable golf scenes, where Matt Mootz and Tour 18 Design Group have delivered the Midwest's first replica course – well, only nine of the holes are reproductions with the other half pure Wisconsin originals; although all of the imitations prove faithful, the most memorable is the par-3 10th, a dead-on copy of TPC Sawgrass' island-green 17th.

Sentryworld ⌖

| ▽ 22 | 21 | 22 | 23 | $79 |

Stevens Point | 601 N. Michigan Ave. | 715-345-1600 | 866-479-6753 | www.sentryworld.com | 6951/5108; 74.4/71; 142/126

"Yes, the 'Flower Hole' makes it a must-play" – the signature par-3 16th features an island green encircled by some 90,000 annuals – "but the whole course" (designed by RTJ Jr.) "is what makes it worth a return"; routed over rolling, tree-dotted terrain two hours north of Madison, this "traditional" track is "an excellent test of golf" with plenty of "personality" courtesy of its "tough greens" and spring-fed lakes.

Trappers Turn

| ▽ 23 | 23 | 24 | 22 | $84 |

Wisconsin Dells | 652 Trappers Turn Dr. | 608-253-7000 | 800-221-8876 | www.trappersturn.com
Arbor/Lake | 6738/5000; 73.3/69.7; 133/123
Canyon/Arbor | 6759/5017; 72.8/69.4; 133/122
Lake/Canyon | 6831/5000; 72.9/69.5; 133/122

A "gorgeous" 27-hole spread that's hosted the Wisconsin PGA Championship, this Dells destination is nevertheless a "very playable" design from two-time U.S. Open champ Andy North and architect Roger Packard; with varied terrain carved out by glacial waters, it offers some "great holes" on its "well-kept" but distinct nines: one is wooded, one is lakeside and a third bounds through a natural canyon; even better than its diversity is its "attentive staff."

University Ridge

| 27 | 22 | 22 | 25 | $74 |

Verona | 9002 County Rd. PD | 608-845-7700 | 800-897-4343 | www.universityridge.com | 6888/5005; 73.2/68.9; 142/121

"Every college should have a course like this!" bellow Badgers about this "awesome" University of Wisconsin spread that "deserves more recognition" for its "diverse", "thoughtful layout"; the "challenging"

Robert Trent Jones Jr. design provides "a great contrast between" the open front and densely wooded back, although both nines are "a pleasure to play" given the "true greens", "excellent conditions" and "scenic vistas"; meanwhile, the "great facilities" include a newly expanded clubhouse with veranda.

Milwaukee

Bog, The

24 | 20 | 19 | 20 | $135

Saukville | 3121 County Hwy. I | 262-284-7075 | 800-484-3264 | www.golfthebog.com | 7221/5110; 75.3/70.3; 143/124

"Challenging" and "well-maintained", this Arnold Palmer design offers "beautiful vistas" as it rambles over wetlands, woodlands and hills 25 miles north of Milwaukee; the "pristine", "gently sloped greens" "roll fast" and are guarded by strategic bunkering, but where some swingers see "real personality", others see "a few goofy holes"; although an "expense account is no handicap here", a 40,000-sq.-ft. practice facility adds to the value.

Bristlecone Pines ♣

▽ 22 | 21 | 19 | 20 | $109

Hartland | 1500 E. Arlene Dr. | 262-367-7880 | www.golfbristlecone.com | 7005/5033; 74.4/69.4; 138/120

Set on glacier-sculpted terrain about 20 minutes west of Milwaukee, this "nicely maintained" daily fee features wide fairways, native fescue and a meandering stream that puts water on 11 holes; the well-endowed facility – it offers a 13-acre practice area, two restaurants and an outdoor pool – will play host to the State Amateur Championship in 2007; N.B. the club intends to go private in the near future.

Brown Deer Park

23 | 14 | 15 | 23 | $84

Milwaukee | 7625 N. Range Line Rd. | 414-352-8080 | www.countyparks.com | 6759/5861; 72.9/73.8; 133/132

Host of the PGA Tour U.S. Bank Championship (where Tiger Woods made his professional debut), this "pleasant" Milwaukee "surprise" proves "tougher than the pros make it look" on TV; considered "one of the country's great munis", the "tree-lined" 1929 classic has "eye appeal" and "deep rough", and although out-of-towners opine it's "overpriced if you're not a county resident", it's still an overall "good value."

NEW Erin Hills

▽ 27 | 21 | 28 | 22 | $150

Hartford | 7169 County Rd. O | 262-646-3331 | 866-724-8822 | www.erinhills.com | 6544/4300; 72/0; 141/110

This "tremendous track" northwest of Milwaukee is truly "Mother Nature's best": a rugged, "visually spectacular" layout that's minimally developed and "not for the faint of heart" with its "rolling hills, woodlands" and wind-swept fescue; some say the young course "needs a few years", which gives early birds plenty of time to "go before the masses find out about this jewel" at the 2008 U.S. Women's Amateur Public Links Championship.

Fire Ridge

▽ 21 | 20 | 22 | 23 | $75

Grafton | 2241 Hwy. W. | 262-375-2252 | www.fireridgegc.com | 7049/5463; 74.5/72.3; 136/126

Located a few miles west of Lake Michigan, this former country-club course gets high marks for its "good variety" of holes nestled amid rolling hills, marshland and ponds (11 have water in play); although the "decent conditions could be better", most find it an all-around "great buy" and an especially "outstanding value before 8 AM" in spring and fall during "their early-bird specials."

Naga-Waukee
▽ 19 | 11 | 13 | 22 | $38

Pewaukee | 1897 Maple Ave. | 262-367-2153 | www.waukeshacountyparks.com | 6830/5817; 71.8/72.4; 125/125

With a "solid design" that features "large greens" ("lots of three-putts") and undulating "terrain changes", this "very good" muni about 30 minutes west of Milwaukee makes for a "challenging" round; it's "hard to get a tee time, though", as the "beautiful" woodlands course gets "crowded on weekends" with players intent on enjoying the "nice views" of Pewaukee Lake; still, "above-average groundskeeping" makes this a particularly "outstanding value."

Northern Wisconsin

NEW Big Fish
- | - | - | - | $49

Hayward | 14122 W. True North Ln. | 715-934-4770 | www.bigfishgolf.com | 7190/4938; 73.9/68.6; 135/116

This relatively new facility about two hours north of the Twin Cities offers "awesome conditions" on a scenic Pete Dye design that blends links and woodland holes; "any player would have a great time" navigating the strategic bunkering, tall fescue and undulating terrain, and the promising addition will play host to qualifying rounds for the 2007 State Amateur and State Match Play Qualifiers.

Northwood
- | - | - | - | $42

Rhinelander | 3131 Golf Course Rd. | 715-282-6565 | www.northwoodgolfclub.com | 6724/5338; 73.1/71.3; 140/129

"It's just you and nature" at this "beautiful", "challenging" layout three-plus hours from Madison in the state's far northern reaches; its short length makes it a fine beginners track, and while you may be "pleasantly surprised" to find "such a technologically advanced course" – the carts are equipped with GPS – in this untouched area, you won't be astonished by the presence of the "annoying deer flies."

Wyoming

Jackson

Jackson Hole Golf & Tennis
▽ 26 | 19 | 22 | 22 | $155

Jackson | 5000 Spring Gulch Rd. | 307-733-3111 | www.jhgtc.com | 7168/5492; 72.5/70.4; 123/123

"Man, the ball goes a long way at 7,000 feet", giving this "beautiful" RTJ Jr. redesign in Jackson "a bit of bite" to go with its "awesome views" of the Grand Tetons; a few consider "course conditions not up to par for the prices", but ongoing renovations – which will revamp the tee boxes and bunkers as well as add a new irrigation system, clubhouse and driving range – may help to ease their minds (and outdate the above Facilities score); N.B. construction will be complete by spring 2007.

Private Courses

Access to play is limited to members and their guests.

Aronimink Golf Club
Newtown Square | 3600 St. Davids Rd. | PA | 610-356-8000 |
www.aronimink.org
Restored to its original Donald Ross design, this 1962 PGA
Championship host features rugged par 4s with elevated greens.

Atlanta Country Club
Marietta | 500 Atlanta Country Club Dr. | GA | 770-953-2100 |
www.atlantacountryclub.org
The PGA Tour's 1967–1996 Atlanta home has a showstopping 13th
featuring pines, wildflowers, a waterfall and a covered bridge.

Atlantic Golf Club
Bridgehampton | 1040 Scuttle Hole Rd. | NY | 631-537-1818
Ocean breezes and native-grass mounding characterize Rees Jones'
linksy spiritual cousin to England's Royal Birkdale.

Augusta National Golf Club
Augusta | 2604 Washington Rd. | GA | 706-667-6000 |
www.masters.org
Home to the Masters Tournament, this hilly beauty at a men-only club
is rich in trees, flowers, creeks and ponds.

Baltimore Country Club, East
Timonium | 11500 Mays Chapel Rd. | MD | 410-561-3381 |
www.bcc1898.com
A.W. Tillinghast crafted this host of the 1928 PGA Championship,
1932 U.S. Amateur, 1965 Walker Cup and 1988 U.S. Women's Open.

Baltusrol Golf Club, Lower
Springfield | 201 Shunpike Rd. | NJ | 973-376-1900 |
www.baltusrol.org
An hour from Manhattan, this club has hosted seven U.S. Opens, four
on the Lower course, which closes with back-to-back par 5s.

Bel-Air Country Club
Los Angeles | 10768 Bellagio Rd. | CA | 310-472-9563 |
www.bel-aircc.org
At this celeb-studded enclave, golfers cross a barranca at the 10th via
the famed 'Swinging Bridge.'

Bellerive Country Club
St. Louis | 12925 Ladue Rd. | MO | 314-434-4400
The 1965 U.S. Open, 1992 PGA Championship and 2004 U.S. Senior
Open were played on RTJ Sr.'s elevated, fiercely trapped greens.

Black Diamond Ranch Golf & Country Club, Quarry
Lecanto | 2600 W. Black Diamond Circle | FL | 352-746-3440 |
www.blackdiamondranch.com
Holes that play up, down and around an old quarry make for a striking
back nine on this Tom Fazio design.

PRIVATE COURSES

Camargo Club
Indian Hill | 8605 Shawnee Run Rd. | OH | 513-561-9292
Golden Age architect Seth Raynor crafted a wonderful variety of ravine-skirting par 3s and par 4s on this 1926 course.

Canterbury Golf Club
Beachwood | 22000 S. Woodland Rd. | OH | 216-561-1000 | www.canterburygc.org
Jack Nicklaus broke Bobby Jones' record for majors won when he took the 1973 PGA Championship on this 1922 woodlander.

Castle Pines Golf Club
Castle Rock | 1000 Hummingbird Dr. | CO | 303-688-6000 | www.castlepines.com
At 7,559 yards, one of the PGA Tour's longest tracks is this 1982 Nicklaus design featuring sharp downhills framed in pines.

Cherry Hills Country Club
Englewood | 4125 S. University Blvd. | CO | 303-761-9900 | www.chcc.com
President Eisenhower's home away from home in the Rockies has hosted numerous championships, including the 1960 U.S. Open.

Chicago Golf Club
Wheaton | 25W253 Warrenville Rd. | IL | 630-668-2000
Considered American golf royalty, this 1892 classic was the first 18-holer in the country and has hosted U.S. Opens three times, in 1897, 1900 and 1911.

Colonial Country Club
Ft. Worth | 3735 Country Club Circle | TX | 817-927-4200
Ben Hogan won the PGA Tour's Colonial National Invitational five times here, providing the track its nickname, 'Hogan's Alley.'

Congressional Country Club, Blue
Bethesda | 8500 River Rd. | MD | 301-469-2000 | www.ccclub.org
This host of the 1964 and 1997 U.S. Opens was redone by Robert Trent Jones Sr. and son Rees in 1960 and 1989, respectively.

Country Club, The, Clyde/Squirrel
Brookline | 191 Clyde St. | MA | 617-566-0240
A Boston Brahmin enclave for more than 100 years, this tree-lined layout has hosted three U.S. Opens and the 1999 Ryder Cup.

Country Club of Fairfield
Fairfield | 936 Sasco Hill Rd. | CT | 203-259-1601
Seth Raynor's 1914 breeze-fueled classic serves up a stout collection of par 4s plus handsome vistas of Long Island Sound.

Creek Club
Locust Valley | 1 Horse Hollow Rd. | NY | 516-676-1405
Wooded and links holes, an island green and lovely views of Long Island Sound are on offer at this short but exciting 1923 layout.

Crooked Stick Golf Club

Carmel | 1964 Burning Tree Ln. | IN | 317-844-9938 |
www.crookedstick.org

This Pete Dye design was the host of the 1991 PGA Championship,
1993 U.S. Women's Open and 2005 Solheim Cup.

Crystal Downs Country Club

Frankfort | 249 E. Crystal Downs Dr. | MI | 231-352-9933

Atop a bluff between Lake Michigan and Crystal Lake, Alister
MacKenzie's windswept gem is thick with native rough.

Cypress Point Club

Pebble Beach | 3150 17-Mile Dr. | CA | 831-624-6444

Alister MacKenzie's seasider near Pebble Beach Resort hosted the
PGA Tour's Bing Crosby National Pro-Am.

Desert Forest Golf Club

Carefree | 37207 N. Mule Train Rd. | AZ | 480-488-4589 |
www.desertforestgolfclub.com

Fairways and back-to-front sloping greens hemmed in by cacti de-
mand accuracy on this desert beauty with mountain views.

Double Eagle Club

Galena | 6025 Cheshire Rd. | OH | 740-548-4017

This Weiskopf/Morrish track boasts dual fairways and conditioning
so superb that the tee boxes could double as greens.

East Lake Golf Club

Atlanta | 2575 Alston Dr. SE | GA | 404-373-5722 |
www.eastlakegolfclub.com

Bobby Jones' boyhood playground is reborn with a 1994 Rees Jones
redesign and a caddie program for local underserved youth.

Estancia Club

Scottsdale | 27998 N. 99th Pl. | AZ | 480-473-4400 |
www.estanciaclub.com

Tom Fazio set the tee boxes and greens on high desert outcroppings at
this enclave that climbs Pinnacle Peak.

Eugene Country Club

Eugene | 255 Country Club Rd. | OR | 541-345-0181 |
www.eugenecountryclub.com

In 1967, Robert Trent Jones Sr. reversed the tees and greens and enlarged the water hazards on this 1924 tree-laden track.

Firestone Country Club, South

Akron | 452 E. Warner Rd. | OH | 330-644-8441 |
www.firestonecountryclub.com

RTJ Sr.'s redesign has hosted PGA Championships, the 2002 Senior
PGA Championship and the World Series of Golf.

Fishers Island Club

Fishers Island | Fishers Island | NY | 631-788-7221

At a society retreat in Long Island Sound, this 1926 Seth Raynor links
design is known for its Atlantic shore vistas.

PRIVATE COURSES

Forest Highlands Golf Club, Canyon
Flagstaff | 657 Forest Highlands | AZ | 928-525-5200 |
www.fhgc.com
Par 5s over 600 yards long are made more manageable by the 7,000-ft.
altitude of this Weiskopf/Morrish design.

Friar's Head
Baiting Hollow | 3000 Sound Ave. | NY | 631-722-5200
Tree-lined dunes, open meadows and blufftop views of CT and Long
Island Sound spice the play on this Coore/Crenshaw design.

Garden City Golf Club
Garden City | 315 Stewart Ave. | NY | 516-747-2880
Host of the 1902 U.S. Open, this Long Island men-only institution
plays like a British links, with tall fescue, bunkers and sea breezes.

Golf Club, The
New Albany | 4522 Kitzmiller Rd. | OH | 614-855-7326
Hidden at a men-only club, this early Pete Dye layout offers tall native
rough, clever bunkers and outstanding par 5s.

Grandfather Golf & Country Club
Linville | 2120 Hwy. 105 | NC | 828-898-4531 |
www.grandfatherclub.org
In a high Blue Ridge valley next to the Linville River, this hilly design
looks up through the pines at Grandfather Mountain.

Hazeltine National Golf Club
Chaska | 1900 Hazeltine Blvd. | MN | 952-448-4929 |
www.hngc.com
Designed by RTJ Sr. and reworked by his son Rees, this farm/forest
blend hosted the 1991 U.S. Open and 2002 PGA Championship.

Honors Course
Ooltewah | 9603 Lee Hwy. | TN | 423-238-4272
Tiger Woods' winning final-round 80 at the 1996 Men's NCAA
Championship testifies to the difficulty of this Pete Dye design.

Interlachen Country Club
Edina | 6200 Interlachen Blvd. | MN | 952-929-1661 |
www.interlachencc.org
Bobby Jones skipped his second shot across the pond at the 9th to win
the 1930 U.S. Open here in his Grand Slam year.

Inverness Club
Toledo | 4601 Dorr St. | OH | 419-578-9000 |
www.invernessclub.com
Donald Ross' centenarian remains a superb test; just ask Bob Tway,
who holed a sand shot here to win the 1986 PGA Championship.

Jupiter Hills Club, Hills
Tequesta | 11800 SE Hill Club Terrace | FL | 561-746-5228 |
www.jupiterhillsclub.org
Bob Hope and auto executive William Clay Ford were among the
founders of this track with 70 feet of elevation changes.

PRIVATE COURSES

Kinloch Golf Club
Manakin-Sabot | 1100 Hockett Rd. | VA | 804-784-8000 |
www.kinlochgolfclub.com
Near Richmond, this millennial design from Lester George and Vinny
Giles offers multiple avenues of play on nearly every hole.

Kittansett Club
Marion | 11 Point Rd. | MA | 508-748-0148 | www.kittansett.org
Windy Buzzards Bay is home to the 1953 Walker Cup Match host,
where the 3rd plays to an island green encircled by sand.

Laurel Valley Golf Club
Ligonier | 175 Palmer Dr. | PA | 724-238-9555
On an old pheasant-hunting preserve is this host of the 1965 PGA
Championship, 1975 Ryder Cup Match and 1989 U.S. Senior Open.

Long Cove Club
Hilton Head Island | 399 Long Cove Dr. | SC | 843-686-1070 |
www.longcoveclub.org
This 25-year-old Pete Dye design is laced with live oaks, palmettos
and waste bunkers on its amazing variety of holes.

Los Angeles Country Club, North
Los Angeles | 10101 Wilshire Blvd. | CA | 310-276-6104
George Thomas' layout sits on pricey real estate at the meeting of
Santa Monica and Wilshire Boulevards near Beverly Hills.

Maidstone Club
East Hampton | 50 Old Beach Ln. | NY | 631-324-0510
The 19th-century links design at this tony Hamptons club is awash in
ocean breezes that make it play much longer than its yardage.

Medinah Country Club, No. 3
Medinah | 6N001 Medinah Rd. | IL | 630-773-1700 |
www.medinahcc.org
Tiger Woods captured both the 1999 and 2006 PGA Championships
on this wooded brute with par 3s that play over Lake Kadijah.

Merion Golf Club, East
Ardmore | 450 Ardmore Ave. | PA | 610-642-5600 |
www.meriongolfclub.com
Bobby Jones clinched his Grand Slam in 1930 at this Main Line
Philadelphia classic's famed 'Babbling Brook' hole.

Milwaukee Country Club
River Hills | 8000 N. Range Line Rd. | WI | 414-362-5200
The host of the 1969 Walker Cup Match features a wooded back nine
that tumbles down to the Milwaukee River.

Muirfield Village Golf Club
Dublin | 5750 Memorial Dr. | OH | 614-889-6700
Jack Nicklaus designed this track to host his own Memorial
Tournament, won by Tiger Woods in 1999, 2000 and 2001.

PRIVATE COURSES

Myopia Hunt Club
South Hamilton | 435 Bay Rd. | MA | 978-468-4433
The hilly host of four U.S. Opens in 1898–1908 provides a solid, old-style test, thanks to bunkering and vexing putting surfaces.

Nantucket Golf Club
Siasconset | 250 Milestone Rd. | MA | 508-257-8520
Coastal gusts complicate this British links–style Rees Jones design, a 7,081-yard-long throwback to an earlier era.

National Golf Links of America
Southampton | Sebonac Inlet Rd. | NY | 631-283-0410
This nonagenarian on Great Peconic Bay is by Charles Blair Macdonald, who modeled creations after the British Isles' best.

NCR Country Club, South
Dayton | 4435 Dogwood Trail | OH | 937-299-3571 | www.ncrcountryclub.com
Dick Wilson sculpted this host of the 1969 PGA Championship, 1986 U.S. Women's Open and 2005 U.S. Senior Open.

Oak Hill Country Club, East
Rochester | 346 Kilbourn Rd. | NY | 585-586-1660 | www.oakhillcc.com
Host to three U.S. Opens and the 1995 Ryder Cup Match, Donald Ross' 1920s design calls for long, accurate shot-making.

Oakland Hills Country Club, South
Bloomfield Hills | 3951 W. Maple Rd. | MI | 248-644-2500 | www.oaklandhillscc.com
Ben Hogan called this track a 'monster', but he tamed its undulating greens and many bunkers to win the 1951 U.S. Open.

Oakmont Country Club
Oakmont | 1233 Hulton Rd. | PA | 412-828-8000 | www.oakmontcc.org
Hosting its eighth U.S. Open in 2007, this centenarian has the most bunkers and the largest, fastest greens in championship golf.

Oak Tree Golf Club
Edmund | 1515 W. Oak Tree Dr. | OK | 405-348-2004 | www.oaktreegolfclub.com
Amid prairie gusts, Pete Dye dishes up undulations, moguls and superb variety for events like the 1988 PGA Championship.

Ocean Forest Golf Club
Sea Island | 200 Ocean Rd. | GA | 912-638-5834
On an Atlantic island, Rees Jones' fairly flat mix of wooded holes and windy, open links hosted the 2001 Walker Cup Match.

Olympia Fields Country Club, North
Olympia Fields | 2800 Country Club Dr. | IL | 708-748-0495 | www.ofcc.info
The North course first hosted the U.S. Open in 1928 and just recently hosted it for a second time in 2003.

PRIVATE COURSES

Olympic Club, The Lake
San Francisco | 524 Post St. | CA | 415-587-4800 | www.olyclub.com
You can see the Golden Gate Bridge from the 3rd tee of this pine-, cedar- and cypress-laced four-time U.S. Open site.

Peachtree Golf Club
Atlanta | 4600 Peachtree Rd. NE | GA | 404-233-4428
A onetime-only Bobby Jones/RTJ Sr. co-design, this hilly, forested Southerner boasts broad fairways and huge greens.

Pete Dye Golf Club
Bridgeport | 801 Aaron Smith Dr. | WV | 304-842-2801 | www.petedye.com
Routed over a former strip coal mine, this undulating namesake forces healthy carries across Simpson Creek.

Pine Valley Golf Club
Pine Valley | E. Atlantic Ave. | NJ | 856-783-3000
This brutal but beautiful favorite dishes out multiple forced carries on holes hopscotching from one island of turf to the next.

Piping Rock Club
Locust Valley | 150 Piping Rock Rd. | NY | 516-676-2332
Near where Matinecock Indians smoked peace pipes, this 1911 design retooled in the '80s pays homage to Britain's best.

Plainfield Country Club
Edison | 1591 Woodland Ave. | NJ | 908-757-1800 | www.plainfieldcc.com
Host of the 1978 U.S. Amateur and 1987 U.S. Women's Open, this classic sports cross bunkers and contoured greens.

Point O'Woods Golf & Country Club
Benton Harbor | 1516 Roslyn Rd. | MI | 269-944-1433 | www.pointowoods.com
Tom Weiskopf, Ben Crenshaw and Tiger Woods are among champs of the Western Amateur, played here since the 1960s.

Prairie Dunes Country Club
Hutchinson | 4812 E. 30th Ave. | KS | 620-662-0581 | www.prairiedunes.com
Amid sandhills, yucca and plum thickets, this rolling, windswept layout proved a formidable test at the 2002 U.S. Women's Open.

Pumpkin Ridge, Witch Hollow
North Plains | 12930 NW Old Pumpkin Ridge Rd. | OR | 503-647-9977 | www.pumpkinridge.com
The 1996 site of Tiger Woods' third U.S. Amateur win also hosted Nancy Lopez's heartbreaking loss at the 1997 U.S. Women's Open.

Quaker Ridge Golf Club
Scarsdale | 146 Griffen Ave. | NY | 914-725-1100 | www.quakerridgegc.org
Hidden next to Winged Foot, this A.W. Tillinghast design boasts outstanding par 4s and was host to the 1997 Walker Cup Match.

Quarry at La Quinta
La Quinta | 1 Quarry Ln. | CA | 760-777-1100 |
www.thequarryinfo.com
Every hole offers scenic desert backdrops at this Palm Springs-area
Tom Fazio course that's draped across mountain slopes.

Ridgewood Country Club, East/West
Paramus | 96 W. Midland Ave. | NJ | 201-599-3900 |
www.ridgewoodclub.com
A.W. Tillinghast's 27-holer hosted the 1935 Ryder Cup, 1990 U.S.
Senior Open and 2001 Senior PGA Championship.

Rim Golf Club, The
Payson | 300 S. Clubhouse Rd. | AZ | 928-472-1480 |
www.therimgolfclub.com
The boulder escarpment backdropping the par-5 13th is just one high
desert wonder on this final Weiskopf/Morrish design.

Riviera Country Club
Pacific Palisades | 1250 Capri Dr. | CA | 310-454-6591 |
www.rccla.com
Host of the PGA Tour's Nissan Open, this eucalyptus-lined layout sits
in a canyon south of Sunset Boulevard.

Robert Trent Jones Golf Club
Gainesville | 1 Turtle Point Dr. | VA | 703-754-4050 |
www.rtjgc.com
Named for the dean of U.S. golf architects, this former Presidents Cup
host is chock-full of water hazards and puzzle-piece bunkers.

Sahalee Country Club, South/North
Sammamish | 21200 NE Sahalee Country Club Dr. | WA |
425-868-8800 | www.sahalee.com
Meaning 'high, heavenly ground' in Chinook, this 1998 PGA
Championship site is bracketed by cedars, firs and hemlocks.

Salem Country Club
Peabody | 133 Forest St. | MA | 978-538-5400 |
www.salemcountryclub.org
Amid maples, oaks and pines, this Donald Ross design has hosted two
U.S. Women's Opens and the 2001 U.S. Senior Open.

Sand Hills Golf Club
Mullen | Hwy. 97, Mile Marker 55 | NE | 308-546-2237 |
www.sandhillsgolfshop.com
This Bill Coore/Ben Crenshaw links, a noteworthy post-World War II
design, takes full advantage of its sandy, rolling terrain.

Sand Ridge Golf Club
Chardon | 12150 Mayfield Rd. | OH | 440-285-8088 |
www.sandridgegolf.com
A modern classic amid aged beauties, this 1998 Tom Fazio design is
dotted with strategically deployed, white-sand bunkers.

PRIVATE COURSES

San Francisco Golf Club
San Francisco | Brotherhood Way & Junipero Sierra Blvd. | CA | 415-469-4100
A.W. Tillinghast designed this beauty that features massive cypresses and sensational bunkering, but nary a water hazard.

Scioto Country Club
Columbus | 2196 Riverside Dr. | OH | 614-486-4341 | www.sciotocc.com
Jack Nicklaus learned to play on this classic that's hosted the U.S. Open, Ryder Cup, PGA Championship and U.S. Senior Open.

Seminole Golf Club
Juno Beach | 901 Seminole Blvd. | FL | 561-626-1331
At a posh retreat, this Donald Ross gem challenges with sea grape bushes, palms, ocean breezes and nearly 200 bunkers.

Shinnecock Hills Golf Club
Southampton | 200 Tuckahoe Rd. | NY | 631-283-1310
Wedged between the Atlantic Ocean and Great Peconic Bay, this links was the site of the U.S. Open in 1986, 1995 and 2004.

Shoal Creek
Shoal Creek | 100 New Williamsburg Dr. | AL | 205-991-9000 | www.shoal-creek.com
The 1984 and 1990 PGA Championships were played on this Nicklaus course carved from dense forest.

Shoreacres
Lake Bluff | 1601 Shore Acres Rd. | IL | 847-234-1470
On Chicago's North Shore, this short but sweet 1921 Seth Raynor masterpiece offers several exciting shots over steep ravines.

Somerset Hills Country Club
Bernardsville | 180 Mine Mount Rd. | NJ | 908-766-0043
Near the USGA headquarters sits this A.W. Tillinghast design featuring a well-bunkered front nine and a heavily wooded back.

Southern Hills Country Club
Tulsa | 2636 E. 61st St. | OK | 918-492-3351 | www.southernhillscc.com
Host of the 2001 U.S. Open, this Perry Maxwell parklander with Bermuda rough and prairie wind will be a solid test during the 2007 PGA Championship.

Stanwich Club
Greenwich | 888 North St. | CT | 203-869-0555 | www.stanwich.com
Fast greens, large bunkers, multiple water hazards and double-dogleg par 5s make this 1962 design the state's toughest course.

Troon Golf & Country Club
Scottsdale | 25000 N. Windy Walk Dr. | AZ | 480-585-4310 | www.trooncc.com
This Weiskopf/Morrish debut is a desert target track sporting a 'Cliff' 14th amid boulders, with McDowell Mountain views.

Trump International Golf Club
West Palm Beach | 3505 Summit Blvd. | FL | 561-682-0700 |
www.trumpnational.com
The host to the LPGA's ADT Championship features risk/reward holes
designed by Jim Fazio, with input from The Donald himself.

Trump National Golf Club
Briarcliff Manor | 339 Pine Rd. | NY | 914-944-0900 |
www.trumpnational.com
A celebrity-laden membership enjoys this Jim Fazio/Donald Trump
design with a spectacular 'waterfall' par-3 13th.

Trump National Golf Club
Bedminster | 567 Lamington Rd. | NJ | 908-470-4400 |
www.trumpnational.com
Hewn from John DeLorean's former estate in rolling horse country is
this sleek, gull-winged Tom Fazio beauty.

Valhalla Golf Club
Louisville | 15503 Shelbyville Rd. | KY | 502-245-4475
This Kentucky thoroughbred's bluegrass rough and split fairways
hosted Tiger Woods' 2000 PGA Championship win.

Valley Club of Montecito
Santa Barbara | 1901 E. Valley Rd. | CA | 805-969-2215 | www.valleyclub.org
Amid sycamore and eucalyptus groves, this 1929 Alister MacKenzie
design offers stylish bunkering and superior par 3s.

Victoria National Golf Club
Newburgh | 2000 Victoria National Blvd. | IN | 812-858-8230 |
www.victorianational.com
Tom Fazio transformed an old strip mine into this gorgeous layout featuring lush mounding and small ponds.

Wade Hampton Golf Club
Cashiers | Hwy. 107 S. | NC | 828-743-5465 | www.wadehamptongc.com
In the Smoky Mountains, Tom Fazio's 1987 design winds through a
valley heavy with pines and crisscrossed by clear streams.

Wannamoisett Country Club
Rumford | 96 Hoyt Ave. | RI | 401-434-1200 |
www.wannamoisett.com
Donald Ross' rare par 69 is crammed into 104 acres yet still packs a
wallop with long, strong par 4s and speedy, undulating greens.

Whisper Rock Golf Club, Lower
Scottsdale | 32002 N. Old Bridge Rd. | AZ | 480-575-8700 |
www.whisperrockgolf.com
Lined in saguaro, prickly pear and ocotillo, Phil Mickelson's debut offers superb par 4s and risk/reward par 5s.

Winged Foot Golf Club, East
Mamaroneck | Fennimore Rd. | NY | 914-698-8400 | www.wfgc.org
West's shorter sister sports handsome par 3s and a tournament pedigree, including the inaugural U.S. Senior Open in 1980.

PRIVATE COURSES

Winged Foot Golf Club, West
Mamaroneck | Fennimore Rd. | NY | 914-698-8400 | www.wfgc.org
A.W. Tillinghast designed this five-time U.S. Open test with pear-shaped greens and deep bunkers on rolling parkland.

Yeamans Hall Club
Hanahan | 900 Yeamans Hall Rd. | SC | 843-744-5555
In 1998, Tom Doak restored this layout to its 1925 glory with huge square greens, yawning traps and aged oaks.

Urban Driving Ranges

Within a short ride from a major business district

Atlanta

Blue Heron Golf Club
Atlanta | 460 Morgan Falls Rd. | 770-390-0424 |
www.blueherongolfclub.com

Charlie Yates Golf Course
Atlanta | 10 Lakeside Village Dr. SE | 404-373-4655 |
www.charlieyatesgolfcourse.com

Boston

Boston Golf Driving Range at The Radisson Hotel
Boston | 200 Stuart St. | 617-457-2699 |
www.bostongolfacademy.com

City Golf Boston
Boston | 38 Bromfield St. | 617-357-4653 | www.citygolfboston.com

Chicago

Diversey Driving Range
Chicago | 141 W. Diversey Pkwy. | 312-742-7929 |
www.diverseygolf.com

Dallas

Hank Haney City Place Golf Center
Dallas | 3637 McKinney Ave. | 214-520-7275 |
www.hankhaney.com

North Texas Golf Center
Dallas | 2101 Walnut Hill Ln. | 972-247-4653 |
www.northtexasgolf.com

Denver

All Golf at Overland
Denver | 1801 S. Huron St. | 303-777-7331 | www.allgolf.com

Kennedy Golf Center
Denver | 10500 E. Hampden Ave. | 303-755-0105 | www.allgolf.com

Honolulu

Coral Creek Golf Club
Honolulu | 91111 Geiger Rd. | 808-441-4653 |
www.coralcreekgolfhawaii.com

Houston

Clear Creek Golf Club
Houston | 3902 Fellows Rd. | 713-738-8000 |
www.clearcreekgolfclub.com

Las Vegas

Badlands Golf Club
Las Vegas | 9119 Alta Dr. | 702-242-4653 | www.troongolf.com

Callaway Golf Center
Las Vegas | 6730 Las Vegas Blvd. S. | 702-896-4100

Los Angeles

Griffith Park Golf Courses
Los Angeles | 4900 Griffith Park Dr. | 323-663-2555 |
www.laparks.org

John Wells Golf Driving Range
Los Angeles | 11501 Strathern St. | 818-767-1954

Lakes at El Segundo, The
El Segundo | 400 S. Sepulveda Blvd. | 310-322-0202 |
www.premiergc.com

Rancho Park Golf Course
Rancho Park | 10460 W. Pico Blvd. | 310-838-7373 |
www.laparks.org

New York City

Alley Pond Golf Center
Queens | 232-01 Northern Blvd. | 718-225-9187 |
www.golfandsportsinfo.com

Brooklyn Golf Center
Brooklyn | 3200 Flatbush Ave. | 718-253-6816 |
www.brooklyngolfcenter.com

Chelsea Piers Golf Club
Manhattan | Pier 59 | 212-336-6400 | www.chelseapiers.com

Randall's Island Golf Center
Manhattan | 1 Randall's Island | 212-427-5689

Philadelphia

FDR Golf Club
Philadelphia | Pattison Ave. & 20th St. | 215-462-8997 |
www.golfphilly.com

Karakung at Cobb's Creek Golf Club
Philadelphia | 7200 Lansdowne Ave. | 215-877-8707 |
www.golfphilly.com

San Diego

Bonita Driving Range
San Diego | 3631 Bonita Rd. | 619-426-2069 | www.golfsd.com

Stadium Golf Center
San Diego | 29-90 Murphy Canyon Rd. | 858-277-6667 |
www.stadiumgolfcenter.com

Seattle

Interbay Golf Center
Seattle | 2501 15th Ave. W. | 206-285-2200 | www.seattlegolf.com

Jefferson Park Golf Course
Seattle | 4101 Beacon Ave. S. | 206-762-4513 | www.seattlegolf.com

Washington, DC

East Potomac Park Golf Course & Driving Range
Washington | 972 Ohio Dr. SW | 202-554-7660 | www.golfdc.com

INDEXES

Listings cover the best in each category, with names followed by nearest major city. ☑ indicates a place with the highest ratings, popularity and importance.

BUDGET

($50 and under)

Aldeen | *Rockford, IL*
Alvamar Public | *Kansas City, KS*
Baker Nat'l | *Minneapolis, MN*
Bear Trace/Harrison Bay | *Chattanooga, TN*
Bear Trace/Ross Creek | *Nashville, TN*
Bethpage, Blue | *Long Island, NY*
Bethpage, Green | *Long Island, NY*
NEW Big Fish | *Northern Wisconsin, WI*
Blue Hill | *NYC Metro, NY*
Bluffs | *Vermillion, SD*
Bretwood, North | *Keene, NH*
Buffalo Dunes | *Garden City, KS*
Buffalo Run | *Denver, CO*
NEW Bully Pulpit | *Bismarck, ND*
Canterbury Woods | *Concord, NH*
Capstone Club/Alabama | *Birmingham, AL*
Chenango Valley | *Finger Lakes, NY*
Chickasaw Pointe | *Durant, OK*
Classic Golf Club | *Tacoma, WA*
Cooks Creek | *Columbus, OH*
Draper Valley | *Roanoke, VA*
Druids Glen | *Seattle, WA*
Eagleglen | *Anchorage, AK*
Eaglesticks | *Columbus, OH*
Edinburgh USA | *Minneapolis, MN*
Forest Akers MSU, East | *Lansing, MI*
Forest Akers MSU, West | *Lansing, MI*
Gauntlet | *DC Metro Area, VA*
Gold Mountain, Cascade | *Bremerton, WA*
Granville | *Columbus, OH*
Gray Plantation | *Lake Charles, LA*
Greystone | *Finger Lakes, NY*
Heritage Bluffs | *Chicago, IL*
Heron Lakes, Great Blue | *Portland, OR*
Heron Lakes, Greenback | *Portland, OR*

Hidden Valley | *Pittsburgh, PA*
Indian Peaks | *Boulder, CO*
Jimmie Austin Univ./OK | *Oklahoma City, OK*
NEW King Carter | *Richmond, VA*
Lake Placid Resort, Mountain | *Adirondacks, NY*
Legacy Ridge | *Denver, CO*
Les Bolstad Univ./MN | *Minneapolis, MN*
Links/North Dakota | *Williston, ND*
Los Verdes | *Los Angeles, CA*
Lyman Orchards, Robert Trent Jones | *Hartford, CT*
Mariana Butte | *Boulder, CO*
Maumee Bay | *Toledo, OH*
NEW Mines | *Grand Rapids, MI*
Moors | *Panhandle, FL*
Murphy Creek | *Denver, CO*
Naga-Waukee | *Milwaukee, WI*
Northwood | *Northern Wisconsin, WI*
OGA Golf Course | *Portland, OR*
Olde Scotland Links | *Boston, MA*
Old Silo | *Lexington, KY*
Old Works | *Butte, MT*
Oxmoor Valley, Ridge | *Birmingham, AL*
Oxmoor Valley, Valley | *Birmingham, AL*
Pacific Grove | *Monterey Peninsula, CA*
Painted Dunes | *El Paso, TX*
Papago Municipal | *Phoenix, AZ*
Piñon Hills | *Farmington, NM*
Piper Glen | *Springfield, IL*
Poquoy Brook | *Boston, MA*
Prairie Highlands | *Kansas City, KS*
Rancho Park | *Los Angeles, CA*
Rawls/Texas Tech | *Lubbock, TX*
Reading Country Club | *Lancaster, PA*
☑ Riverdale, Dunes | *Denver, CO*
Rock Hollow | *Indianapolis, IN*
Saddle Rock | *Denver, CO*

Rawls/Texas Tech | *Lubbock, TX*

🟦 Red Sky, Norman | *Vail, CO*

Red Tail | *Worcester, MA*

Reserve Vineyards, South | *Portland, OR*

🆕 Reunion Resort, Independence | *Orlando, FL*

Ridge/Castle Pines N. | *Denver, CO*

Royal Kunia | *Oahu, HI*

Rustic Canyon | *Los Angeles, CA*

Saddle Creek | *Stockton, CA*

Sand Barrens | *Cape May, NJ*

🟦 Sea Island, Seaside | *Lowcountry, GA*

🟦 Shadow Creek | *Las Vegas, NV*

Shore Gate | *Atlantic City, NJ*

Southern Dunes | *Orlando, FL*

🟦 Spyglass Hill | *Monterey Peninsula, CA*

Talega | *Orange County, CA*

Talking Stick, North | *Scottsdale, AZ*

Tanglewood Park, Championship | *Winston-Salem, NC*

🟦 TPC Sawgrass, Stadium | *Jacksonville, FL*

TPC Tampa Bay | *Tampa, FL*

Troon North, Pinnacle | *Scottsdale, AZ*

🆕 Trump Nat'l | *Los Angeles, CA*

🟦 Twisted Dune | *Atlantic City, NJ*

Venetian Golf | *Sarasota, FL*

Victoria Hills | *Daytona Beach, FL*

Walt Disney World, Magnolia | *Orlando, FL*

Wente Vineyards | *San Francisco Bay Area, CA*

Westin Innisbrook, Copperhead | *Tampa, FL*

🟦 Whistling Straits, Irish | *Kohler, WI*

🆕 Windswept Dunes | *Panhandle, FL*

Wintonbury Hills | *Hartford, CT*

🟦 World Woods, Pine Barrens | *Tampa, FL*

CELEBRITY DESIGNS

ARNOLD PALMER
Bluffs | *Baton Rouge, LA*

Bog | *Milwaukee, WI*

Bridges/Hollywood Casino | *Gulfport, MS*

Carolina Club | *Pinehurst, NC*

Cherokee Run | *Atlanta, GA*

🆕 Classic Club | *Palm Springs, CA*

Craft Farms, Cotton Creek | *Mobile, AL*

Geneva Nat'l, Palmer | *Lake Geneva, WI*

Gillette Ridge | *Hartford, CT*

Kapalua, Bay | *Maui, HI*

Keswick Club | *Charlottesville, VA*

Kingsmill, Plantation | *Williamsburg, VA*

Legacy/Lakewood Ranch | *Sarasota, FL*

Marriott's Wildfire, Palmer Signature | *Phoenix, AZ*

Mauna Kea, Hapuna | *Big Island, HI*

Myrtle Beach Nat'l, King's North | *Myrtle Beach, SC*

Myrtle Beach Nat'l, SouthCreek | *Myrtle Beach, SC*

Oasis, Palmer | *Las Vegas, NV*

Orange Lake, Legends | *Orlando, FL*

Osage Nat'l | *Lake of the Ozarks, MO*

PGA Nat'l, General | *Palm Beach, FL*

Resort Semiahmoo, Semiahmoo Course | *Vancouver Area, WA*

🆕 Reunion Resort, Legacy | *Orlando, FL*

Running Y Ranch | *Klamath Falls, OR*

Shanty Creek, The Legend | *Traverse City, MI*

🆕 SilverRock Resort, Arnold Palmer Classic | *Palm Springs, CA*

Spencer T. Olin | *St. Louis Area, IL*

Starr Pass | *Tucson, AZ*

Stonewall Resort, Palmer | *Weston, WV*

🆕 Suncadia Inn, Prospector | *Seattle, WA*

Turtle Bay, Arnold Palmer | *Oahu, HI*

World Golf Village, King & Bear | *Jacksonville, FL*

ARTHUR HILLS
Bay Harbor | *Petoskey, MI*

Black Gold | *Orange County, CA*

Grand Cypress, New | *Orlando, FL*

Grand Traverse, The Bear | *Traverse City, MI*

Z Hualalai | *Big Island, HI*

Kauai Lagoons, Kiele | *Kauai, HI*

Kauai Lagoons, Mokihana | *Kauai, HI*

Kiawah Island, Turtle Point | *Charleston, SC*

La Cantera, Palmer | *San Antonio, TX*

La Paloma | *Tucson, AZ*

Long Bay | *Myrtle Beach, SC*

Mansion Ridge | *NYC Metro, NY*

May River/Palmetto Bluff | *Hilton Head, SC*

Nicklaus/Birch River | *Atlanta, GA*

NEW North Palm Beach Club, Jack Nicklaus Signature | *Palm Beach, FL*

Z Ocean Hammock | *Daytona Beach, FL*

NEW Old Greenwood | *Lake Tahoe, CA*

Old Works | *Butte, MT*

Pawleys Plantation | *Pawleys Island, SC*

Reflection Bay/Lake Las Vegas | *Las Vegas, NV*

Z Reynolds, Great Waters | *Lake Oconee, GA*

Rocky Gap Lodge | *Cumberland, MD*

Stonewolf | *St. Louis Area, IL*

World Golf Village, King & Bear | *Jacksonville, FL*

PETE DYE

Amelia Island, Oak Marsh | *Jacksonville, FL*

Amelia Island, Ocean Links | *Jacksonville, FL*

ASU Karsten | *Phoenix, AZ*

Avalon Lakes | *Cleveland, OH*

Barefoot, Dye | *Myrtle Beach, SC*

NEW Big Fish | *Northern Wisconsin, WI*

Z Blackwolf Run, Meadow Valleys | *Kohler, WI*

Z Blackwolf Run, River | *Kohler, WI*

Brickyard Crossing | *Indianapolis, IN*

Z Bulle Rock | *Baltimore, MD*

Fort | *Indianapolis, IN*

Fowler's Mill | *Cleveland, OH*

Grand Geneva, Highlands | *Lake Geneva, WI*

Z Kiawah Island, Ocean | *Charleston, SC*

Kingsmill, River | *Williamsburg, VA*

La Quinta, Dunes | *Palm Springs, CA*

La Quinta, Mountain | *Palm Springs, CA*

Las Vegas Paiute, Snow Mountain | *Las Vegas, NV*

Las Vegas Paiute, Sun Mountain | *Las Vegas, NV*

Las Vegas Paiute, Wolf | *Las Vegas, NV*

Lost Canyons, Shadow | *Los Angeles, CA*

Lost Canyons, Sky | *Los Angeles, CA*

Luana Hills | *Oahu, HI*

Nemacolin Woodlands, Mystic Rock | *Pittsburgh, PA*

Pete Dye/Virginia Tech | *Roanoke, VA*

PGA Golf Club, Dye | *Port St. Lucie, FL*

Z PGA West, TPC Stadium | *Palm Springs, CA*

Pinehills, Nicklaus | *Boston, MA*

Z Riverdale, Dunes | *Denver, CO*

Ruffled Feathers | *Chicago, IL*

Rum Pointe | *Ocean City, MD*

Z Sea Pines, Harbour Town Golf Links | *Hilton Head, SC*

TPC Louisiana | *New Orleans, LA*

Z TPC Sawgrass, Stadium | *Jacksonville, FL*

TPC Sawgrass, Valley | *Jacksonville, FL*

Walt Disney World, Eagle Pines | *Orlando, FL*

Westin Mission, Pete Dye | *Palm Springs, CA*

Z Whistling Straits, Irish | *Kohler, WI*

Z Whistling Straits, Straits | *Kohler, WI*

Wintonbury Hills | *Hartford, CT*

Waikoloa Beach, Beach | *Big Island, HI*

Wailea, Emerald | *Maui, HI*

Wailea, Gold | *Maui, HI*

ROBERT TRENT JONES SR.

Boyne Highlands, Heather | *Petoskey, MI*

Bristol Harbour | *Finger Lakes, NY*

Broadmoor, East | *Colorado Springs, CO*

Broadmoor, West | *Colorado Springs, CO*

Z Cambrian Ridge | *Montgomery, AL*

Capitol Hill, Judge | *Montgomery, AL*

Capitol Hill, Legislator | *Montgomery, AL*

Capitol Hill, Senator | *Montgomery, AL*

Carambola | *St. Croix, USVI*

Celebration | *Orlando, FL*

Z Crumpin-Fox | *Berkshires, MA*

Dorado Beach Resort, East | *Dorado, PR*

Dorado Beach Resort, West | *Dorado, PR*

Duke Univ. Golf | *Raleigh-Durham, NC*

Dunes Golf & Beach | *Myrtle Beach, SC*

Z Golden Horseshoe, Gold | *Williamsburg, VA*

Grand Nat'l, Lake | *Auburn, AL*

Z Grand Nat'l, Links | *Auburn, AL*

Hampton Cove, Highlands | *Huntsville, AL*

Hampton Cove, River | *Huntsville, AL*

Homestead, Lower Cascades | *Roanoke, VA*

Hominy Hill | *Freehold, NJ*

Horseshoe Bay, Applerock | *Austin, TX*

Horseshoe Bay, Ram Rock | *Austin, TX*

Horseshoe Bay, Slick Rock | *Austin, TX*

Lely, Flamingo Island | *Naples, FL*

Lodge/Four Seasons, Witch's Cove | *Lake of the Ozarks, MO*

Lyman Orchards, Robert Trent Jones | *Hartford, CT*

Mauna Kea, Mauna Kea Course | *Big Island, HI*

Z Montauk Downs | *Long Island, NY*

Otter Creek | *Indianapolis, IN*

Oxmoor Valley, Ridge | *Birmingham, AL*

Oxmoor Valley, Valley | *Birmingham, AL*

Palmetto Dunes, Robert Trent Jones | *Hilton Head, SC*

Portsmouth Country Club | *Portsmouth, NH*

NEW Ross Bridge | *Birmingham, AL*

SCGA Golf | *San Diego, CA*

Seven Oaks | *Finger Lakes, NY*

Silver Lakes | *Birmingham, AL*

Z Spyglass Hill | *Monterey Peninsula, CA*

Sugarbush | *Northern Vermont, VT*

Tanglewood Park, Championship | *Winston-Salem, NC*

Tanglewood Park, Reynolds | *Winston-Salem, NC*

Treetops, Robert Trent Jones Masterpiece | *Gaylord, MI*

Wigwam, Gold | *Phoenix, AZ*

Woodstock Country Club | *Southern Vermont, VT*

TOM FAZIO

Amelia Island, Long Point | *Jacksonville, FL*

Barefoot, Fazio | *Myrtle Beach, SC*

Z Barton Creek, Fazio Canyons | *Austin, TX*

Barton Creek, Fazio Foothills | *Austin, TX*

NEW Beau Rivage Resort, Fallen Oak | *Gulfport, MS*

Belterra | *Cincinnati Area, IN*

Z Branson Creek | *Springfield, MO*

Camp Creek | *Panhandle, FL*

Cordillera, Valley | *Vail, CO*

Dancing Rabbit, Azaleas | *Jackson, MS*

Dancing Rabbit, Oaks | *Jackson, MS*

Frog at The Georgian | *Atlanta, GA*

Glen Club | *Chicago, IL*

Grayhawk, Raptor | *Scottsdale, AZ*

Karsten Creek | *Stillwater, OK*

Kiawah Island, Osprey Point | *Charleston, SC*

Mahogany Run | *St. Thomas, USVI*

Missouri Bluffs | *St. Louis, MO*

Oak Creek | *Orange County, CA*

Oyster Bay Town Golf | *Long Island, NY*

PGA Golf Club, Ryder | *Port St. Lucie, FL*

PGA Golf Club, Wanamaker | *Port St. Lucie, FL*

PGA Nat'l, Champion | *Palm Beach, FL*

PGA Nat'l, Haig | *Palm Beach, FL*

PGA Nat'l, Squire | *Palm Beach, FL*

🄩 Pine Hill | *Camden, NJ*

Pinehurst, No. 4 | *Pinehurst, NC*

Pinehurst, No. 6 | *Pinehurst, NC*

🄩 Pinehurst, No. 8 | *Pinehurst, NC*

Porters Neck | *Myrtle Beach Area, NC*

Primm Valley, Desert | *Las Vegas, NV*

Primm Valley, Lakes | *Las Vegas, NV*

🄩 Red Sky, Fazio | *Vail, CO*

Reynolds | *Lake Oconee, GA*

NEW Ritz-Carlton Members Club | *Sarasota, FL*

Sawmill Creek | *Cleveland, OH*

🄩 Sea Island, Seaside | *Lowcountry, GA*

🄩 Shadow Creek | *Las Vegas, NV*

TPC Myrtle Beach | *Myrtle Beach, SC*

Treetops, Tom Fazio Premier | *Gaylord, MI*

Turning Stone, Atunyote | *Finger Lakes, NY*

Ventana Canyon, Canyon | *Tucson, AZ*

Ventana Canyon, Mountain | *Tucson, AZ*

Walt Disney World, Osprey Ridge | *Orlando, FL*

Westin Rio Mar, Ocean | *Rio Grande, PR*

Westin Stonebriar, Fazio | *Dallas, TX*

Wild Dunes, Harbor | *Charleston, SC*

Wild Dunes, Links | *Charleston, SC*

🄩 World Woods, Pine Barrens | *Tampa, FL*

World Woods, Rolling Oaks | *Tampa, FL*

Wynn Las Vegas | *Las Vegas, NV*

TOM WEISKOPF/ JAY MORRISH

Buffalo Creek | *Dallas, TX*

Daufuskie Island, Bloody Point | *Hilton Head, SC*

Harbor Club | *Lake Oconee, GA*

La Cantera, Resort | *San Antonio, TX*

TPC Scottsdale, Stadium | *Scottsdale, AZ*

🄩 Troon North, Monument | *Scottsdale, AZ*

Troon North, Pinnacle | *Scottsdale, AZ*

Waikoloa Beach, Kings' | *Big Island, HI*

Wilds | *Minneapolis, MN*

CONDITIONING

Arnold Palmer/Bay Hill | *Orlando, FL*

Augustine | *DC Metro Area, VA*

🄩 Aviara | *San Diego, CA*

🄩 Bandon Dunes, Bandon Dunes Course | *Coos Bay, OR*

🄩 Bandon Dunes, Pacific Dunes | *Coos Bay, OR*

Barton Creek, Fazio Foothills | *Austin, TX*

Baywood Greens | *Rehoboth Beach, DE*

Bear's Best Vegas | *Las Vegas, NV*

🄩 Belgrade Lakes | *Central Maine, ME*

🄩 Bethpage, Black | *Long Island, NY*

🄩 Blackwolf Run, River | *Kohler, WI*

Boulders, North | *Phoenix, AZ*

Boulders, South | *Phoenix, AZ*

Broadmoor, East | *Colorado Springs, CO*

Broadmoor, West | *Colorado Springs, CO*

Z Bulle Rock | *Baltimore, MD*

Z Caledonia Golf & Fish | *Pawleys Island, SC*

Z Cascata | *Las Vegas, NV*

Z Challenge/Manele | *Lanai, HI*

Z Coeur d'Alene | *Coeur d'Alene, ID*

CordeValle | *San Francisco Bay Area, CA*

Z Crystal Springs, Ballyowen | *NYC Metro, NJ*

Desert Willow, Firecliff | *Palm Springs, CA*

Duke Univ. Golf | *Raleigh-Durham, NC*

Edgewood Tahoe | *Reno, NV*

Frog at The Georgian | *Atlanta, GA*

Gleneagles/Equinox | *Southern Vermont, VT*

Z Gold Canyon, Dinosaur Mountain | *Phoenix, AZ*

Z Golden Horseshoe, Gold | *Williamsburg, VA*

Grand Cypress | *Orlando, FL*

Grand Cypress, New | *Orlando, FL*

Z Greenbrier, Old White | *White Sulphur Springs, WV*

Z Homestead, Cascades | *Roanoke, VA*

Karsten Creek | *Stillwater, OK*

Kauai Lagoons, Kiele | *Kauai, HI*

Z Kiawah Island, Ocean | *Charleston, SC*

Z Kiva Dunes | *Mobile, AL*

Z NEW Lake of Isles, North | *New London, CT*

NEW Lansdowne, Norman | *Leesburg, VA*

Las Vegas Paiute, Snow Mountain | *Las Vegas, NV*

Las Vegas Paiute, Sun Mountain | *Las Vegas, NV*

Leatherstocking | *Albany, NY*

Legend Trail | *Scottsdale, AZ*

Little Mountain | *Cleveland, OH*

Z Longaberger | *Columbus, OH*

Maderas | *San Diego, CA*

Mauna Kea, Mauna Kea Course | *Big Island, HI*

Mauna Lani, North | *Big Island, HI*

Mauna Lani, South | *Big Island, HI*

Nemacolin Woodlands, Mystic Rock | *Pittsburgh, PA*

Oak Valley | *San Bernardino, CA*

Ocean Ridge, Tiger's Eye | *Myrtle Beach Area, NC*

NEW Old Greenwood | *Lake Tahoe, CA*

Z Old Kinderhook | *Lake of the Ozarks, MO*

Orchards | *Detroit, MI*

Orchard Valley | *Chicago, IL*

PGA West, Jack Nicklaus Tournament | *Palm Springs, CA*

Z PGA West, TPC Stadium | *Palm Springs, CA*

Phoenician | *Scottsdale, AZ*

Z Pine Hill | *Camden, NJ*

Pinehills, Jones | *Boston, MA*

Z Pinehurst, No. 2 | *Pinehurst, NC*

Pinehurst, No. 4 | *Pinehurst, NC*

Z Pinehurst, No. 8 | *Pinehurst, NC*

Pine Needles Lodge, Pine Needles | *Pinehurst, NC*

Z Poppy Hills | *Monterey Peninsula, CA*

Primm Valley, Lakes | *Las Vegas, NV*

Z Pumpkin Ridge, Ghost Creek | *Portland, OR*

Raspberry Falls | *Leesburg, VA*

Z Red Sky, Fazio | *Vail, CO*

Resort Semiahmoo, Loomis Trail | *Vancouver Area, WA*

Z Reynolds, Great Waters | *Lake Oconee, GA*

Ridge/Castle Pines N. | *Denver, CO*

NEW Ritz-Carlton Members Club | *Sarasota, FL*

Ritz-Carlton Orlando | *Orlando, FL*

Rock Hill | *Long Island, NY*

Sagamore | *Adirondacks, NY*

Sand Barrens | *Cape May, NJ*

Z Sea Island, Plantation | *Lowcountry, GA*

Z Sea Island, Seaside | *Lowcountry, GA*

Z Shadow Creek | *Las Vegas, NV*

Z Spyglass Hill | *Monterey Peninsula, CA*

Stonewall | *Leesburg, VA*

StoneWater | *Cleveland, OH*

Sunriver, Crosswater | *Bend, OR*
🔲 Taconic | *Berkshires, MA*
ThunderHawk | *Chicago, IL*
Tiburón, Black | *Naples, FL*
Tidewater | *Myrtle Beach, SC*
TPC Myrtle Beach | *Myrtle Beach, SC*
🔲 TPC Sawgrass, Stadium | *Jacksonville, FL*
TPC Sawgrass, Valley | *Jacksonville, FL*
Treetops, Robert Trent Jones Masterpiece | *Gaylord, MI*
🔲 Troon North, Monument | *Scottsdale, AZ*
Troon North, Pinnacle | *Scottsdale, AZ*
NEW Trump Nat'l | *Los Angeles, CA*
Turning Stone, Kaluhyat | *Finger Lakes, NY*
Vistoso | *Tucson, AZ*
Wailea, Gold | *Maui, HI*
Walt Disney World, Osprey Ridge | *Orlando, FL*
🔲 We-Ko-Pa, Cholla | *Scottsdale, AZ*
🔲 Whistling Straits, Straits | *Kohler, WI*
Whitehawk Ranch | *Lake Tahoe, CA*
Wintonbury Hills | *Hartford, CT*
🔲 Wolf Creek | *Las Vegas, NV*
World Golf Village, Slammer & Squire | *Jacksonville, FL*
🔲 World Woods, Pine Barrens | *Tampa, FL*
World Woods, Rolling Oaks | *Tampa, FL*
Wynn Las Vegas | *Las Vegas, NV*

EASIEST

(Courses with the lowest slope ratings from the back tees)
🔲 Coeur d'Alene | *Coeur d'Alene, ID*
Forest Akers MSU, East | *Lansing, MI*
Gold Mountain, Cascade | *Bremerton, WA*
Los Verdes | *Los Angeles, CA*
Mt. Mitchell | *Asheville, NC*
Pacific Grove | *Monterey Peninsula, CA*

Peninsula Golf | *Mobile, AL*
Pinehurst, No. 1 | *Pinehurst, NC*
Pinehurst, No. 3 | *Pinehurst, NC*
Schaumburg | *Chicago, IL*
Windham | *Catskills, NY*

ENVIRONMENTALLY FRIENDLY

(As certified by Audubon International)
Aldeen | *Rockford, IL*
Amana Colonies | *Cedar Rapids, IA*
Amelia Island | *Jacksonville, FL*
Augustine | *DC Metro Area, VA*
Baker Nat'l | *Minneapolis, MN*
Barona Creek | *San Diego, CA*
Barton Creek | *Austin, TX*
Beaver Creek | *Vail, CO*
Bethpage | *Long Island, NY*
Birdwood | *Charlottesville, VA*
Black Butte Ranch | *Bend, OR*
Black Lake | *Gaylord, MI*
Blue Heron Pines | *Atlantic City, NJ*
Breckenridge | *Vail, CO*
Brickyard Crossing | *Indianapolis, IN*
Bridges/Hollywood Casino | *Gulfport, MS*
Broadmoor | *Colorado Springs, CO*
NEW Callippe Preserve | *San Francisco Bay Area, CA*
Camp Creek | *Panhandle, FL*
Cantigny | *Chicago, IL*
Carolina Nat'l | *Myrtle Beach Area, NC*
Classic Golf Club | *Tacoma, WA*
Colbert Hills | *Topeka, KS*
Cordillera | *Vail, CO*
Coyote Moon | *Lake Tahoe, CA*
Crandon | *Miami, FL*
Crystal Springs | *NYC Metro, NJ*
Currituck | *Outer Banks, NC*
Eagle's Landing | *Ocean City, MD*
Fire Ridge | *Milwaukee, WI*
Fowler's Mill | *Cleveland, OH*
Fox Hollow/Lakewood | *Denver, CO*
Glen Annie | *Santa Barbara, CA*
Golden Horseshoe | *Williamsburg, VA*
Greenbrier | *White Sulphur Springs, WV*
Green Valley Ranch | *Denver, CO*

Harbor Pines | *Atlantic City, NJ*
Heritage Bluffs | *Chicago, IL*
Hermitage | *Nashville, TN*
Heron Lakes | *Portland, OR*
Hyatt Hill Country | *San Antonio, TX*
Jackson Hole Golf | *Jackson, WY*
Kapalua | *Maui, HI*
Keswick Club | *Charlottesville, VA*
Keystone Ranch | *Vail, CO*
Kiawah Island | *Charleston, SC*
Kingsmill | *Williamsburg, VA*
La Cantera | *San Antonio, TX*
La Quinta | *Palm Springs, CA*
Leatherstocking | *Albany, NY*
Longaberger | *Columbus, OH*
McCormick Woods |
    Bremerton, WA
Murphy Creek | *Denver, CO*
Newport National | *Newport, RI*
OGA Golf Course | *Portland, OR*
Olde Scotland Links | *Boston, MA*
NEW Old Greenwood | *Lake
    Tahoe, CA*
Palmetto Hall | *Hilton Head, SC*
Pasatiempo | *Santa Cruz, CA*
Pebble Beach | *Monterey
    Peninsula, CA*
PGA Golf Club | *Port St. Lucie, FL*
PGA of So. Cal. | *San Bernardino, CA*
Pinehurst | *Pinehurst, NC*
Port Ludlow | *Bremerton, WA*
Powder Horn | *Sheridan, WY*
Prairie Landing | *Chicago, IL*
Presidio | *San Francisco Bay Area, CA*
Pumpkin Ridge | *Portland, OR*
Red Hawk Run | *Toledo, OH*
Red Tail | *Worcester, MA*
Regatta Bay | *Panhandle, FL*
Resort Semiahmoo | *Vancouver
    Area, WA*
Reynolds | *Lake Oconee, GA*
Ridge/Castle Pines N. | *Denver, CO*
Robinson Ranch | *Los Angeles, CA*
Running Y Ranch | *Klamath Falls, OR*
Saddle Rock | *Denver, CO*
Salishan | *Central Coast, OR*
Sanctuary/Westworld |
    Scottsdale, AZ
Sea Pines | *Hilton Head, SC*
Shaker Hills | *Worcester, MA*

Shennecossett | *New London, CT*
Sonnenalp | *Vail, CO*
Spanish Bay | *Monterey
    Peninsula, CA*
Spyglass Hill | *Monterey
    Peninsula, CA*
Stevinson Ranch | *Stockton, CA*
St. James | *Myrtle Beach Area, NC*
Stonewall Resort | *Weston, WV*
ThunderHawk | *Chicago, IL*
Tiburón | *Naples, FL*
Timbers at Troy | *Baltimore, MD*
TPC Canyons | *Las Vegas, NV*
TPC Deere Run | *Moline, IL*
TPC Heron Bay | *Ft. Lauderdale, FL*
TPC Myrtle Beach | *Myrtle
    Beach, SC*
TPC Sawgrass | *Jacksonville, FL*
TPC Scottsdale | *Scottsdale, AZ*
TPC Tampa Bay | *Tampa, FL*
Troon North | *Scottsdale, AZ*
Turning Stone | *Finger Lakes, NY*
Univ. of MD Golf | *DC Metro
    Area, MD*
Venetian Golf | *Sarasota, FL*
Walt Disney World | *Orlando, FL*
Wilderness/Fortune Bay |
    Duluth, MN
Wintonbury Hills | *Hartford, CT*

EXCEPTIONAL CLUBHOUSES

Amelia Island | *Jacksonville, FL*
Arcadia Bluffs | *Traverse City, MI*
Arnold Palmer/Bay Hill | *Orlando, FL*
Barefoot Resort | *Myrtle Beach, SC*
Bear's Best Vegas | *Las Vegas, NV*
Big Creek | *Mt. Home, AR*
Blackwolf Run | *Kohler, WI*
Boca Raton Resort | *Palm Beach, FL*
Boulders | *Phoenix, AZ*
Breakers | *Palm Beach, FL*
Broadmoor | *Colorado Springs, CO*
Caledonia Golf & Fish | *Pawleys
    Island, SC*
Camelback | *Scottsdale, AZ*
Carter Plantation | *Baton Rouge, LA*
Cascata | *Las Vegas, NV*
ChampionsGate | *Orlando, FL*
CordeValle | *San Francisco Bay
    Area, CA*

Desert Willow | *Palm Springs, CA*
Doral | *Miami, FL*
Edinburgh USA | *Minneapolis, MN*
Elk Ridge | *Gaylord, MI*
Falls/Lake Las Vegas | *Las Vegas, NV*
Fox Hopyard | *East Haddam, CT*
Glen Club | *Chicago, IL*
Golf Club/Newcastle | *Seattle, WA*
Grand Cypress | *Orlando, FL*
Grayhawk | *Scottsdale, AZ*
Great River | *New Haven, CT*
Greystone | *Baltimore, MD*
Harvester | *Des Moines, IA*
Heritage Club | *Pawleys Island, SC*
Keswick Club | *Charlottesville, VA*
Kiawah Island | *Charleston, SC*
Kierland | *Scottsdale, AZ*
Kingsmill | *Williamsburg, VA*
La Costa | *San Diego, CA*
La Quinta | *Palm Springs, CA*
Las Vegas Paiute | *Las Vegas, NV*
Legends Club | *Minneapolis, MN*
Lost Canyons | *Los Angeles, CA*
Maderas | *San Diego, CA*
Marriott Desert Springs | *Palm Springs, CA*
Myrtle Beach Nat'l | *Myrtle Beach, SC*
Ojai Valley Inn | *Los Angeles, CA*
Olde Stonewall | *Pittsburgh, PA*
Pebble Beach | *Monterey Peninsula, CA*
PGA Nat'l | *Palm Beach, FL*
Phoenician | *Scottsdale, AZ*
Pine Hill | *Camden, NJ*
Poppy Hills | *Monterey Peninsula, CA*
Ranch | *Springfield, MA*
Red Hawk | *Bay City, MI*
Red Sky | *Vail, CO*
Resort Semiahmoo | *Vancouver Area, WA*
Reynolds | *Lake Oconee, GA*
Ridge/Castle Pines N. | *Denver, CO*
Sea Island | *Lowcountry, GA*
Seaview Marriott | *Atlantic City, NJ*
Shadow Creek | *Las Vegas, NV*
NEW Soldier Hollow | *Salt Lake City, UT*
Spanish Bay | *Monterey Peninsula, CA*

StoneWater | *Cleveland, OH*
Talking Stick | *Scottsdale, AZ*
Tiburón | *Naples, FL*
TPC Heron Bay | *Ft. Lauderdale, FL*
TPC Sawgrass | *Jacksonville, FL*
TPC Scottsdale | *Scottsdale, AZ*
Tribute | *Dallas, TX*
Troon North | *Scottsdale, AZ*
NEW Trump Nat'l | *Los Angeles, CA*
Turning Stone | *Finger Lakes, NY*
Walt Disney World | *Orlando, FL*
We-Ko-Pa | *Scottsdale, AZ*
Whirlwind | *Phoenix, AZ*
World Golf Village | *Jacksonville, FL*

EXPENSE ACCOUNT
($200 and over)
Arnold Palmer/Bay Hill | *Orlando, FL*
Atlantic City Country Club | *Atlantic City, NJ*
Z Aviara | *San Diego, CA*
Bali Hai | *Las Vegas, NV*
Z Bandon Dunes, Bandon Dunes Course | *Coos Bay, OR*
Z Bandon Dunes, Bandon Trails | *Coos Bay, OR*
Z Bandon Dunes, Pacific Dunes | *Coos Bay, OR*
Z Barton Creek, Fazio Canyons | *Austin, TX*
Barton Creek, Fazio Foothills | *Austin, TX*
Bear's Best Vegas | *Las Vegas, NV*
NEW Beau Rivage Resort, Fallen Oak | *Gulfport, MS*
Boulders, North | *Phoenix, AZ*
Boulders, South | *Phoenix, AZ*
Z Cascata | *Las Vegas, NV*
Z Challenge/Manele | *Lanai, HI*
Z Coeur d'Alene | *Coeur d'Alene, ID*
CordeValle | *San Francisco Bay Area, CA*
Cordillera, Mountain | *Vail, CO*
Cordillera, Summit | *Vail, CO*
Cordillera, Valley | *Vail, CO*
Z Doral, Blue Monster | *Miami, FL*
Doral, Gold | *Miami, FL*
Doral, Great White | *Miami, FL*
Edgewood Tahoe | *Reno, NV*
Experience/Koele | *Lanai, HI*

Falls/Lake Las Vegas | *Las Vegas, NV*

Grand Cypress | *Orlando, FL*

Grand Cypress, New | *Orlando, FL*

Grayhawk, Raptor | *Scottsdale, AZ*

Grayhawk, Talon | *Scottsdale, AZ*

☑ Homestead, Cascades | *Roanoke, VA*

Kapalua, Bay | *Maui, HI*

☑ Kapalua, Plantation | *Maui, HI*

Karsten Creek | *Stillwater, OK*

Kiawah Island, Cougar Point | *Charleston, SC*

☑ Kiawah Island, Ocean | *Charleston, SC*

Kiawah Island, Osprey Point | *Charleston, SC*

Kiawah Island, Turtle Point | *Charleston, SC*

La Costa, North | *San Diego, CA*

La Costa, South | *San Diego, CA*

La Paloma | *Tucson, AZ*

Las Vegas Paiute, Wolf | *Las Vegas, NV*

Marriott's Wildfire, Faldo Championship | *Phoenix, AZ*

Marriott's Wildfire, Palmer Signature | *Phoenix, AZ*

Mauna Kea, Mauna Kea Course | *Big Island, HI*

Mauna Lani, North | *Big Island, HI*

Mauna Lani, South | *Big Island, HI*

May River/Palmetto Bluff | *Hilton Head, SC*

Monarch Beach | *Orange County, CA*

☑ Ocean Hammock | *Daytona Beach, FL*

Palos Verdes Golf | *Los Angeles, CA*

☑ Pebble Beach | *Monterey Peninsula, CA*

PGA Nat'l, Champion | *Palm Beach, FL*

PGA Nat'l, General | *Palm Beach, FL*

PGA Nat'l, Haig | *Palm Beach, FL*

PGA Nat'l, Squire | *Palm Beach, FL*

PGA West, Jack Nicklaus Tournament | *Palm Springs, CA*

☑ PGA West, TPC Stadium | *Palm Springs, CA*

☑ Pinehurst, No. 2 | *Pinehurst, NC*

Pinehurst, No. 4 | *Pinehurst, NC*

Pinehurst, No. 6 | *Pinehurst, NC*

Pinehurst, No. 7 | *Pinehurst, NC*

☑ Pinehurst, No. 8 | *Pinehurst, NC*

Pine Needles Lodge, Pine Needles | *Pinehurst, NC*

Quail Lodge | *Monterey Peninsula, CA*

☑ Red Sky, Fazio | *Vail, CO*

☑ Red Sky, Norman | *Vail, CO*

Reflection Bay/Lake Las Vegas | *Las Vegas, NV*

Revere, Lexington | *Las Vegas, NV*

☑ Reynolds, Great Waters | *Lake Oconee, GA*

☑ Reynolds, Oconee | *Lake Oconee, GA*

Rio Secco | *Las Vegas, NV*

NEW Ritz-Carlton Members Club | *Sarasota, FL*

Ritz-Carlton Orlando | *Orlando, FL*

Royal Links | *Las Vegas, NV*

☑ Sea Island, Plantation | *Lowcountry, GA*

Sea Island, Retreat | *Lowcountry, GA*

☑ Sea Island, Seaside | *Lowcountry, GA*

☑ Sea Pines, Harbour Town Golf Links | *Hilton Head, SC*

☑ Shadow Creek | *Las Vegas, NV*

☑ Spanish Bay | *Monterey Peninsula, CA*

☑ Spyglass Hill | *Monterey Peninsula, CA*

Tiburón, Black | *Naples, FL*

Tiburón, Gold | *Naples, FL*

☑ TPC Sawgrass, Stadium | *Jacksonville, FL*

TPC Scottsdale, Stadium | *Scottsdale, AZ*

☑ Troon North, Monument | *Scottsdale, AZ*

Troon North, Pinnacle | *Scottsdale, AZ*

NEW Trump Nat'l | *Los Angeles, CA*

Turning Stone, Atunyote | *Finger Lakes, NY*

Ventana Canyon, Canyon | *Tucson, AZ*

Ventana Canyon, Mountain | *Tucson, AZ*

Westin Innisbrook, Copperhead | *Tampa, FL*

Westin Innisbrook, Island | *Tampa, FL*

☑ Whistling Straits, Straits | *Kohler, WI*

Wynn Las Vegas | *Las Vegas, NV*

FINE FOOD TOO

Arizona Biltmore | *Phoenix, AZ*

Arroyo Trabuco | *Orange County, CA*

Aviara | *San Diego, CA*

Bali Hai | *Las Vegas, NV*

Balsams | *Colebrook, NH*

Bandon Dunes | *Coos Bay, OR*

Barnsley Gardens | *Atlanta, GA*

Big Creek | *Mt. Home, AR*

Biltmore | *Miami, FL*

Blackwolf Run | *Kohler, WI*

Boca Raton Resort | *Palm Beach, FL*

Boulders | *Phoenix, AZ*

Breakers | *Palm Beach, FL*

Broadmoor | *Colorado Springs, CO*

Caledonia Golf & Fish | *Pawleys Island, SC*

Camelback | *Scottsdale, AZ*

Cascata | *Las Vegas, NV*

Château Élan | *Atlanta, GA*

CordeValle | *San Francisco Bay Area, CA*

Cordillera | *Vail, CO*

Eagle Ridge | *Freehold, NJ*

Edgewood Tahoe | *Reno, NV*

Farm Neck | *Martha's Vineyard, MA*

Four Seasons/Las Colinas | *Dallas, TX*

Fox Hopyard | *East Haddam, CT*

Geneva Nat'l | *Lake Geneva, WI*

Grand Cypress | *Orlando, FL*

Grayhawk | *Scottsdale, AZ*

Great River | *New Haven, CT*

Greenbrier | *White Sulphur Springs, WV*

Half Moon Bay | *San Francisco Bay Area, CA*

Harvester | *Des Moines, IA*

Homestead | *Roanoke, VA*

Keswick Club | *Charlottesville, VA*

Keystone Ranch | *Vail, CO*

Kiawah Island | *Charleston, SC*

La Costa | *San Diego, CA*

La Paloma | *Tucson, AZ*

La Quinta | *Palm Springs, CA*

Legends Club | *Minneapolis, MN*

Lely | *Naples, FL*

Links/Lighthouse Sound | *Ocean City, MD*

Linville | *Asheville, NC*

Lodge/Four Seasons | *Lake of the Ozarks, MO*

Marriott Desert Springs | *Palm Springs, CA*

Mauna Lani | *Big Island, HI*

May River/Palmetto Bluff | *Hilton Head, SC*

Mid Pines Inn | *Pinehurst, NC*

Nemacolin Woodlands | *Pittsburgh, PA*

Ocotillo | *Phoenix, AZ*

Ojai Valley Inn | *Los Angeles, CA*

Pebble Beach | *Monterey Peninsula, CA*

PGA Nat'l | *Palm Beach, FL*

Phoenician | *Scottsdale, AZ*

Pine Hill | *Camden, NJ*

Pointe/Lookout Mtn. | *Phoenix, AZ*

Poppy Hills | *Monterey Peninsula, CA*

Princeville | *Kauai, HI*

Quail Lodge | *Monterey Peninsula, CA*

Rancho Bernardo | *San Diego, CA*

Raven/Snowshoe Mtn. | *Elkins, WV*

Raven/Verrado | *Phoenix, AZ*

NEW Raven's Claw | *Philadelphia, PA*

Reserve Vineyards | *Portland, OR*

Reynolds | *Lake Oconee, GA*

Ridge/Castle Pines N. | *Denver, CO*

NEW Ritz-Carlton Members Club | *Sarasota, FL*

Sagamore | *Adirondacks, NY*

Samoset | *Southern Maine, ME*

Saratoga Nat'l | *Albany, NY*

Sea Island | *Lowcountry, GA*

Seaview Marriott | *Atlantic City, NJ*

Shadow Creek | *Las Vegas, NV*

Spanish Bay | *Monterey Peninsula, CA*

Starr Pass | *Tucson, AZ*

Strawberry Farms | *Orange County, CA*
SunRidge Canyon | *Scottsdale, AZ*
Sunriver | *Bend, OR*
Temecula Creek Inn | *San Diego, CA*
Tiburón | *Naples, FL*
Torrey Pines | *San Diego, CA*
TPC Sawgrass | *Jacksonville, FL*
TPC Scottsdale | *Scottsdale, AZ*
Treetops | *Gaylord, MI*
Troon North | *Scottsdale, AZ*
NEW Trump Nat'l | *Los Angeles, CA*
Twin Warriors | *Albuquerque, NM*
Ventana Canyon | *Tucson, AZ*
Walt Disney World | *Orlando, FL*
Wente Vineyards | *San Francisco Bay Area, CA*
Westin Mission Hills | *Palm Springs, CA*
Whirlwind | *Phoenix, AZ*
Whistling Straits | *Kohler, WI*
Wigwam | *Phoenix, AZ*
World Golf Village | *Jacksonville, FL*

FINISHING HOLES

Arizona Nat'l | *Tucson, AZ*
Arnold Palmer/Bay Hill | *Orlando, FL*
Z Aviara | *San Diego, CA*
Z Bulle Rock | *Baltimore, MD*
Z Cambrian Ridge | *Montgomery, AL*
Camp Creek | *Panhandle, FL*
Capitol Hill, Judge | *Montgomery, AL*
Z Cascata | *Las Vegas, NV*
Daufuskie Island, Melrose | *Hilton Head, SC*
Z Doral, Blue Monster | *Miami, FL*
Eagle Mountain | *Scottsdale, AZ*
NEW Erin Hills | *Milwaukee, WI*
Fox Hopyard | *East Haddam, CT*
Z Grand Nat'l, Links | *Auburn, AL*
Grayhawk, Raptor | *Scottsdale, AZ*
Half Moon Bay, Old Course | *San Francisco Bay Area, CA*
Industry Hills, Eisenhower | *Los Angeles, CA*
Z Kapalua, Plantation | *Maui, HI*
Kauai Lagoons, Kiele | *Kauai, HI*
Z NEW Lake of Isles, North | *New London, CT*

Leatherstocking | *Albany, NY*
Mid Pines Inn | *Pinehurst, NC*
Z Ocean Hammock | *Daytona Beach, FL*
Omni Tucson Nat'l, Catalina | *Tucson, AZ*
Z Pebble Beach | *Monterey Peninsula, CA*
Pete Dye/Virginia Tech | *Roanoke, VA*
PGA Nat'l, Champion | *Palm Beach, FL*
Z PGA West, TPC Stadium | *Palm Springs, CA*
Pine Meadow | *Chicago, IL*
Reflection Bay/Lake Las Vegas | *Las Vegas, NV*
Z Sea Pines, Harbour Town Golf Links | *Hilton Head, SC*
St. Ives Resort, Tullymore | *Grand Rapids, MI*
SunRidge Canyon | *Scottsdale, AZ*
ThunderHawk | *Chicago, IL*
Z Torrey Pines, South | *San Diego, CA*
Z TPC Sawgrass, Stadium | *Jacksonville, FL*
TPC Scottsdale, Stadium | *Scottsdale, AZ*
Z Troon North, Monument | *Scottsdale, AZ*
Troon North, Pinnacle | *Scottsdale, AZ*
NEW Trump Nat'l | *Los Angeles, CA*
Turning Stone, Atunyote | *Finger Lakes, NY*
Ventana Canyon, Canyon | *Tucson, AZ*
Wild Dunes, Links | *Charleston, SC*
Wynn Las Vegas | *Las Vegas, NV*

INSTRUCTION

Amelia Island | *Jacksonville, FL*
Arnold Palmer/Bay Hill | *Orlando, FL*
ASU Karsten | *Phoenix, AZ*
Aviara | *San Diego, CA*
Baywood Greens | *Rehoboth Beach, DE*
Black Bear | *Orlando, FL*
Black Gold | *Orange County, CA*
Black Lake | *Gaylord, MI*

FEATURES INDEX

Univ. Park Golf | *Sarasota, FL*
Walt Disney World | *Orlando, FL*
Westin Innisbrook | *Tampa, FL*
Westin Mission Hills | *Palm Springs, CA*
Whirlwind | *Phoenix, AZ*
Whiskey Creek | *Frederick, MD*
Whiteface | *Adirondacks, NY*
Wilds | *Minneapolis, MN*
World Golf Village | *Jacksonville, FL*
Wyncote | *Lancaster, PA*

JUNIOR-FRIENDLY

Alvamar Public | *Kansas City, KS*
Annbriar | *St. Louis Area, IL*
Apple Tree | *Seattle, WA*
Arrowhead | *Myrtle Beach, SC*
Arroyo Trabuco | *Orange County, CA*
ASU Karsten | *Phoenix, AZ*
Barton Creek, Crenshaw Cliffside | *Austin, TX*
Bay Creek, Arnold Palmer | *Virginia Beach, VA*
Baywood Greens | *Rehoboth Beach, DE*
Bear Trace/Ross Creek | *Nashville, TN*
Big Mountain | *Kalispell, MT*
Blackmoor | *Myrtle Beach, SC*
Boyne Highlands, Moor | *Petoskey, MI*
☒ Caledonia Golf & Fish | *Pawleys Island, SC*
NEW Callippe Preserve | *San Francisco Bay Area, CA*
Cantigny | *Chicago, IL*
Cape May Nat'l | *Cape May, NJ*
Celebration | *Orlando, FL*
Center Valley Club | *Allentown, PA*
Cinnabar Hills | *San Francisco Bay Area, CA*
Cobblestone | *Atlanta, GA*
Colbert Hills | *Topeka, KS*
☒ Crumpin-Fox | *Berkshires, MA*
Eagle Vail | *Vail, CO*
Golden Bear/Indigo Run | *Hilton Head, SC*
Gray Plantation | *Lake Charles, LA*
Grossinger, Big G | *Catskills, NY*
Harbor Pines | *Atlantic City, NJ*

☒ Harding Park | *San Francisco Bay Area, CA*
Hog Neck | *Easton, MD*
Howell Park | *Freehold, NJ*
Hyatt Hill Country | *San Antonio, TX*
Indian Peaks | *Boulder, CO*
Kebo Valley | *Central Maine, ME*
☒ Kiva Dunes | *Mobile, AL*
Kona Country Club, Mountain | *Big Island, HI*
Kona Country Club, Ocean | *Big Island, HI*
NEW Lederach | *Philadelphia, PA*
Legacy Ridge | *Denver, CO*
Longbow | *Phoenix, AZ*
Makaha | *Oahu, HI*
Memorial Park | *Houston, TX*
Murphy Creek | *Denver, CO*
Myrtle Beach Nat'l, SouthCreek | *Myrtle Beach, SC*
Oyster Bay Town Golf | *Long Island, NY*
Pacific Grove | *Monterey Peninsula, CA*
Palmetto Dunes, Robert Trent Jones | *Hilton Head, SC*
Penn Nat'l, Founders | *Gettysburg, PA*
PGA Golf Club, Ryder | *Port St. Lucie, FL*
Pinehurst, No. 1 | *Pinehurst, NC*
Pinehurst, No. 3 | *Pinehurst, NC*
Poipu Bay | *Kauai, HI*
Sandestin, Baytowne | *Panhandle, FL*
Smithtown Landing | *Long Island, NY*
SouthWood | *Panhandle, FL*
Spencer T. Olin | *St. Louis Area, IL*
Sterling Farms | *Stamford, CT*
Tan-Tar-A, The Oaks | *Lake of the Ozarks, MO*
Valley View | *Salt Lake City, UT*

LINKS-STYLE

Amelia Island, Ocean Links | *Jacksonville, FL*
☒ Arcadia Bluffs | *Traverse City, MI*
☒ Bandon Dunes, Bandon Dunes Course | *Coos Bay, OR*

Kiawah Island | *Charleston, SC*

Kierland | *Scottsdale, AZ*

Kingsmill | *Williamsburg, VA*

Kiva Dunes | *Mobile, AL*

La Costa | *San Diego, CA*

La Quinta | *Palm Springs, CA*

Legends Club | *Minneapolis, MN*

Links/Bodega Harbour | *Santa Rosa, CA*

Lodge/Four Seasons | *Lake of the Ozarks, MO*

Lost Canyons | *Los Angeles, CA*

May River/Palmetto Bluff | *Hilton Head, SC*

Monarch Beach | *Orange County, CA*

Neshanic Valley | *Bridgewater, NJ*

Ocotillo | *Phoenix, AZ*

Ojai Valley Inn | *Los Angeles, CA*

Orange County Nat'l | *Orlando, FL*

Pebble Beach | *Monterey Peninsula, CA*

PGA Nat'l | *Palm Beach, FL*

PGA West | *Palm Springs, CA*

Phoenician | *Scottsdale, AZ*

Pine Needles Lodge | *Pinehurst, NC*

Poppy Hills | *Monterey Peninsula, CA*

Raven/Verrado | *Phoenix, AZ*

Revere | *Las Vegas, NV*

Reynolds | *Lake Oconee, GA*

Sedona Golf | *Sedona, AZ*

Spanish Bay | *Monterey Peninsula, CA*

SunRidge Canyon | *Scottsdale, AZ*

ThunderHawk | *Chicago, IL*

Tiburón | *Naples, FL*

Torrey Pines | *San Diego, CA*

TPC Heron Bay | *Ft. Lauderdale, FL*

TPC Myrtle Beach | *Myrtle Beach, SC*

TPC Sawgrass | *Jacksonville, FL*

TPC Scottsdale | *Scottsdale, AZ*

Treetops | *Gaylord, MI*

Troon North | *Scottsdale, AZ*

NEW Trump Nat'l | *Los Angeles, CA*

Ventana Canyon | *Tucson, AZ*

Wente Vineyards | *San Francisco Bay Area, CA*

Whirlwind | *Phoenix, AZ*

Whistling Straits | *Kohler, WI*

World Golf Village | *Jacksonville, FL*

NOTEWORTHY NEWCOMERS

Atchafalaya/Idlewild | *New Orleans, LA*

Bay Creek, Jack Nicklaus | *Virginia Beach, VA*

Bayside | *Rehoboth Beach, DE*

Beau Rivage Resort, Fallen Oak | *Gulfport, MS*

Big Fish | *Northern Wisconsin, WI*

Blue Heron, Highlands/Lakes | *Akron, OH*

Broadmoor, Mountain | *Colorado Springs, CO*

Bully Pulpit | *Bismarck, ND*

Callippe Preserve | *San Francisco Bay Area, CA*

Classic Club | *Palm Springs, CA*

Club/Morgan Hill | *Allentown, PA*

Erin Hills | *Milwaukee, WI*

Escena | *Palm Springs, CA*

Golf Resort/Indian Wells, Celebrity | *Palm Springs, CA*

Juniper | *Bend, OR*

Kinderlou Forest | *Valdosta, GA*

King Carter | *Richmond, VA*

Z Lake of Isles, North | *New London, CT*

Lakota Canyon Ranch | *Grand Junction, CO*

Lansdowne, Norman | *Leesburg, VA*

Laughlin Ranch | *Bullhead City, AZ*

Lederach | *Philadelphia, PA*

Marquette, Greywalls | *Upper Peninsula, MI*

Meadows at Mystic Lake | *Minneapolis, MN*

Mines | *Grand Rapids, MI*

Monarch Dunes | *San Luis Obispo, CA*

Northern Bay | *Madison, WI*

North Palm Beach Club, Jack Nicklaus | *Palm Beach, FL*

Oasis, Canyons | *Las Vegas, NV*

Old Greenwood | *Lake Tahoe, CA*

Omni Tucson Nat'l, Sonoran | *Tucson, AZ*

Oxford Greens | *New Haven, CT*

Raven's Claw | *Philadelphia, PA*

Redstone, Tournament | *Houston, TX*

Reunion Resort, Independence | *Orlando, FL*

Reunion Resort, Legacy | *Orlando, FL*

Ritz-Carlton Members Club | *Sarasota, FL*

Ross Bridge | *Birmingham, AL*

Sand Creek Station | *Wichita, KS*

Sandia | *Albuquerque, NM*

Shoals, Fighting Joe | *Huntsville, AL*

SilverRock Resort, Arnold Palmer Classic | *Palm Springs, CA*

Soldier Hollow, Gold | *Salt Lake City, UT*

Soldier Hollow, Silver | *Salt Lake City, UT*

Suncadia Inn, Prospector | *Seattle, WA*

Sunday River | *Central Maine, ME*

Tamarack Resort, Osprey Meadows | *Boise, ID*

Trump Nat'l | *Los Angeles, CA*

We-Ko-Pa, Saguaro | *Scottsdale, AZ*

Windswept Dunes | *Panhandle, FL*

Wolfdancer | *Austin, TX*

OPENING HOLES

Arizona Nat'l | *Tucson, AZ*

Arnold Palmer/Bay Hill | *Orlando, FL*

Atlantic Golf/South River | *DC Metro Area, MD*

Augustine | *DC Metro Area, VA*

Bay Creek, Arnold Palmer | *Virginia Beach, VA*

NEW Bayside | *Rehoboth Beach, DE*

Beaver Creek | *Vail, CO*

Berkshire Valley | *NYC Metro, NJ*

Z Bethpage, Red | *Long Island, NY*

Black Mesa | *Santa Fe, NM*

Boulders, South | *Phoenix, AZ*

Z Cambrian Ridge | *Montgomery, AL*

Capitol Hill, Judge | *Montgomery, AL*

Capitol Hill, Legislator | *Montgomery, AL*

CrossCreek | *San Diego, CA*

Crystal Springs, Great Gorge | *NYC Metro, NJ*

Desert Willow, Firecliff | *Palm Springs, CA*

Diamondback | *Orlando, FL*

El Diablo | *Ocala, FL*

Fossil Trace | *Denver, CO*

Garrison Golf | *Hudson Valley, NY*

Glen Annie | *Santa Barbara, CA*

Gleneagles/Equinox | *Southern Vermont, VT*

Grand Cypress, New | *Orlando, FL*

Grayhawk, Talon | *Scottsdale, AZ*

Z Greenbrier, Old White | *White Sulphur Springs, WV*

Keystone Ranch, Ranch | *Vail, CO*

Keystone Ranch, River | *Vail, CO*

La Cantera, Resort | *San Antonio, TX*

NEW Laughlin Ranch | *Bullhead City, AZ*

Little Mountain | *Cleveland, OH*

Z Madden's/Gull Lake, Classic | *Brainerd, MN*

NEW Monarch Dunes | *San Luis Obispo, CA*

Murphy Creek | *Denver, CO*

Newport Nat'l, Orchard | *Newport, RI*

Z Pasatiempo | *Santa Cruz, CA*

PGA Golf Club, Dye | *Port St. Lucie, FL*

Poipu Bay | *Kauai, HI*

Z Poppy Hills | *Monterey Peninsula, CA*

Raven/Snowshoe Mtn. | *Elkins, WV*

Z Red Sky, Norman | *Vail, CO*

NEW Ritz-Carlton Members Club | *Sarasota, FL*

Sagamore | *Adirondacks, NY*

Sandestin, Burnt Pine | *Panhandle, FL*

Seven Oaks | *Finger Lakes, NY*

Shennecossett | *New London, CT*

Silver Lakes | *Birmingham, AL*

Z Spanish Bay | *Monterey Peninsula, CA*

Z Spyglass Hill | *Monterey Peninsula, CA*

Sun Valley | *Sun Valley, ID*

Talamore | *Pinehurst, NC*

Tot Hill Farm | *Greensboro, NC*

TPC Sawgrass, Valley | Jacksonville, FL

NEW Trump Nat'l | Los Angeles, CA

Victoria Hills | Daytona Beach, FL

Walt Disney World, Magnolia | Orlando, FL

Z We-Ko-Pa, Cholla | Scottsdale, AZ

Wente Vineyards | San Francisco Bay Area, CA

Westin Innisbrook, Island | Tampa, FL

Whitehawk Ranch | Lake Tahoe, CA

NEW Windswept Dunes | Panhandle, FL

Z World Woods, Pine Barrens | Tampa, FL

OUTSTANDING ACCOMMODATIONS

Aviara | San Diego, CA

Barnsley Gardens | Atlanta, GA

Bay Harbor | Petoskey, MI

Blackwolf Run | Kohler, WI

Boulders | Phoenix, AZ

Breakers | Palm Beach, FL

Broadmoor | Colorado Springs, CO

Challenge/Manele | Lanai, HI

Cordillera | Vail, CO

Experience/Koele | Lanai, HI

Falls/Lake Las Vegas | Las Vegas, NV

Four Seasons/Las Colinas | Dallas, TX

Golden Horseshoe | Williamsburg, VA

Grand Cypress | Orlando, FL

Greenbrier | White Sulphur Springs, WV

Half Moon Bay | San Francisco Bay Area, CA

Homestead | Roanoke, VA

Hualalai | Big Island, HI

Kiawah Island | Charleston, SC

La Cantera | San Antonio, TX

La Costa | San Diego, CA

Lake Placid | Adirondacks, NY

La Quinta | Palm Springs, CA

Monarch Beach | Orange County, CA

Nemacolin Woodlands | Pittsburgh, PA

Ojai Valley Inn | Los Angeles, CA

Pebble Beach | Monterey Peninsula, CA

Phoenician | Scottsdale, AZ

Poipu Bay | Kauai, HI

Princeville | Kauai, HI

Red Sky | Vail, CO

Reflection Bay/Lake Las Vegas | Las Vegas, NV

Resort Semiahmoo | Vancouver Area, WA

Reynolds | Lake Oconee, GA

NEW Ritz-Carlton Members Club | Sarasota, FL

Ritz-Carlton Orlando | Orlando, FL

Sea Island | Lowcountry, GA

Shadow Creek | Las Vegas, NV

Spanish Bay | Monterey Peninsula, CA

Tiburón | Naples, FL

Torrey Pines | San Diego, CA

TPC Scottsdale | Scottsdale, AZ

Troon North | Scottsdale, AZ

Twin Warriors | Albuquerque, NM

Wailea | Maui, HI

Walt Disney World | Orlando, FL

Whistling Straits | Kohler, WI

Wynn Las Vegas | Las Vegas, NV

PACE OF PLAY

Atlantic City Country Club | Atlantic City, NJ

Balsams, Panorama | Colebrook, NH

Black Mesa | Santa Fe, NM

Boulders, North | Phoenix, AZ

Boulders, South | Phoenix, AZ

Broadmoor, East | Colorado Springs, CO

Broadmoor, West | Colorado Springs, CO

Bull Run | Leesburg, VA

Camp Creek | Panhandle, FL

Z Cascata | Las Vegas, NV

Z Circling Raven | Coeur d'Alene, ID

CordeValle | San Francisco Bay Area, CA

Diablo Grande, Legends West | Sacramento, CA

Diablo Grande, Ranch | Sacramento, CA

NEW Escena | Palm Springs, CA

☒ Sea Pines, Harbour Town Golf
  Links | *Hilton Head, SC*
Sedona Golf | *Sedona, AZ*
☒ Spanish Bay | *Monterey
  Peninsula, CA*
☒ Spyglass Hill | *Monterey
  Peninsula, CA*
NEW Sunday River | *Central
  Maine, ME*
SunRidge Canyon | *Scottsdale, AZ*
Tot Hill Farm | *Greensboro, NC*
☒ TPC Sawgrass, Stadium |
  Jacksonville, FL
☒ Troon North, Monument |
  Scottsdale, AZ
Twin Warriors | *Albuquerque, NM*
Ventana Canyon, Mountain |
  Tucson, AZ
World Golf Village, Slammer &
  Squire | *Jacksonville, FL*
Wynn Las Vegas | *Las Vegas, NV*

PAR-4 HOLES

Apache Stronghold | *San Carlos, AZ*
Arnold Palmer/Bay Hill | *Orlando, FL*
Barona Creek | *San Diego, CA*
Bear Trace/Ross Creek |
  Nashville, TN
☒ Bethpage, Black | *Long Island, NY*
Boulders, North | *Phoenix, AZ*
Bull at Pinehurst | *Kohler, WI*
Capitol Hill, Judge |
  Montgomery, AL
Capstone Club/Alabama |
  Birmingham, AL
☒ Challenge/Manele | *Lanai, HI*
Desert Willow, Firecliff | *Palm
  Springs, CA*
NEW Erin Hills | *Milwaukee, WI*
Falls/Lake Las Vegas | *Las
  Vegas, NV*
Giants Ridge, Quarry | *Duluth, MN*
☒ Gold Canyon, Dinosaur
  Mountain | *Phoenix, AZ*
☒ Grand Nat'l, Links | *Auburn, AL*
☒ Harding Park | *San Francisco Bay
  Area, CA*
Harvester | *Des Moines, IA*
Kauai Lagoons, Kiele | *Kauai, HI*
☒ Kiawah Island, Ocean |
  Charleston, SC

La Purisima | *Santa Barbara, CA*
Little Mountain | *Cleveland, OH*
☒ Madden's/Gull Lake, Classic |
  Brainerd, MN
Mansion Ridge | *NYC Metro, NY*
☒ Montauk Downs | *Long
  Island, NY*
Murphy Creek | *Denver, CO*
☒ Ocean Hammock | *Daytona
  Beach, FL*
Old Silo | *Lexington, KY*
Palmetto Dunes, Arthur Hills |
  Hilton Head, SC
☒ Pasatiempo | *Santa Cruz, CA*
☒ Pebble Beach | *Monterey
  Peninsula, CA*
PGA Nat'l, Champion | *Palm
  Beach, FL*
PGA West, Jack Nicklaus
  Tournament | *Palm Springs, CA*
☒ PGA West, TPC Stadium | *Palm
  Springs, CA*
Purgatory | *Indianapolis, IN*
Rawls/Texas Tech | *Lubbock, TX*
Redlands Mesa | *Grand Junction, CO*
Red Tail | *Worcester, MA*
Ridge/Castle Pines N. | *Denver, CO*
Sagamore | *Adirondacks, NY*
San Juan Oaks | *Monterey
  Peninsula, CA*
☒ Spanish Bay | *Monterey
  Peninsula, CA*
☒ Spyglass Hill | *Monterey
  Peninsula, CA*
ThunderHawk | *Chicago, IL*
☒ Torrey Pines, South | *San
  Diego, CA*
☒ TPC Sawgrass, Stadium |
  Jacksonville, FL
TPC Scottsdale, Stadium |
  Scottsdale, AZ
☒ Troon North, Monument |
  Scottsdale, AZ
Troon North, Pinnacle |
  Scottsdale, AZ
NEW Trump Nat'l | *Los Angeles, CA*
Ventana Canyon, Canyon |
  Tucson, AZ
Walt Disney World, Palm |
  Orlando, FL

FEATURES INDEX

Gaylord Springs | *Nashville, TN*

Golden Horseshoe | *Williamsburg, VA*

Golf Club/Newcastle | *Seattle, WA*

Grand Cypress | *Orlando, FL*

Grande Dunes | *Myrtle Beach, SC*

Grayhawk | *Scottsdale, AZ*

Great River | *New Haven, CT*

Greenbrier | *White Sulphur Springs, WV*

Harborside Int'l | *Chicago, IL*

Hawk Hollow | *Lansing, MI*

Homestead | *Roanoke, VA*

Hyatt Hill Country | *San Antonio, TX*

Jimmie Austin Univ./OK | *Oklahoma City, OK*

Karsten Creek | *Stillwater, OK*

Kiawah Island | *Charleston, SC*

Kingsmill | *Williamsburg, VA*

La Cantera | *San Antonio, TX*

Legends | *Myrtle Beach, SC*

Limestone Springs | *Birmingham, AL*

Longaberger | *Columbus, OH*

Lost Canyons | *Los Angeles, CA*

LPGA Int'l | *Daytona Beach, FL*

Lyman Orchards | *Hartford, CT*

Marriott Shadow Ridge | *Palm Springs, CA*

Murphy Creek | *Denver, CO*

Neshanic Valley | *Bridgewater, NJ*

Oak Creek | *Orange County, CA*

Orange County Nat'l | *Orlando, FL*

Peninsula Golf | *Mobile, AL*

PGA Golf Club | *Port St. Lucie, FL*

PGA Nat'l | *Palm Beach, FL*

PGA of So. Cal. | *San Bernardino, CA*

PGA West | *Palm Springs, CA*

Pinehills | *Boston, MA*

Pinehurst | *Pinehurst, NC*

Pinewild | *Pinehurst, NC*

Poppy Ridge | *San Francisco Bay Area, CA*

Princeville | *Kauai, HI*

Pumpkin Ridge | *Portland, OR*

Ranch | *Springfield, MA*

Raven/Verrado | *Phoenix, AZ*

Rawls/Texas Tech | *Lubbock, TX*

Reynolds | *Lake Oconee, GA*

Royce Brook | *Bridgewater, NJ*

Rum Pointe | *Ocean City, MD*

Sea Island | *Lowcountry, GA*

Seaview Marriott | *Atlantic City, NJ*

Shell Landing | *Pascagoula, MS*

Silver Lakes | *Birmingham, AL*

StoneRidge | *Minneapolis, MN*

StoneWater | *Cleveland, OH*

SunRidge Canyon | *Scottsdale, AZ*

Sunriver | *Bend, OR*

Talking Stick | *Scottsdale, AZ*

Tanglewood Park | *Winston-Salem, NC*

Tiburón | *Naples, FL*

Tiffany Greens | *Kansas City, MO*

TPC Sawgrass | *Jacksonville, FL*

TPC Scottsdale | *Scottsdale, AZ*

TPC Tampa Bay | *Tampa, FL*

Treetops | *Gaylord, MI*

Troon North | *Scottsdale, AZ*

Univ. of NM Championship | *Albuquerque, NM*

Univ. Ridge | *Madison, WI*

Victoria Hills | *Daytona Beach, FL*

We-Ko-Pa | *Scottsdale, AZ*

Whistling Straits | *Kohler, WI*

World Golf Village | *Jacksonville, FL*

World Woods | *Tampa, FL*

PRIVATE FUNCTIONS

Aldeen | *Rockford, IL*

Angeles Nat'l | *Los Angeles, CA*

Angel Park | *Las Vegas, NV*

Arizona Biltmore | *Phoenix, AZ*

Aviara | *San Diego, CA*

Bald Head Island | *Myrtle Beach Area, NC*

Barnsley Gardens | *Atlanta, GA*

Barton Creek | *Austin, TX*

Boca Raton Resort | *Palm Beach, FL*

Boulders | *Phoenix, AZ*

Boyne Highlands | *Petoskey, MI*

Breakers | *Palm Beach, FL*

Brickyard Crossing | *Indianapolis, IN*

Broadmoor | *Colorado Springs, CO*

Callaway Gardens | *Columbus, GA*

Carambola | *St. Croix, USVI*

Challenge/Manele | *Lanai, HI*

Coeur d'Alene | *Coeur d'Alene, ID*

DarkHorse | *Sacramento, CA*

Druids Glen | *Seattle, WA*

Four Seasons/Las Colinas | *Dallas, TX*

PRO-EVENT HOSTS

NEW Golf Resort/Indian Wells, Celebrity | *Palm Springs, CA*

Grayhawk, Raptor | *Scottsdale, AZ*

Z Hualalai | *Big Island, HI*

Z Kapalua, Plantation | *Maui, HI*

Z Kiawah Island, Ocean | *Charleston, SC*

NEW Kinderlou Forest | *Valdosta, GA*

Kingsmill, River | *Williamsburg, VA*

Ko Olina | *Oahu, HI*

La Cantera, Resort | *San Antonio, TX*

Z Ocean Hammock | *Daytona Beach, FL*

Omni Tucson Nat'l, Catalina | *Tucson, AZ*

Orange County Nat'l, Crooked Cat | *Orlando, FL*

Z Pebble Beach | *Monterey Peninsula, CA*

PGA Nat'l, Champion | *Palm Beach, FL*

PGA West, Jack Nicklaus Tournament | *Palm Springs, CA*

Pine Needles Lodge, Pine Needles | *Pinehurst, NC*

Z Poppy Hills | *Monterey Peninsula, CA*

NEW Redstone, Tournament | *Houston, TX*

NEW Reunion Resort, Independence | *Orlando, FL*

NEW Reunion Resort, Legacy | *Orlando, FL*

Z Reynolds, Oconee | *Lake Oconee, GA*

NEW Ross Bridge | *Birmingham, AL*

Sandestin, Raven | *Panhandle, FL*

Z Sea Pines, Harbour Town Golf Links | *Hilton Head, SC*

Sonoma Golf | *San Francisco Bay Area, CA*

Z Spyglass Hill | *Monterey Peninsula, CA*

StoneWater | *Cleveland, OH*

Sunriver, Crosswater | *Bend, OR*

Z Torrey Pines, North | *San Diego, CA*

Z Torrey Pines, South | *San Diego, CA*

TPC Deere Run | *Moline, IL*

TPC Louisiana | *New Orleans, LA*

Z TPC Sawgrass, Stadium | *Jacksonville, FL*

TPC Scottsdale, Stadium | *Scottsdale, AZ*

TPC Tampa Bay | *Tampa, FL*

Turning Stone, Atunyote | *Finger Lakes, NY*

Turtle Bay, Arnold Palmer | *Oahu, HI*

Wailea, Gold | *Maui, HI*

Walt Disney World, Magnolia | *Orlando, FL*

Walt Disney World, Palm | *Orlando, FL*

Wente Vineyards | *San Francisco Bay Area, CA*

Westin Innisbrook, Copperhead | *Tampa, FL*

Z Whistling Straits, Straits | *Kohler, WI*

PRO SHOPS

Angel Park | *Las Vegas, NV*

Arizona Nat'l | *Tucson, AZ*

Arnold Palmer/Bay Hill | *Orlando, FL*

ASU Karsten | *Phoenix, AZ*

Aviara | *San Diego, CA*

Bali Hai | *Las Vegas, NV*

Bandon Dunes | *Coos Bay, OR*

Barton Creek | *Austin, TX*

Bay Harbor | *Petoskey, MI*

Big Creek | *Mt. Home, AR*

Blackwolf Run | *Kohler, WI*

Boulders | *Phoenix, AZ*

Breakers | *Palm Beach, FL*

Breckenridge | *Vail, CO*

Broadmoor | *Colorado Springs, CO*

Callaway Gardens | *Columbus, GA*

Camelback | *Scottsdale, AZ*

Cantigny | *Chicago, IL*

Capitol Hill | *Montgomery, AL*

Carter Plantation | *Baton Rouge, LA*

Challenge/Manele | *Lanai, HI*

ChampionsGate | *Orlando, FL*

Club/Savannah Harbor | *Savannah, GA*

Coeur d'Alene | *Coeur d'Alene, ID*

Cordillera | *Vail, CO*

Crystal Springs/Great Gorge | *NYC Metro, NJ*

FEATURES INDEX

Whistling Straits | *Kohler, WI*
Whitetail | *Allentown, PA*
Wild Wing | *Myrtle Beach, SC*
Windmill Lakes | *Akron, OH*
World Golf Village | *Jacksonville, FL*

PUTTING COURSES

Angel Park | *Las Vegas, NV*
Arizona Biltmore | *Phoenix, AZ*
Desert Canyon | *Wenatchee, WA*
Golf Club/Newcastle | *Seattle, WA*
Hawk Hollow | *Lansing, MI*
Horseshoe Bay | *Austin, TX*
Marriott Desert Springs | *Palm Springs, CA*
Orange County Nat'l | *Orlando, FL*
Quail Lodge | *Monterey Peninsula, CA*
Running Y Ranch | *Klamath Falls, OR*
Sunriver | *Bend, OR*
Turtle Creek | *Philadelphia, PA*
Waikoloa Beach | *Big Island, HI*
World Golf Village | *Jacksonville, FL*

REPLICAS

Bear's Best Atlanta | *Atlanta, GA*
Bear's Best Vegas | *Las Vegas, NV*
Boyne Highlands, Donald Ross Memorial | *Petoskey, MI*
McCullough's Emerald | *Atlantic City, NJ*
NEW Northern Bay | *Madison, WI*
Royal Links | *Las Vegas, NV*
Tour 18 Dallas | *Dallas, TX*
Tour 18 Houston | *Houston, TX*
Tribute | *Dallas, TX*

RESORT

Amelia Island | *Jacksonville, FL*
Apache Stronghold | *San Carlos, AZ*
Arizona Biltmore | *Phoenix, AZ*
Arnold Palmer/Bay Hill | *Orlando, FL*
Aviara | *San Diego, CA*
Bald Head Island | *Myrtle Beach Area, NC*
Balsams | *Colebrook, NH*
Bandon Dunes | *Coos Bay, OR*
Barefoot Resort | *Myrtle Beach, SC*
Barnsley Gardens | *Atlanta, GA*
Barton Creek | *Austin, TX*
Bay Creek | *Virginia Beach, VA*
Bay Harbor | *Petoskey, MI*

NEW Beau Rivage Resort | *Gulfport, MS*
Beaver Creek | *Vail, CO*
Belterra | *Cincinnati Area, IN*
Black Butte Ranch | *Bend, OR*
Blackwolf Run | *Kohler, WI*
Bluffs, The | *Baton Rouge, LA*
Boca Raton Resort | *Palm Beach, FL*
Boulders | *Phoenix, AZ*
Boyne Highlands | *Petoskey, MI*
Brasstown Valley | *Atlanta, GA*
Breakers | *Palm Beach, FL*
Brickyard Crossing | *Indianapolis, IN*
Bridges/Hollywood Casino | *Gulfport, MS*
Bristol Harbour | *Finger Lakes, NY*
Broadmoor | *Colorado Springs, CO*
Callaway Gardens | *Columbus, GA*
Camelback | *Scottsdale, AZ*
Camp Creek | *Panhandle, FL*
Carroll Valley | *Gettysburg, PA*
Carter Plantation | *Baton Rouge, LA*
Cascata | *Las Vegas, NV*
Challenge/Manele | *Lanai, HI*
ChampionsGate | *Orlando, FL*
Château Élan | *Atlanta, GA*
Circling Raven | *Coeur d'Alene, ID*
Cliffs | *Dallas, TX*
Club/Savannah Harbor | *Savannah, GA*
Coeur d'Alene | *Coeur d'Alene, ID*
Concord Resort | *Catskills, NY*
CordeValle | *San Francisco Bay Area, CA*
Cordillera | *Vail, CO*
Craft Farms | *Mobile, AL*
Crystal Springs | *NYC Metro, NJ*
Crystal Springs/Great Gorge | *NYC Metro, NJ*
Dancing Rabbit | *Jackson, MS*
Daufuskie Island | *Hilton Head, SC*
Desert Canyon | *Wenatchee, WA*
Desert Willow | *Palm Springs, CA*
Diablo Grande | *Sacramento, CA*
Dorado Del Mar | *Dorado, PR*
Doral | *Miami, FL*
Double JJ Ranch | *Muskegon, MI*
Eagle Ridge | *Galena, IL*
Edgewood Tahoe | *Reno, NV*
El Conquistador | *Tucson, AZ*

FEATURES INDEX

Palmetto Dunes Arthur Hills | *Hilton Head, SC*

Pawleys Plantation | *Pawleys Island, SC*

Pebble Beach | *Monterey Peninsula, CA*

Penn Nat'l | *Gettysburg, PA*

PGA Golf Club | *Port St. Lucie, FL*

PGA Nat'l | *Palm Beach, FL*

PGA West | *Palm Springs, CA*

Phoenician | *Scottsdale, AZ*

Pinehurst | *Pinehurst, NC*

Pine Needles Lodge | *Pinehurst, NC*

Pointe/Lookout Mtn. | *Phoenix, AZ*

Poipu Bay | *Kauai, HI*

Port Ludlow | *Bremerton, WA*

Primm Valley | *Las Vegas, NV*

Princeville | *Kauai, HI*

Quail Lodge | *Monterey Peninsula, CA*

Rancho Bernardo | *San Diego, CA*

Raven/Snowshoe Mtn. | *Elkins, WV*

Red Sky | *Vail, CO*

Reflection Bay/Lake Las Vegas | *Las Vegas, NV*

Resort Semiahmoo | *Vancouver Area, WA*

NEW Reunion Resort | *Orlando, FL*

Reynolds Landing | *Lake Oconee, GA*

Reynolds | *Lake Oconee, GA*

NEW Ritz-Carlton Members Club | *Sarasota, FL*

Ritz-Carlton Orlando | *Orlando, FL*

River Marsh | *Easton, MD*

Robert Trent Jones/Palmetto Dunes | *Hilton Head, SC*

Rocky Gap Lodge | *Cumberland, MD*

NEW Ross Bridge | *Birmingham, AL*

Running Y Ranch | *Klamath Falls, OR*

Saddlebrook | *Tampa, FL*

Sagamore | *Adirondacks, NY*

Salishan | *Central Coast, OR*

Samoset | *Southern Maine, ME*

Sandestin | *Panhandle, FL*

NEW Sandia | *Albuquerque, NM*

Sandpines | *Eugene, OR*

Sawmill Creek | *Cleveland, OH*

Sea Island | *Lowcountry, GA*

Sea Pines | *Hilton Head, SC*

Sea Trail | *Myrtle Beach Area, NC*

Seaview Marriott | *Atlantic City, NJ*

Sedona Golf | *Sedona, AZ*

Seven Springs Mtn. | *Pittsburgh, PA*

Shadow Creek | *Las Vegas, NV*

Shanty Creek | *Traverse City, MI*

Shawnee Inn | *Poconos, PA*

NEW SilverRock | *Palm Springs, CA*

Sonnenalp | *Vail, CO*

Spanish Bay | *Monterey Peninsula, CA*

Spyglass Hill | *Monterey Peninsula, CA*

Starr Pass | *Tucson, AZ*

St. Ives Resort | *Grand Rapids, MI*

St. Ives Resort | *Grand Rapids, MI*

Stonehenge/Fairfield | *Knoxville, TN*

Stonewall Resort | *Weston, WV*

Stratton Mtn. | *Southern Vermont, VT*

Sugarbush | *Northern Vermont, VT*

Sugarloaf | *Central Maine, ME*

NEW Suncadia Inn | *Seattle, WA*

NEW Sunday River | *Central Maine, ME*

Sunriver | *Bend, OR*

Sun Valley | *Sun Valley, ID*

NEW Tamarack Resort | *Boise, ID*

Tan-Tar-A | *Lake of the Ozarks, MO*

Temecula Creek Inn | *San Diego, CA*

Tennanah Lake Golf | *Hudson Valley, NY*

TimberStone | *Upper Peninsula, MI*

Toftrees | *State College, PA*

Tom's Run/Chestnut Ridge | *Pittsburgh, PA*

TPC Canyons | *Las Vegas, NV*

TPC Sawgrass | *Jacksonville, FL*

Treetops | *Gaylord, MI*

Tribute | *Dallas, TX*

Troon North | *Scottsdale, AZ*

True Blue | *Pawleys Island, SC*

Turning Stone | *Finger Lakes, NY*

Turtle Bay | *Oahu, HI*

Twin Warriors | *Albuquerque, NM*

Wachesaw Plantation E. | *Myrtle Beach, SC*

Waikoloa Beach | *Big Island, HI*

Wailea | *Maui, HI*

Walt Disney World | *Orlando, FL*

Westfields | *DC Metro Area, VA*

Leatherstocking | Albany, NY

Links/Bodega Harbour | Santa Rosa, CA

☑ Links/Lighthouse Sound | Ocean City, MD

Linville | Asheville, NC

Mahogany Run | St. Thomas, USVI

Makena, North | Maui, HI

Mauna Kea, Mauna Kea Course | Big Island, HI

Mauna Lani, South | Big Island, HI

May River/Palmetto Bluff | Hilton Head, SC

Monarch Beach | Orange County, CA

☑ Montauk Downs | Long Island, NY

Nemacolin Woodlands, Mystic Rock | Pittsburgh, PA

☑ Ocean Hammock | Daytona Beach, FL

Ojai Valley Inn | Los Angeles, CA

☑ Paa-Ko Ridge | Albuquerque, NM

Pacific Grove | Monterey Peninsula, CA

☑ Pasatiempo | Santa Cruz, CA

☑ Pebble Beach | Monterey Peninsula, CA

Phoenician | Scottsdale, AZ

Poipu Bay | Kauai, HI

Port Ludlow | Bremerton, WA

Primm Valley, Lakes | Las Vegas, NV

Princeville, Makai | Kauai, HI

☑ Princeville, Prince | Kauai, HI

Puakea | Kauai, HI

Raven/Snowshoe Mtn. | Elkins, WV

Redlands Mesa | Grand Junction, CO

☑ Red Sky, Fazio | Vail, CO

☑ Red Sky, Norman | Vail, CO

Reflection Bay/Lake Las Vegas | Las Vegas, NV

☑ Reynolds, Great Waters | Lake Oconee, GA

☑ Reynolds, Oconee | Lake Oconee, GA

Ridge/Castle Pines N. | Denver, CO

Running Y Ranch | Klamath Falls, OR

Sagamore | Adirondacks, NY

Samoset | Southern Maine, ME

Sandpiper | Santa Barbara, CA

☑ Sea Island, Seaside | Lowcountry, GA

☑ Sea Pines, Harbour Town Golf Links | Hilton Head, SC

Sedona Golf | Sedona, AZ

☑ Shadow Creek | Las Vegas, NV

Shennecossett | New London, CT

☑ Spanish Bay | Monterey Peninsula, CA

☑ Spyglass Hill | Monterey Peninsula, CA

Stonewall Resort, Palmer | Weston, WV

Sugarbush | Northern Vermont, VT

Sugarloaf | Central Maine, ME

NEW Sunday River | Central Maine, ME

Sunriver, Crosswater | Bend, OR

Sun Valley | Sun Valley, ID

☑ Taconic | Berkshires, MA

NEW Tamarack Resort, Osprey Meadows | Boise, ID

Tiburón, Black | Naples, FL

Tidewater | Myrtle Beach, SC

Tokatee | Eugene, OR

☑ Torrey Pines, North | San Diego, CA

☑ Torrey Pines, South | San Diego, CA

☑ TPC Sawgrass, Stadium | Jacksonville, FL

Treetops, Robert Trent Jones Masterpiece | Gaylord, MI

☑ Troon North, Monument | Scottsdale, AZ

NEW Trump Nat'l | Los Angeles, CA

Ventana Canyon, Mountain | Tucson, AZ

Wailea, Emerald | Maui, HI

Wailua | Kauai, HI

☑ We-Ko-Pa, Cholla | Scottsdale, AZ

NEW We-Ko-Pa, Saguaro | Scottsdale, AZ

Wente Vineyards | San Francisco Bay Area, CA

☑ Whistling Straits, Straits | Kohler, WI

☑ Wolf Creek | Las Vegas, NV

☒ World Woods, Pine Barrens | *Tampa, FL*

Wynn Las Vegas | *Las Vegas, NV*

STORIED

Arizona Biltmore, Adobe | *Phoenix, AZ*

Arnold Palmer/Bay Hill | *Orlando, FL*

Atlantic City Country Club | *Atlantic City, NJ*

☒ Bethpage, Black | *Long Island, NY*

Biltmore | *Miami, FL*

Boca Raton Resort, Resort Course | *Palm Beach, FL*

Breakers, Ocean | *Palm Beach, FL*

Brickyard Crossing | *Indianapolis, IN*

Broadmoor, East | *Colorado Springs, CO*

Broadmoor, West | *Colorado Springs, CO*

☒ Cog Hill, No. 4 (Dubsdread) | *Chicago, IL*

Crandon | *Miami, FL*

☒ Doral, Blue Monster | *Miami, FL*

Dunes Golf & Beach | *Myrtle Beach, SC*

French Lick, Donald Ross | *French Lick, IN*

☒ Golden Horseshoe, Gold | *Williamsburg, VA*

Grayhawk, Talon | *Scottsdale, AZ*

☒ Greenbrier, Greenbrier Course | *White Sulphur Springs, WV*

☒ Greenbrier, Old White | *White Sulphur Springs, WV*

☒ Harding Park | *San Francisco Bay Area, CA*

Hershey, West | *Harrisburg, PA*

☒ Homestead, Cascades | *Roanoke, VA*

Homestead, Old | *Roanoke, VA*

Hominy Hill | *Freehold, NJ*

☒ Kapalua, Plantation | *Maui, HI*

Kebo Valley | *Central Maine, ME*

☒ Kiawah Island, Ocean | *Charleston, SC*

La Cantera, Resort | *San Antonio, TX*

La Costa, North | *San Diego, CA*

La Costa, South | *San Diego, CA*

Memorial Park | *Houston, TX*

Mid Pines Inn | *Pinehurst, NC*

☒ Montauk Downs | *Long Island, NY*

Ojai Valley Inn | *Los Angeles, CA*

Omni Tucson Nat'l, Catalina | *Tucson, AZ*

☒ Pasatiempo | *Santa Cruz, CA*

☒ Pebble Beach | *Monterey Peninsula, CA*

Pecan Valley | *San Antonio, TX*

PGA Nat'l, Champion | *Palm Beach, FL*

PGA West, Jack Nicklaus Tournament | *Palm Springs, CA*

☒ PGA West, TPC Stadium | *Palm Springs, CA*

☒ Pinehurst, No. 2 | *Pinehurst, NC*

Pine Needles Lodge, Pine Needles | *Pinehurst, NC*

Poipu Bay | *Kauai, HI*

☒ Poppy Hills | *Monterey Peninsula, CA*

Presidio | *San Francisco Bay Area, CA*

Puakea | *Kauai, HI*

☒ Pumpkin Ridge, Ghost Creek | *Portland, OR*

Rancho Park | *Los Angeles, CA*

Red Tail | *Worcester, MA*

Sagamore | *Adirondacks, NY*

☒ Sea Island, Plantation | *Lowcountry, GA*

☒ Sea Island, Seaside | *Lowcountry, GA*

☒ Sea Pines, Harbour Town Golf Links | *Hilton Head, SC*

Seaview Marriott, Bay | *Atlantic City, NJ*

Shawnee Inn | *Poconos, PA*

Shennecossett | *New London, CT*

☒ Spyglass Hill | *Monterey Peninsula, CA*

Sun Valley | *Sun Valley, ID*

☒ Taconic | *Berkshires, MA*

Tanglewood Park, Championship | *Winston-Salem, NC*

☒ Torrey Pines, South | *San Diego, CA*

TPC Heron Bay | *Ft. Lauderdale, FL*

☒ TPC Sawgrass, Stadium | *Jacksonville, FL*

TPC Scottsdale, Stadium | *Scottsdale, AZ*

TPC Tampa Bay | *Tampa, FL*

Triggs Memorial | *Providence, RI*

🆕 Trump Nat'l | *Los Angeles, CA*

Turtle Bay, Arnold Palmer | *Oahu, HI*

Wachusett | *Worcester, MA*

Walt Disney World, Magnolia | *Orlando, FL*

Westin Innisbrook, Copperhead | *Tampa, FL*

Wigwam, Gold | *Phoenix, AZ*

Woodstock Country Club | *Southern Vermont, VT*

World Golf Village, King & Bear | *Jacksonville, FL*

TOUGHEST

(Courses with the highest slope ratings from the back tees)

Apache Stronghold | *San Carlos, AZ*

🄳 Arcadia Bluffs | *Traverse City, MI*

Arizona Nat'l | *Tucson, AZ*

🆕 Atchafalaya/Idlewild | *New Orleans, LA*

🄳 Aviara | *San Diego, CA*

Barefoot, Dye | *Myrtle Beach, SC*

🆕 Bay Creek, Jack Nicklaus | *Virginia Beach, VA*

Bay Harbor | *Petoskey, MI*

Bear's Best Vegas | *Las Vegas, NV*

Bear Trace/Ross Creek | *Nashville, TN*

🄳 Bethpage, Black | *Long Island, NY*

🄳 Blackwolf Run, Meadow Valleys | *Kohler, WI*

🄳 Blackwolf Run, River | *Kohler, WI*

🆕 Blue Heron, Highlands/Lakes | *Akron, OH*

Bluffs | *Baton Rouge, LA*

Boyne Highlands, Arthur Hills | *Petoskey, MI*

Breckenridge | *Vail, CO*

Bridges | *San Francisco Bay Area, CA*

🆕 Broadmoor, Mountain | *Colorado Springs, CO*

Bull at Pinehurst | *Kohler, WI*

🄳 Bulle Rock | *Baltimore, MD*

Camp Creek | *Panhandle, FL*

Capitol Hill, Judge | *Montgomery, AL*

🄳 Centennial | *NYC Metro, NY*

Club/Emerald Hills | *Ft. Lauderdale, FL*

Colbert Hills | *Topeka, KS*

Cordillera, Mountain | *Vail, CO*

Crandon | *Miami, FL*

Diablo Grande, Legends West | *Sacramento, CA*

Diablo Grande, Ranch | *Sacramento, CA*

Double JJ Ranch, Thoroughbred | *Muskegon, MI*

Dunes Golf & Beach | *Myrtle Beach, SC*

Edgewood Tahoe | *Reno, NV*

Edinburgh USA | *Minneapolis, MN*

El Diablo | *Ocala, FL*

Elk Ridge | *Gaylord, MI*

Giants Ridge, Quarry | *Duluth, MN*

Glen Dornoch | *Myrtle Beach, SC*

🄳 Golden Horseshoe, Gold | *Williamsburg, VA*

Grand Traverse, The Bear | *Traverse City, MI*

Grand View Lodge, Deacon's Lodge | *Brainerd, MN*

Grand View Lodge, Pines | *Brainerd, MN*

Great River | *New Haven, CT*

Heritage Club | *Pawleys Island, SC*

Kelly Plantation | *Panhandle, FL*

🄳 Kiawah Island, Ocean | *Charleston, SC*

🆕 Kinderlou Forest | *Valdosta, GA*

Ko'olau | *Oahu, HI*

🆕 Lansdowne, Norman | *Leesburg, VA*

La Paloma | *Tucson, AZ*

Las Sendas | *Phoenix, AZ*

Las Vegas Paiute, Wolf | *Las Vegas, NV*

Legacy Ridge | *Denver, CO*

Legends Club | *Minneapolis, MN*

🄳 Links/Lighthouse Sound | *Ocean City, MD*

Links/Madison Green | *Palm Beach, FL*

Lost Canyons, Shadow | *Los Angeles, CA*

FEATURES INDEX

Wilderness/Fortune Bay |
  Duluth, MN
Wilds | *Minneapolis, MN*
Willingers | *Minneapolis, MN*
Z Wolf Creek | *Las Vegas, NV*
Worthington Manor | *Frederick, MD*

UNIVERSITY

Duke Univ. Golf | *Raleigh-
  Durham, NC*
Forest Akers MSU | *Lansing, MI*
Jimmie Austin Univ./OK |
  Oklahoma City, OK
Les Bolstad Univ./MN |
  Minneapolis, MN
Pete Dye River/VA Tech |
  Roanoke, VA
Rawls/Texas Tech | *Lubbock, TX*
Seven Oaks | *Finger Lakes, NY*
Taconic | *Berkshires, MA*
Univ. of MD Golf | *DC Metro
  Area, MD*
Univ. of NM Championship |
  Albuquerque, NM
Univ. Ridge | *Madison, WI*

WALKING ONLY

Z Bandon Dunes, Bandon Dunes
  Course | *Coos Bay, OR*
Z Bandon Dunes, Bandon Trails |
  Coos Bay, OR
Z Bandon Dunes, Pacific Dunes |
  Coos Bay, OR
Z Bethpage, Black | *Long Island, NY*
Z Whistling Straits, Straits |
  Kohler, WI

WOMEN-FRIENDLY

Amelia Island, Ocean Links |
  Jacksonville, FL
Angel Park, Palm | *Las Vegas, NV*
Barona Creek | *San Diego, CA*
Bay Creek, Arnold Palmer | *Virginia
  Beach, VA*
Baywood Greens | *Rehoboth
  Beach, DE*
Bear Trace/Ross Creek |
  Nashville, TN
Big Mountain | *Kalispell, MT*
Big Run | *Chicago, IL*
Birdwood | *Charlottesville, VA*
Black Lake | *Gaylord, MI*

Boca Raton Resort, Resort Course |
  Palm Beach, FL
Boulders, South | *Phoenix, AZ*
Boyne Highlands, Heather |
  Petoskey, MI
Breakers, Ocean | *Palm Beach, FL*
Bridges | *Gettysburg, PA*
Broadmoor, East | *Colorado
  Springs, CO*
Z Bulle Rock | *Baltimore, MD*
Camelback, Club | *Scottsdale, AZ*
Camelback, Resort | *Scottsdale, AZ*
Carroll Valley, Carroll Valley
  Course | *Gettysburg, PA*
Celebration | *Orlando, FL*
Z Challenge/Manele | *Lanai, HI*
Château Élan, Château |
  Atlanta, GA
Château Élan, Woodlands |
  Atlanta, GA
Z Coeur d'Alene | *Coeur d'Alene, ID*
Coral Canyon | *St. George, UT*
Cowboys | *Dallas, TX*
Desert Willow, Mountain View |
  Palm Springs, CA
Eagle Ridge | *Freehold, NJ*
Eaglesticks | *Columbus, OH*
NEW Escena | *Palm Springs, CA*
Farm Neck | *Martha's Vineyard, MA*
Glen Annie | *Santa Barbara, CA*
Z Golf Club/Newcastle, China
  Creek | *Seattle, WA*
Grand Cypress | *Orlando, FL*
Z Greenbrier, Meadows | *White
  Sulphur Springs, WV*
Z Greenbrier, Old White | *White
  Sulphur Springs, WV*
Z Half Moon Bay, Ocean | *San
  Francisco Bay Area, CA*
Harvester | *Des Moines, IA*
Hershey, West | *Harrisburg, PA*
Hog Neck | *Easton, MD*
Homestead, Old | *Roanoke, VA*
Keystone Ranch, River | *Vail, CO*
Kiawah Island, Osprey Point |
  Charleston, SC
Kierland | *Scottsdale, AZ*
Kingsmill, Plantation |
  Williamsburg, VA

ALPHABETICAL
PAGE INDEX

Private courses are listed beginning on page 224.

ALPHA INDEX

ALPHA INDEX

ALPHA INDEX

ALPHA INDEX

ALPHA INDEX

ALPHA INDEX

ALPHA INDEX

ALPHA INDEX

ALPHA INDEX

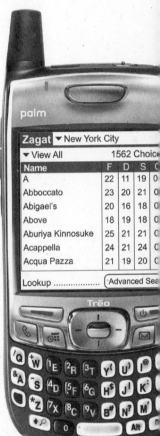